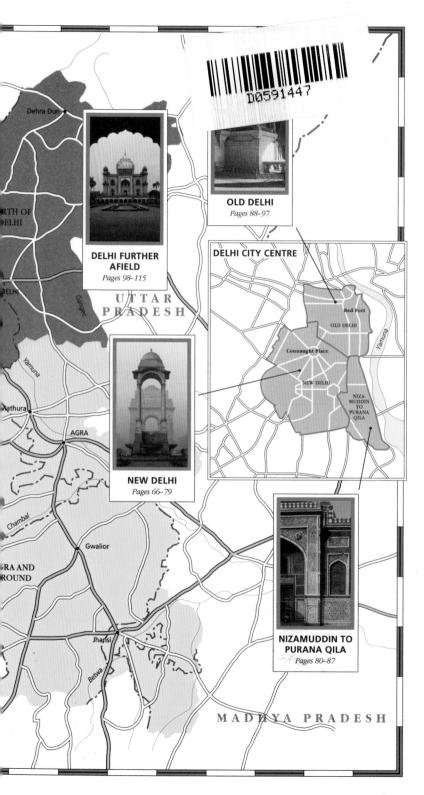

Dehra Dun

OLD DELHI
Pages 88–97

DELHI FURTHER
AFIELD
Pages 98–115

RTH OF
ELHI

DELHI

Ganges

UTTAR
PRADESH

Yamuna

DELHI CITY CENTRE

Red Fort
OLD DELHI

Yamuna

Connaught Place

NEW DELHI

NIZA-
MUDDIN
TO
PURANA
QILA

Mathura

AGRA

NEW DELHI
Pages 66–79

Chambal

GRA AND
ROUND

Gwalior

NIZAMUDDIN TO
PURANA QILA
Pages 80–87

Jhansi

Betwa

MADHYA PRADESH

EYEWITNESS TRAVEL

DELHI
AGRA & JAIPUR

EYEWITNESS TRAVEL

DELHI
AGRA & JAIPUR

MAIN CONTRIBUTORS: ANURADHA CHATURVEDI
DHARMENDAR KANWAR & RANJANA SENGUPTA

DK

LONDON, NEW YORK,
MELBOURNE, MUNICH AND DELHI
www.dk.com

PROJECT EDITOR Aruna Ghose
ART EDITOR Alpana Khare
EDITORS Ira Pande, Madhulita Mohapatra, Razia Grover
DESIGNERS Anand Naorem, Benu Joshi, Mugdha Sethi
CARTOGRAPHY Uma Bhattacharya
PICTURE EDITOR Radhika Singh

MAIN CONTRIBUTORS
Anuradha Chaturvedi, Dharmendar Kanwar, Partho Datta,
Premola Ghose, Ranjana Sengupta, Subhadra Sengupta

PHOTOGRAPHERS
Aditya Patankar, Amit Pashricha, Dinesh Khanna,
Fredrick & Laurence Arvidsson, Ram Rahman

ILLUSTRATORS
Ajay Sethi, Ampersand, Ashok Sukumaran, Avinash,
Dipankar Bhattacharya, Gautam Trivedi, Mark Warner

Reproduced by Colourscan, Singapore
Printed and bound by South China Printing Co. Ltd., China

First published in Great Britain in 2000
by Dorling Kindersley Limited
80 Strand, London WC2R 0RL

Reprinted with revisions 2001, 2003, 2007

Copyright 2000, 2007 © Dorling Kindersley Limited, London
A Penguin Company

ISBN 978-1-4053-2092-4

FLOORS ARE REFERRED TO THROUGHOUT IN
ACCORDANCE WITH EUROPEAN USAGE; IE THE "FIRST FLOOR"
IS THE FLOOR ABOVE GROUND LEVEL.

Front cover main image: The Taj Mahal at sunset, Agra

**The information in this
DK Eyewitness Travel Guide is checked regularly.**
Every effort has been made to ensure that this book is as up-to-date
as possible at the time of going to press. Some details, however,
such as telephone numbers, opening hours, prices, gallery hanging
arrangements and travel information are liable to change. The
publishers cannot accept responsibility for any consequences arising
from the use of this book, nor for any material on third party
websites, and cannot guarantee that any website address in this
book will be a suitable source of travel information. We value the
views and suggestions of our readers very highly. Please write to:
Publisher, DK Eyewitness Travel Guides,
Dorling Kindersley, 80 Strand, London WC2R 0RL, Great Britain.
**The external boundaries of India as shown on the maps are
neither correct nor authentic.**

◁ **A view of Taj Mahal from the river**

A bullock-cart and mustard fields

CONTENTS

HOW TO USE THIS GUIDE 6

Kishangarh miniature

INTRODUCING DELHI, AGRA & JAIPUR

FOUR GREAT DAYS IN DELHI, AGRA & JAIPUR **10**

PUTTING DELHI, AGRA & JAIPUR ON THE MAP **12**

A PORTRAIT OF DELHI, AGRA & JAIPUR **16**

DELHI, AGRA & JAIPUR THROUGH THE YEAR **38**

THE HISTORY OF DELHI, AGRA & JAIPUR **42**

DELHI AREA BY AREA

DELHI AT A GLANCE **64**

NEW DELHI **66**

NIZAMUDDIN TO PURANA QILA **80**

OLD DELHI **88**

FURTHER AFIELD **98**

DAY TRIPS FROM DELHI **116**

SHOPPING IN DELHI **118**

ENTERTAINMENT IN DELHI **120**

DELHI STREET FINDER **122**

Image of the young Krishna

BEYOND DELHI AREA BY AREA

BEYOND DELHI AT A GLANCE **134**

NORTH OF DELHI **136**

AGRA AND AROUND **146**

JAIPUR AND ENVIRONS **178**

A hand painted ceramic tile

TRAVELLERS' NEEDS

WHERE TO STAY **228**

WHERE TO EAT **248**

SHOPS AND MARKETS **264**

A sandstone *jaali*

ENTERTAINMENT **270**

SPORTS AND OUTDOOR ACTIVITIES **272**

SURVIVAL GUIDE

PRACTICAL INFORMATION **278**

TRAVEL INFORMATION **292**

GENERAL INDEX **302**

ACKNOWLEDGMENTS **316**

FURTHER READING & GLOSSARY **318**

PHRASE BOOK **320**

Humayun's Tomb

HOW TO USE THIS GUIDE

This guide helps you to get the most from your visit to the region. It provides both detailed practical information and expert recommendations. *Introducing Delhi, Agra and Jaipur* maps the region and sets it in its historical and cultural context. The three regional sections, plus *Delhi,* describe important sights, using maps, photographs and illustrations. Features cover topics from music and dance to food and festivals. Restaurant and hotel recommendations can be found in *Travellers' Needs.* The *Survival Guide* has tips on everything from transport to using the telephone, and the *Glossary* explains Indian terms and words.

DELHI

The city is divided into areas, each with its own chapter. A last chapter, *Further Afield,* covers peripheral sights. All sights are numbered and plotted on the chapter's area map. Information on each sight is easy to locate as it follows the numerical order on the map.

Sights at a Glance lists the chapter's sights by category: Mosques and Tombs, Museums and Galleries, Streets and Gardens, Historic Sites, Monuments and Markets.

Stars indicate the sights that no visitor should miss.

2 Street-by-Street Map
This gives a bird's-eye view of the key areas in each chapter.

All pages relating to Delhi have red thumb tabs.

A locator map shows where you are in relation to other areas of the city centre.

1 Area Map
For easy reference, sights are numbered and located on a map. City centre sights are also marked on the Delhi Street Finder map (pages 122–31).

A suggested route for a walk is shown in red.

3 Detailed information
The sights in Delhi are described individually. Useful addresses, telephone numbers, opening hours and other practical information are also provided. The key to the symbols used is on the back flap of the book.

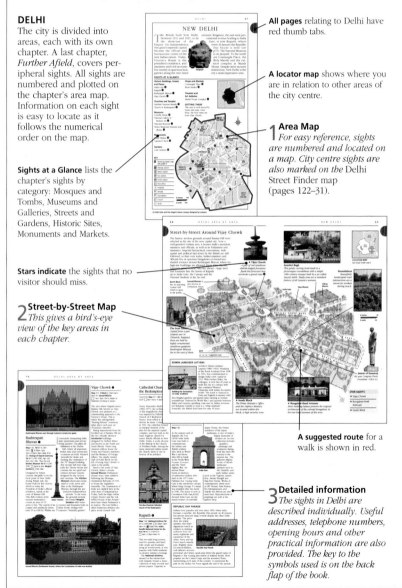

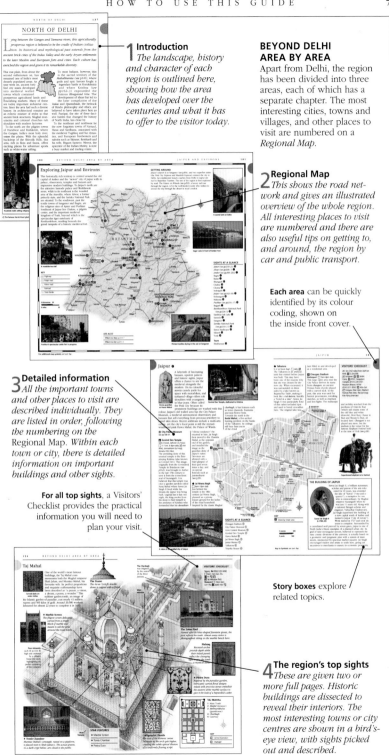

NORTH OF DELHI

1 Introduction
The landscape, history and character of each region is outlined here, showing how the area has developed over the centuries and what it has to offer to the visitor today.

BEYOND DELHI AREA BY AREA
Apart from Delhi, the region has been divided into three areas, each of which has a separate chapter. The most interesting cities, towns and villages, and other places to visit are numbered on a *Regional Map*.

Exploring Jaipur and Environs

2 Regional Map
This shows the road network and gives an illustrated overview of the whole region. All interesting places to visit are numbered and there are also useful tips on getting to, and around, the region by car and public transport.

Each area can be quickly identified by its colour coding, shown on the inside front cover.

3 Detailed information
All the important towns and other places to visit are described individually. They are listed in order, following the numbering on the Regional Map. Within each town or city, there is detailed information on important buildings and other sights.

For all top sights, a Visitors' Checklist provides the practical information you will need to plan your visit.

Jaipur

Story boxes explore related topics.

Taj Mahal

4 The region's top sights
These are given two or more full pages. Historic buildings are dissected to reveal their interiors. The most interesting towns or city centres are shown in a bird's-eye view, with sights picked out and described.

INTRODUCING DELHI AGRA & JAIPUR

FOUR GREAT DAYS IN DELHI,
AGRA & JAIPUR 10–11

PUTTING DELHI, AGRA & JAIPUR
ON THE MAP 12–15

A PORTRAIT OF THE REGION 16–37

THROUGH THE YEAR 38–41

THE HISTORY OF
DELHI, AGRA & JAIPUR 42–61

FOUR GREAT DAYS IN DELHI, AGRA AND JAIPUR

Called the Golden Triangle, this circuit has a bewildering array of things to do and see. A lifetime will be insufficient to take in all its treasures, which include the best Mughal architecture and monuments and the most tempting food and shopping. With a bit of

Pietra dura, Taj Mahal

planning, it's possible to get a general feel of the region. These itineraries will help you plan your stay without missing out on any of the essential experiences. For convenience, hire a car or taxi. The price guides include cost of travel, food and admission fees.

Humayun's Tomb in Delhi, inspiration for the Taj Mahal

A FAMILY DAY OUT IN DELHI

- **Rail Museum and Nehru Planetarium**
- **Santushti Shopping Complex**
- **Humayun's Tomb**

FAMILY OF 4 allow at least Rs3,000

Morning

Start the day by viewing vintage trains at the **Rail Museum** *(see p104)*. A toy train takes visitors around, and on some days, the old Patiala State Steam Monorail is steamed up as well. A must-see is the *Fairy Queen*, manufactured in 1855 and listed in the *Guinness Book of Records* as the world's oldest working locomotive. Next, visit the **Nehru Memorial Museum and Library** *(see p78)*, once the official residence of India's first prime minister, Pandit Jawaharlal Nehru, and now a museum. Within its grounds

is the **Nehru Planetarium** *(see p78)*. A dome-shaped screen and a sky theatre hold live and taped shows on astronomy, with a Carl Zeiss Spaceflight master projector to view the sky. You can also see the historic module, Soyuz T-10, which carried Rakesh Sharma, India's first cosmonaut to space in 1984.

Afternoon

Take a lunch break at **Basil and Thyme** *(see p601)* at the nearby **Santushti Shopping Complex** *(p118)*, where some of the city's best boutiques provide a tempting distraction. After a delicious meal and bit of shopping, head for **Humayun's Tomb** *(see p83)*. Set in the centre of a stylised garden, India's first great Mughal garden tomb is a tranquil place. Pause to examine the fine trellis-work of the stone screens. The lawns provide space for children to run around and enjoy themselves after a morning spent indoors.

MUSEUMS AND SHOPPING IN DELHI

- **Short historical walk to the National Museum**
- **Al fresco lunch at Lodi Gardens**
- **Crafts Museum and Shopping in Khan Market**

TWO ADULTS allow at least Rs2,500

Morning

Start the day with a walk down majestic **Rajpath** *(see p71)*, New Delhi's main ceremonial street, to **India Gate** *(see p71)*. The lawns here are a great vantage point to view the magnificent sweep of Lutyens's capital complex. A brisk walk to Janpath will bring you to the **National Museum** *(see pp72–3)*. Highlights include the Indus Valley Civilization, miniature paintings and the Indo-Chinese Buddhist art sections. A short drive from here will bring

India Gate, surrounded by lawns, is a pleasant picnic spot

◁ Miniature painting of a Rajput prince, surrounded by female attendants in a garden pavilion

Taj Mahal at sunrise, a sublime experience

A DAY IN JAIPUR

- A Dramatic Rajput Fort-Palace
- Palace-Hopping in Jaipur
- Lunch at a Heritage Hotel
- A Traditional Indian Bazaar

TWO ADULTS allow at least Rs2,500

Morning
Begin your day with a trip to the dramatic 16th century hill fort of **Amber** *(see pp200-201)*. An elephant ride takes you to the complex, with courtyards, private gardens and pillared apartments. Back in Jaipur, a city of pink palaces, start palace-hopping by first going to the **City Palace** *(see pp188-9)*, a part of which still houses the erstwhile royal family. Close by, is the **Jantar Mantar** *(see pp192-3)*, still used to calculate astronomical events. Finally, visit **Hawa Mahal** *(see p186)*, a whimsical façade of windows and quite unlike any other palace.

Afternoon
A leisurely lunch at the **Rambagh Palace Hotel** *(see p195)* comes with all the trappings of a royal feast, including splendidly attired waiters. However, don't miss out an afternoon of shopping at the lively bazaars around **Bari Chaupar** *(see pp184-5)* for brightly printed textiles, hand-made paper and silver jewellery. Also check out Johar Bazaar's jewellery shops, showcasing the famous *kundan* and precious stone work.

---

you to **Lodi Gardens** *(see p79)* for a delicious al fresco lunch at **Lodi, The Garden Restaurant** *(see p603)*.

Afternoon
After lunch, visit the **Crafts Museum** *(see pp86-7)*, to see an unusual art collection. Open courtyards with shady trees provide good resting places for children and the elderly. End your day at lively **Khan Market** *(see p79)*, exploring the excellent bookshops, boutiques and cafés to be found there.

A DAY IN AGRA

- Sunrise over the Taj Mahal
- The Glories of the Itmad-ud-Daulah Tomb
- Goodbye to the Taj, Shah Jahan style

TWO ADULTS allow at least Rs2,000

Morning
Try and reach Agra the evening before so that you watch the sun rise over the **Taj Mahal** *(see pp154-5)*. The changing colours of the marble at this hour are an unforgettable experience. It is also the best time of the day to see the Taj as the

afternoon sun heats the marble and makes it difficult to walk barefoot (mandatory here). Nothing can top this experience, so break off for lunch to recover your breath.

Afternoon
Head for **Itmad-ud-Daulah's Tomb** *(see p158)* to see the superb *pietra dura* interiors and the delicate marble screens, that almost rival the Taj's. The last lap of the day must belong to historic **Agra Fort** *(see p150)*. Shah Jahan was imprisoned by his son in the fort's Moti Masjid. He spent his last days gazing lovingly at the Taj, across the river. You can stand at the same window to say your final goodbye to the Taj.

Elephants waiting for visitors outside Amber Fort, Jaipur,

Putting Delhi, Agra & Jaipur on the Map

The Delhi, Agra and Jaipur region lies in the heart of
North India. It covers an area of about 114,000 sq
km (44,000 sq miles) and has a population of over
23 million. Delhi is the capital of India, while Jaipur
is the capital of Rajasthan. Agra is a major district
headquarters in Uttar Pradesh. Delhi has an
international airport. Agra and Jaipur are serviced by
domestic flights. The region also has good road and
railway connections, with Agra about three hours
and Jaipur about four by train from Delhi.

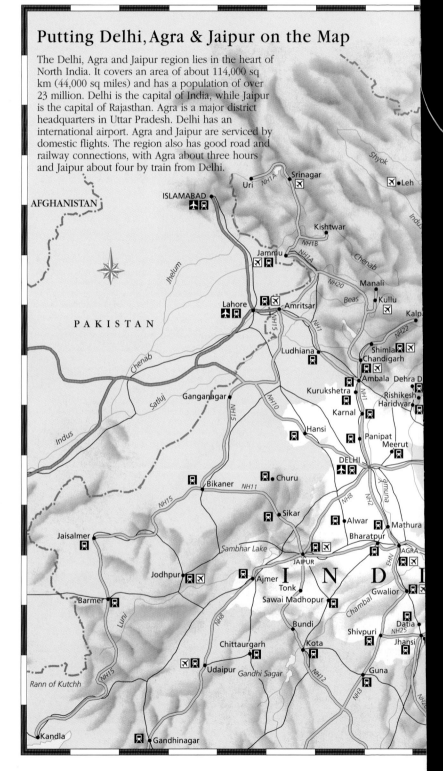

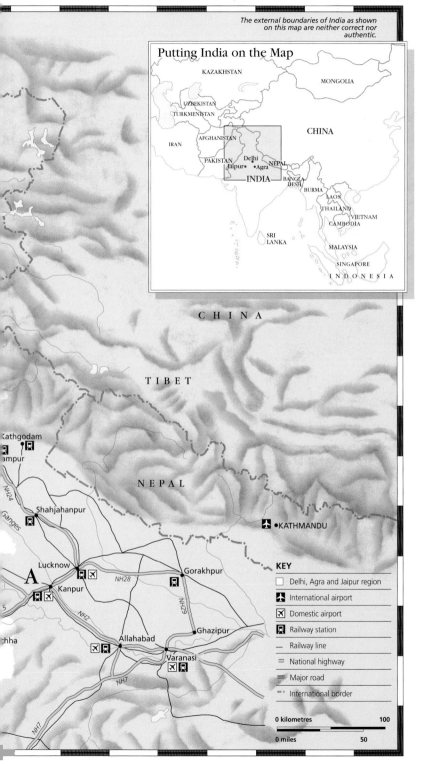

The external boundaries of India as shown on this map are neither correct nor authentic.

Putting India on the Map

KAZAKHSTAN

MONGOLIA

UZBEKISTAN

TURKMENISTAN

CHINA

IRAN

AFGHANISTAN

PAKISTAN

Delhi

NEPAL

Jaipur

Agra

INDIA

BANGLA-
DESH

BURMA

LAOS

THAILAND

VIETNAM

CAMBODIA

SRI
LANKA

MALAYSIA

SINGAPORE

I N D O N E S I A

C H I N A

T I B E T

Kathgodam

ampur

N E P A L

Ganges

Shahjahanpur

KATHMANDU

Lucknow

A

Kanpur

NH28

Gorakhpur

NH29

5

NH7

chha

Allahabad

Ghazipur

Varanasi

NH7

KEY

☐   Delhi, Agra and Jaipur region

✈   International airport

☒   Domestic airport

🚉   Railway station

—   Railway line

=   National highway

=   Major road

···   International border

0 kilometres   100

0 miles   50

Delhi City Centre and Greater Delhi

Some of Delhi's most impressive buildings can be seen in this area. The sights described in this book are grouped within three areas, each of which can be explored on foot. Vijay Chowk is the vantage point for the grand sweep of Raj buildings grouped on Raisina Hill. To the north, the magnificent Jami Masjid with its busy hive of lanes, was once the heart of the Mughal empire and is still the focus of Old Delhi. The past and present mingle here and yet preserve their own space and identity. To the east, the medieval quarter around the *dargah* of the Sufi Nizamuddin Auliya leads along Mathura Road to the ruined Purana Qila. This ancient site has interesting origins, going back to a distant mythological past.

Vijay Chowk *(see p70),* at the base of Raisina Hill, surrounded by government offices

Buddha Jayanti Park *(see p104),* created on the Ridge in northwest Delhi

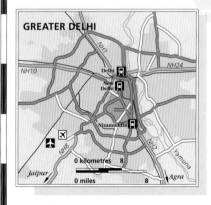

GREATER DELHI

Greater Delhi
North Delhi houses the university and historic sites associated with the Old City. South Delhi, around the Qutb Minar and Mehrauli, has grown into a busy commercial and residential area.

Jami Masjid *(see p92)* **the city's main mosque near Chandni Chowk**

Purana Qila *(see p84),* **Delhi's oldest historical site, now an integral part of the city**

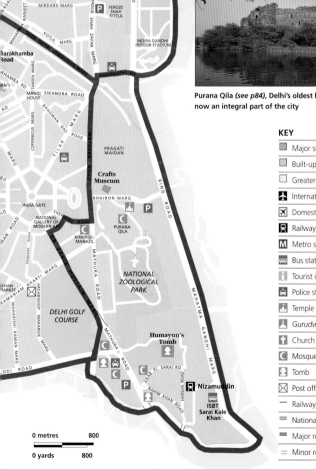

KEY

▢	Major sight
▢	Built-up area
▢	Greater Delhi
✈	International airport
⊠	Domestic airport
▯	Railway station
M	Metro station
▦	Bus station
ℹ	Tourist information
▣	Police station
▲	Temple
▲	Gurudwara
✚	Church
C	Mosque
▲	Tomb
⊠	Post office
—	Railway line
═	National highway
▬	Major road
=	Minor road

0 metres   800

0 yards   800

A PORTRAIT OF DELHI, AGRA & JAIPUR

The Delhi, Agra and Jaipur region lies at the geographical heart of North India. Its strategic location along the north-south and east-west routes has given it a focal position in Indian history and many great empires have been ruled from here. What we see today is a dynamic blend of the old and the new, a proudly traditional social structure within a modern liberalized economy.

This landlocked region is enclosed by mountains to the north, the desert and the forested Aravallis to the west. To the east are the agriculturally rich riverine plains, with vast fields of sugarcane, wheat, mustard and lentils. Southwards, these flat plains dramatically metamorphose into the earth pillars of the Chambal ravines, a rugged landscape once inhabited by fierce bandits. Invaders, entering the subcontinent from the mountain passes of the northwestern frontiers, conquered this region centuries earlier and made it their home.

Ganesha mask

THE LEGACY OF THE PAST

The earliest civilization in this region was the Harappan culture in the second millennium BC. However, it was the Aryan settlements in the next millennium that provided the region with its philosophical moorings, epic literature, such as the *Ramayana* and *Mahabharata,* and its early Hindu kingdoms. In the first and second centuries, the area was the centre of a Buddhist empire when the Kushana emperors who ruled from Taxila (now in Pakistan) made Mathura their second capital. After the decline of the great Hindu and

Men in colourful turbans at the village square

◁ A young Rajasthani girl at work in a mustard field

Cenotaphs of the Bharatpur kings at Kusum Sarovar near Brindavan

Buddhist empires, powerful Rajput rulers seized control of parts of North India. Many of the magnificent forts from which their feudal kingdoms were ruled can still be seen today.

Religion has always been the cultural link between the epochs, and by the 13th century, Hinduism had been influenced by the Bhakti Movement which stressed the need for a personal god. This resulted in the Krishna cult, centred around Mathura and Brindavan – places associated with the youth of this popular god. Even as the Bhakti Movement flourished, invaders from Afghanistan and Central Asia conquered the north. Delhi, and later Agra, became the capitals of the Muslim sultans. The cross-fertilization of indigenous and Islamic cultures bred a unique hybrid that influenced art, architecture, music and cuisine, reaching its zenith with the Mughals.

The 19th century saw the decline of the Mughal empire and the growing

An open-air village school near Neemrana

power of the British East India Company. In 1858, the East India Company's territories in India were transferred to the British Crown, and the country settled down to a 90-year span of Pax Britannica. The legacy of the British Raj lives on in modern India's administrative and educational systems, and English is today the common language of communication between India's different linguistic regions and states.

In 1947, British rule came to an end and India became an independent nation. Since then, the country has faced the challenge of building industries, and tackling the social problems of illiteracy, poverty and the caste system. As the population of India raced towards one billion, these problems became more pressing. So, in the 1990s, India adopted an open-market economy, adding yet another dimension of change to a land that is constantly on the move.

PEOPLE AND CULTURE

The capital of India, New Delhi, is known as a city of migrants. After the violent Partition of India and Pakistan in 1947, millions of people, mainly from West Punjab, flocked here in search of a new life. Since then, there has been a continuing influx of people from all over India. The majority of Delhi's 12 million citizens have settled here primarily for economic reasons – the average wage here is twice that of the country as a whole.

This mega-city nevertheless retains a small-town friendliness in its different neighbourhoods. Life still centres around the family, even though the joint family system is breaking down here, as is the case in all big Indian cities. Beyond the family is the larger world of the regional com-munity which plays a significant role in the city's social and cultural life. Diaspora groups very often come together for auspicious occasions such as marriages or festivals, with which the Indian calendar is punctuated.

Its mixed population has made Delhi a resolutely cosmopolitan city where Hindus, Muslims, Christians and Sikhs live side by side. Yet, each community has retained its distinct cultural identity, and the city is less a melting pot than

Bullock carts transporting rural goods

A fashion model

a *thali* (plate) whose offerings may either be savoured singly or in interesting combinations.

Different levels of development are evident in Delhi, Agra and Jaipur. But in all three cities, with the liberalized economy bringing in a sudden flood of consumer goods, and cable television channels beaming foreign cultures into their homes, the lifestyles and expectations of the people are rapidly changing.

What makes the region so interesting is that contrasts often exist here in perfect harmony – a bullock cart plods placidly beside the latest luxury car; weather forecasts are made both by satellite imaging and astrological calculations; and jeans-clad youngsters eating pizza in fast food joints are just as much at ease in a sari or *dhoti*, sitting cross-legged on the floor at home, to participate in traditional ceremonies or rituals.

A religious procession in Jaipur moving along in traditional splendour

Landscape and Wildlife

The Delhi, Agra and Jaipur region lies at the heart of Northern India and covers a wide ecological zone, flanked by the Himalayas to the north and the ravines of the River Chambal to the south. To the west are the Aravalli mountain range and the Thar Desert, and to the east stretch the riverine plains watered by the Yamuna and the Chambal. Forests once covered much of this area but, with growing urbanization, have now been reduced to a few pockets around the national parks. These are the habitats of many prized species, like the endangered tiger.

The peacock, India's national bird

INDIAN TREES

The region's rich variety of trees has local species as well as some of recent import. Some are sacred, others are valued for their healing qualities.

Banyan leaves

SUB-HIMALAYAN REGION

The Indian pine *(chir)* and sal *(Shorea robusta)* once formed thick forests that covered this area, but few remain today. However, there are still areas with sufficient forest cover to support a varied wildlife.

Indian elephants *are smaller than the African species and are found on the lower Himalayan slopes. These gentle, intelligent animals are easy to train and domesticate.*

Cheetal, *the graceful Indian spotted deer, is found in herds in the grassland areas.*

Monkeys *of two types, the rhesus and the langur, are found here.*

DRY DECIDUOUS FORESTS

This ecological zone covers the arid and semi-arid tracts along the Aravallis. The mixed vegetation of scrub and deciduous trees, comprises acacias, cassia and *dhak (Butea monosperma)*, cacti and wild grasses.

Sambar, *India's largest deer, is crowned with impressive antlers.*

Tiger, *the national animal, is now a protected species. Loss of forest cover today has brought it to the brink of extinction.*

Crested serpent eagle, *with its underwing pattern of black and white bands, is a large raptor often seen in the Ranthambhore forests.*

Ashoka (Saraca indica), *one of India's five sacred trees, is extolled in Indian literature.*

Pipal (Ficus religiosa), *a hardy tree that grows anywhere, is also the sacred Bodhi tree under which the Buddha attained enlightenment in Bodh Gaya.*

Neem *(Azadirachta indica). This large, shade-giving tree has an extraordinary range of medicinal, antiseptic and disinfectant properties.*

Kadamba (Anthocephalus cadamba) *is a tall majestic tree associated with Krishna and Brindavan.*

WETLANDS

In the southwest are shallow, inland lakes, marshes and swamps that have been formed from subterranean artesian wells. This is the habitat of otters and a wide variety of resident and migratory birds who feed on fish and aquatic plants.

RIVERINE AREAS

These lie to the south and east along the Yamuna and Chambal rivers. The southern area is marked by desolate ravines, formed by erosion and covered with tufts of wiry grass, but to the east the rich alluvial plains form a thriving agricultural belt. The rivers support a rich aquatic wildlife.

Painted stork *with its black and pink plumage, keeps its long beak immersed in water, probing the sediment at the bottom for food.*

Gharial (Gavialis gangeticus) *is a species of crocodile found in the Ganges and its tributaries. It is named after the pitcher-like (ghara) hump on its long, lean snout.*

Darter or snake bird *is a bird with dark, glossy plumage. Large flocks can be found in marshy areas, spearing fish with their sharp beaks and then swallowing them.*

King cobra *is the world's largest venomous snake. This lethal reptile has a characteristic mark on its hood and is considered to be one of Shiva's sacred creatures.*

Religions

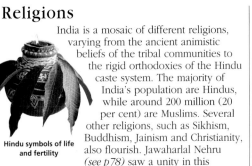

India is a mosaic of different religions, varying from the ancient animistic beliefs of the tribal communities to the rigid orthodoxies of the Hindu caste system. The majority of India's population are Hindus, while around 200 million (20 per cent) are Muslims. Several other religions, such as Sikhism, Buddhism, Jainism and Christianity, also flourish. Jawaharlal Nehru *(see p78)* saw a unity in this diversity, and the Constitution of India declares it to be a secular republic, where the state has no official religion and all faiths can be freely practised.

Hindu symbols of life and fertility

Sufi mystic at a *dargah*

HINDUISM

The bedrock of Hinduism constitutes the four *Vedas* and the *Upanishads,* which are a holistic compilation of knowledge, philosophy and ethics. Yet, Hinduism is not a religion of the Book, but a way of life that has systematically evolved over the past 5,000 years.

In practice, Hindus worship a huge pantheon of gods and goddesses *(see pp22–3)*. Socially, they can be divided into four castes – the upper caste Brahmins (priests), the Kshatriyas (warriors), the Vaishyas (merchants and traders), and the lowest caste, Sudras (workers). The caste system envisioned society as an organic whole with each part or caste performing a vital function.

The sacred feet of Vishnu

The traditional family structure was that of a joint family presided over by its patriarch. This is now fast disappearing in urban areas. Yet, *sanskara*, traditional values, are still instilled into children, and complicated rites mark each stage of orthodox Hindu life. There is also an aspect of Hinduism which shuns idol-worship, and prefers to concentrate on larger philosophical issues. Sadhus, who wear saffron to indicate their retreat from the material world, are its most visible practitioners. They hold a most respected position in Hindu society.

ISLAM

Islam was introduced into Western India in the 8th century by Arab traders, but it gained prominence in the north only after the 12th century, when it was declared the state religion under the medieval Muslim rulers.

Today, Muslims are India's second largest religious community, despite a large exodus to Pakistan after the traumatic Partition of 1947 *(see pp58–9)*. Muslims can be broadly divided into two sects, the Sunnis and the Shias. The latter believe that Prophet Mohammed's cousin Ali and his descendents are the true imams. Traditional Muslim education, based on the Koran, is still imparted by the clergy in *madrasas* near mosques, which are central to the entire community. In India, the Friday public prayers, led by the local imam, are only open to men, and nearly all Muslim places of worship follow strict rules of segregation.

Sufism is a less orthodox mystic Islamic order. Its teachings emphasize direct experience of god, and Sufis believe that mystical ecstasy can be attained even through music and dance. Sufi saints like Nizamuddin Auliya *(see p82)* attracted many converts from Hinduism, and the fusion of the two religious traditions led to a flowering of poetry, music and art.

Matted hair, saffron clothes and ash-smeared bodies mark sadhus

SIKHISM

Sikhism is a reformist religion founded by Guru Nanak in the 15th century. Eschewing idol worship, rituals and the caste system, it believes in a formless god. The Sikh, with his characteristic turban, is easy to identify. He is supposed to abide by the five "k"s': *kesh* (long hair), *kachha* (underpants), *kirpan* (small sword), *kangha* (comb) and *kara* (bracelet). The Sikhs follow the teachings of ten gurus that are contained in their holy book, the *Adi Granth*, kept in the Golden Temple at Amritsar (Punjab).

Religious persecution by the later Mughals led the tenth guru, Gobind Singh, to reorganize the community in 1699 as a military order called the Khalsa, based on the principles of *sangat* (congregation), *simran* (meditation), *kirtan* (hymn singing), *langar* and *pangat* (sharing and partaking of food in a common kitchen).

Sikh priest reciting verses from the *Adi Granth*

CHRISTIANITY

The rise of Christianity in this region dates to the late-15th century when Catholic missionaries travelled to India in the wake of Portuguese traders. About this time, Christian Armenian communities also settled in Mughal India, procuring a licence to trade. There is evidence that the

Church services are often conducted in local dialects

Mughal emperor Akbar *(see pp52–3)* invited Jesuit priests to religious discussions held in Fatehpur Sikri *(see pp170–71)*. With the coming of the East India Company, Protestant missionaries spread across the country, setting up educational institutions and hospitals in the 18th and 19th centuries. Many are still run by dedicated workers. They also involved themselves with reform movements and influenced the government to take measures against practices such as *sati (see p48)*. Marriages between Indians and the Europeans who came led to the birth of the Anglo-Indian community. During the Raj *(see pp56–7)*, the railways and many of the subordinate civil services were run by them.

Indian Christians believe that the apostle St Thomas brought the religion to South India in the 1st century AD. Today, church services have been Indianized to a large extent by absorbing some dialects, practices and rituals to make it easier for local worshippers to follow them.

OTHER RELIGIONS

Apart from these four major groups, India has other smaller though distinct religious communities. **Buddhists** are followers of Gautam Buddha who lived and preached the gospel of non-violence and peace. From India, Buddhism spread to other countries in Asia but, ironically, it has now nearly vanished in the land of its birth. The 14th Dalai Lama, the spiritual leader of the Tibetan Buddhists, now lives in India with his followers in exile and is a widely respected figure. **Jains**, the followers of Mahavira, are a pacific and non-violent community who respect life in every form, and observe rigid fasts and self-denial. They are divided into the Svetambaras (dressed in white) and the Digambaras (who shun clothing). The **Parsis** are followers of Zoroaster and came from Persia in the 7th century. A small community, they have nevertheless played a significant role in Indian industry and are known for their philanthropy. The first **Jews** came to India in about 587 BC and now live mainly in Mumbai and Cochin.

A golden Buddha statue

Jain nuns cover their mouths to avoid swallowing insects

The Pantheon of Gods and Goddesses

The great pantheon of Hindu gods and goddesses is a bewildering array, ranging from anthropomorphic symbols and shapes to exotic half-human, half-animal forms. Each god has a personal *vahana* (vehicle) and symbols of power. Although community worship takes place in temples, especially on festivals, for most Hindus, the home with its own shrine and personal deities is where the daily *puja* (prayer) is conducted.

Lakshmi, *the goddess of wealth, is also the consort of Vishnu. Her vahana is an owl.*

Shesh Nag is the hundred-headed leviathan on whose coils Vishnu reclines.

Narada, the sage, accompanies Vishnu.

Ganesha, remover of obstacles.

Saraswati, *the goddess of learning and music, is the consort of Brahma and has a swan as her vahana. Seated on a lotus, with a garland of white flowers, she is seen as the embodiment of purity.*

Hanuman, the monkey god, is a faithful attendant of Lord Rama.

Vishnu, the Preserver, floats on Kshirsagar (the sacred ocean), the source of all life.

RELIGIOUS SYMBOLS

Om, *a symbol of the primal sound, is recited to start all religious ceremonies.*

Kamal *("lotus") is a Vaishnavite symbol for purity.*

Trishul *("trident") is a Shaivite symbol of asceticism.*

Chakra *("wheel") is a universal symbol of the wheel of life.*

Shankh *("conch shell") is a Vaishnavite symbol of the life-giving ocean.*

Ganesha, *the elephant-headed son of Shiva, is invoked at the start of any auspicious task.*

Hanuman *the monkey god (see p197), is invoked by those in need of courage and fortitude.*

Rama (right), *the epitome of virtue, was Vishnu's seventh avatara (incarnation), and* **Krishna** (left), *the embodiment of love, was the eighth. Vishnu is said to assume these avataras to save the world from destruction. The last avatara, Kalki, will fashion a new world when this one reaches the end of its time.*

Brahma sits on a lotus attached to Vishnu's navel.

Shiva lives atop Mount Kailash. The River Ganges flows from his matted locks.

Nandi, the bull, is Shiva's vehicle and is always present at Shiva temples.

Garuda is Vishnu's vehicle on his travels through the cosmos.

Parvati *lives in the Himalayan hills with Shiva. This gentle daughter of the mountains is worshipped in many forms, which collectively represent the Devi (goddess) cult.*

Durga *rides a tiger with her deadly arsenal of weapons and destroys evil, in the form of the buffalo-demon Mahishasura. She is the fierce persona of the gentle Parvati.*

THE HOLY TRINITY

A popular calendar picture depicts the Holy Trinity that comprises Brahma the Creator, Vishnu the Preserver, and Shiva the Destroyer. Vishnu mediates between Brahma and Shiva to preserve life. The world was created when the ocean was churned by the gods and demons *(see p45)* to extract the divine nectar *(amrit)*. The present age (Kaliyuga) is only one stage of the unending cycle of life.

Kali, *wearing a garland of skulls, rampages through creation, annihilating evil. Along with Durga, she is the patron goddess of many Rajput clans who lived by the sword.*

Architecture: A Brief History

In North India, monumental architecture followed historical and political change. The wide variety of styles that emerged were executed in a distinctly "Indian" way, influenced by climate and local building traditions. Sadly, few buildings before the 12th century survived the ravages of time, war and climate, but the region is rich in medieval remains, of which the Taj Mahal is the centrepiece. An interesting feature is the mingling of Hindu and Islamic styles, which blends the sensuous beauty of temple sculpture with the austere grandeur of Islamic architecture. Gardens, fountains, screened arches and shaded interiors are some features used for keeping buildings cool.

Carved niche at Agra Fort

EARLY INDIAN ARCHITECTURE (UP TO 12TH CENTURY)

The temple was the social and economic focus of a town. Early Hindu temples, built on a square base, follow sacred building rules. The deity lies within the sanctum, and the outer surface is profusely decorated.

Carved frieze on *shikhara*

The **shikhara** is a pointed arch that meets over the sanctum.

Garbhagriha, the womb-like inner sanctum sanctorum.

The **mandapa** is a hall in front of the sanctum.

Piled stone blocks raise the temple's height

The **entrance** is spanned by a square stone lintel, carved with sacred images.

Teli ka Mandir *(9th century) at Gwalior (see p174) is a rare example of a North Indian temple of that time.*

SULTANATE ARCHITECTURE (13TH TO 15TH CENTURIES)

A sandstone and marble panel

Techniques for constructing true arches and domes were learnt by Indian masons from the Muslims after the 12th century. Mortar, another significant technology transfer, made it possible to build high structures. Hindu carving skills added a new element to the Islamic architectural lexicon.

The **dome** is crowned with a finial.

Islamic arches are often trimmed with a Hindu lotus bud fringe.

Geometric ornamentation is an Islamic feature.

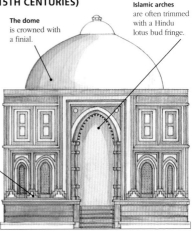

Detail of a geometric panel

Alai Darwaza *(c.1311) in Delhi, with one of the oldest surviving domes, is one of the gems of early Islamic architecture (see p112).*

MUGHAL ARCHITECTURE (16TH TO LATE 18TH CENTURIES)

Mughal buildings awe the viewer and assert the exalted status of their imperial patron. Whether built of red sandstone or marble, symmetry, grandeur and landscaping are some common features. Inlay work, decorative *jaalis* and cusped arches give these buildings an ethereal grace that offsets their massive size.

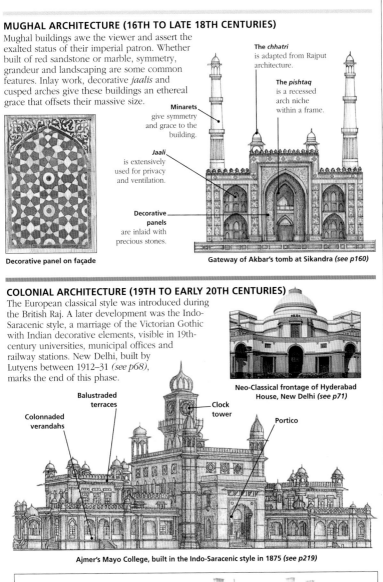

Minarets give symmetry and grace to the building.

Jaali is extensively used for privacy and ventilation.

Decorative panels are inlaid with precious stones.

The *chhatri* is adapted from Rajput architecture.

The *pishtaq* is a recessed arch niche within a frame.

Decorative panel on façade

Gateway of Akbar's tomb at Sikandra *(see p160)*

COLONIAL ARCHITECTURE (19TH TO EARLY 20TH CENTURIES)

The European classical style was introduced during the British Raj. A later development was the Indo-Saracenic style, a marriage of the Victorian Gothic with Indian decorative elements, visible in 19th-century universities, municipal offices and railway stations. New Delhi, built by Lutyens between 1912–31 *(see p68)*, marks the end of this phase.

Neo-Classical frontage of Hyderabad House, New Delhi *(see p71)*

Balustraded terraces

Colonnaded verandahs

Clock tower

Portico

Ajmer's Mayo College, built in the Indo-Saracenic style in 1875 *(see p219)*

BUNGALOWS

An architectural legacy of the Raj, originally designed to house Europeans living in remote outposts, bungalows have broad, covered verandahs, a front porch and a balustraded roof. The term

Government bungalow in New Delhi *(see p69)*

was a corruption of "Bangla", or Bengal, for its basic structure was derived from the indigenous, Bengali rural hut. Until 1947, few bungalows outside towns had running water or electricity but their high ceilings and shaded interiors kept them dark and cool in summer. However, when Herbert Baker *(see p68)* designed a bungalow for New Delhi's mandarins, its unhappy occupants christened his airless edifice "Baker's Oven".

Architectural Styles

Some of the country's finest forts and palaces lie in this region. Forts often served both as defensive buildings and as self-sufficient walled cities, built along natural outcrops or near rivers. Palaces were either part of a fort complex, or individual royal residences with public and private spaces separated by gardens and courtyards. Later, during the Raj, fortified palaces gave way to stately mansions inspired by European models. The beautiful garden tombs, of which the Taj is the most famous example, were a Mughal innovation. In contrast to these are rural houses that blend into the landscape. These eco-friendly structures, based on indigenous building skills are well-insulated, and both cheap and easy to build.

Marble podium at Delhi's Jami Masjid

FORTS

Most Mughal forts, built of red sandstone with marble trimmings, contained a city complex, with private and public areas and were seats of imperial power. Rajput forts, like Amber *(see pp200–201)* and Gwalior, on the other hand, follow a different plan and their solid bastions were built primarily for self-defence.

Foundation inscription from the Red Fort

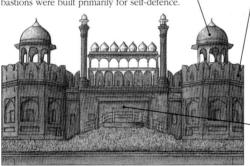

Ramparts have pierced holes for cannons.

The burj acted as a watchtower.

Lahore Gate is named after the direction it faced.

Red Fort at Delhi *(see pp94–5)*

PALACES

Some of the region's most spectacular palaces date to the 19th century in a style that imitated English stately homes. The older, medieval palaces nestle within forts and had separate quarters for men *(mardana)* and women (zenana) with landscaped gardens and private mosques or temples.

The bangaldar roof is crowned with decorative spikes.

A grand flight of steps leads to the gorgeous interior.

The simple exterior conceals a rich interior.

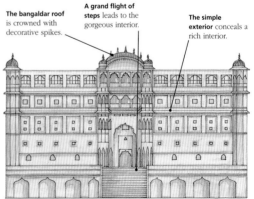

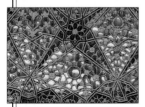

Detail from a mirrored room

Samode Palace, *built in the 19th century and now a heritage hotel (see pp232–3), has fabulously gilded and mirrored rooms. It is built in the traditional design but has period furniture rather than the usual cushions and floor coverings used in older palaces.*

THE GARDEN TOMB

The charbagh (see p167) is a terraced garden that surrounds the tomb to give its austere lines a soft focus. The Taj Mahal, set at the edge of one, is the most famous example of this style.

The dome surmounts the central space.

Arched cloisters lead to the crypt.

Humayun's tomb (see p83) *is one of the earliest Mughal garden tombs, which were set on a raised plinth within a charbagh. Other features include a private mosque and crypts for other royal graves.*

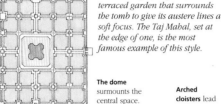

TRADITIONAL HOUSES

Indian villagers usually live in simple houses made of local material, often mud and thatch. They have cool, shaded interiors and are brightly decorated on the outside. Building materials come from the land and are renewed annually at Diwali (*see p37*).

Thatched roofs keep the interiors cool and shaded.

Mud walls are reinforced with straw and cowdung.

Ritual paintings brighten mud walls.

A rural Indian house at Mandawa (*see p213*)

HAVELIS

The *haveli*, a multi-storeyed mansion for wealthy merchant families, was usually built around one or more courtyards which formed a focal point for the domestic activity of the joint family. Shekhawati's painted *havelis* (*see pp212–13*) are examples of this architectural style.

The terrace gave an airy overview of the surroundings.

Covered verandahs separated living areas into smaller private units.

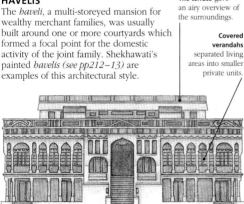

Haveli of the Bhartiya family, Shekhawati region

GLOSSARY OF TERMS

Baoli Underground stepwell, such as Ugrasen's Baoli (*see p76*).

Burj Residential or fortificatory tower; also bastion.

Chajja Overhanging eaves or cornices to protect buildings from the sun and rain.

Chhatri Open square or octagonal pavilion, literally an umbrella.

Diwan-i-Aam Hall of Public Audience.

Diwan-i-Khas Hall of Private Audience.

Gumbad/gumbaz Dome, often crowned with a finial; the term is also used for a mausoleum.

Chhatri

Gumbad

Jharokha Overhanging oriel window supported on brackets; some were used for the official appearances of the ruler.

Masjid Mosque.

Mihrab Arched niche facing Mecca in a mosque.

Jharokha

Minar Free-standing tower such as the Qutb Minar (*see p112*).

Mohalla Quarter of town inhabited by members of one caste.

Namazgah Space near mosque for celebration of major Muslim festivals.

Qila Castle, fortress, citadel.

Sheesh Mahal Chamber profusely decorated with mirror mosaic; glass palace.

Minaret

Stambha Stately pillar, post or column.

Stupa Tumulus, burial or reliquary mound.

Stambha

Music, Dance and Theatre

India's performing arts are simultaneously modes of worship and a joyous celebration of life. Music and dance originated in the temples, gradually acquiring a secular, more sensuous character as royal patrons founded individual schools *(gharanas)*. Two prominent classical forms in this region are Kathak and Hindustani music. The artiste creates a mood *(rasa)* which invites the audience to participate in it so as to make the performance a mutually shared experience.

Sarangi and bow

***Qawwalis and** bhajans are devotional songs that go back to medieval Sufi and Bhakti cults. Sung intensely to arouse mystical ecstasy, they celebrate the power of divine love.*

***Raslila**, a folk variation of Kathak, narrates the life of Lord Krishna. Traditionally, the Ramlila (below) and the Raslila featured young boys.*

Hands are used in stylized mudras, symbolic movements that follow the *Natya Shastra*, a classic treatise on the performing arts.

***Lehenga**, a long skirt worn over tight pyjamas, accentuates the swirling movement of the dancer.*

Ramlila *enacts the story of the epic* Ramayana *in a cycle of ten episodic folk plays during the Dussehra festival (see p37).*

HINDUSTANI MUSIC

The origins of Hindustani music date to about 3000 BC and the *Sama Veda (see p319)*. The *raga* (melodic mode) and *tala* (rhythmic cycle) are the foundation of Indian classical music, of which the Dhrupad and the Khayal are two major vocal styles. Indian classical music has no formal notational score, giving artistes a wide scope to elaborate the mood of a *raga*, each with its own set of notes. To preserve individuality, knowledge was passed down orally from teacher to pupil through schools called *gharanas*. The Gwalior *gharana (see p174)* is said to be the oldest one in the region.

Ravi Shankar, *one of India's foremost sitar players, introduced classical music to the West.*

Amjad Ali Khan *belongs to a famous family of sarod players, who developed the rabab, a medieval lute from Central Asia, to its present form.*

Nine rasas *(moods) are mentioned in the 4th-century treatise* Natya Shastra. *From the erotic, comic and pathetic to the odious, marvellous and quiescent,* rasa *covers every mood and expression, whether in music or painting. This 17th-century* Ragamala painting *(see pp30–31) depicts the mood of the morning* Raga Todi.

BAYADÈRE OF MEWAT.

Nautch Girl *was the pejorative title given to dancing girls in the 19th century when Kathak became mere entertainment.*

Rapid body movements keep time with the beat of the accompanying percussionist.

Ghungroos are brass bells that aid the rhythmic beat. Foot stamping controls and varies their sound.

Gorgeous jewellery and the colour red on the hands and feet make the intricacies of the dance easy to see.

KATHAK

This North Indian classical dance form, that received lavish patronage in the court of Jaipur, derives from the epic tales *(kathas)* narrated by balladeers. A typical Kathak performance is a blend of complex footwork and facial expressions *(abhinaya)* to enact an episode, often from Krishna's life.

Bismillah Khan *played the* shehnai, *a ceremonial reed pipe which the late maestro popularized into a concert instrument.*

Zakir Hussain *plays the* tabla, *a pair of drums that provide percussion to most music and dance performances.*

Contemporary theatre *draws on classical Sanskrit drama. Avant-garde street plays are popular with fringe and protest theatre groups. The National School of Drama Repertory (see p120) often produces Indian adaptations of classical plays, such as* King Lear, *seen above.*

Painting

A bird by Mansur

Two distinct schools of painting, Rajput and Mughal, emerged in 16th-century North India. The meteoric growth and popularity of miniature painting was due to the introduction of paper as well as the lavish patronage of Muslim and Rajput rulers. The Mughals encouraged Persian miniature painters to settle in India where they came into contact with indigenous traditions. A fusion of the two styles under Akbar, Jahangir and Shah Jahan led to a burst of artistic activity when court painters, such as Mansur, produced folios of birds, flowers, royal portraits and illustrated manuscripts. As Mughal patronage declined in the 18th century, other regional centres of art developed in North India.

Jain palm leaf manuscripts, *such as this piece (c.1439), use bright primary colours. Their large-eyed human figures and narrative depiction of themes influenced early Rajput art.*

Monsters symbolize the threats to Krishna at birth.

Early Mughal paintings *were pictorial narratives of historical events and literary texts. This leaf from a 16th-century* Babur Nama *shows Babur crossing the River Son. Mughal landscapes are rendered realistically, unlike the more romantic Rajput allegories.*

Space is divided into units, each dealing with a separate episode of the story.

Rajput paintings *are known for their bright colours and stylized figures. Classical texts and religious figures are recurrent subjects, such as this 18th-century page from the* Rasikapriya *romance of the Bundi School.*

Ragamalas *are sets of paintings strung like a garland, that depict the mood of individual ragas (see p28). This 17th-century* Ragini Dev-Gandhari, *an early morning* raga, *has dainty figures, and the delicate floral border that was a hallmark of Mughal paintings.*

Pahari painting *emerged from the hill (pahari) states of the western Himalayas, where many artists went in search of work after the decline of Mughal patronage. Raja Sansar Chand of Kangra, a patron of this style, can be seen in this late 18th-century Pahari painting.*

Nature is depicted in metaphorical terms, as in the snake-like ripples of lightning.

Narrative progression shows the growth of Krishna from infancy to boyhood.

Human faces are drawn in profile and space lacks perspective.

Colours and pigments were extracted from precious stones and plants.

The Company School *flourished in the colonial period. This portrait of King Edward VII and Queen Alexandra, attired in Indian clothes and ornaments, was painted by a local artist as a specially commissioned work.*

RAJPUT MINIATURES

Rajput ateliers were named after their patron courts *(see p215)*, each with a distinctive style, such as this 18th-century Mewar miniature, *Krshna Revealing his Divinity as Visnu to his Parents*. Rajput paintings have a narrative theme – a court episode or a mythological tale. Unlike Mughal paintings, their treatment of space and the natural world is poetic rather than realisitic and evokes a musical mood or *rasa (see p29)*. *Baramasa* (cycle of seasons) and *Ragamala* (garland of *ragas*) paintings are famous examples of this romantic style.

CONTEMPORARY INDIAN ART

A nationalist poet, musician, philosopher and educationalist, Rabindranath Tagore (d.1943) pioneered the 19th-century Bengal Renaissance art movement, which was a step towards the modernist impulse in Indian art. He drew heavily on the rich mythic content of folk art. Later, Amrita Shergill (d.1940) brought a European style to Indian themes and scenes. Contemporary Indian art evolved from the work of these and other seminal artists. Yet it retained an Indian identity even when experimenting with fashionable European styles. Modern Indian artists have experimented with Tantric symbols, mythology and miniature paintings to produce a vibrant art style which has tried to retain the richness of its folk and classical art forms even as they work with different media and materials.

Head Study,
Rabindranath Tagore

Indian Design

Indian design has evolved out of a very close bond between the artist and his craft, in which the skill of the hand is regarded as a sacred gift, passed down from father to son in an unbroken line. This has ensured a design tradition that is both a living art form as well as a means of fulfilling the everyday needs of the community, be they sacred or functional. Freely enriched by the traditions of other races and cultures, India's artistic heritage is renowned throughout the world for its vibrancy and creativity.

Mughal flower motif

Geometric designs *form the base of traditional decoration.*

Mud and thatch are regarded as sacred media, being the gift of Mother Earth.

The rounded shape of the pot has not changed since 2500 BC.

Pottery *has a 5,000-year-old history (see pp44–5) making it one of the world's oldest skills. The potter's wheel produces cheap, eco-friendly objects of daily use.*

The wheel or *chakra* is regarded as a symbol of the eternal circle of life and death.

Lime wash applied on the mud surface adds colour and repels pests.

The living space *is embellished with surface decorations ranging from relief carvings to mirror-work. Whether a mud hut or palace, the Indian home is the origin of most forms of art.*

COLOUR

The colours of Indian design are taken from nature, with names to match. The five shades of white are lyrically compared to the clouds when the rain is spent, the August moon, conch shell, jasmine flower and the surf of the sea. Indigo, madder and turmeric are valued for their dyes, and the crushed flowers of the flame of the forest *(Butea monosperma)* yield a soft yellow colour still used in rural India for playing Holi *(see p36)*. Each colour has a ritual significance as well: red is associated with weddings and festivals, saffron is the colour of warriors and ascetics, yellow is worn during the spring festival of Vasant, and green in the monsoon. The Indian dyer *(right)* uses plants and roots for extracting colour.

A dyer at work

The peacock is a popular symbol of royalty.

The lotus is associated with grace and purity.

Paisley motifs are stylized representations of the mango and cypress.

Animal and flower motifs *can be seen everywhere. The most elegant floral patterns were perfected in Mughal and Rajput painting (see pp30–31), while the popular lotus and peacock motifs are inherent to Buddhist and Hindu temple iconography. Worked in a variety of forms these motifs are most visible in textiles, carpets, painting, jewellery, ceramics and* zardozi *(see p153).*

The poppy, the iris, narcissus and tulip are textile motifs inspired by Mughal art.

Marble inlay *can be traced to Mughal* pietra dura *(see pp156–7). Agra still has families of craftsmen whose ancestors worked at the Mughal court.*

Precious stones such as amethyst, lapis, carnelian and jade are inlaid by hand on marble.

Floral patterns, inspired by the Islamic paradise garden concept, are common.

HOME AND FAMILY

The earliest art objects were those needed for everyday life. Emerging from the home and its daily rituals, the shape and form of articles was based on religious symbols which ensured their survival down the ages. With time, sophisticated materials and techniques learnt from royal courts enhanced design consciousness, resulting in a more exclusive range of decorative art.

Wall paintings are often inspired by nature.

Flame of the forest

Spices

Saffron turban for warriors

A vermilion-daubed shrine

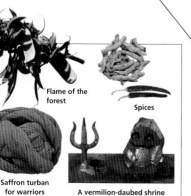

Form and function *are equally important in Indian design, endowing even everyday utility objects with beauty. As architectural skills developed over the centuries, basic forms and materials became more sophisticated. This graceful trellised stone window is an example of this change.*

Festivals in India

Indians love celebrations. Festivals are both religious and social events, where ritual fasting and joyful feasting often go hand in hand. Hindu festivals usually follow the lunar calendar and both the full moon *(purnima)* and the new moon *(pradosh)* are considered auspicious. Some fairs and festivities are connected to the pantheon of gods and goddesses, others to ancient pastoral, fertility or martial rites. Muslim festivals, too, are determined by the new moon. This means that the dates of festivals vary from year to year.

Effigy of Ravana

SHISHIR (JAN–MAR)

This is the most auspicious period in the Indian calendar. **Lohri** and **Makar Sankranti** follow one another in early January. The former is observed mainly by Punjabis as the height of winter, and the latter, confined to Jaipur, marks the movement of the sun from the equator to the Tropic of Capricorn. The wind usually changes direction on this day and colourful kites fill the sky. **Vasant Panchami**, towards the end of January, is said to

Child sports Holi colours

be the first day of spring. In January Shia Muslims also observe **Muharram**, a ten-day period of mourning for the martyrdom of the Prophet's grandson, Hazrat Imam Hussain, at Karbala (Iraq). On the tenth and final day, impressive processions of *tazias* (replicas of his tomb) are taken out and young boys and men dressed in black, flagellate themselves in a frenzy of religious fervour. In February, devotees of Shiva observe **Shivaratri**, or the night of his celestial wedding to Parvati. **Holi**, one of the most important Hindu festivals in this region, takes place on a full-

moon night, and is celebrated as the end of winter. On the eve of Holi, bonfires are lit and an effigy of the demon Holika is burnt to signify the triumph of good over evil. The next day, people swarm the streets, sprinkling coloured water and powder *(gulal)* on each other. This lively festival was especially dear to Lord Krishna.

VASANT (MAR–MAY)

The Hindu year begins with Vasant (spring). Nine days of fasting *(navaratris)* precede the birth of Rama *(see p23)* on **Ramnavami**. During this period, most households prepare special vegetarian foods, which are cooked in *ghee* (clarified butter) without garlic or onions.

Muslims celebrate **Milad-ul-Nabi**, the birthday of the Prophet in March. The pastoral festival of **Baisakhi** on 13 April heralds the harvest season in North India, and is celebrated with singing and dancing. Later in in the month comes **Shitala Ashtami**, a Rajasthani folk festival to commemorate Shitala Devi, goddess of smallpox and a manifestation of Durga. A religious fair that is attended by many villagers, is held at the Chaksu temple *(see p222)*.

Holi celebrations in the villages of Brajbhumi, near Mathura

GRISHMA (MAY–JUN)

As the heat intensifies, the festival season comes to a halt. The most sacred of Buddhist festivals, **Buddha Jayanti** or **Buddha Purnima** is celebrated (*see p38*).

VARSHA (JUL–SEP)

With the monsoon comes **Janmashtami**, the birth of Lord Krishna on a moonless night. Celebrations reach their peak at midnight, while the day is given to fasting.

The **Urs**, one of the biggest Muslim fairs in the subcontinent, takes place in Ajmer. It is held over 13 days at the *dargah* of the great Sufi saint Moinuddin Chishti (*see pp220–21*).

Dussehra images being prepared

SHARAD (SEP–OCT)

This season of festivals begins with **Dussehra**. For ten days, Ramlilas (*see p28*) are held and fairs organized to celebrate the legend of Rama. These dramatize episodes from the *Ramayana*: the exile of Rama, his brother Lakshman and wife Sita. Her abduction by the demon-king Ravana of Lanka and the epic battle for her rescue glorifies the monkey god, Hanuman, who helped Rama defeat Ravana and return in triumph to Ayodhya. Huge effigies of Ravana, his brother and son are stuffed with fireworks to be set alight on the last day,

Muslim pilgrims at the Urs at Ajmer

Vijaya Dashami. Dussehra is preceded by the *navaratri* fasts. Bengalis celebrate this period as **Durga Puja**, when grand marquees (*pandals*) are erected over images of the goddess Durga.

In October, **Id-ul-Fitr** marks the end of Ramadan or Ramzan, the month of fasting for Muslims, commemorating the period when the Prophet received the message of the Koran from Allah. The actual day of celebration varies according to the sighting of the new moon. A special *namaaz* is held at Delhi's Jami Masjid. This festival is also called Mithi (sweet) Id, as *sewian*, a delicacy made with sweetened vermicelli, is distributed at all homes.

HEMANT (NOV–JAN)

The onset of the winter season ushers in cool days and a large number of festivals. **Diwali**, or the

Diwali crackers on sale at pavement stalls

festival of lights, marks Rama's joyous entry into Ayodhya when the town was lit with lamps to greet him. It also heralds the Hindu New Year when old accounts are closed. Hindus believe that Lakshmi, the goddess of wealth, visits her devotees on that night, so houses are painted, sweets exchanged, and a profusion of *melas* encourages wild spending on homes and clothes.

Bhai Duj, two days later, is a family festival in honour of brothers, who give gifts to their sisters.

Another festival soon after Diwali is **Govardhan Puja** or Annakut, celebrated in both Rajasthan and Mathura. It commemorates the day Lord Krishna lifted the Govardhan hillock on his little finger to protect the area from a deluge sent by an irate Indra, the god of rain. On the full moon after Diwali, Sikhs celebrate **Guru Purab**, the birthday of Guru Nanak, the founder of Sikhism. In Rajasthan, the **Pushkar Fair** (*see pp216–17*) attracts throngs of tourists as well as pilgrims and herdsmen. **Christmas** and New Year, now national festivals, are celebrated with flair all over the country. At this time, restaurants fill and brightly-lit streets bustle with throngs of busy shoppers.

Paper kite

DELHI, AGRA & JAIPUR THROUGH THE YEAR

Three definite seasons, the summer, monsoon and winter, with a brief but glorious spring and autumn, span the year in the region. The calendar is filled with festivals and fairs celebrated by each of the diverse religious

Bauhinia blossom

or local communities. Some follow the changing seasons and mark pastoral occasions, while others celebrate anniversaries and events of national importance such as the Republic Day (see p71). Most cultural shows are held during the winter.

SUMMER (MAR–JUN)

From mid-March until June the North Indian plains experience a hot and dry summer. The temperatures in March and April can be mild and variable, but by May and June the heat builds up to a crescendo with the mercury rising above 40° C (104° F). This is a signal for many residents to move to the Himalayan hill stations. Those who stay back remain indoors and only venture out after sunset. Most festivities, too, come to a halt during this period.

Holi *(Mar)*. This exuberant festival of colour marks the end of winter. In and around Brindavan *(see p162)* Holi celebrations last two weeks.

Elephant Festival *(Mar)*, Jaipur. Around Holi, 60 decorated elephants parade through the streets bearing revellers who throw colour at one another. Elephant polo matches are also held at Chaugan Stadium.

Nauchandi Mela *(Mar)*, Meerut. Held around the shrine of a Muslim saint and a

Procession of Buddhist lamas on Buddha Jayanti

temple, this fair has come to symbolize Hindu-Muslim unity. Its origins date to the late-17th century when local leaders decided to merge festivities held concurrently at both shrines. Today, this is more a fun-filled carnival than a religious event.

Jahan e Khusrau *(Mar)*, Delhi. The three-day international Sufi music festival is one of the city's most eagerly awaited events. Performances are held at Humayun's tomb.

ITC Sangeet Sammelan *(Mar)*, Delhi. This important Hindustani classical music event, sponsored by a major Indian industrial house, attracts all music-lovers in the capital.

Elephant Festival

Gangaur Festival *(Mar/Apr)*, Jaipur. For 18 days, new brides and young girls worship Gauri, one of the manifestations of Parvati, the

consort of Shiva. Bejewelled images of the goddess are carried through the city, escorted by bullock-drawn chariots, bands of musicians and women singing hymns.

Shankarlal Sangeet Sammelan *(Mar)*, Delhi. This is the capital's oldest classical vocal and instrumental music festival.

Baisakhi *(13 Apr)*. On this day Gobind Singh, the last Sikh guru, founded the Khalsa, the "Holy Army of the Pure". Gala processions, dancing and feasting mark the occasion. It also signals the onset of summer and the start of the harvest season.

Urs *(Apr)*, Delhi. For three days devotees of the Sufi saint Nizamuddin Auliya *(see p82)* celebrate his birth anniversary with night-long qawwalis and a funfair.

Buddha Jayanti *(May)*, Delhi. The Buddha was born, attained enlightenment and died on the full moon of the fourth lunar month. Prayer meetings are held at Delhi's Buddha Jayanti Park.

AVERAGE DAILY HOURS OF SUNSHINE

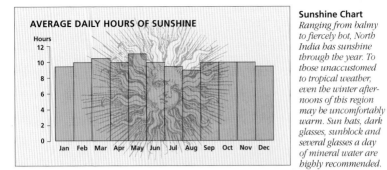

Sunshine Chart
Ranging from balmy to fiercely hot, North India has sunshine through the year. To those unaccustomed to tropical weather, even the winter afternoons of this region may be uncomfortably warm. Sun hats, dark glasses, sunblock and several glasses a day of mineral water are highly recommended.

Summer Theatre Festival
(May/Jun), Delhi. A theatre festival is organized by the National School of Drama.

MONSOON (JUL–AUG)

July, August and most of September are hot and humid with intermittent showers. All newspapers eagerly report the progress of the southwest monsoon and though rainfall is scanty in the region, this season is celebrated for its magical transformation of the earth.

Mango Festival *(early Jul)*, Delhi. Held at the peak of the mango season, over 1,000 varieties of delicious mangoes grown in North India are on view at the Talkatora Stadium.

National Film Festival *(Jul)*, Delhi. During this two-week-long festival, regional films from India that have won awards and have been made by prominent directors, are screened at the large Siri Fort Auditorium.

Shehnai player at Teej

Teej *(Aug)*, Jaipur. Young girls, dressed in green, sing songs and play on specially erected swings. This joyous event venerates Parvati, the goddess of marital harmony. It also heralds the advent of the much awaited monsoon.

Independence Day *(15 Aug)*. This is a national

A dancing peacock announcing the coming of the monsoon

holiday, commemorating India's freedom from British rule in 1947. The Prime Minister addresses the nation from the ramparts of the historic Red Fort in Delhi.

Raksha Bandhan *(full moon in Aug)*. Young girls tie sacred threads *(rakhis)* on their brothers' wrists as a token of love, and receive in exchange, gifts and a promise of everlasting protection.

Independence Day celebration

Janmashtami *(Aug)*. Krishna's birth is celebrated all over India. In Brindavan, Raslilas are performed, and in Delhi, there are shows of *Krishna Katha*, a dance-drama on the Krishna story.

NATIONAL HOLIDAYS
Republic Day (26 Jan)
Independence Day (15 Aug)
Gandhi Jayanti (2 Oct)

PUBLIC HOLIDAYS
Shivaratri (Feb)
Holi (Mar)
Id-ul-Zuha (Mar)
Good Friday (Apr)
Baisakhi (13 April)
Ramnavami (Apr)
Mahavir Jayanti (Apr/May)
Buddha Jayanti (May)
Milad-ul-Nabi (May/Jun)
Janmashtami (Aug)
Dussehra (Oct)
Diwali (Oct/Nov)
Guru Purab (Nov)
Christmas (25 Dec)

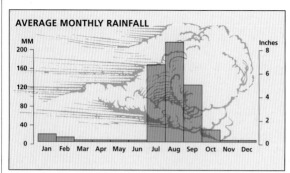

AVERAGE MONTHLY RAINFALL

MM
200
160
120
80
40
0

Inches
8
6
4
2
0

Jan Feb Mar Apr May Jun Jul Aug Sep Oct Nov Dec

Rainfall Chart
Apart from local showers, this region receives its rain mostly during the southwest monsoon, which lasts from July to September. The landscape turns lush green but the humidity, sometimes as high as 90 per cent, makes this the wrong season for travelling in the plains of North India.

WINTER (OCT–FEB)

This is the most perfect season when the monsoon has cleared the dust haze and the days begin to grow cooler. The onset of winter also marks the sowing of winter crops such as mustard and wheat.

The winter chill is at its worst between mid-December and mid-January, and though temperatures often fall below 3° C (37° F), the days are sunny. Spring is the main season for weddings, parades, picnics, polo and cricket matches, flower shows and various cultural events.

Cricket, the national obsession

Gandhi Jayanti *(2 Oct)*. Mahatma Gandhi's birthday is widely celebrated as a national holiday.

Phoolwalon ki Sair *(early Oct)*, Delhi. A colourful procession of floral banners and fans from the Jogmaya Temple and the Sufi shrine of Qutbuddin Bakhtiyar Kaki culminates at Jahaz Mahal in Mehrauli *(see pp110–13)*. Music and poetry recitations *(mushairas)* are also held.

The IIC Experience *(mid Oct)*, Delhi. Organized by the India International Centre, the festival celebrates world music, dance, theatre, film, literature and special cuisine.

Qutb Festival *(Oct)*, Delhi. A feast of Indian classical music and dance, organized by Delhi Tourism, is held against the dramatic backdrop of the Qutb Minar.

Dussehra *(Oct)*. A nine-day festival enacting episodes from the *Ramayana* depicting Rama's battle against Ravana. The tenth day, Vijaya Dashami, celebrates Rama's defeat of Ravana, and huge effigies of the demon-king, his brother and son are burnt. In Delhi, the Shriram Bharatiya Kala Kendra's month-long dance-drama encapsulates the much-loved epic.

Diwali *(Oct/Nov)*. Oil lamps illuminate each home to commemorate Rama's return to Ayodhya after 14 years of exile. Firecrackers are lit and

Balloon Mela

sweets exchanged. During this period every locality holds Diwali *melas*.

Parampara Festival *(Nov)*, Delhi. A cultural event for lovers of classical music and dance, it involves some of the country's leading artistes.

Pushkar Fair *(Nov)*, Pushkar. Asia's largest camel and cattle fair, takes place in this pilgrim town *(see pp216–17)*.

International Trade Fair *(14–21 Nov)*, Delhi. Pragati Maidan hosts this major event for Indian industry, exhibiting goods manufactured in India and abroad. Cultural events are also held in the fair grounds.

Balloon Mela *(14 Nov)*, Delhi. This festival coincides with Nehru's birthday, celebrated as Children's Day.

Tansen Festival *(Nov)*, Gwalior. Classical singers pay homage to the most famous of Indian musicians, Tansen, Mughal emperor Akbar's favourite singer.

Chrysanthemum Show *(1st week Dec)*, Delhi. The YWCA organizes a display of magnificent blooms.

Kathak Utsav *(Dec)*, Delhi. Exponents of this North Indian dance form enthrall audiences with their artistry.

The Prithvi Theatre Festival *(Dec)*, Delhi. Mumbai-based group, formed in memory of Prithviraj Kapoor, hosts a two-day feast of plays.

Car display at the Trade Fair

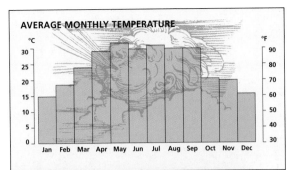

AVERAGE MONTHLY TEMPERATURE

°C
30
25
20
15
10
5
0

Jan Feb Mar Apr May Jun Jul Aug Sep Oct Nov Dec

°F
90
80
70
60
50
40
30

Temperature Chart
This region is hot and dry throughout the year, barring October to February. The mercury begins to rise from March, and by May heat wave conditions prevail with hot and dusty gusts of the "loo" winds. By the end of June, however, dark clouds signal the onset of monsoon.

Bagpipers at the Beating Retreat ceremony

Christmas *(25 Dec)*.
A public holiday, Christmas is celebrated all over and is an occasion for everyone to shop, feast and party.
New Year's Eve *(31 Dec)*.
All hotels and clubs organize New Year's Eve balls.
Lohri *(13 Jan)* . Bonfires are lit amidst song and dance to mark the height of winter.
Makar Sankranti *(14 Jan)*, Jaipur. Kites are flown to celebrate the return of the sun from the equator to the Tropic of Capricorn.
Jaipur Festival *(mid Jan)* Jaipur. A ten-day cultural extravaganza of music, dance and craft exhibitions celebrating Rajasthan's and the Pink City's rich heritage.
Republic Day *(26 Jan)*. A national holiday. Pomp and pageantry mark India's birth as an independent republic. In Delhi, a colourful military parade is held at Rajpath.
Beating Retreat *(29 Jan)*, Delhi. A moving ceremony that recalls the end of the day's battle when armies

retreated to their camps. There is a grand display of regimental bands performing against the spectacular backdrop of North and South Blocks. As the sun sets, a bugle sounds the retreat, fireworks are lit and fairy-lights outline the buildings.
Surajkund Crafts Mela *(1–14 Feb)*, Surajkund. This handicrafts fair is held at an 11th-century historic site on the outskirts of the capital.
International Yoga Week *(Feb)*, Rishikesh. On the

banks of the Ganges, scholars and students from all over the world participate in yoga classes and seminars.
Vintage Car Rally *(Feb)*, Delhi. *The Statesman* newspaper organizes this event when vintage cars, or the "grand old ladies", are flagged off from Rajpath to embark on a 20-km (12-mile) race. Their owners often dress up in period costumes.
Vasant Panchami *(Feb)*.
A spring festival when crops ripen and nature is in full bloom. People wear yellow and worship Saraswati.
Taj Mahotsav *(18–27 Feb)*, Agra. A ten-day cultural fiesta of music and dance in the vicinity of the Taj Mahal.
Shivaratri *(Feb)*. Night-long celebrations mark the marriage of Shiva on the 14th day of a lunar fortnight.
Kathak Bindadin Mahotsav *(Feb)*, Delhi. A five-day dance festival organized by the Kathak Kendra.
Dhrupad Festival *(Feb)*, Delhi. Leading exponents of this ancient musical tradition present a series of recitals.

Vintage cars testing their strength on an uphill road outside Delhi

THE HISTORY OF DELHI, AGRA & JAIPUR

North Indian society sprang from the wide plains of the Indus and Ganges rivers, sites of continuous human settlement since about 2500 BC, when a sophisticated urban culture flourished along the Indus Valley. After 600 BC, powerful empires such as the Mauryas, Kushanas and Guptas presided over the rise of Buddhism and Hinduism, two major religions that emerged from North India.

Statue of the Holy Trinity, Gupta Age

Overland trade with Central Asia and the Far East invited conquest and settlement as well. Interestingly, India is a derivative of "Indoi", a Greek word given to people who lived across the River Sindhu, or Indus. From 1500 BC on, North India was home to immigrants. These included the Aryans, Greeks and Parthians, Scythians, Huns and Mongols.

An important development took place in AD 1192 when Muhammad Ghori displaced the Rajputs from Delhi to found the first major Islamic kingdom in the region. Later, with the coming of the Mughals in 1526, North India underwent a process of social and political change that lasted nearly 300 years, as a vibrant Indo-Islamic cultural fusion took place. Imperial centralization under the Mughals brought peace and prosperity in its wake, while art and architecture scaled new heights of excellence.

The rise of the British East India Company in the 18th century, after the decline of the Mughals, was the start of 200 years of British rule in India. The colonial period, which also marks the political unification of the subcontinent, ended in 1947 when India became independent. Today a mature democracy, India is trying to tackle poverty and illiteracy with economic and political reform in this rapidly expanding nation.

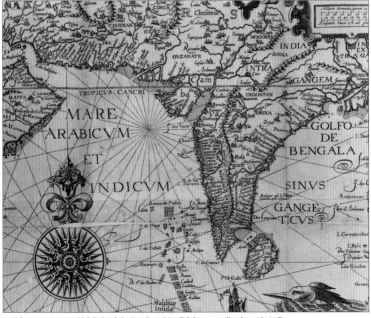

A 16th-century map, which helped the Dutch and English locate trading bases in India

◁ Royal procession, a mid-19th-century mural in the Moti Mahal, Gwalior

Early Civilizations

Indian civilization first flourished between 2500 and 1500 BC in the Harappan settlements along the River Indus. These sophisticated urban settlements, with an underground drainage system and well laid out streets, were spread over an area much larger than either ancient Egypt or Mesopotamia. The reasons for the decline of this early civilization are still unclear, but by 1500 BC, the Aryans, who had entered India through the passes of the Hindu Kush, had settled down in Northwest India. Sacred texts such as the *Rig Veda* record aspects of their culture. By 600 BC, with the gradual adoption of widespread crop cultivation, several new urban sites had emerged in the Ganges Valley. Many of these were capitals of independent kingdoms, and some cities of that age, such as Mathura, Patna and Varanasi, still exist.

Mother Goddess icon, Indus Valley

EARLY CIVILIZATIONS

— *Extent of Indus Valley Civilization*

☐ *Extent of Aryan settlements*

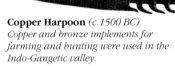

Copper Harpoon *(c.1500 BC)*
Copper and bronze implements for farming and hunting were used in the Indo-Gangetic valley.

Burial urn from a Harappan site.

Indus Seal (Tree)
Over 2,000 steatite seals have been found in the Indus Valley, each with an emblem and a script that has still not been fully deciphered.

Platter *(c.800 BC)*
A Painted Grey Ware platter from the Ganges Valley area. Austere and functional, such objects were made of baked clay.

TIMELINE

Early Stone Age relics

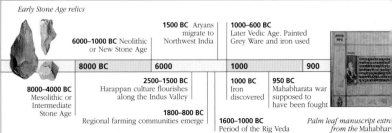

		1500 BC Aryans migrate to Northwest India	**1000–600 BC** Later Vedic Age. Painted Grey Ware and iron used	
	6000–1000 BC Neolithic or New Stone Age			
8000 BC	**6000**		**1000**	**900**
8000–4000 BC Mesolithic or Intermediate Stone Age	**2500–1500 BC** Harappan culture flourishes along the Indus Valley		**1000 BC** Iron discovered	**950 BC** Mahabharata war supposed to have been fought
	1800–800 BC Regional farming communities emerge		**1600–1000 BC** Period of the Rig Veda	*Palm leaf manuscript extra from the* Mahabhar

Beliefs and Ideas
*Sacred Rig Vedic hymns,
composed by the Aryans in
praise of Nature and various
gods, were later absorbed
into Hinduism. Several
Hindu gods and rituals,
even the caste system
(see p22), can be
traced to Aryan beliefs.*

WHERE TO SEE HARAPPAN ARTIFACTS

Harappan dice at the National Museum

The finest collection of Indus Valley artifacts, arranged chronologically, is in New Delhi's National Museum *(see pp 72–3)*. Some archaeological finds, especially Painted Grey Ware from the site of Indraprastha mentioned in the epic *Mahabharata*, are lodged in a small museum in Delhi's Purana Qila itself *(see p84)*. The state museums at Kurukshetra *(see p140)* and Mathura *(see p161)* have a good collection of statues and archaeological finds excavated from this region.

This **toy cart** indicates the use of the wheel.

Toy animals testify to the Harappan artisan's skill.

Baked clay was used by the Harappans to shape various objects such as this anteater.

Grain was stored in wide-mouthed jars.

HARAPPAN CULTURE
The Indus Valley (or Harappan) Civilization (2500–1500 BC) had an efficient system of government based on trade and a thriving agricultural economy. Worshippers of a mother goddess and trees, they used water for ritual practice. These Harappan artifacts are in the National Museum.

The Origin of Life
An 18th-century painting depicting the popular Hindu myth that life was created when the divine nectar (amrit), hidden in the Ocean of Milk, was won by the gods from the demons (see p25).

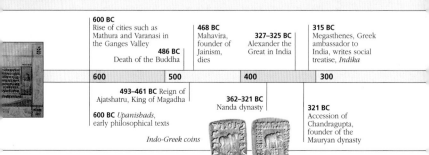

600 BC
Rise of cities such as Mathura and Varanasi in the Ganges Valley

486 BC
Death of the Buddha

468 BC
Mahavira, founder of Jainism, dies

327–325 BC
Alexander the Great in India

315 BC
Megasthenes, Greek ambassador to India, writes social treatise, *Indika*

600	500	400	300

493–461 BC Reign of Ajatshatru, King of Magadha

600 BC *Upanishads*, early philosophical texts

Indo-Greek coins

362–321 BC
Nanda dynasty

321 BC
Accession of Chandragupta, founder of the Mauryan dynasty

Ancient Empires

Ashokan capital

Under the Mauryan Emperor Ashoka, North India saw its first large-scale empire. Contact with Central Asia, which began around 200 BC, determined crucial political alliances after the Mauryas, and by the 1st century AD, the Kushanas from Central Asia had an empire that extended up to the Ganges Valley. This period also saw the rise and spread of Buddhism. In the 4th century, the Gupta kings presided over the flowering of classical Sanskrit at the hands of writers such as Kalidasa. The emergence of the Holy Trinity *(see pp24–5)* and temple worship also date from the Gupta Age.

EARLY EMPIRES

☐ Mauryan Empire

— Kushana Empire

— Gupta Empire

Buddhism
A peaceful, non-violent religion, its message of tolerance and social equality won Buddhism many followers, among them the Mauryan emperor Ashoka. Its rise had a profound impact on social, political and cultural life.

Speckled red sandstone was extensively used in Mathura art.

The human form, sensuously carved, has expressive lines. The gold ornaments and elaborate hair styles of the figures reflect the court fashions of the age.

Ashokan Edict
(3rd century BC) Considered valuable historical records, such rock edicts, installed throughout his kingdom, proclaim Ashoka's ethical code (dhamma) *as well as important events.*

TIMELINE

273–232 BC
Ashoka's reign

260 BC Battle of Kalinga leads Ashoka to embrace Buddhism

180–165 BC Foundation of Indo-Greek empire by Demetrius

80 BC Maues, Shaka king in Northwest India

AD 78–110 Reign of Kushana king Kanishka; Fourth Buddhist Council held in Kashmir

2nd-century Buddh[ist] begging bowl

200 BC	100 BC	AD 1	AD 100	200

185 BC Accession of Sungas in Magadha

165–145 BC Menander, Indo-Greek king, rules over the northwest

AD 20–46 Gondophernes, Indo-Parthian king in Taxila; St Thomas comes to South India

150 Rudradaman, th[e] king in West India; f[...] Sanskrit inscription [...] imperishable materia[l] from his reign

Mauryan sculpture

Kanishka *(AD 78–110)*
This famous Kushana king came from Central Asia (as the boots and cloak of his headless statue reveal) to control a large part of North India. Another great patron of Buddhism, his reign presided over its spread to China, Central Asia and Afghanistan, along the famous Silk Route.

WHERE TO SEE ANCIENT ART

The Government Museum, Mathura *(see p161)* and the National Museum, New Delhi *(see pp72–3)* have fine collections of Mauryan, Kushana, Gupta and Sunga sculptures. The Northern Ridge *(see p103)* and Feroze Shah Kotla *(see p97)* have well-preserved Ashokan pillars.

Sunga pillar, National Museum

Yakshas and **yakshis**, male and female nature spirits, as well as the foliage behind them, represent fertility and an abundance of life. Their presence highlights the mood of revelery and fecundity.

Greek features like curly hair and sharp noses distinguish Gandhara sculpture.

Vasantasena, a courtesan, slumped in a drunken state, is helped to her feet.

MATHURA SCHOOL OF ART

Between the 1st and 6th centuries AD, a renowned school of art flourished at Mathura *(see p161)*. Statues of Jain, Buddhist and Hindu divinities, with remarkably expressive faces, were produced along with secular art such as this dramatic 2nd-century Kushana panel, *The Drunken Courtesan.*

Gandhara Sculpture

After the 1st century AD, a distinct Hellenistic style first emerged in Gandhara in the northwest. The Buddha was now depicted in a sublime human form, rather than through symbols such as the lotus and chakra, with expressions that recall classical Greek sculpture.

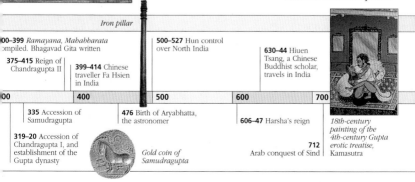

Iron pillar

00–399 *Ramayana, Mahabharata* compiled. *Bhagavad Gita* written

375–415 Reign of Chandragupta II

399–414 Chinese traveller Fa Hsien in India

500–527 Hun control over North India

630–44 Hiuen Tsang, a Chinese Buddhist scholar, travels in India

| **00** | **400** | **500** | **600** | **700** |

335 Accession of Samudragupta

476 Birth of Aryabhatta, the astronomer

606–47 Harsha's reign

319–20 Accession of Chandragupta I, and establishment of the Gupta dynasty

Gold coin of Samudragupta

712 Arab conquest of Sind

18th-century painting of the 4th-century Gupta erotic treatise, Kamasutra

Rajput Dynasties

Rajput shield with sun emblem

Rajput clans rose to prominence in North India from the late 7th century. Claiming a high caste warrior status (*kshatriya*), they traced their lineage to the sun and moon to firmly establish their legitimacy, and ruled over North, West and Central India. After losing Delhi and Kannauj to the Muslims, they confined their activities to the western region, now Rajasthan, where rival clans fought for supremacy. Widely renowned for their loyalty and valour, most Rajput clans were welcomed as allies by Mughal rulers.

LOCATOR MAP

☐ *Extent of Rajput Kingdoms*

Turbans indicate the home, region and status of a person.

Prithviraj Chauhan of Ajmer
The last Rajput ruler of Delhi, he was defeated in 1192 by Muhammad Ghori. The Qutb Minar and a mosque were built over his citadel, Rai Pithora.

Pageantry was a vital part of the Rajput concept of kingship.

Sacred Beliefs
Rajput kings were patrons of Hinduism and worshipped martial gods such as Hanuman (see p197) and Shakti. They were also prolific builders of beautiful temples.

Sati Sites
Hand imprints mark the sites where women immolated themselves by jumping into their husbands' funeral pyres. This cruel practice, called sati, *was made illegal in 1829.*

TIMELINE

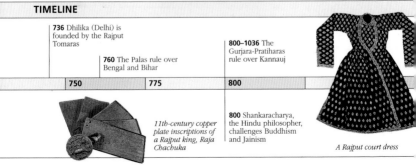

736 Dhilika (Delhi) is founded by the Rajput Tomaras

760 The Palas rule over Bengal and Bihar

800–1036 The Gurjara-Pratiharas rule over Kannauj

| 750 | 775 | 800 |

11th-century copper plate inscriptions of a Rajput king, Raja Chachuka

800 Shankaracharya, the Hindu philosopher, challenges Buddhism and Jainism

A Rajput court dress

Rajput Art
Rajput rulers were great patrons of architecture and painting. This unusual 18th-century miniature from Jaipur shows Rajput women playing polo (see p195).

Man Singh I of Amber
This loyal Mughal ally, one of the "nine jewels" (navaratna) of Akbar's court, was among the first Rajputs to befriend the Mughals. Such alliances paved the way for peace in North India and a fusion of Hindu and Islamic cultures, especially in architecture.

Palanquins, such as this fanciful one, were carried by a retinue of clansmen during ceremonial processions.

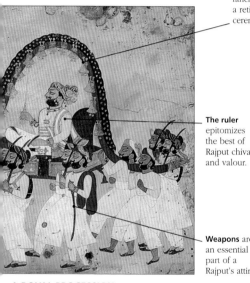

The ruler epitomizes the best of Rajput chivalry and valour.

Weapons are an essential part of a Rajput's attire.

WHERE TO SEE RAJPUT INDIA

Amber *(see pp200–201)* and the jungle fort at Ranthambhore *(see pp 224–5)* are some famous Rajput forts in this region. The museum inside the City Palace, Jaipur *(see pp188–91)* and Alwar *(see p206)* display private collections. The National Museum, New Delhi, also has a wide display of Rajput miniature paintings *(see pp30–31)*, sculpture and jewellery.

Amber Fort *(see pp200–201)*

A ROYAL PROCESSION

Rajput princes enjoyed a divine status in the eyes of their clan. Rajputana, literally the land of princes, once had some 21 kingdoms ruled by rival clans which included the Sisodias of Mewar, Kachhawahas of Amber and Jaipur, Rathors of Marwar and Bikaner, Haras of Kota and Bundi, Chauhans of Ajmer, and Bhattis of Jaisalmer.

883–1026 The Hindu Shahis rule over Kabul and the Punjab

973–1192 The Chahamanas of Sakambhari rule over Ajmer, Rajasthan

974–1238 The Solankis rule Anhilwad in Gujarat

| 75 | 900 | 925 | 950 | 975 |

916–1202 The Chandellas rule over Bundelkhand and build the Khajuraho temples in Central India

974–1233 The Paramars rule Dhar in Central India

Phad, *a Rajput folk painting*

10th-century Khajuraho temple

The Delhi Sultans

Astrolabe

The fabulous wealth of India attracted Arab traders and raiders, such as Mahmud of Ghazni. A slave general of Muhammad Ghori, called Qutbuddin Aibak, established himself in North India and founded the Mamluk (Slave) Dynasty. Followed by the Khiljis, Tughlaqs, Sayyids and Lodis, these Muslim rulers, called the Sultans of Delhi, established an empire that survived into the early 16th century and changed the cultural and urban milieu of much of the subcontinent by introducing new technologies and customs.

COMING OF ISLAM

— *Empire of Mamluks (1236)*

☐ *Empire of Tughlaqs (1335)*

Illustrated Koran *(17th century)*
The noble Islamic art of calligraphy was introduced by Muslim rulers and used to embellish royal decrees, manuscripts and copies of the Koran, as well as buildings.

Ceramic Tiles
Jamali Kamali (see p111) *has fine examples of this Islamic art.*

Qutbuddin Aibak built the first storey of the Qutb Minar and a mosque to proclaim his victory over the Rajputs.

Quwwat-ul-Islam, which means "Might of Islam", was the first congregational mosque in Delhi.

Madrasa and tomb of Alauddin Khilji

Persian Wheel
The water wheel came in the wake of Muslim rule. Its simple technology is still used in rural areas to draw underground water for irrigation.

TIMELINE

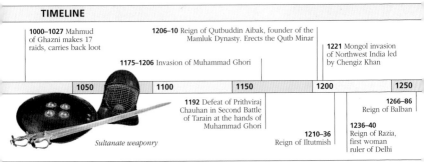

1000–1027 Mahmud of Ghazni makes 17 raids, carries back loot

1175–1206 Invasion of Muhammad Ghori

1206–10 Reign of Qutbuddin Aibak, founder of the Mamluk Dynasty. Erects the Qutb Minar

1221 Mongol invasion of Northwest India led by Chengiz Khan

| 1050 | 1100 | 1150 | 1200 | 1250 |

1192 Defeat of Prithviraj Chauhan in Second Battle of Tarain at the hands of Muhammad Ghori

Sultanate weaponry

1210–36 Reign of Iltutmish

1266–86 Reign of Balban

1236–40 Reign of Razia, first woman ruler of Delhi

Feroze Shah Tughlaq added the topmost storeys in 1368.

Iltutmish, Qutbuddin's successor, built the second and third storeys.

Alai Darwaza was built by Alauddin Khilji in 1311.

Nizamuddin Auliya
Mystic sages called Sufis were among the immigrants from Central Asia. This 17th-century miniature shows Nizamuddin Auliya (see p82) with the poet Amir Khusrau. Together, they raised metaphysical love, poetry and music to the level of divine worship.

WHERE TO SEE THE DELHI SULTANATE

The Mehrauli area *(see pp110–13)*, Hauz Khas *(see p106)*, Tughlaqabad *(see p114)*, Feroze Shah Kotla *(see p97)*, Purana Qila *(see p84)* and Lodi Gardens *(see p79)* show the various architectural styles of the Sultanate. The National Museum *(see pp72–3)* has a fine collection of artifacts dating to this period.

Begampuri Masjid (see p109)

Music
Amir Khusrau, poet and musician, is said to have introduced the multi-stringed sitar and the raga style to North Indian music.

THE QUTB MINAR
In 1193, Qutbuddin Aibak built the Qutb Minar *(see p112)* and a mosque to announce the advent of the Muslim sultans. This 19th-century lithograph shows a part of the Qutb complex that was built over the remains of an earlier Rajput citadel at Mehrauli *(see pp110–11)*.

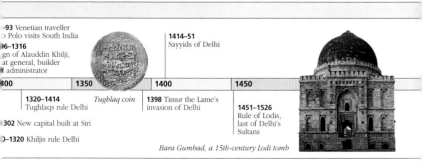

-93 Venetian traveller
Polo visits South India

96–1316
gn of Alauddin Khilji,
at general, builder
administrator

Tughlaq coin

1414–51
Sayyids of Delhi

00	1350	1400	1450

1320–1414
Tughlaqs rule Delhi

1398 Timur the Lame's
invasion of Delhi

1451–1526
Rule of Lodis,
last of Delhi's
Sultans

302 New capital built at Siri

0–1320 Khiljis rule Delhi

Bara Gumbad, a 15th-century Lodi tomb

The Great Mughals

Mughal cooking vessel

The Mughals, like the Ottomans of Turkey, the Safavids of Iran and the Tudors of England, were one of the greatest medieval dynasties. For over 200 years they held firm political control over the subcontinent, establishing a stable administrative system and a rich pluralistic culture blending the best of Hindu and Islamic traditions. Great patrons of art and architecture, they also encouraged the translation of Sanskrit texts into Persian. Markets and cities flourished under them, making India famous.

MUGHAL EMPIRE

☐ *Mughal Empire at the end of the 17th century*

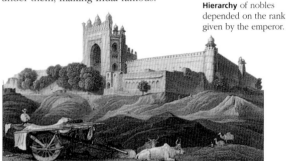

Hierarchy of nobles depended on the rank given by the emperor.

Buland Darwaza at Fatehpur Sikri
Erected to celebrate Akbar's victory over Gujarat in 1572–3, Buland Darwaza (see p173) is part of the great Mughal architectural legacy that still dominates the region.

Rajput princes were often loyal Mughal supporters. Shah Jahan's grandmother was a Rajput princess.

Mughal Art
A ruby-studded ceremonial gold spoon, Jahangir's jade wine cup, a gold enamelled glass hookah base and Mughal miniature paintings (see pp30–31) offer vivid glimpses of their extravagant patronage of art.

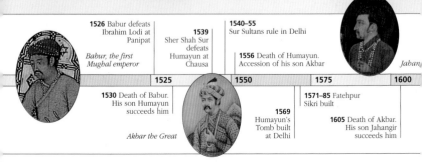

1526 Babur defeats Ibrahim Lodi at Panipat

Babur, the first Mughal emperor

1539 Sher Shah Sur defeats Humayun at Chausa

1540–55 Sur Sultans rule in Delhi

1556 Death of Humayun. Accession of his son Akbar

Jahan

1525	1550	1575	1600

1530 Death of Babur. His son Humayun succeeds him

Akbar the Great

1569 Humayun's Tomb built at Delhi

1571–85 Fatehpur Sikri built

1605 Death of Akbar. His son Jahangir succeeds him

Order and Symmetry
The "taming of the land" that took place under the Mughals, whether it was their landscaped gardens or their system of justice and revenue settlement, was founded on this dual principle.

WHERE TO SEE MUGHAL INDIA

Fatehpur Sikri *(see pp170–73)* and the Taj Mahal *(see pp154–5)* are among the finest examples of Mughal architecture in this region. The area around Delhi's Red Fort *(see pp94–5)* also has several Mughal relics. Important collections of Mughal art, manuscripts, coins, jewellery, costumes and armoury are housed in both the National Museum, Delhi *(see pp72–3)* and the City Palace Museum, Jaipur *(see pp188–9).*

Mughal necklace

Shah Jahan with his son in the foreground receiving a gift from a noble.

Diwan-i-Khas was used for special audience with the emperor and his advisors.

Court robes and turbans indicated status and religion.

A railing separated the imperial circle from lower state officials.

Military Organization
All senior administrators (mansabdars) maintained an armed retinue (sawars) and rank (zat) determined salary.

SHAH JAHAN'S COURT

The splendour of the Mughal court is illustrated in this 17th-century painting of Shah Jahan among his nobles, grouped in strict hierarchical order round the throne. Mughal emperors, seated in an elevated alcove, used glittering court rituals to display their supreme political position as they took stock of the state affairs from their officials.

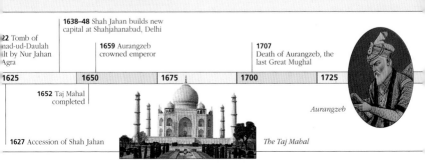

22 Tomb of mad-ud-Daulah lt by Nur Jahan Agra

1638–48 Shah Jahan builds new capital at Shahjahanabad, Delhi

1659 Aurangzeb crowned emperor

1707 Death of Aurangzeb, the last Great Mughal

| 1625 | 1650 | 1675 | 1700 | 1725 |

1652 Taj Mahal completed

Aurangzeb

1627 Accession of Shah Jahan

The Taj Mahal

European Traders, Colonizers and Mercenaries

Sahib and mahout

Crippled by the sack of Delhi in 1739 by Nadir Shah of Persia, Mughal power declined rapidly. This was exploited by petty rulers, European mercenaries, and the British East India Company, set up in the 1690s to trade in spices and cotton. Its commercial success led to the rise of the Company as a political power, which ushered in some social reforms and new power equations. Yet, the social instability engendered by the Company's unpopular trade and political practices erupted in the Indian Mutiny or Great Revolt of 1857.

THE INDIAN MUTINY OF 1857

☐ *Areas where British administration was disputed*

• *Site of major revolt in 1857*

British officer killing a rebel leader at Fatehpur.

The Decline of the Mughals
Nadir Shah's plunder of Delhi (see p92) was the signal for the rise of the Jats and Marathas. Suraj Mal Jat (see p166) filled Bharatpur Fort, seen above, with looted Mughal treasures.

Sepoys mutinied against animal grease on bullets as it violated religious taboos.

Economic Exploitation
A 19th-century lithograph shows the impoverishment of cotton ginners as cheap English mill-made cloth flooded the Indian market.

Indian rebels led by disgruntled princes ultimately lost the war.

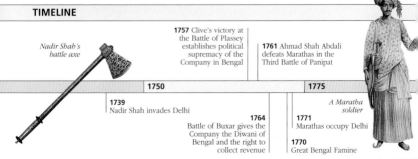

TIMELINE

Nadir Shah's battle axe

1757 Clive's victory at the Battle of Plassey establishes political supremacy of the Company in Bengal

1761 Ahmad Shah Abdali defeats Marathas in the Third Battle of Panipat

1750

1775

1739 Nadir Shah invades Delhi

1764 Battle of Buxar gives the Company the Diwani of Bengal and the right to collect revenue

1771 Marathas occupy Delhi

1770 Great Bengal Famine

A Maratha soldier

A Nabob and his Concubines
A corruption of nawab, this name described officials who made huge fortunes from the East India Company's cotton and spice trade in India. Many adopted the feudal lifestyles of the Indian princes as this 19th-century painting shows.

The plains of North India were the main battle areas.

Palanquins transported rebel princes and gentlefolk to the scene of battle.

Indian Sepoys
The Company's commercial interests were protected by its military establishment, which employed Indian foot soldiers called sepoys.

WHERE TO SEE EUROPEAN INDIA

Sardhana *(see p142)* has a cathedral built by Begum Samroo, the Indian wife of Walter Reinhardt, a European mercenary. Meerut's church, where the first shots of the sepoy mutiny were fired, survives in mint condition *(see p142)*. The cantonments in Meerut and Agra, the Agra cemetery *(see p152)* and St James's Church in Delhi *(see p101)* are other sites that go back to the time of the Indian Mutiny.

Sardhana Cathedral *(see p142)*

SEPOYS REBELLING AT FATEHPOOR
This lithograph of a pitched battle during the Mutiny show sepoys and Indian leaders being tackled by the Company's troops. The Indian Mutiny or Great Revolt of 1857 was seen as India's first war of independence from colonial rule by some nationalists as it shook the foundation of the East India Company's rule in India.

---

4 William Jones elected first president
he Asiatic Society of Bengal

1803 Delhi captured by the British

1829 *Sati* abolished

1853 First railway from Bombay to Thana

1857–8 The Indian Mutiny

1800 **1825** **1850**

1835 Company strikes its own coins omitting Mughal emperor's name

1856 Annexation of Oudh leads to wide public outrage against the Company

Queen Victoria's head on a Company coin

Oudh's Nawab Wajid Ali Shah

Pax Britannica

The Victoria Cross

The foundation of British rule, or the Raj, was laid only after the Indian Mutiny, which truly revealed the unpopularity of the East India Company. An Act of Parliament in 1858 brought its rule to a close and its Indian territories became part of Britain's empire. India was now ruled directly by the Crown through a viceroy. Though the Raj was unabashedly Victorian and conservative, and its *raison d'être* was economic profit and political control, its abiding legacy was the political unification of the subcontinent, and the introduction of modern Western education, a centralized civil administration and judicial system, along with a wide network of railways and postal services.

BRITISH INDIA

☐ *British territory, 1858*

The Steel Frame
Some 2,000 British officers ruled over a subcontinent of 300 million people. The paternalistic civil service brought order and justice even to remote outposts.

Indian attendants in viceregal livery re-enact a Mughal procession.

Old Delhi is relegated to the background.

Memsahib with her Tailor
Despite the climate, the English clung to their own dress styles. Children were sent "home" to study, and a large Indian staff enabled a luxurious lifestyle.

TIMELINE

Lord Canning, the first Viceroy

1859 Withdrawal of Doctrine of Lapse, a major cause of the 1857 revolt

1861 Indian Council Act

Lord Dalhousie, author of notorious Doctrine of Lapse (see p319)

1875

1858 Victoria proclaims Lord Canning first Viceroy of India

1865 Telegraphic communication is established with Europe

1876 Victoria proclaims herself Empress of India

1877 Lytton's Delhi Durbar

A Sahib Travelling
A vast rail network was set up by the British to facilitate commerce and travel. This lithograph of first-class travel, a privilege of "whites only", is from the 19th century.

Raj Cuisine
While kababs, curry and rice became a part of British culinary preference, Westernized Indians took to drinking tea and nibbling biscuits. An early 20th-century biscuit tin label reflects this exchange of tastes.

Caparisoned elephants carry the new rulers.

Crowds line the streets to see the grand spectacle.

WHERE TO SEE BRITISH INDIA

Raisina Hill and the surrounding area *(see pp68–9)*, Agra's St John's College *(see p152)*, Mayo College *(see p219)* in Ajmer are examples of colonial architecture. Delhi's Coronation Park *(see p103)* and the University area *(see p103)* are other sites with a Raj connection.

Detail of India Gate *(see p71)*

THE DURBAR, 1903

This painting of Curzon's Delhi Durbar (1903), held to celebrate the coronation of Edward VII, shows a procession winding through the historic streets of Delhi. Held periodically, such assemblies announced both the grandeur and the political might of British rule in India.

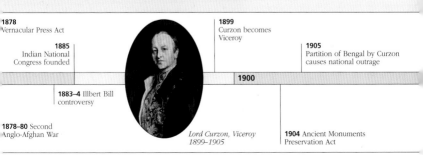

1878 Vernacular Press Act

1885 Indian National Congress founded

1883–4 Illbert Bill controversy

1878–80 Second Anglo-Afghan War

1899 Curzon becomes Viceroy

1905 Partition of Bengal by Curzon causes national outrage

1900

Lord Curzon, Viceroy 1899–1905

1904 Ancient Monuments Preservation Act

The Freedom Movement

Gandhi's spinning wheel

The founding of the Indian National Congress in 1885 gave Indians a platform from which to demand freedom from foreign rule. Their ideology was provided by Gandhi, whose message of non-violence and economic self-reliance gave them moral confidence, and united castes and communities under a common cause. At first the movement for freedom was ruthlessly suppressed, but by the 1930s it became too large for the British to handle. Finally, weakened by World War II and under growing international pressure, England granted India formal independence in 1947.

FREEDOM MOVEMENT

- *Major towns associated with the Freedom Movement*

Khadi, homespun cloth, was worn as a statement of patriotism.

Huge crowds turned out to register their support. Gandhi united castes and communities as never before.

Round Table Conference (1931)
The British tried to work out a settlement with Gandhi, accompanied by formidable campaigner and poet, Sarojini Naidu.

The police dogged public assemblies, often brutally beating the audience.

The Cellular Jail, Andaman Islands
Hundreds of freedom fighters were shipped here by the British. Many were hanged, some died of diseases such as malaria. Now a national monument, the jail's popular name, Kala Pani ("black waters"), recalls its dark past.

TIMELINE

Rabindranath Tagore

1906 Muslim League formed at Dacca

1907 Congress splits at Surat between the moderates and extremists

1908 Tilak, a prominent nationalist, sentenced to six years transportation on charges of sedition

1910

1913 Rabindranath Tagore wins the Nobel Prize for Literature

1914 Canada refuses Indians aboard the ship *Kamagata Maru* permission to land

1915 Home Rule League started by Annie Besant

1917 Gandhi takes up the cause of indigo farmers at Champaran, Bihar

1919 Police fires at unarmed crowd at Jallianwala Bagh in Amritsar, Punjab

1920 Non-cooperation Movement launched by Gandhi

1920

New Delhi
New Delhi was declared the Raj's capital in 1911. This early photo shows Parliament House, then the Legislative Assembly building.

WHERE TO SEE THE FREEDOM MOVEMENT
The National Archives *(see p71)* and the Gandhi Smriti *(see p78)* have a permanent exhibition on the Freedom Movement. Panels on this theme are also displayed at the Jawahar Pavilion in Pragati Maidan *(see p85)*. Teen Murti House *(see p78)* offers a view of Nehru's life.

Nehru and Jinnah
Brilliant lawyers who joined Gandhi's national movement, they enjoyed an iconic status in India and Pakistan after Independence.

Gandhi delivered his powerful message of freedom at public meetings.

Gandhi Samadhi, Rajghat *(see p97)*

The Partition (1947)
A huge displacement of people across the borders took place at the division of the subcontinent into India and Pakistan, leading to an eruption of violent communal riots.

MAHATMA GANDHI
Called Mahatma ("great spirit"), MK Gandhi returned to India from South Africa in 1915 as a protest against apartheid. He travelled across the subcontinent, launching a moral crusade that encouraged non-violent Civil Disobedience against colonial rule.

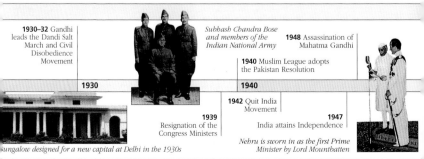

1930–32 Gandhi leads the Dandi Salt March and Civil Disobedience Movement

Subhash Chandra Bose and members of the Indian National Army

1948 Assassination of Mahatma Gandhi

1940 Muslim League adopts the Pakistan Resolution

1930

1940

1942 Quit India Movement

1939 Resignation of the Congress Ministers

1947 India attains Independence

...ungalow designed for a new capital at Delhi in the 1930s

Nehru is sworn in as the first Prime Minister by Lord Mountbatten

India Today

Cell-phones are a familiar sight

India celebrated 50 years of independence in 1997. Nehru, the first prime minister, laid the foundations for a modern nation state with a democratic, secular polity, a strong industrial base and a planned economy, with non-alignment as the keystone of its foreign policy. India's 1.1 billion people speak 18 languages, and though many of them are illiterate and unemployed, a vigorous and free press and electoral system ensure that their interests and rights are safeguarded and well represented. The two major national political parties are the Congress, and the more right-wing Bharatiya Janata Party.

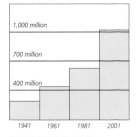

1,000 million

700 million

400 million

1941   1961   1981   2001

POPULATION FIGURES

☐ *Growth of population*

New Delhi
was built between 1911 and 1933 by Lutyens and Baker.

Rural India
More than half the country's population lives in its villages. An adult literacy programme is under way to educate the disadvantaged, particularly women.

The Nehru Family
Jawaharlal Nehru is seen here with his daughter Indira Gandhi (who was not related to Mahatma Gandhi), and her son Rajiv Gandhi. All three were prime ministers of India. Rajiv's Italian-born widow, Sonia, now heads the Congress Party.

The Indian flag
is a tricolour of saffron, white and green, with a *chakra* (wheel) in the centre.

TIMELINE

1952 First General Election

1953 Mount Everest scaled by Hillary and Tenzing

1964 Death of Jawaharlal Nehru, first prime minister

1971 War with Pakistan, birth of Bangladesh

1977 Janata Party, the first non-Congress coalition, takes power

Indian flag

1960	1965	1970	1975	1980

1955 Bandung Conference on Non-Alignment

1962 India-China War

1966 Indira Gandhi becomes prime minister

1965 War with Pakistan

1974 First nuclear test, Pokhran

1975 Indira Gandhi declares the unpopular Emergency

1980 Indira Gandhi returns as prime minister

1982 India sends scientific team to Antarctica

1950 India becomes a Republic

Cricket
Introduced by the British, this game is now a national obsession. Sachin Tendulkar, the "little master", is regarded by many as the greatest batsman since Donald Bradman.

Industrial Development
Nehru, the architect of the country's industrial base, hailed factories as the new temples of modern India. India is now a major industrial power with a huge workforce of skilled workers.

The Indian Army is one of the largest in the world.

South Block and its twin, North Block, were designed to flank Raisina Hill.

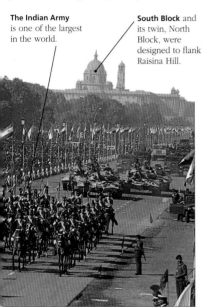

Protest Rallies
India's vibrant democracy expresses itself through popular protest (dharna) in which women figure prominently. The Narmada Bachao activists, seen here, have mobilized women and displaced tribal people against the World Bank-funded Narmada Dam.

Amartya Sen
He won the Nobel Prize for Economics in 1998 for his work on development economics, based on studies of India's literacy, population, famine and the status of women.

THE REPUBLIC DAY PARADE
A magnificent parade on 26 January celebrates the day when India became a republic in 1950. A colourful flypast, folk dances and floats celebrate its pluralistic society, and the president, as head of the republic, takes the salute at Rajpath.

4 Indira Gandhi ssinated, her son Gandhi succeeds as prime minister

1990 VP Singh becomes prime minister; announcement of reservation for backward classes

1998 The right-wing Bharatiya Janta Party (BJP) comes to power for the first time; AB Vajpayee becomes prime minister

2001 Earthquake in Gujarat

2005 Indo-US nuclear deal signed

| 985 | 1990 | 1995 | 2000 | 2005 |

1992 Destruction of Babri Masjid in the state of Uttar Pradesh leads to communal riots

2004 Manmohan Singh elected Prime Minister; UPA government in power

1991 Rajiv Gandhi assassinated; New Liberalization Policy under Prime Minister Narasimha Rao

1999 Conflict with Pakistan over Kashmir at Kargil; 13th General Elections re-elect a BJP-led government

woman casts her vote

DELHI
AREA BY AREA

DELHI AT A GLANCE 64–65

NEW DELHI 66–79

NIZAMUDDIN TO PURANA QILA 80–87

OLD DELHI 88–97

FURTHER AFIELD 98–115

DAY TRIPS FROM DELHI 116–117

SHOPPING IN DELHI 118–119

ENTERTAINMENT IN DELHI 120–121

DELHI STREET FINDER 122–131

Delhi at a Glance

Situated along the Yamuna river, New Delhi was
built by the British in the 1930s and is the
youngest of several historic cities that have
occupied this site. Now a noisy and chaotic
metropolis of 15 million people and a mélange
of shanty settlements and smart colonies, it is
still dotted with the remains of its interesting
past. There are museums and art galleries with
impressive collections, and its shops offer a
tempting array of handicrafts. Delhi is a major
cultural centre of the country with music, dance
and art events held throughout the year.

The Jami Masjid
(see p92) *is the
largest congre-
gational mosque in
Asia with lively
bazaars in the
surrounding lanes.*

Connaught Place
(see p76), *was
built in the 1930s
as the business
centre of New
Delhi, in
concentric circles
round a central
park. Its stately
colonnaded
corridors contain
shops and offices.*

NEW DELHI
(see pp66–79)

Rashtrapati Bhavan (see pp68–70) *is the
official residence of the President of India.
Called Viceroy's House in colonial times, it
was designed by Edwin Lutyens and occupies
the crest of Raisina Hill. Its forecourt is the
venue for colourful state pageantry.*

**The National
Museum** (see
pp72–5) *houses the
most comprehensive
collection of
antiquities in the
country. This 2nd-
century Sunga panel
of a grieving woman is part
of a stunning section on sculpture
from various periods and places.*

0 kilometres		1
0 miles		

◁ Swirling traffic in the narrow lanes of the old city around Jami Masjid

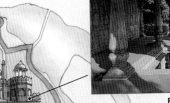

Red Fort (see pp94–5), *an impressive fort-palace built by Shah Jahan, was the seat of Mughal power. After the Indian Mutiny of 1857, the British converted it into a garrison and it was stripped of many precious treasures.*

OLD DELHI
(see pp88–97)

The Crafts Museum (see pp86–7) *complex offers an insight into India's cultural, craft and rural traditions. The museum exhibits textiles, folk art and objects of everyday use in terracotta, metal and wood.*

NIZAMUDDIN TO PURANA QILA
(see pp80–87)

Humayun's Tomb (see p83) *is where the second Mughal emperor Humayun is buried. This garden tomb with its imposing double dome is considered by many to be the first great Mughal mausoleum in this region.*

NEW DELHI

The British built New Delhi, between 1911 and 1931, to be the showcase of the Empire. On Independence, this grand imperial capital became the official and bureaucratic centre of the new Indian nation. Today, Viceroy's House is the president's residence, and ministers and civil servants live nearby in spacious bungalows along the tree-lined avenues.

Gargoyle

Kingsway, the east-west processional avenue leading to India Gate, is now Rajpath, where every 26 January the Republic Day Parade is held *(see p71)*. The National Museum is on Janpath. To the north are Connaught Place, the Birla Mandir and the cultural complex at Mandi House. Despite strict security restrictions, New Delhi is the city's most impressive area.

SIGHTS AT A GLANCE

Historic Buildings, Streets and Plazas
India Gate **6**
Rajpath **4**
Rashtrapati Bhavan **1**
Vijay Chowk **2**

Churches and Temples
Lakshmi Narayan Mandir **11**
Church of Redemption **3**

Museums
Gandhi Smriti **14**
National Gallery of Modern Art **7**
National Museum **5**
Nehru Memorial Museum and Library **13**

Monuments
Jantar Mantar **12**
Ugrasen's Baoli **9**

Gardens
Lodi Gardens **15**

Shops and Markets
Connaught Place **10**
Khan Market **16**

Theatres and Art Galleries
Mandi House Complex **8**

GETTING THERE
This area is well served by buses, the safe and efficient metro rail and taxis.

KEY

▨	Street-by-Street map *See pp68–9*
▤	Railway station
M	Metro station
▥	Bus station
▣	Police station
⊠	Post office
✚	Hospital
▦	Temple
▧	Gurudwara
▤	Church
▨	Tomb

0 metres 750
0 yards 750

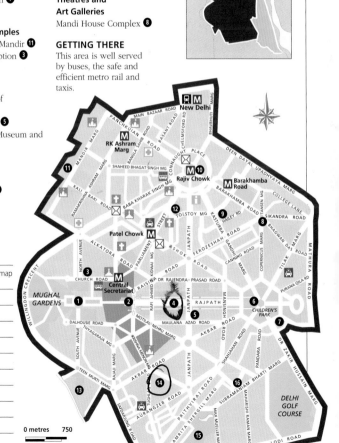

◁ **India Gate and the elegant statue canopy designed by Lutyens**

Street-by-Street: Around Vijay Chowk

The barren, treeless grounds around Raisina Hill were selected as the site of the new capital city. Now a well-guarded verdant area, it houses India's president, ministers and officials, as well as its Parliament and ministries. Imperial hierarchical conventions, both spatial and political laid down by the British are still followed, so that even today, Indian ministers and officials live in spacious bungalows on broad tree-shaded avenues around Rashtrapati Bhavan where no high-rise buildings are allowed. From Vijay Chowk, Lutyens's grand central vista lies ahead – large trees and fountains line the lawns of Rajpath up to India Gate, the Canopy and the National Stadium at the far end.

★ **Vijay Chowk**
A pair of red sandstone obelisk-shaped fountains flank this forecourt that overlooks a grand vista ❷

North Block has an imposing Central Hall which is open to the public.

Sansad Bhavan is also known as Parliament House.

The Iron Gates
Copied from a pair Lutyens saw in Chiswick, England, these are held by highly ornamental sandstone gateposts. Rashtrapati Bhavan lies to the west of them.

DALHOUSIE ROAD

THYAGARAJ MARG

KEY

– – – Suggested route

EDWIN LANDSEER LUTYENS

Building the Secretariats on rocky scrubland

Architect Edwin Landseer Lutyens (1869–1944), President of the Royal Academy from 1938 to 1944, was commissioned to design India's new capital in 1911. With Herbert Baker, his colleague, it took him 20 years to build the city in a unique style that combined Western Classicism with Indian decorative motifs. The result is classical in form and English in manner with Neo-Mughal gardens and grand vistas meeting at verdant roundabouts. Delayed by World War I and quarrels between Baker and Lutyens, spiralling costs met by Indian revenues led Mahatma Gandhi to term it a "white elephant". Ironically, the British lived here for only 16 years.

★ **South Block**
The Prime Minister's Office and the Defence Ministry are located within this block, a high security zone.

Sunehri Bagh
This gently curving street leads to a picturesque roundabout with a simple 18th-century mosque built by a pir called Sayyid Sahib. Shady trees are a standard feature of all Lutyens's avenues.

LOCATOR MAP
See Street Finder map 4

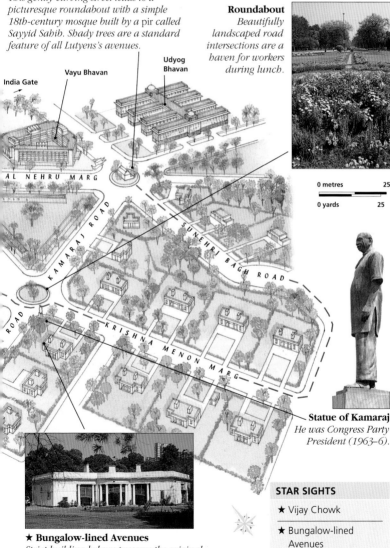

Roundabout
Beautifully landscaped road intersections are a haven for workers during lunch.

Udyog Bhavan

Vayu Bhavan

India Gate

AL NEHRU MARG

KAMARAJ ROAD

SUNEHRI BAGH ROAD

ROAD

KRISHNA MENON MARG

| 0 metres | 25 |
| 0 yards | 25 |

Statue of Kamaraj
He was Congress Party President (1963–6).

★ **Bungalow-lined Avenues**
Strict building bylaws preserve the original architecture of the colonial bungalows in the tree-lined avenues of this area.

STAR SIGHTS

★ Vijay Chowk

★ Bungalow-lined Avenues

★ South Block

Rashtrapati Bhavan seen through Lutyens's ornate iron gates

Rashtrapati Bhavan ❶

Map 4 E2. **Tel** *(011) 2301 5321.* ⬚ *9.30am–1pm, 2pm–4.30pm: Mon, Wed, Fri & Sat.* **Change of Guard Ceremony Tel** *(011) 2301 3592. Apr–Oct: 8am; Nov–Mar: 10am Sat only.* **Kitchen Museum Tel** *(011) 2301 3592.* ⬚ *Same as tour.* **Mughal Gardens** ⬚ *Feb–Mar.*

Designed by Edwin Lutyens *(see p68)* to be the focal point of New Delhi during British rule, the house built for the viceroy, which is today the President of India's official residence, stands at the crest of Raisina Hill. This 20th-century architectural masterpiece covers an area of 4.5 acres (2 ha). The cupola of its copper and sandstone dome rises 55 m (180 ft). Within are

Jaipur Column

courtyards, banqueting halls, state apartments and private living quarters. The *pièce de résistance* is the Durbar Hall, where all important Indian state and ceremonial occasions are held. Situated beneath the dome and forming the centrepiece of the "H"-shaped building, this circular hall was originally the Throne Room and contains the two gold and crimson thrones Lutyens designed for the viceroy and vicereine. The **Kitchen Museum** showcases items used to cook, serve and dine at the Rashtrapati Bhavan, through the pre- and post-Independence periods. To the west of the grounds are the formal **Mughal Gardens** with water-courses and fountains built on three levels, ending with Lutyens's "butterfly garden".

Vijay Chowk ❷

Map 4 F2. **N Block** ⬚ *9am–6pm Mon–Fri.* **Sansad Bhavan** ⬚ *11am–5pm. Visit is subject to Parliament not being in session.*

The area where Rajpath meets Raisina Hill, known as Vijay Chowk, was planned as a commanding approach to the Viceroy's House. This is where the unforgettable "Beating Retreat" ceremony takes place each year on 29 January *(see p41)*.

Rising impressively from the levelled top of Raisina Hill are the two virtually identical **Secretariat** buildings designed by Herbert Baker and known as the North and South Blocks. These long classical edifices house the Home and Finance ministries and the Ministry of Foreign Affairs. The stately Central Hall of North Block (to the left, if facing Vijay Chowk) is open to the public.

Sited to the north of Vijay Chowk, Baker's circular **Sansad Bhavan** (Parliament House) was a later addition following the Montagu-Chelmsford Reforms of 1919, to house the Legislative Assembly. The Constitution of India was drafted here in the early days of Independence. Today, both the Rajya Sabha (Upper House) and the Lok Sabha (House of the People) meet here when Parliament is in session. The Lok Sabha's often boisterous debates take place in the Central Hall.

Sansad Bhavan (Parliament House), where the Constitution of India was drafted

Cathedral Church of the Redemption ❸

Church Rd. **Map** 4 E1. **Tel** (011) 2309 4229. ⬜ 8am–noon; 4–6pm daily.

Henry Alexander Medd (1892–1977), the architect of this magnificent church, was inspired by Palladio's Church of Il Redentore in Venice, from which it also derives its name. Consecrated in 1931, the cathedral formed an integral element of the plan for the imperial capital complex, and was built as the main Anglican church for senior British officials in New Delhi. Today, it is the diocese of the Bishop of the Church of Northern India. Among the many memorial tablets inside the church, there is one in honour of its architect.

The Neo-Classical Cathedral Church of the Redemption

Rajpath ❹

Map 5 A2. **National Archives Tel** (011) 2338 5000. ⬜ 9.30am–6pm Mon–Fri. 🌑 Public hols. **Indira Gandhi National Centre for the Arts Tel** (011) 2338 9216. ⬜ 9am–5.30pm Mon–Fri.

This two-mile-long avenue, used for parades and lined with canals and fountains along its lovely lawns, is very popular with Delhi residents on steamy summer evenings.

The **National Archives**, situated at the intersection with Janpath, houses a major collection of state records and private papers. Opposite is the **Indira Gandhi National Centre for the Arts** (IGNCA), with an archive of rare manuscripts. It holds many national and international exhibitions and symposia.

National Museum ❺

See pp72–3.

India Gate ❻

Map 5 B2.

At the eastern end of Rajpath, the 9-m (30-ft) wide India Gate was built to commemorate the Indian and British soldiers who died in World War I and those who fell in battle in the North-West Frontier Province and the Third Afghan War. An eternal flame burns in memory of unknown soldiers who died in the 1971 Indo-Pakistan war. Facing India Gate is the sandstone canopy where King George V's statue was installed after his death in 1936. The statue is now at Coronation Park (see p103). Around India Gate are the stately homes of erstwhile Indian princes, including Hyderabad House where official state banquets are held, and Jaipur, Bikaner, Patiala and Baroda Houses.

India Gate

National Gallery of Modern Art ❼

Jaipur House, near India Gate. **Map** 5 C2. **Tel** (011) 2338 2835. ⬜ 10am–5pm Tue–Sun. 🌑 Mon & public hols. 🎟 👥

Jaipur House, the former residence of the Jaipur maharajas, is one of India's largest museums of modern art. Its vast collection includes graphics, paintings and sculptures dating from the mid-19th century to the present day. The galleries display works of British landscape painters such as the Daniells, and early Indian artists such as the Tagores, Jamini Roy, Amrita Shergill and Raja Ravi Varma. Works of contemporary artists such as MF Husain, Ram Kumar, KG Subramanyam and Anjolie Ela Menon are also seen here. Reproductions of paintings are sold at the gallery shop.

REPUBLIC DAY PARADE

Indians love parades and ever since 1950, when India became a republic, the Republic Day parade on 26 January has always attracted large crowds despite the often chilly weather. The president, the prime minister and other dignitaries watch as soldiers in dashing uniforms from the many regiments and squadrons of the Army, Navy and Air Force march smartly past. Brightly dressed schoolchildren, civil defence services personnel and others quick-step down the grand vistas of Rajpath to the rousing percussion of military bands. Most popular are the Camel Corps and the inventive floats representing each state of the country. A ceremonial fly-past by the Indian Air Force signals the end of the parade.

Republic Day Parade

The National Museum ❺

Dancing girl from 2500 BC

Five millennia of Indian history can be explored at the National Museum, with a collection of more than 200,000 pieces of Indian art. The nucleus collection of about 1,000 artifacts was sent to London in the winter of 1948–9 for an exhibition at the Royal Academy's Burlington House. After its return, it was housed in the Durbar Hall of Rashtrapati Bhavan until the present building, built of the same beige and pink stone as the imposing new capital, was complete in 1960. The Museum's collection of Indus Valley relics and Central Asian treasures from the Silk Route is considered among the finest in the world.

★ Dara Shikoh's Marriage Procession
An 18th-century Mughal miniature painting in gold and natural pigments.

★ Nataraja
This 12th-century Chola statue of the cosmic dance of Lord Shiva is the centre-piece of the museum's South Indian bronzes.

The Coins and Indian Scripts Gallery displays an impressive collection of coins and the evolution of the Indian script.

Jewellery Gallery

Ground floor

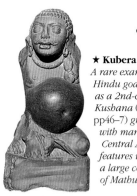

★ Kubera
A rare example of a Hindu god shown as a 2nd-century Kushana (see pp46–7) grandee with marked Central Asian features is among a large collection of Mathura Art.

Entrance

THE SERINDIAN COLLECTION

Silk painting, 7th–8th century

Almost 700 years after the Silk Route fell into disuse, Sir Aurel Stein, a British archae-ologist, led a series of expeditions (1900–16) to un-cover its treasures. On view at the National Museum, Stein's Central Asian collec-tion of the artifacts he found in the Taklamakan Desert has silk paintings, Buddhist manuscripts and valuable records of life along this ancient trade route.

Terracotta Mask
This unusual human mask made of terracotta dates back to 2700 BC, and was unearthed in Mohenjodaro in the early 20th century.

Aurangzeb's Sword

The personal sword of the Mughal emperor Aurangzeb, crafted in 1675 in the Indo-Persian style, has quotations from the Koran inscribed on it.

Gold Brocade

This 19th-century silk wedding sari woven in Varanasi is embellished with motifs in gold thread.

Wood carvings in the form of religious statues, carved doors and lintels are some of the exhibits here.

Second floor

First floor

★ Illuminated Koran

A superb example of the elegant Islamic art of calligraphy, this gilded 18th-century Koran is one of a collection that also has a 8th-century Koran in the ancient Kufic script. The latter is among the oldest of its kind in the world.

GALLERY GUIDE

The collection is displayed on three floors, grouped according to theme, epoch and style. The central foyer itself has a display of sculptures from various parts of the country. The museum also has a library and auditorium where film shows and lectures are regularly held. Information on these is published in the newspapers. Information regarding catalogues and souvenirs can be had at the ticket office in the foyer. The display is changed from time to time for variety, and special exhibitions are also mounted.

KEY TO FLOORPLAN

- ☐ Indus Valley Culture
- ☐ Ancient and Medieval Sculpture
- ☐ Chola Bronzes
- ☐ Buddhist Art
- ☐ Indian Miniatures
- ☐ Decorative Arts
- ☐ Manuscripts and Wall Paintings
- ☐ Central Asian Antiquities
- ☐ Textiles, Arms and Armour, Musical Instruments

STAR EXHIBITS

- ★ Dara Shikoh's Marriage Procession
- ★ Nataraja
- ★ Kubera
- ★ Illuminated Koran

Exploring the National Museum Collection

Spread over three floors radiating from an octagonal courtyard, the museum has 30 galleries (some closed for renovation or devoted to temporary exhibitions). The impressive collection includes sculpture, paintings, jewellery, decorative arts and textiles. These represent the finest examples of each style and period from all over the country.

2nd-century Kushana sculpture

INDUS VALLEY CULTURE

Excavations in the 1920s at Harappa and Mohenjodaro (now in Pakistan) revealed the remains of a sophisticated urban culture that existed between 2500–1500 BC along the Indus Valley *(see pp44–5)*. The museum's collection of relics from these sites is among the finest in the world. Although the Indus copper and bronze instruments are less opulent than the later Mesopotamian and Egyptian ones, other items, such as the figure of a dancing girl and a headless female torso, show enormous artistic skill.

Also on display are soapstone seals, used perhaps by merchants and officials, whose pictographic script remains undeciphered. Particularly notable is the display of Harappan pottery which ranges from functional items such as pots to charming toys, beads, necklaces and weights.

ANCIENT AND MEDIEVAL SCULPTURE

Six galleries on the ground floor trace the growth of Indian sculpture over 1,500 years. Among the earliest pieces is a rare terracotta fertility goddess from Mathura dating to the 3rd century BC. From Amaravati in Andhra Pradesh (1st century AD), is a superb sculpted panel depicting its now vanished reliquary mound *(stupa)*. The 2nd-century AD Kushana frieze of Vasantasena, an inebriated courtesan *(see pp46–7)*, is an amusing comment on court life, while the splendid collection of Gandhara art, with its marked Hellenistic style, shows the evolution of the human form in North Indian sculpture after the 1st century. Its delicately draped statues are the first representations of the Buddha in human form. After the great stone-carved Hindu temples and images of the Gupta period (3rd–5th centuries), regional styles emerged in the south and the east. Successive galleries trace sculptural developments of the Pallava, Chalukya and the Hoysala dynasties.

BRONZES

Indian bronzes, executed through the *cire perdue* or "lost wax" process as an alternative to stone temple sculptures, developed in South India under the Chola and Pallava dynasties. Idols made of bronze, an alloy of eight metals with copper as the base, were less weighty than stone and could either be worshipped at home or taken out for festive processions. The gallery's collection covers 600 years (5th–11th centuries). The pride of place belongs to a 10th-century Chola Nataraja, the name given to the Lord of Dance, Shiva. This shows him dancing the Chaturatandava, a classic representation of his cosmic dance of life and death. The circle of flames that surrounds the dancer represents the entire cosmos.

Devi, 15th-century bronze

Another 11th-century Chola bronze, *Kaliyamardan Krishna*, is a superb study of the balance and poise of the young Lord Krishna as he dances on the hood of the five-headed serpent, Kaliya, holding his tail in triumph.

MANUSCRIPTS AND WALL PAINTINGS

Among the wealth of rare manuscripts in the museum are the *Bustan-e-sadi* (1502), one of the few dated and illustrated manuscripts of pre-Mughal India. Leaves from the 16th-century *Babur Nama*, a biography of the first Mughal emperor, illustrate the style of early Mughal painting. A *Rig Veda Samita* (1514) and a beautiful 18th century cloth scroll of the *Bhagvat Purana* are also part of this collection.

Also on display is an unparalleled *Hunting Scene* (c.1810) from the Kota School of Painting, salvaged from the Jhala Jhalim Singh Haveli in Kota, Rajasthan.

2nd-century Jain votive plaque from Mathura

DECORATIVE ARTS

The immense variety of India's decorative arts fills two adjoining galleries. Even everyday objects, such as a 19th-century silver rosewater sprinkler from Delhi, or a hookah base enamelled in blue and green from 18th-century Rajasthan have individual flourishes.

Court patronage ensured that artists fashioned innumerable *objets d'art* to delight royal whims. Thus, floral arabesques adorn a 17th-century Mughal *degcha* (cooking pot). Daintily carved ivory statues and artifacts and elegant Hyderabad *bidri* ware, delicately inlaid with silver, are also on display.

Durga Killing Demon Raktabija, Malwa, c.1640

An 18th-century *bidri ware* jewel box

INDIAN MINIATURES

Over 350 paintings from a large collection of 18,000 are on display in the new miniature gallery. There are some Mughal masterpieces from the Jahangir and Shah Jahan period, including the famous *Jahangir Holding the Picture of Madonna* (c.1620) and *Camel Fight* (c.1615-20). Insightful portraits of the Mughal rulers Babur, Jahangir, Shah Jahan, and other court personalities such as Tansen, the legendary court musician of Akbar's time, bring Mughal history to life.

Also on view are a selection of *Ragamala* series depicting the mood of each *raga*. The Rajasthani miniatures illustrate Hindu mythological themes, particularly the devotional love between Krishna and Radha. The Kishangarh paintings, *Boat of Love* and *Radha and Krishna*, both mid-18th

century, bring lyricism and beauty to this timeless relationship. There are also hunting scenes from Kota where the depiction of nature is real and vibrant. Court painters at Mewar produced detailed depictions of a variety of royal pursuits ranging from the court to recreation and leisure.

Basholi paintings with their bold and intense colours, and delicate portraits from Guler are part of the large collection of Pahari paintings from the northern hill states. Deccani art from Hyderabad, a fusion of the Islamic idiom with indigenous styles, produced masterpieces such as *A Picnic Party* (early 18th century). Also on display are later provincial schools that developed after the Mughals, as well as Company art, produced for the British from the mid-18th century.

CENTRAL ASIAN ANTIQUITIES

Sir Aurel Stein's collection of treasures (see p72) discovered from the fabled Silk Route in Chinese Turkestan comprises this invaluable section. Included are paintings on silk (3rd century) and a 10th-century caravan scene on paper from Dunhuang in China that re-create the romance of those times. Fragments of another fabulous silk painting, *Ladies in a Garden*, from Astana, show lovely women in elaborate coiffures with impressive gold filigree pins, lounging among blossoms.

TEXTILES, ARMS AND ARMOUR, MUSICAL INSTRUMENTS

The textile collection displays a selection of Indian weaving techniques, including the world famous gold and silk brocades of Varanasi from the Mughal period; *ikat* and tie-and-dye from Andhra Pradesh and Gujarat; and 19th-century *kantha* embroidery from Bengal in intricate hemstitch. Also worth noting is a hand-embroidered *rumal* from Golconda dating to 1640.

The Arms and Armour Gallery has the 18th-century painted rhinohide shield of the Rajput king, Maharana Sangram Singh.

The Musical Instruments Gallery has some artifacts that are over 200 years old, including an ivory inlaid *tanpura* (a stringed instrument) from the 18th century. The core collection was donated by Sharan Rani, a famous *sarod* player.

17th-century jamawar shawl

Mandi House Complex ❽

Map 2 D5.
Triveni Kala Sangam Tansen Marg.
Tel *(011) 2371 8833.*
⬜ *9.30am–5pm Mon–Sat.* ◑
Public hols. 🚽 🅿
Rabindra Bhavan Ferozeshah Rd.
Tel *(011) 2338 6626.*
Kamani Auditorium Copernicus
Marg. ***Tel*** *(011) 2338 8084.*
Sri Ram Centre Safdar Hashmi
Marg. ***Tel*** *(011) 2371 4307.* 🚽 🅿
National School of Drama Bhagwan
Das Rd. ***Tel*** *(011) 2338 9402.*
For ***Tickets*** *see* ***Entertainment***
pp120–21.

Mandi House, once the palace of the ruler of a small principality in Himachal Pradesh and today the offices of the state-owned television centre, lends its name to this cultural complex encircling the roundabout.
Triveni Kala Sangam's various art galleries hold regular contemporary art exhibitions. A pleasant open air auditorium here stages dance and theatre performances. Well-known artistes and writers can often be glimpsed in the popular café, and there is also a bookshop specializing in Indian arts publications.

The state-sponsored arts complex, **Rabindra Bhavan**, houses the three national academies of literature (Sahitya Akademi), fine arts and sculpture (Lalit Kala Akademi), and the performing arts (Sangeet Natak Akademi) in separate wings. All have libraries and display galleries which also sell reproductions and postcards. The Lalit Kala is the site of the international Triennale exhibition in which painters and sculptors from more than 30 countries participate. Exhibitions of photography, graphics and ceramics are also held here.
Kamani Auditorium, the **Sri Ram Centre** and the **National School of Drama** host theatrical, classical music and dance events in their auditoria. The latter two have their own repertory companies which stage plays in many regional languages.

Ugrasen's Baoli in the heart of New Delhi

Ugrasen's Baoli ❾

Off Hailey Rd. **Map** 2 D5.

This stepwell *(see p27)* is reached by turning left on Hailey Road into a narrow lane without a signpost just before the Consulate General of Malta. A little way along on the right are the remains of an old stone wall; the *baoli* is behind them and can be entered through a narrow buttressed gateway, usually locked, but the *chowkidar* will open the gate. Considered one of Delhi's finest stepwells, its architectural features suggest a 15th-century date, though popular myth holds that it was built in the 14th century by Raja Ugrasen, an ancestor of the mercantile Aggarwal community, to provide water and shelter for travellers.

Mirror-work skirts on sale at Janpath

Connaught Place ❿

Map 1 C4.
Shops ⬜ *10:30am–8pm Mon–Sat.*
◑ *Sun & public hols.*

Robert Tor Russell, one of New Delhi's architects, designed this imperial plaza named after the Duke of Connaught, an uncle of King George V. Noble Palladian archways and stuccoed colonnades deliberately recalled the very English terraces of Cheltenham and Bath; and when the first shops raised their shutters in 1931, they had names such as "Empire Stores" to distinguish them from the local shops selling Indian goods in shopping areas like Gole Market and Chandni Chowk. Today there are as many offices as shops in the central circle, officially renamed Rajiv Chowk. (The outer circle is now Indira Chowk.) The shops are an eclectic mix of travel agencies, banks, outlets for several leading international brands and the ubiquitous gift kiosks. Though Connaught Place has, in recent years, lost out to other local markets, its shaded arcades offer a pleasant atmosphere to stroll in and to browse through the pavement book stalls. There are many restaurants also located here, as well as a number of cinema halls. The central lawns, earlier a venue

Connaught Place, the British-built shopping complex in New Delhi

The brick and plaster astronomical instruments in Jantar Mantar

for street theatre, shoeshine boys and self-styled "ear cleaners", have made way for the Delhi Metro. The recently built Central Park features an amphitheatre, 21 fountains and flowered lawns. Nearby popular shopping centres include the state emporia at **Baba Kharak Singh Marg** and the stalls along Janpath.

Lakshmi Narayan Mandir ⓫

Mandir Marg. **Map** 1 A4.

The prominent industrialist GD Birla built this temple dedicated to Lakshmi Narayan in 1938. Mahatma Gandhi attended its first *puja* as this was among the country's first temples that had no caste restrictions. Popularly known as Birla Mandir, it is a fairly typical example of contemporary Indian temple architecture.

Approached by a flight of marble stairs, the main shrine has images of Vishnu and his consort, Lakshmi. It is surmounted by ochre and maroon *shikharas* (temple towers). Subsidiary shrines dedicated to Radha-Krishna, Hanuman, Shiva and Durga *(see pp22–3)* are set around the courtyard. On the walls are inscriptions from Hindu scriptures, often with English translations. They are also decorated with paintings from the *Mahabharata (see p141)* and *Ramayana (see p37).*

Surrounded by a peaceful park with a pleasant marble pavilion on one side and a large *dharamshala* (resthouse) on the other, this popular temple is a good place to visit as it is spotlessly clean and very well-maintained.

The popular Lakshmi Narayan Mandir

Jantar Mantar ⓬

Sansad Marg. **Map** 1 C5.

Sawai Jai Singh II of Jaipur built this observatory in 1724 when commissioned by the then Mughal emperor Muhammad Shah. A keen astronomer, the maharaja felt that the existing instruments were not accurate enough to calculate the eclipses and planetary positions required to set the timings of his *pujas* and other sacred rituals. To solve the problem he erected five observatories *(see pp192–3)* with instruments that were sufficiently large and fixed to the site to be both exact and not prone to vibration. The instruments are the Samrat Yantra, a right-angled triangle whose hypotenuse is parallel to the earth's axis. This is, in fact, a gigantic sundial, and there are two brick quadrants on either side which measure its shadow. The others are the Jai Prakash Yantra, Jai Singh's invention, which, among other functions, verifies the time of the spring equinox; the Ram Yantra which reads the altitude of the sun; and the Misra Yantra, a group of instruments for a variety of purposes. Today, the observatory lies obsolete, in the centre of a pleasant park, surrounded by high-rises.

The Nehru Memorial Museum and Library at Teen Murti Bhavan

Nehru Memorial Museum and Library ⓭

Teen Murti Marg. **Map** 4 E3.
Tel (011) 2301 5191. **Museum**
◯ 9am–6.30pm Tue–Sun. ◉ public
hols. **Nehru Planetarium**
Tel (011) 2301 4504. ▣ **Shows**
11:30am, 3pm. ◉ Mon & public hols.

Jawaharlal Nehru lived in this house, then called Teen Murti Bhavan, while he was India's first prime minister (1947–64). On his death, the house was converted into a national memorial comprising a **Museum** and a library for research scholars.

Originally the residence of the Commander-in-Chief of British Forces in India and located directly south of Rashtrapati Bhavan, the house was designed by Robert Tor Russell, the architect of Connaught Place and the Eastern and Western Courts on Janpath. Its design follows the established Lutyens-style classicism with a teak panelled interior and vaulted reception rooms. Nehru's bedroom and study, still exactly as he left them, are an austere centre in a grand house. Especially interesting are the bookshelves containing Nehru's large private collection, an eclectic mix of English classics, Left Book Club editions and treatises on the Cold War.

This home has a special place in modern Indian history as it once housed,

not just the incumbent prime minister, but two future ones as well, his daughter, Indira Gandhi, and grandson, Rajiv. Both mother and son were assassinated *(see pp60–61)*.

The extensive grounds are home to the **Nehru Planetarium** and the square, three-arched **Kushak Mahal**, a 14th-century hunting lodge built by the Tughlaq sultan, Feroze Shah *(see p97)*.

On the roundabout, in front of the house, is the memorial known as Teen Murti ("three statues") dedicated to the men of the Indian regiments who died in World War I. It was from this landmark that the house derived its name.

Teen Murti Memorial

Gandhi Smriti ⓮

Tees January Marg. **Map** 4 F3.
Tel (011) 2301 1480. ◯ 10am–5pm.
▨ ▣ ◉ Mon & public hols.

On 30 January 1948, at 11am, Nathuram Godse assassinated Mahatma Gandhi as he was going to his daily prayer meeting in the gardens of this house, once the residence of the Birla family *(see p77)*. A simple sandstone pillar marks the spot.

Now a museum commemorating Gandhi's life and final hours, the ambience here reflects Gandhi's philosophy of lofty political principles and down to earth common sense. A series of appealing dioramas made up of dolls in glass cabinets, tell the story of his eventful life through such defining moments as bidding farewell to his parents while going to England and the death of Kasturba, his beloved wife. The rooms where he used to stay when in Delhi are memorably austere and do convey a sense of his history. In the garden, footsteps, cast in red sandstone, lead to the site of his final martyrdom.

The museum complex has shops selling inexpensive editions of Gandhi's writings as well as items made from khadi, the simple homespun cloth he always wore, and which became one of the important symbols of the Freedom Movement *(see pp58–9)*.

Lodi Gardens ⓯

Map 5 A4. ◻ *sunrise–sunset daily.*

Lodi Gardens, located in the heart of residential New Delhi, was built at the behest of Lady Willingdon, the Vicereine, in 1936. Originally the site of two villages, their inhabitants were shifted elsewhere and lawns and pathways were laid out around the tombs belonging to the 15th-century Sayyid and Lodi dynasties. Inside, the bridge called **Athpula**, literally "eight piers", near the entrance on South End Road, is said to date from the 17th century. To the west of it are the ramparts of the **tomb of Sikandar Lodi** (r.1489–1517) which enclose an octagonal tomb at the centre of some rather overgrown gardens. Inside it, traces of turquoise tilework and calligraphy are just about visible.

To the south of Sikandar Lodi's Tomb are the **Bara Gumbad** ("big dome") and **Sheesh Gumbad** ("glazed dome"). The names of the nobles buried within have long been forgotten, but the Bara Gumbad is an imposing structure with an attached mosque built in 1494, and a *mehmankhana* (guesthouse). The Sheesh Gumbad derives its name from the glazed turquoise tiles that still cling to its outer walls along with blue calligraphic panels.

Recent research claims that this is Bahlol Lodi's tomb. The **tomb of Muhammad Shah** (r.1434–44), the third ruler of the Sayyid dynasty, is said to be the oldest in the garden. The dome of this octagonal structure is surrounded by *chhatris*, and *jaalis* once filled the spaces between the pillars. The graves inside are said to be those of the sultan himself and some of the most favoured nobles of his court.

Today, with its tree-lined pathways and well-kept lawns and flower beds, the park acts as a "green lung" for the people of Delhi. It is one of the city's most picturesque parks and a favourite haunt of joggers, yoga-enthusiasts and families who come here to picnic on weekends. Vendors selling balloons, ice-creams and snacks from handcarts are popular with children.

Muhammad Shah's Tomb

Khan Market ⓰

Subramaniam Bharti Marg. **Map** 5 B3. **Shops** ◻ 10.30am–8pm Mon–Sat. ● Sun.

This market was built in the early 1940s to serve the needs of the British forces living in the hurriedly constructed barracks at Lodi Estate. Its na_ is in honour of th_ Pathan nationalist and reformer, Dr Khan Sahib, the brother of Khan Abdul Gaffar Khan, the "Frontier Gandhi". Both men were revered for their role for independence among the warlike tribes of the North-West Frontier Province (now in Pakistan).

This popular market is much frequented by Indians and foreigners alike. There is a wide range of Indian and Western merchandise on offer here, from crockery, cakes and dog leashes to boutiques selling exquisite jewellery and designer clothes. There are also traditional sari shops, as well as Anokhi *(see p266)*, selling blockprinted linen and garments in both Western and Indian styles. There are a number of excellent places to buy shoes, as well as good book-shops – Bahri & Sons, Full Circle and Faqir Chand's, one of the oldest shops in the market. Its other charming features are the groceries and the colourful flower shops. A number of cafés such as Barista, Café Turtle and Market Café are located here for shoppers in search of a quick snack, as well as Delhi's popular delicatessen, Sugar & Spice.

Athpula, the 17th-century bridge near the entrance to Lodi Gardens on South End Road

NIZAMUDDIN TO PURANA QILA

The Nizamuddin area, named after the famous 14th-century Sufi saint, Nizamuddin Auliya, is bisected by Mathura Road and has a clearly visible split personality. East Nizamuddin is the quieter half, with Humayun's Tomb *(see p83)* resting peacefully at the centre of a Persian garden. West Nizamuddin, the old Muslim quarter around the saint's *dargah,* is a lively *basti* which still retains its medieval character. This important pilgrim centre also has the graves of famous poets such as Amir Khusrau and Mirza Ghalib, as well as the tombs of Jahanara, the daughter of Shah Jahan *(see pp154–5),* and the dilettante Muhammad Shah Rangila,

Marble inlay

a later Mughal emperor. In this neighbourhood, the medieval and modern co-exist harmoniously. Busy Mathura Road swirls past the Subz Burj with its blue-tiled dome, today a traffic island. Humayun's Tomb and the Sundar Horticulture Nursery is off to the west. Further north is the up-market residential colony of Sundar Nagar with antique shops, Delhi Zoo and Purana Qila, the "old fort", *(see p84).* The crumbling battlements of the fort overlook the Crafts Museum, the small shrine of Matka Pir, a Sufi saint, and the exhibition grounds of Pragati Maidan. To the east stands the Khair-ul-Manazil Mosque, built by Maham Anga in the mid-16th century.

SIGHTS AT A GLANCE

Historic Site
Nizamuddin **1**

Tomb
Humayun's Tomb p83 **2**

Monuments
Purana Qila **3**
Khair-ul-Manazil Mosque **4**

Museums
Crafts Museum pp86–7 **5**

Exhibition Grounds
Pragati Maidan **6**

KEY

🚉	Railway station
🚌	Bus station
🛕	Temple
🕌	Mosque
🪦	Tomb

GETTING THERE
Take a taxi or autorickshaw to Nizamuddin to visit both the village and Humayun's Tomb. To get to Purana Qila, hire another taxi or auto from one of the many stands. Once at Purana Qila, most of the sights are easily accessible by foot.

0 metres 750
0 yards 750

◁ Inlaid marble and tiles decorating the façade of Atgah Khan's Tomb in Nizamuddin

Nizamuddin Complex ❶

West of Mathura Rd. **Map** 6 D5. **Dargah** ◯ *daily.* **Qawwali** *6:30pm Thurs.* 📷 *Urs (Apr).*

This medieval settlement, or *basti,* is named after Sheikh Hazrat Nizamuddin Auliya, whose grave and hospice are located here. Nizamuddin belonged to a fraternity of Sufi mystics, the Chishtiyas *(see p319),* respected for their austerity, piety and disdain for politics and material desires. His daily assemblies drew both the rich and the poor, who believed that he was a "friend of God" and so a master who would intercede on their behalf on Judgement Day. Nizamuddin died in 1325 but his disciples call him a *zinda pir,* a living spirit, who heeds their pleas and alleviates their misery.

Colourful stalls lining the alley leading to Nizamuddin's *dargah*

Congregational area, Nizamuddin

The Urs *(see p38)* is held on the anniversary of his birth and death, and celebrated by his disciples with qawwalis and offerings of *chadors.*

A winding alley leads to the saint's grave. It is crowded with mendicants and lined with stalls selling flowers and *chadors,* polychrome clocks and prints of Mecca. The main congregational area is a marble pavilion (rebuilt in 1562) where, every Thursday evening, devotees sing devotional songs composed by the celebrated Persian poet, Amir Khusrau (1253–1325). Women are denied entry beyond the outer verandah but may peer through *jaalis* into the small, dark chamber where the saint's grave lies draped with a rose petal-strewn cloth and where imams continuously recite verses from the Koran. The complex also contains the graves of several eminent

Tomb of the famous poet Mirza Ghalib

disciples, such as Jahanara Begum and Amir Khusrau.

Across the western side of the open courtyard is the red sandstone Jama't Khana Mosque, built in 1325. To its north is a *baoli,* secretly excavated while Tughlaqabad *(see p114)* was being built because Ghiyasuddin Tughlaq had banned all building activities elsewhere. Legend has it that labourers worked here at night with the help of lamps lit, not by oil, but water blessed by Nasiruddin, Nizamuddin's successor *(see p108).* The mid-16th-century tomb of Atgah Khan, Akbar's minister and the husband of one of his wet nurses, who was murdered by Adham Khan *(see p113),* is to the north. An open marble pavilion, the Chaunsath Khamba ("64 pillars"), is close by. Just outside, is an enclosure containing the simple grave of Mirza Ghalib (1786–1869). One of the greatest poets of his time, Ghalib wrote in both Urdu and Persian, and his verses are still recited today. Nearby is the Ghalib Academy, a repository of paintings and manuscripts.

Always crowded, the *basti* preserves with miraculous serenity, the legend of this *pir,* who was called "a king without throne or crown, with kings in need of the dust of his feet" by his disciple, Amir Khusrau.

NIZAMUDDIN COMPLEX

One of Delhi's historic necropolises, many of the *pir's* disciples, such as Amir Khusrau and Jahanara Begum, Shah Jahan's favourite daughter, are buried close to their master. Jahanara's epitaph echoes her master's teachings: "Let naught cover my grave save the green grass, for grass well suffices as a covering for the grave of the lowly".

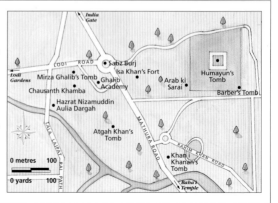

India Gate

LODI ROAD

Lodi Gardens

Sabz Burj

Mirza Ghalib's Tomb   Isa Khan's Fort

Ghalib Academy

Chausanth Khamba

Arab ki Sarai

Humayun's Tomb

Hazrat Nizamuddin Aulia Dargah

Barber's Tomb

LALA LAJPAT RAI PATH

MATHURA ROAD

Atgah Khan's Tomb

RADIO KHAN ROAD

Khan i Khanan's Tomb

Baba's Temple

0 metres   100
0 yards   100

Humayun's Tomb ❷

Marble star inlaid on panel

Humayun, the second Mughal emperor *(see p84)*, is buried in this tomb, the first great example of a Mughal garden tomb and inspiration for several later monuments, such as the incomparable Taj Mahal. Built in 1565 by a Persian architect Mirak Mirza Ghiyas, it was commissioned by Humayun's senior widow, Haji Begum. Often called "a dormitory of the House of Timur", the graves in its chambers include Humayun's wives and Dara Shikoh, Shah Jahan's scholarly son. Also in the complex are the Afsarwala Tomb, the octagonal tomb and mosque of Isa Khan, a noble at Sher Shah's court, and the tomb of Humayun's favourite barber. The Arab ki Sarai housed the Persian masons who built the tomb.

VISITORS' CHECKLIST

Off Mathura Rd. **Map** 6 D4.
Tel (011) 2435 5275.
◯ sunrise–sunset daily.
🎞 📷 *extra charges.*

The tomb as seen from the entrance

The Dome
This imposing white marble double dome is a complete half-sphere, and is surmounted by a finial with a crescent in the Persian style. Later Mughal finials, such as the one at the Taj Mahal, used a lotus.

Geometric designs inlaid on panels

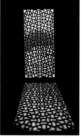

Jaalis
Such fine trellis work in stone later became a signature Mughal feature.

The Tomb Chamber
The plain white marble sarcophagus stands on a simple black and white marble platform. The grave itself lies in the rather dark, bat-filled basement below.

The imposing plinth is decorated with red sandstone arches and consists of multiple chambers, a departure from the single chamber of previous tombs.

Purana Qila ❸

Mathura Rd. **Map** 6 D2. **Tel** *(011) 2435 4260.* ☐ *sunrise–sunset daily.* **Museum** *Tel (011) 2435 5387.* ☐ *10am–5pm.* ◑ *Friday.* 🖾

Purana Qila, literally "old fort", stands on an ancient mound. Excavations near its eastern wall reveal that the site has been continuously occupied since 1000 BC. It is also believed to be the place where Indraprastha, the Pandava capital mentioned in the epic, the *Mahabharata (see p141),* once stood.

It was here that Humayun, the second Mughal emperor, began to construct his city, Dinpanah ("Asylum of Faith"), just four years after his father Babur established the Mughal dynasty in 1526 *(see pp52–3).* However, his reign was short-lived and, in 1540, he was dispossessed of his kingdom by the ambitious Afghan chieftain, Sher Shah Sur (r.1540–45). When Sher Shah took possession of the citadel, he strengthened its forti-fications, added several new structures and renamed it Shergarh. After his death, his successors were defeated by Humayun who recaptured his domains in 1555. Today, of the many palaces, barracks and houses that once existed, only Sher Shah's mosque and the building said to be Humayun's library remain.

The Yamuna once flowed on the fort's eastern side and formed a natural moat: a small lake to the west facing busy Mathura Road is all that remains today. The present entrance, an imposing red

Boating outside Purana Qila

sandstone gate on the western wall called the **Bara Darwaza**, is one of the three principal gates of Shergarh. Its double-storeyed façade, surmounted by *chhatris* and approached by a steep ramp, still displays traces of tiles and carved foliage. **Humayun's Gate**, on the southern wall, has an inscription bearing Sher Shah's name and the date 950 AH (1543–4). To the north, the **Taliqi Darwaza** (the so-called "forbidden gate") has carved reliefs, and across the road is the red sandstone **Lal Darwaza**, or Sher Shah Gate, one of the entrances to the township that grew around the fort.

Chhatri with decorative tilework

The single-domed **Qila-i-Kuhna Mosque**, built by Sher Shah in 1541, is an excellent example of a pre-Mughal

design. Its prayer hall inside has five elegant arched niches or *mihrabs* set in its western wall. Marble in shades of red, white and slate is used for the calligraphic inscriptions and marks a transition from Lodi to Mughal architecture. A second storey provided space for female courtiers to pray, while the arched doorway on the left wall, framed by ornate *jharokhas*, was reserved for members of the royal family.

The **Sher Mandal** stands to the south of the mosque. This double-storeyed octagonal tower of red sandstone was built by Sher Shah and was used as a library by Humayun after he recaptured the fort.

The tower is topped by an octagonal *chhatri*, supported by eight pillars and decorated with white marble. Inside, there are remnants of the decorative plaster-work and traces of the stone shelving where, presumably, the emperor's books were placed. This was also the tragic spot where, on 24 January 1556, on hearing the muezzin's call, the devout Humayun hurried to kneel on the stairs, missed his footing and tumbled to his death. His tomb can be seen from the southern gate. Purana Qila flourished as the sixth city of Delhi *(see p107)* and traces of walls still stand in the area. There is a small **Museum** at the entrance displaying items excavated from the site.

Sher Shah's mosque at Purana Qila

The single dome surmounting the prayer hall at Khair-ul-Manazil

Khair-ul-Manazil ❹

Mathura Rd. **Map** 5 C2.
◯ sunrise–sunset.

This mosque, "the most auspicious of houses", was constructed in 1561 by Akbar's influential wet nurse, Maham Anga, and a courtier, Shiha-bu'd-Din Ahmed Khan. An imposing, double-storeyed red sandstone gateway leads into a large courtyard ringed by cloisters, two storeys high, one of which was used as a *madrasa*. The prayer hall with its five-arched openings is topped by a single dome. Above the central archway, a marble inscription mentions Maham Anga's and Shiha-bu'd-Din's names. Inside, the central *mihrab* is decorated with bands of blue and green calligraphy. Maham Anga is buried in Mehrauli with her son, Adham Khan *(see p113)*, who was killed by Akbar.

Crafts Museum ❺

See pp86–7.

Pragati Maidan ❻

Mathura Rd. **Map** 6 D1. *Tel* (011) 2337 1540. *Fax* (011) 2337 1492/3. ◯ 10am–5pm daily. 🖼 📷 🖥 🍴 **Hamsadhwani, Falaknuma** and **Shakuntalam** *Tel* (011) 2337 1849. **National Science Centre** *Tel* (011) 2337 1893. ◯ 10am–5pm daily. 🖼

India's largest exhibition centre, covering nearly 150 acres (61 ha), Pragati Maidan is the venue for numerous

exhibitions and trade fairs organized by the India Trade Promotion Organization. The work of some of India's most eminent architects can be seen here. Raj Rewal has designed the Hall of Nations and Industries and Joseph Allen Stein, the World Trade Centre. Among other notable

buildings are those by Charles Correa, Achyut Kanvinde and Satish Grover. All the Indian states have pavilions spread across the fair's extensive grounds, linked by 16 km (10 miles) of roads.

Exhibitions are held here throughout the year and cover a range of products from textiles, jewellery, automobiles to mining equipment and food products. Every two years the World Book Fair and the India International Travel and Tourism Show are held, drawing international delegates. Within the grounds are Appu Ghar, a children's amusement park, and the **National Science Centre** *(see* p273*)*. Two theatres, the **Falaknuma** and **Shakuntalam**, screen a cross-section of Indian and foreign films, while the **Hamsadhwani Auditorium** is the venue for various cultural events.

A view of Pragati Maidan from Purana Qila

MATKA PIR

Rows of *matkas* (earthenware pots) line the entrance to the shrine of Matka Pir, a Sufi saint. According to legend, a man and his wife came to the saint to seek his help for the birth of a son. Being poor, they could only offer a humble pot of dal and jaggery. The saint asked them to place the pot in the courtyard and leave the rest to God. A year later, their wish fulfilled, they returned with another pot, a tradition that has continued since then. The pot motif leads all the way up the wide marble stairs to the *dargah*, standing on a ridge overlooking Mathura Road. The saint's powers still attract many pilgrims.

The shrine of the Sufi saint, Matka Pir

Crafts Museum ❺

Wooden doll on toy swing

For centuries, Indian craftsmen, such as potters and weavers, masons and carvers, have created a range of objects for everyday use that are both beautiful and practical. A unique project was started in 1956 to promote indigenous artisans by displaying their work in one place, and by the early 1980s, over 20,000 objects had been collected. This was the core around which grew India's first Crafts Museum.

Sarota
A late 19th-century betel nut cracker from South India.

★ Bandhini Odhni
This exquisite veil is the work of the Bhansali tribe in Kutch, Gujarat. In tie-and-dye (bandhini), grains are used to set the pattern. Threads are tied around them and the cloth dyed in different colours.

Mukhalinga
A rare, late 19th-century brass and silver phallic image (linga) with a human face (mukha). Tiny snakes as earrings and the third eye are symbols of Shiva.

Amphitheatre

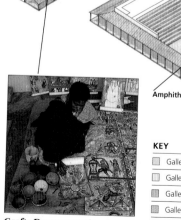

Crafts Demonstration Area
Artisans from all over India set up workshops each month (barring the monsoon) to display their skill to visitors.

STAR EXHIBITS

★ Bandhini Odhni

★ Bhuta Figure

★ Charrake

KEY

☐	Gallery of Aristocratic Arts
☐	Gallery of Ritual Arts
☐	Gallery of Folk and Tribal Cultures
☐	Gallery of Popular Culture
☐	Gallery of Textiles
☐	Administration Block
☐	Temporary Exhibition Gallery
☐	Visual Store

Yashoda and Krishna
This mid-20th-century plaster cast statuette from South India is an interesting example of popular kitsch, inspired by gods and mythology. It is cheap and easy to reproduce for use in a domestic shrine.

VISITORS' CHECKLIST

Bhairon Marg. **Map** 6 D2. *Tel*
(011) 2337 1887. 🔲 10am–5pm
Tue–Sun. ⬤ Mon, public hols.
🅿 🔲 **Crafts demonstration**
🔲 daily. ⬤ Jul–Sep.

★ Charrake
These enormous, circular vessels are cast of an alloy known as bell metal. They are still used in Kerala for wedding feasts or at temples for making payasam *(a type of rice pudding) for devotees during festivals.*

Madhubani Painting
A stunning wall painting in natural pigments depicting a wedding scene by Ganga Devi, a famous woman painter of this traditional art form from Bihar in Eastern India.

★ Bhuta Figure
These life-sized wooden figures were made 200 years ago as part of the Bhuta cult of spirit worship in the southern state of Karnataka.

Library

Entrance

GALLERY GUIDE
The museum's display is spread over two floors of the complex, divided into separate areas by courtyards that also double up as exhibition spaces. A large open area is designated for live art displays by visiting artisans each month, except during the rainy season.

The Crafts Museum Shop
Located on the premises of the Crafts Museum, the shop sells a wide selection of fine Indian folk crafts and textiles.

OLD DELHI

What is known as Old Delhi today was originally the Mughal capital of Shahjahanabad, built by Shah Jahan when he moved the imperial court from Agra to Delhi. Construction began in 1638, and ten years later the Red Fort, Jami Masjid, Chandni Chowk and the surrounding residential and mercantile quarters were ready for occupation.

Detail of a door in Red Fort

The city was surrounded by a rubble wall pierced by 14 gates of which three – Delhi, Turkman and Ajmeri – survive. An elegant, mannered lifestyle flourished, enriched by the courtiers and merchants, artists and poets who lived in the lanes and quarters, called *galis* and *katras*, of the walled city. In 1739, the Persian freebooter Nadir Shah came to plunder the city of Shahjahanabad and left a bleeding ruin behind him. The final deathblow was, however, dealt when the British troops moved into the Red Fort after the Mutiny of 1857, turning it into a military garrison, while a railway line cut the walled city in half. Yet, the spirit of the place has survived all these vicissitudes and its busy *galis* continue to support a vibrant life. Modernity has brought a new urgency to the pace of the traditional traders who still live and operate from here.

SIGHTS AT A GLANCE

Mosques
Jami Masjid ❶
Zinat-ul Masjid ❻

Historic Streets and Sites
Ajmeri Gate ❹
Chandni Chowk ❷
Turkman Gate ❺

Monuments
Feroze Shah Kotla ❽
Red Fort pp94–5 ❸

Memorial
Rajghat ❼

GETTING THERE

The most convenient way to get to Red Fort and Chandni Chowk is by car, metro rail or auto-rickshaw. You may also join one of the many day tours to the Old City. Once there, explore the area by foot or cycle-rickshaw.

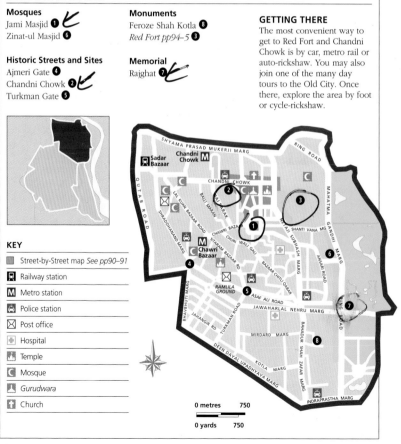

KEY

▨	Street-by-Street map *See pp90–91*
🚉	Railway station
Ⓜ	Metro station
🚓	Police station
⊠	Post office
✚	Hospital
🛕	Temple
C	Mosque
🛕	Gurudwara
✛	Church

0 metres 750

0 yards 750

◁ The white marble throne-balcony, Diwan-i-Aam, Red Fort

Street-by-Street: Chandni Chowk

Now a busy commercial centre, Chandni Chowk was once a grand processional thoroughfare that led from Red Fort to Jami Masjid. When it was laid out in 1648 by Jahanara Begum, Shah Jahan's favourite daughter, a canal ran down the centre of the tree-lined stately avenue. Chandni Chowk, or the "silvery, moonlit square", was then lined with merchants' shops and the grand residences or *havelis* of noblemen and merchants.

Sisganj Gurudwara
Guru Tegh Bahadur, the ninth Sikh guru, was beheaded at this site. The gurudwara marks the site of his martyrdom.

Sunehri Masjid
The "Golden Mosque", with three gilt domes, was built in 1722. On 22 March 1739, Nadir Shah stood on its roof to watch the massacre of Delhi's citizens.

Fatehpuri Masjid ←

CHANDNI CHOWK

KINARI BAZAAR

DARIBA KA

Nai Sarak

★ Kinari Bazaar
Tightly packed stalls sell all manner of glittering gold and silver trimmings such as braids, tinsel garlands and turbans for weddings and festivals.

BAZAAR GULI

CHEL PURI

Shiv Temple

Karim's
Tucked away in a narrow lane to the south of Jami Masjid is Delhi's most authentic Mughlai eatery. Named after a legendary 19th-century chef, the restaurant is now run by his descendants.

STAR SIGHTS

★ Jami Masjid

★ Lahore Gate

★ Kinari Bazaar

★ Lahore Gate
This imposing red sandstone gateway is the main entrance to Red Fort. The Prime Minister addresses the Independence Day rally here.

LOCATOR MAP
See Street Finder map 2

Dariba Kalan
Gold and silver ornaments are sold in this lane. Gulab Singh's famous attar shop (see p119) is located here.

Charity box at the Bird Hospital on Netaji Subhash Marg

★ Jami Masjid
India's largest mosque stands on a mound. Its two slender minarets flank three marble domes ❶

Govt Girls Senior Secondary School

Karim's

0 metres	25
0 yards	25

KEY

– – – Suggested route

Jami Masjid, built by Shah Jahan, the largest mosque in India

Jami Masjid ❶

Off Netaji Subhash Marg. **Map** 2 E2.
⬤ for non-Muslims during prayer time & after 5pm. 📷 extra charges.

This grand mosque, built in 1656 by the Emperor Shah Jahan on a natural rocky outcrop, took six years and 5,000 workmen to construct at the cost of nearly a million rupees. A magnificent flight of red sandstone steps leads to the great arched entrances where, in Aurangzeb's time, horses were sold and jugglers performed. Today, sweet-sellers, shoe-minders and beggars mill around here. The huge 28 m (300 ft) square courtyard accommodates up to 20,000 people at prayer times, especially during Friday prayers and on Id, when it looks like a sea of worshippers. Next to the ablution tank in the centre is the *dikka* platform where, before loudspeakers took over, a second prayer leader

echoed the imam's words and actions for worshippers too far from the pulpit.

Three imposing black and white marble domes surmount the enormous prayer hall, and two minarets frame the great central arch. From the top of the southern minaret, a steep climb of 20 minutes, there are remarkable views of the roof-line of Old Delhi giving way to the high-rises of New Delhi. Women require a male escort to enter the minaret.

Chandni Chowk ❷

Map 2 D2.

Once Shahjahanabad's most elegant boulevard, this wide avenue extending from Red Fort to Fatehpuri Masjid, is still the heart of Old Delhi, where both religious activity

and commerce mix happily together. All along its length are shrines sacred to various communities. The first is the Digamber Jain Mandir. Next to it is the Bird Hospital for sick and wounded birds. Loud chants, clanging bells and calls of vendors selling flowers and vermilion powder surround the Gauri Shankar Mandir, dedicated to Shiva and Parvati, which has a linga said to be 800 years old. Still further, close to the Sisganj Gurudwara, is the Kotwali (police station), the scene of British reprisal after 1857 *(see p55)*. Nearly a century before, another gruesome spectacle took place nearby when one afternoon in 1739, the Persian chieftain Nadir Shah stood on the roof of the Sunehri Masjid and watched his men kill nearly 30,000 of Delhi's citizens. The actual Moonlit Square (Chandni Chowk), is the open space in front of the very British Town Hall, now the Hardayal Library. Just behind it is the Mahatma Gandhi Park, which was called Begum Bagh in Mughal times. Further down, and commanding the end of this charming quarter, stands the Fatehpuri Masjid, constructed in 1650 by Fatehpuri Begum, one of Emperor Shah Jahan's wives. Nearby are the spice markets of Khari Baoli.

Swami Shraddhanand's statue, Chandni Chowk

Chandni Chowk, a vibrant centre of commerce and religious activity

Bazaars of Old Delhi

Old Delhi's bazaars are legendary. An English visitor to these bazaars over a hundred years ago, wrote in praise of the "Cashmere shawls, gold and silver embroidery, jewellery, enamels and carpets" to be found here. Today, the

A cycle-rickshaw puller

great wholesale *katras* of Chandni Chowk and Jami Masjid still retain that souk-like quality. Their narrow streets are lined with shops whose goods spill out onto the pavement; and shopping still means vigorous bargaining for a bewildering array of goods.

Khari Baoli *is Asia's biggest spice market. It spills across this street which derives its name from a stepwell that no longer exists.*

Katra Neel *is reminiscent of Middle Eastern souks. The tiny shops sell a wide variety of textiles, such as brocades from Varanasi, silk, cotton and voile.*

Kinari Bazaar *specializes in tinsel accessories, and attracts trousseau shoppers.*

Katra Neel

Jami Masjid

Dariba Kalan *is the jewellers' lane where artisans have worked for over two centuries.*

Nai Sarak *is very popular among students as school and college textbooks and stationery are sold on this street.*

Chawri Bazaar *has every conceivable variety of paper, sold here by weight.*

Churiwali Gali *has garlands of glass bangles strung along rods to match every sari or lehenga. It is popularly called the "lane of bangle-sellers".*

0 metres   500

0 yards   500

The Red Fort ③

A panel in Diwan-i-Aam

Red sandstone battlements give this imperial citadel its name, Red Fort (Lal Qila). Commissioned by Shah Jahan in 1639, it took nine years to build and was the seat of Mughal power until 1857, when the last emperor, Bahadur Shah Zafar, was dethroned and exiled. Lahore Gate, one of fort's six gateways, leads on to the covered bazaar of Chatta Chowk, where brocades and jewels were once sold. Beyond this lies the Naqqar Khana, from where musicians played three times a day.

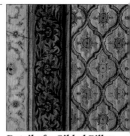

Detail of a Gilded Pillar
The Mughal love of opulence visible in the lavish use of marble and gold in the fort.

Moti Masjid
Named after the pearly sheen of its marble, the tiny "pearl mosque" was added by Emperor Aurangzeb in 1659.

★ **Hamams**
The royal bath has three enclosures. The first provided hot vapour baths, the second sprayed rose-scented water through sculpted fountains, and the third contained cold water.

★ **Diwan-i-Aam**
The emperor gave daily audiences to all his subjects in this 60-pillared hall. The intricately carved throne canopy stands on a platform, while the low marble bench was for the chief minister (wazir).

STAR FEATURES

★ Diwan-i-Khas

★ Diwan-i-Aam

★ Hamams

★ Diwan-i-Khas
The legendary Peacock Throne, one of Shah Jahan's seven jewelled thrones, was housed in this exclusive pavilion where the emperor met his most trusted nobles. The walls and pillars were once inlaid with gems and the ceiling was of silver inlaid with precious stones.

VISITORS' CHECKLIST

Chandni Chowk. **Map** 2 D2.
Tel (011) 2327 7705.
◻ 6am–7pm daily. 🎟 🖼 📷
Son et Lumière Feb–Apr &
Sep–Oct: 8.30pm; May–Aug: 9pm;
Nov–Jan: 7.30pm. 🎟 ⬤ Mon.
Museum ◻ 10am–5pm Tue–Sun.

Khas Mahal
The royal apartments were divided by the "Stream of Paradise". The emperor's prayer room (Tasbih Khana) was flanked by his sleeping chamber (Khwabgah) and sitting room (Baithak). This overlooked the Yamuna and led to a balcony where he appeared before his subjects at sunrise.

Rang Mahal
Inside these gilded chambers, once exclusively for women, is an inlaid marble fountain shaped like an open lotus.

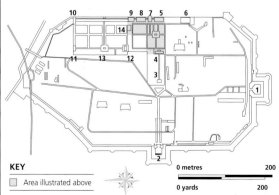

THE RED FORT

1 Delhi Gate
2 Lahore Gate
3 Naqqar Khana
4 Diwan-i-Aam
5 Rang Mahal
6 Moti Mahal
7 Khas Mahal
8 Diwan-i-Khas
9 *Hamams*
10 Shah Burj (Tower)
11 Sawan (Pavilion)
12 Bhadon (Pavilion)
13 Zafar Mahal
14 Moti Masjid

KEY
◻ Area illustrated above

0 metres 200
0 yards 200

Ajmeri Gate ❹

Ajmeri Gate Rd. **Map** 1 C3.

This is one of the 14 gates encircling Shahjahanabad that has survived more than 300 years and today stands in the midst of the city's congested commercial centre. Diagonally opposite Ajmeri Gate is **Ghazi-ud-Din's Tomb** and **Madrasa**. Ghazi-ud-Din Khan was an eminent courtier during the reign of the sixth Mughal emperor Aurangzeb, and his son, Mir Qamar-ud-Din, established the dynasty that ruled the southern state of Hyderabad until Independence in 1947.

The imposing, red sandstone *madrasa* has several arcades and a mosque on its western side. Founded in the late 17th century, this was at one time Delhi's foremost *madrasa* and after 1824 came to be known as the Anglo-Arabic School. English classes were held here, and British teachers also introduced mathematics and science texts to students, which were then translated into Urdu. Ghazi-ud-Din's grave is in a marble enclosure at the mosque's southern end. Athough this complex is surrounded by today's urban congestion, it still performs the noble function it was meant to. The three-domed mosque is in regular use and students crisscross the courtyard, while

Ghazi-ud-Din's *madrasa*

striped towels hang from the hostel balconies where glorious silks may once have billowed. Until recently, the esteemed Delhi College, now the Zakir Husain College, was also located on the premises.

A cycle-rickshaw from Ajmeri Gate will take you past tiny shops to the teeming lanes of Lal Kuan Bazaar where the **Zinat Mahal** is situated. Built in 1846, this was the eponymous home of the favourite wife of the last Mughal emperor Bahadur Shah Zafar. Today, it houses a school, lawyers' offices and shops. The original façade was wonderfully carved and arcaded with an oriel window. The beautiful verse by Bahadur Shah Zafar that was inscribed over the arched gateway can still be seen.

Turkman Gate ❺

Asaf Ali Rd. **Map** 2 D3.

The solid, square-shaped, red sandstone Turkman Gate stands in splendid isolation among the modern high-rise buildings of busy Asaf Ali Road. It marked the southern boundary of Shahjahanabad and was named after a Muslim *pir*, Hazrat Shah Turkman Bayabani, whose 13th-century tomb and *dargah* stand to the east. The serpentine lanes behind the gateway are home to two medieval monuments. **Kalan Masjid** ("black mosque"), in the Bulbulekhan area, was built in 1387 by Khan-i-Jahan Junan Shah, Feroze Shah Tughlaq's prime minister. This is one of the seven mosques he built in Delhi; the others are at Khirkee and Begumpuri *(see p109)*. A short walk away lies what is believed to be the **grave of Sultana Razia** Delhi's only medieval woman ruler *(see pp50–51)*. Her brief reign was bedevilled by revolts and she was killed at Karnal in 1240 while fleeing from Delhi. Her plain rubble-stone grave lies open to the sky in a cramped enclosure amidst houses and shops. The atelier of the last practising craftsman of Delhi's blue pottery, Hazarilal, is situated in the congested alleys of Hauz Suiwalan, located behind Turkman Gate.

Traffic swirling around the Mughal Turkman Gate

Zinat-ul Masjid ⑥

Daryaganj. **Map** 2 F3.

This mosque was built in 1710 by Princess Zinat-un-Nisa Begum, one of Emperor Aurangzeb's daughters. The gracefully proportioned red sandstone mosque has a spacious courtyard built over a series of basement rooms. Its seven-arched prayer hall is surmounted by three domes, with alternating stripes of black and white marble. The locals who worship here have a more lyrical name for it, the Ghata ("Cloud") Mosque because its striped domes simulate the monsoon sky.

Zinat-ul Masjid, also known as the Ghata or "Cloud" Mosque

Rajghat

Rajghat ⑦

Mahatma Gandhi Rd. **Map** 2 F3.
◯ sunrise–sunset daily.
Prayer meetings 5pm Fri.
National Gandhi Museum Tel (011) 2331 1793. ◯ 9:30am–5:30pm Tue–Sun. ◼ Mon & public hols.
Film shows 4–5pm Sat & Sun.

Rajghat, India's most revered symbol of nationalism, is the site of Mahatma Gandhi's cremation. A sombre black granite platform inscribed with his last words *He Ram!* ("Oh God!") now stands here. The only splash of colour comes from the garlands of orange marigolds draped over it. Devotees sing *bhajans* and the steady beat of the *dholak* lends the scene a dolorous melancholy. All visiting heads of state are taken to this *samadhi* ("memorial") to lay wreaths in memory of the "Father of the Nation". On Gandhi's birthday (2 Oct) and death anniversary (30 Jan), the nation's leaders gather here for prayer meetings.

Just across the road is the **Gandhi National Museum**, crammed with memorabilia connected with Gandhi's life, including his letters and diaries. A framed plaque on the stairs explains his simple philosophy: "Non-violence is the pitting of one's whole soul against the will of the tyrant… it is then possible for a single individual to defy the might of an unjust empire."

Feroze Shah Kotla ⑧

Bahadur Shah Zafar Marg. **Map** 2 F4.

Only some ramparts and ruined structures remain of Feroze Shah Kotla, the palace complex of Ferozabad, Delhi's fifth city erected by that indefatigable builder, Feroze Shah Tughlaq *(see p107)*. Entry is from the gate next to the Indian Express Building. Towards the very end of the walled enclosure stand the partial ruins of the Jami Masjid. Roofless, with only the rear wall still extant, this was at one time Delhi's largest mosque where as legend says, Timur the Lame, the Mongol conqueror who sacked Delhi in 1398, came to say his Friday prayers. Next to the Jami Masjid is a rubble pyramidal structure topped by one of the Mauryan emperor Ashoka's polished stone pillars *(see pp46–7)*, brought from the Punjab and installed here in 1356 by Feroze Shah. It was from the inscriptions on this pillar that James Prinsep, the Oriental linguist, deciphered the Brahmi script, a forerunner of the modern Devanagari, in 1837.

Khuni Darwaza (the "bloodstained gate"), opposite the Indian Express Building, was built by Sher Shah Sur as one of the gates to his city *(see p84)*. This was where Lieutenant Hodson shot Bahadur Shah Zafar's sons after the Mutiny of 1857 was quashed. Across the road is Delhi's main cricket stadium, named after the palace complex, where world-class test matches are held.

The Ashokan Pillar at Feroze Shah Kotla

FURTHER AFIELD

Detail, Moth ki Masjid

There is much to see and explore beyond the city centre. An undulating wooded area, the Ridge, sweeps across Delhi from the southwest to the north. The north contains the university campus and Civil Lines, an orderly civilian enclave created by the British, and the west houses the army Cantonment. South Delhi, juxtaposed between the old cities of Siri, Jahanpanah and

Tughlaqabad, is a more recent addition, with many affluent suburbs, smart residential colonies, shops, cinemas and restaurants. Further south, the historic Mehrauli Archaeological Park encompasses 19th-century hunting lodges, tombs, pavilions and the towering Qutb Minar. This picturesque area was the site of Delhi's first city, Qila Rai Pithora built around Lal Kot, a Tomar Rajput fortress.

SIGHTS AT A GLANCE

Historic Buildings and Sites
Chiragh Delhi ⑰
Civil Lines ⑤
Delhi Cantonment ⑩
Delhi University ⑧
Hauz Khas ⑮
Jahanpanah ⑲
Khirkee ⑱
Mehrauli Archaeological Park pp110–13 ⑳
Old Delhi GPO ②
Siri Fort ⑯
Tughlaqabad ㉓

Temples, Churches and Mosques
Baha'i House of Worship ㉕
Kalkaji Temple ㉔
Moth ki Masjid ⑭
St James's Church ①

Cemeteries
Nicholson Cemetery ③

Parks and Gardens
Northern Ridge ⑦
Qudsia Gardens ④
The Ridge ⑨

Monuments
Coronation Memorial ⑥

Museums
National Rail Museum ⑪
Sanskriti ㉑

Tombs
Safdarjung's Tomb ⑫
Sultan Ghari ㉒

Markets
INA Market ⑬

GETTING THERE
A private car, taxi, metro rail or auto-rickshaw is the best way of exploring the area. Private tour operators also run coaches to some sites.

0 kilometres   3
0 miles   3

SIGHTS OUTSIDE THE CENTRE

KEY
▪	Delhi city centre
▫	Built-up area
▫	Greater Delhi
🚉	Railway station
▬	Major road
═	Minor road

◁ **Safdarjung's Tomb, the last great Mughal garden tomb, built in the mid-18th century**

Street-by-Street: Around Kashmiri Gate

Delhi's Kashmiri Gate area resonates with memories of 1857. Many of the dramatic events between the months of May and September took place on the short stretch between Kashmiri Gate and the Old Delhi General Post Office (GPO). In the 1920s, this was also a favourite watering hole of the British residents living in nearby Civil Lines. Then the street was lined with smart shops and restaurants, few of which survive now.

Shop Façades
The grand old shops are now shabby and derelict.

★ Kashmiri Gate
The Mughals used to set off from this gate to spend the summer in Kashmir. In 1857, it was the scene of a bitter battle and a plaque on the western side honours "the engineers and miners who died while clearing the gate for British forces on September 14, 1857".

Nicholson Cemetery ❸

NICHOLSON RD

CHURCH ROAD

LOTHIAN

RAMLAL CHANDHOK MARG

Fakr-ul-Masjid
The domes and minarets of this small mosque rise above the rows of shops and offices along this busy street. Local residents come here to worship every Friday.

BARA BA

| 0 metres | | 15 |
| 0 yards | | 15 |

Old Hindu College

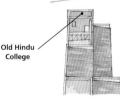

Old St Stephen's College

STAR SIGHTS

★ Kashmiri Gate

★ St James's Church

KEY

– – – Suggested route

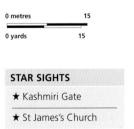

★ **St James's Church**
Delhi's oldest and most historic church, consecrated in 1836, is an impressive edifice, painted yellow and white ❶

Northern Railways Office
This Indo-Saracenic fantasy was once the residence of the British Commissioner, William Fraser, one of Skinner's closest friends.

CHURCH ROAD

Delhi College of Engineering

Dara Shikoh's library

Old Delhi GPO ❷

St James's Church ❶

Lothian Rd. **Tel** *(011) 2386 2539.*
◯ *8am–12 noon; 2–5pm daily.*
Services *9am Sun.*

A tablet in the church founded by Colonel James Skinner explains: "This church is erected at the sole expense of Colonel James Skinner" in fulfilment of a vow made on the battlefield. Built at the cost of Rs 80,000, the church is in the shape of a Greek cross, surmounted by an imposing eight-leafed dome. The two stained-glass windows were installed in the 1860s. Skinner died at Hansi *(see p140)*. A marble tablet, in front of the altar, marks his simple grave.

The imposing Old Delhi General Post Office

Old Delhi GPO ❷

Lothian Rd. ◯ *9:30am–6pm Mon–Fri; 9:30am–1pm Sat.*

To the south of Kashmiri Gate is the Old Delhi General Post Office, an old fashioned establishment caught in a time warp. This stucco-fronted colonial edifice is significant because it faces a traffic island on which stand two structures dating to the Indian Mutiny of 1857. The Telegraph Memorial is a memorial obelisk dedicated to the officers of the Telegraph Department. The inscription on it honours the telegraph operators, Brendish and Pilkington, who flashed news of the Indian Mutiny to the British garrison at Ambala. Nearby lies the ruined British Magazine. It was blown up by a Captain Willoughby on 11 May 1857 to prevent it from falling into the hands of the rebelling sepoys.

JAMES SKINNER

One of the Empire's most swashbuckling adventurers, Skinner was the son of a Scotsman and a Rajput. Rejected by the British Army because of his mixed parentage, he raised his own cavalry regiment, Skinner's Horse, whose flamboyant yellow uniforms gave rise to the name Yellow Boys. His troops fought with distinction and are still part of the Indian Army. On his death he was honoured as a Commander of the Order of the Bath. His descendants still live on an estate in Mussoorie, Uttar Pradesh.

James Skinner (1778–1841)

Graves at Nicholson Cemetery

Nicholson Cemetery ❸

Lala Hardev Sahai Marg.
⬛ 10am–5pm.

In the recently renovated walled cemetery named after him, surrounded by brisk traffic and overlooked by the huge Inter State Bus Terminus (ISBT), lies the flamboyant Brigadier General John Nicholson, the British commander. The headstone on his grave, which is to the right of the entrance, records that he "led the assault on Delhi but fell mortally wounded and died 3rd September 1857, aged 35". The surrounding graves belong to others like him who died at the time of the Indian Mutiny, between 10 May and 30 September 1857. The saddest, though, are the tiny graves of children, such as the headless angel mourning over Alfred and Ida Scott's little daughter: "We gave her back to bloom in heaven".

To enter the cemetery, knock on the gate and the *chowkidar* will open it. Even though there are no entrance charges, a small tip (10–20 rupees) to the *chowkidar* and a donation to the Church of North India will be welcome.

Qudsia Gardens ❹

Shamnath Marg. ⬛ sunrise–sunset.

Qudsia Begum, the dancing girl who became the wife of Emperor Muhammad Shah (r.1719–48), laid out these gardens in around 1748, and although the Inter State Bus Terminus and the Tourist Park now occupy much of the original site, the imposing gateway still stands. The rest of the present park is more modern with a children's playground and a rather formidable statue of the great Rajput king, Maharana Pratap. North of the gardens is the children's home run by Mother Teresa's Missionaries of Charity, where abandoned children are cared for.

Civil Lines ❺

Bounded by Shamnath Marg and Mahatma Gandhi Marg.

Old Delhi's Civil Lines were inhabited by the British civilian population while the Cantonment (*see p104*) was the military enclave. They lived in spacious bungalows, shopped at the Exchange Stores, dined at Maidens Hotel and worshipped at St James's Church. The old "temporary" Secretariat (built in 1912) is also located here on Mahatma Gandhi Marg. This long white building with its two towers, where the former Legislative Assembly once sat, also housed the offices of the Delhi Administration at one time. When the British moved into New Delhi, established Indian professional and merchant families settled here. Several old bungalows have been redeveloped as modern blocks of flats, yet some areas, such as Rajpur Road, still retain their essential colonial character.

To the east of Civil Lines, near the Delhi-Chandigarh bypass, is Metcalfe House, a sprawling mansion built in the 1830s by Sir Thomas Metcalfe, Delhi's eccentric British Resident from 1835–53. This house, once the hub of British social life, can be seen from the highway. It is now owned by the Defence Ministry and not open to the public.

White-plastered façade of the Oberoi Maidens Hotel in the Civil Lines area

Statues of former viceroys in the Coronation Durbar site

still visible. Feroze Shah also had a large hunting estate here where he built a lodge called Kushak-i-Shikar, a mosque, as well as a double-storeyed mansion, the Pir Ghaib, now in the grounds of the Hindu Rao Hospital (enter the main gate and turn right at the Cardiac Unit). The name, Pir Ghaib, derives from the tale of a resident *pir* who one day, simply vanished *(ghaib)* while meditating at this site. A cenotaph in one of the rooms marks the spot.

Coronation Memorial 6

S of NH1 Bypass. ☐ *sunrise–sunset.*

This was the site of the Royal Durbar held in 1911 to proclaim the accession of George V as King Emperor of India. A red sandstone obelisk records that the King Emperor proclaimed his coronation to the "governors, princes and peoples of India" (in that order) and "received their dutiful homage". He also announced the transfer of the capital from Calcutta to Delhi and two days later laid the foundation stones for the new city *(see pp68–9)*. On 12 December 1911, more than 100,000 people thronged the site where the King Emperor and Queen Empress sat beneath a golden dome mounted on a crimson canopy. Today, the site is a flat, dusty and forlorn spot, and ranged round in a pathetic semi-circle are statues of former viceroys, evicted from their perches in the city to make way for later Indian leaders. These include Lords Hardinge and Willingdon (distinguished for their role in the construction of New Delhi). Towering over them all is the 22 m (73 ft) statue of the King Emperor himself, draped in his Durbar robes, which was removed from the canopy at India Gate *(see p71)* and installed here in the 1960s.

The Northern Ridge 7

Rani Jhansi Rd, Ridge Rd, Magazine Rd. ☐ *sunrise–sunset.*

The northern end of the Ridge is a forested park cut through by Ridge Road and Rani Jhansi Road, with the small clearing of Bara Hindu Rao in the middle. This area still resounds with memories of 1857. It was around Flagstaff Tower, to the far north, that British women and children took shelter before they were evacuated to Karnal near Panipat *(see p140)*.

The Mutiny Memorial (known locally as Ajitgarh), at the southern end, is a red sandstone Victorian Gothic spire built by the British to commemorate "the soldiers, British and native … who were killed" in 1857, and lists separately the names of those who died. At the entrance is a plaque, dated 1972, which points out: "The enemy of the in-scriptions were those who fought bravely for national liberation in 1857". There are pano-ramic views of Old Delhi from the platform at the base of the tower. Nearby is a 3rd-century Ashokan Pillar, one of the two Feroze Shah Tughlaq *(see p97)* brought from Meerut in 1356. Faint inscriptions in Brahmi, extolling the virtues of practising *dhamma* (the Buddhist Way of Truth), are

Coronation Memorial

St Stephen's College

Delhi University 8

Vishwavidyalaya Marg.

The university area runs parallel to the Northern Ridge, and colleges dot the vast campus. Arguably the most attractive of these is St Stephen's College, designed by Walter George in 1938. With its long corridors built in quartzite and its well-kept gardens, it has some deliber-ately cultivated Oxbridge associations. At one time this was one of India's premier institutions, with renowned scholars such as the historian Percival Spear on its staff. The office of the Vice Chancellor was once the guesthouse for British officials. It was here, in what is now the registrar's office, that the young Lord Louis Mountbatten proposed to, and was accepted by, Edwina Ashley. A plaque celebrates the event. They eventually became India's last viceroy and vicereine.

The image of the Buddha installed at Buddha Jayanti Park

The Ridge ❾

Upper Ridge Rd. ⬤ sunrise–sunset.

Delhi's Ridge, the last outcrop of the Aravalli Hills extending northwards from Rajasthan, runs from southwest to northeast. The area was originally developed by Feroze Shah Tughlaq, some 600 years ago as his hunting resort. He erected many lodges, the ruins of which can still be seen here and towards the northern end of the Ridge (see p103). This green belt of undulating, rocky terrain is covered by dense scrub forest consisting mainly of laburnum (Cassia fistula), kikar (Acacia arabica) and flame of the forest (Butea monosperma) trees, interspersed with bright splashes of bougainvillea.

A memorial tablet

A large portion in the southwest is now the **Buddha Jayanti Park**, a peaceful, well-manicured enclave, criss-crossed with paved paths. Pipal (Ficus religiosa) trees abound, and on a small ornamental island is a simple sandstone pavilion shading the large gilt-covered statue of the Buddha, installed by the 16th Dalai Lama in October 1993. An inscription nearby quotes the Dalai Lama: "Human beings have the capacity to bequeathe to future generations a world that is truly human". Every May, Buddhist monks and devotees celebrate Buddha Jayanti (see p38) here.

Delhi Cantonment ❿

Bounded by NH8, MG Rd and Sadar Bazaar Marg. **St Martin's Church** Church Rd. **Tel** (011) 2569 4632. **War Graves Cemetery** Brar Square. **Tel** (011) 2569 1958. ⬤ 8am–5pm daily.

The cantonment in Delhi was planned by John Begg and built by the Military Works Department in the 1930s. With its straight roads, neat, whitewashed walls, well-clipped hedges, parade ground and shooting-range, it epitomizes the quint-essential spit and polish of the military.

The garrison **Church of St Martin's**, probably the most original modern church in India, was designed by Lutyens's close associate, Arthur Gordon Shoosmith (1888–1974). Consecrated in 1931 and built from three and a half million bricks, it rises straight-walled with small, recessed windows and a 39 m (128 ft) tower, the lines between the bricks being the only ornamentation. Within is a stark classical interior with a plaque in honour of the architect and a haunting tablet in memory of the three children of Private Spier who died within days of each other at Abbottabad (now in Pakistan) in 1938. If the church is locked, contact the Presbyter-in-Charge who lives in the adjacent cottage.

A short distance from Dhaula Kuan Circle is the **War Graves Cemetery** where lie the Commonwealth soldiers and airmen who died on the Eastern Front in World War II. A monument at the entrance proudly declares: "Their Name Liveth Ever-more". The graves are set in neat rows with matching headstones; only the regi-mental insignia and biblical texts are different. Every Remembrance Day (11 Nov), wreaths are laid at the Memorial Column, followed by a short prayer.

The National Rail Museum ⓫

Chanakyapuri. **Tel** (011) 2688 1816. ⬤ 9:30am–5pm Tue–Sun. ⬤ 1:30–2:30pm & public hols. 📷 extra for video and train rides. 🚻

India's railway network gives rise to astonishing statistics. It has a route length of 63,360 km (39,370 miles) and tracks that cover 108,513 km (67,427 miles). There are about 7,150 stations, 12,600 passenger trains, and 1,350 goods trains

The War Graves Cemetery

that run every day. The railways employ 1.6 million people, while 13 million passengers travel by train each day and eat 6 million meals through the journey.

This museum encapsulates the history of Indian railways. Steam locomotive enthusiasts will appreciate the collection that traces the development of the Indian railways from 1849, when the first 34 km (21 miles) of railway between Bombay (now Mumbai) and Kalyan was planned. The wealth of memorabilia on display inside includes the skull of an elephant which collided with a mail train at Golkara in 1894, and a realistic model of an 1868 first-class passenger coach with separate compartments for accompanying servants. Outside, are several retired steam locomotives built in Manchester, Glasgow and Darlington in the late 19th century, and the splendid salon that carried the Prince of Wales (later King Edward VII) on his travels during the 1876 Royal Durbar.

A "toy train" offers rides around the compound, and the shop sells model locomotives, ranging from Rs1,000 to 3,000.

Safdarjung's Tomb ⑫

Aurobindo Marg. ◯ *sunrise–sunset.* 🎦 📷 *extra charges for video photography.* **Tel** *(011) 2301 7293.*

This is the last of Delhi's garden tombs and was built in 1754 for Safdarjung, the powerful prime minister of Muhammad Shah, the emperor between 1719–48. Marble was allegedly stripped from the tomb of Abdur Rahim Khan-i-Khanan in Nizamuddin *(see p82)* to construct this rather florid example of late Mughal architecture. Approached by an ornate gateway, the top storey of which houses the Archaeological Survey of India's library, the tomb, with its exaggerated onion-shaped dome, stands in a *charbagh* cut by water channels. Its red and buff stone façade is extensively ornamented with well-preserved plaster carving, and the central chamber itself is unusually light and airy with some fine stone inlay work set into the floor.

A well-stocked shop at INA Market

INA Market ⑬

Aurobindo Marg. **Shops** ◯ *9am–9pm Tue–Sun.* ⬤ *Mon.*

This lively bazaar retains all the trappings of a traditional Indian market but also sells imported foodstuffs such as cheese, pasta and exotic varieties of seafood. The stalls are crammed together under a ramshackle roof, mostly corrugated iron and oilcloth. Shops selling stainless steel utensils, spices, ready-made garments, live chickens and tiny restaurants offering Indian fast food, co-exist cheek by jowl. Ingredients for regional Indian cuisine, such as South Indian *sambhar* (curry) powder, Bengali spices or massive red chillies from Kashmir are also available. Great pots of Punjabi pickles, made from cauliflower, carrots, radish and mustard seeds are sold by weight. Diplomats, out-of-town shoppers and locals all patronize this market for its reasonable prices and variety of products.

The name derives from Indian National Airports, as people working at nearby Safdarjung Aerodrome lived in the adjacent colony. The aerodrome, further down Aurobindo Marg, was built in the 1930s. During World War II, it was the headquarters of the South Eastern Command Air Wing. It now houses offices of the Ministry of Civil Aviation and the Delhi Gliding Club. Indian Airlines also has a 24-hour booking office here *(see p293)*.

A steam engine at the National Rail Museum

CANTONMENT TOWNS

After the 1860s, over 170 cantonments (pronounced "cantoonment") were built on the outskirts of major towns to impress Indians with the seriousness of British military might. Each was a self-contained world, with symmetrical rows of barracks, finely graded bungalows, clubs and regimental messes, bazaars, hospitals and churches. Military hierarchies, too, were rigidly followed. Even after Independence, the military is mostly stationed in cantonment areas.

Indian cavalry officer, pre-World War II

Moth ki Masjid ⓮

South Extension, Part II.

Built in 1505 by Miyan Bhuwa, Sikander Lodi's prime minister, the design of this graceful red sandstone structure with its five-arched, three-domed prayer hall was developed further in later Mughal mosques. Over the central arch is a fine

Detail of Moth ki Masjid

jharokha with traces of the original plaster decoration. The red sandstone gateway and the ornate decorations on the mosque's façade are also noteworthy. It is said that Sikander Lodi gave Miyan Bhuwa a *moth* (lentil seed) which reaped him such rich returns that he was able to endow this mosque. Sadly, he annoyed Sikander's successor, Ibrahim Lodi (r.1517–26), who had him put to death.

Hauz Khas ⓯

W of Aurobindo Marg.

Beyond the boutiques, art galleries and restaurants that have taken over the former village of Hauz Khas, are the medieval monuments from Feroze Shah Tughlaq's reign. In 1352, the sultan constructed a number of buildings on the banks of Hauz Khas, the large tank (now dry) excavated by Alauddin Khilji for his city of Siri *(see p108)*. Contemporary accounts claim that Feroze Shah was a prolific builder, and during his 37-year reign he constructed an astounding 40 mosques, 200 towns, 100 public baths and about 30 reservoirs.

Among the buildings here are a *madrasa,* Feroze Shah's tomb and the ruins of a small mosque at the extreme north of the complex. The double storeyed *madrasa* was built so that the tank and lower storey were at the same level, while the upper floor was at ground level. Refreshing breezes across the water must have once cooled the theological discussions held there by scholars. The low domes, colonnades and *jharokhas* relieve the severity of its façade, while plaster carvings and deep niches for books embellish the interior. The *chhatris* in the entrance forecourt are said to cover the teachers' burial mounds. The tomb of Feroze Shah lies at one end of the *madrasa.* Wine-red painted plaster calligraphy decorates the interior of the austere tomb.

The complex is best viewed in the afternoon when sunlight filters through the *jaalis* carved into the linteled archway, to cover the graves of the sultan, his sons and grandson with delicate star-shaped shadows.

East of Hauz Khas, off Aurobindo Marg, is a small rubble-built tapering structure called **Chor Minar** ("tower of thieves") with a staircase, now locked, leading to the top. This dates to the 14th-century Khilji period and its walls, pockmarked with holes, are said to have held the severed heads of thieves to deter others from crime.

Close by, to the northwest, is the **Nili Masjid** ("blue mosque"), named after the blue tiles above its *chhajja.* The inscription on the central of its three arches reveals that it was built in 1505 by one Kasumbhil, the nurse of the son of the governor of Delhi. Nearby is an Idgah, whose remaining long wall is carved with 11 mihrabs and an inscription proclaiming that it was built in 1404–5 by Iqbal Khan, a Tughlaq noble.

The double-storeyed *madrasa* at Hauz Khas

Early Capitals of Delhi

Delhi's famous "seven cities" range from the 12th-century Qila Rai Pithora, built by Prithviraj Chauhan *(see p48)*, to the imperial Shahjahanabad, constructed in the 17th century. Each of these cities comprised the settlements that grew around the forts and palaces erected by powerful sultans with territorial

Purana Qila

ambitions. As the Sultanate was consolidated, the rulers moved their capitals from those defensively situated in the rocky outcrops of the Aravallis, northwards towards the open plains by the banks of the Yamuna. Today, Delhi is an amalgam of medieval citadels, palaces, tombs and mosques, and a spreading, modern concrete jungle.

Ferozabad, *stretching north from Hauz Khas to the banks of the Yamuna, is Delhi's fifth city built by Feroze Shah Tughlaq (r.1351–88).*

Shahjahanabad *was Delhi's seventh city, built between 1638 and 1649 by Shah Jahan who shifted the Mughal capital here from Agra (see pp150–51).*

Siri, *Delhi's second city can still be seen near the Siri Fort Auditorium and the adjacent village of Shahpur Jat (see p108). The once prosperous city of Siri was built by Alauddin Khilji in 1303.*

Purana Qila, *the citadel (see p84) of Delhi's sixth city, was built by Humayun. It was captured and occupied by the Afghan chieftain, Sher Shah Sur (r.1540–45) who called it Shergarh.*

Jahanpanah *was built by Muhammad-bin-Tughlaq (r.1325–51) as a walled enclosure to link Qila Rai Pithora and Siri. The ruined battlements of Delhi's fourth city stand near Chiragh (see p108).*

Qila Rai Pithora *was the first of Delhi's seven cities, built by the Chauhans in about 1180. In 1192, it was captured by Qutbuddin Aibak who established his capital here (see pp110–11).*

Tughlaqabad, *a dramatic fortress (see p114) on the foothills of the Aravallis, was Delhi's third city built during Ghiyasuddin Tughlaq's four-year reign (1321–5).*

Ruins of Siri, Delhi's second city built by Alauddin Khilji

Siri Fort ⑯

Siri Fort Rd. **Siri Fort Auditorium**
Tel (011) 2649 3370.

Some crumbling ramparts are
all that remain of Alauddin
Khilji's 14th-century city of
Siri *(see p107)*. The ruins of
mosques and tombs can be
found in the adjoining village
of Shahpur Jat, today a
shopper's paradise with many
up-market boutiques, offices
and a few art galleries. Siri
Fort is commonly associated
with the Siri Fort Auditorium
which regularly hosts concerts
and film festivals. It is directly
adjacent to the Asian Games
Village complex where there
are speciality restaurants
serving Indian, Chinese and
Mexican cuisine.

Chiragh Delhi ⑰

Bordered by Outer Ring Rd & LB
Shastri Marg.

The *dargah* of the Sufi saint
Nasiruddin Mahmud (died
1356), who succeeded Hazrat
Nizamuddin Auliya *(see p82)*
as spiritual leader of the
Chishti sect, lies in the once
secluded village of Chiragh
Delhi. This saint, known as
Raushan Chiragh-i-Dehlvi
("illuminated lamp of Delhi"),
was buried here and the
village that grew around his
tomb was named after him.
Muhammad-bin-Tughlaq, the
sultan at that time, built the
original village walls in the
14th century.

The shrine itself is small
and should be approached on
foot through the narrow,
congested village lanes, past
rows of tailoring establishments (including one
specializing in *burqas*) and
shops selling varieties of
mithai ("sweetmeats"),
chadors, flower garlands and
other religious offerings.
Some ruined *havelis*, which
must have once been very
beautiful, also line the street.
A huge arched doorway leads
to the *dargah*, a quieter and
simpler shrine than that of
Hazrat Nizamuddin. Shaded
by trees, the tomb is set in a
12-pillared square chamber,
enclosed by *jaali* screens and
surmounted by a large
plastered dome rising from an
octagonal drum. Small domed
turrets stand at the four
corners. The roof inside has
been embellished with fine
painted plaster carvings set
with mirrors, clearly a recent
addition. Within the enclosure
are several smaller mosques
and halls, added over the
years for religious discourses.

At the far end from the
gateway is a partially ruined
tomb that is locally claimed
to be that of Bahlol Lodi
(r.1451–88), the founder of
the Lodi dynasty. The *chhajja*
has collapsed, but the square
chamber is still surmounted
by five domes, the central
being the largest. The arches
have engraved inscriptions.

Women devotees worshipping at Chiragh Delhi

Covered corridors with arches in the 14th-century Begumpuri Mosque

Khirkee ⑱

N of Press Enclave Marg.

The village adjacent to Chiragh Delhi is called "Khirkee" after the huge mosque built by Feroze Shah Tughlaq's prime minister, Khan-i-Jahan Junan Shah (*see p96*) in the mid-14th century. Standing today in a declivity and surrounded by village houses, is the unusual two-storeyed Khirkee ("windows") Mosque. It has a sombre fortress-like appearance with bastions on all four corners, and its severe façade is broken by rows of arched windows that are covered by portcullis-like *jaalis* which give the mosque its name. Built on a high plinth, flights of stairs lead up to imposing gateways on the north, south and east sides. The inner courtyard is partly covered, its roof supported by monolithic stone pillars, and crowned by nine sets of nine small domes. Only four courtyards remain open to the sky. This was the first example of this type of mosque design. But the division of open space by pillars was found

Detail of an arched window with *jaali*

unsuitable for large congregations, so this design was never repeated.

Satpula ("seven-arches"), the dam and stone weir built by Muhammad-bin-Tughlaq in 1326, is located a few metres down the same road. It formed part of the reservoir which was used for irrigation, and the grooves, meant for sliding the shutters that regulate the flow of water, can still be seen on the seven arches. The weir also formed a portion of the fortified wall enclosing the city of Jahanpanah (*see p107*). Its upper storey was used during Muhammad-bin-Tughlaq's time as a *madrasa*.

The fortress-like Khirkee Mosque

Jahanpanah ⑲

S of Panchsheel Park.

In the heart of Jahanpanah, Muhammad-bin-Tughlaq's capital, stands **Begumpuri Mosque**, also built by Khan-i-Jahan Junan Shah. (When asking for directions, it is advisable to specifically ask for the old mosque, as a new one is located nearby.) Built on a high plinth with massive, typically Tughlaq walls, the mosque has a single imposing doorway at the head of a flight of stairs leading into the vast rectangular courtyard surrounded by arched cloisters, surmounted by 44 small domes. The prayer hall has 24 arched openings, the central one surmounted by a large dome. It is said that in times of need, this mosque also functioned as a treasury, granary and meeting place.

Nearby, to the north, is the palace of **Bijay Mandal**, a derelict, brooding octagonal structure rising from a high plinth. It is worth climbing the broken stone-cut stairs to the upper platform to get a sense of its size. According to the famed 14th-century Arab traveller, Ibn Batuta, it was from these very bastions that Muhammad-bin-Tughlaq held public audience and reviewed his troops. Later, in the early 16th century, the palace is believed to have been used as a residence by Sheikh Hasan Tahir, a much revered saint who visited Delhi during the reign of Sikandar Lodi. Panoramic views of the city of Delhi, extending from the Qutb Minar to Humayun's Tomb and beyond, can be seen from its upper platform.

Mehrauli Archaeological Park ⑳

Chhatri outside Jamali-Kamali

Best known for the Qutb Minar, a World Heritage monument, Mehrauli was built over Rajput territories known as Lal Kot and Qila Rai Pithora. In 1193, Qutbuddin Aibak made this the centre of the Sultanate of Delhi and by the 13th century a small village, Mehrauli, had grown around the shrine of the Sufi saint, Qutb Sahib. Later, Mughal princes came to Mehrauli to hunt and some 19th-century British officials built weekend houses here, attracted by its orchards, ponds and abundant game *(shikar)*. It is still a popular weekend retreat for Delhi's rich and famous.

Dargah Qutb Sahib
This 13th-century dargah is still a pilgrim point.

Zafar Mahal is a palace named after the *nom de plume* of the last Mughal emperor, Bahadur Shah Zafar.

Mehrauli village

Hauz-i-Shamsi is a large reservoir built in 1230 by Iltutmish, who is supposed to have been guided to this site by the Prophet in a dream.

★ **Jahaz Mahal**
Venue of the Phoolwalon ki Sair (see p40), this square pleasure pavilion, built during the Lodi era (1451–1526), seems to float on the Hauz-i-Shamsi tank.

Jharna (waterfall) was so-called because after the monsoon, water from the Hauz-i-Shamsi would flow over an embankment into a garden.

Bagichi Masjid

Madhi Masjid
Surrounded by bastions and a high wall, this fortress-like mosque has a large open courtyard and a three-arched, profusely ornamented prayer hall.

STAR FEATURES

- ★ Qutb Minar
- ★ Jamali-Kamali Mosque and Tomb
- ★ Jahaz Mahal

Adham Khan's Tomb
Built by Akbar in the 16th century, this was rescued from decay by Curzon (see pp56–7).

★ Qutb Minar
The Qutb (Arabic for pole or axis) area saw the advent of Islamic rule in India. The world's highest single tower, this is the focus of an early Islamic complex (see p112).

| 0 metres | 250 |
| 0 yards | 250 |

Dilkusha

New Delhi

Rajon ki Bain
This dramatic three-storeyed stepwell was also called Sukhi Baoli (dry well). Nearby is the five-storeyed Gandhak ki Baoli, named after its strong sulphur (gandhak) smell. These baolis once supplied fresh water to the area.

Balban's Tomb
Balban's 13th-century tomb lies in a square rubble-built chamber, open to the sky.

★ Jamali-Kamali Mosque and Tomb
The tomb of Jamali (the court poet during the late Lodi and early Mughal age) is inscribed with some of his verses. Its well-preserved interior has coloured tiles and richly decorated painted plasterwork. The second grave is unidentified but is widely believed to be that of his brother, Jamali.

The Qutb Complex

Floral motif

The Qutb Minar towers over this historic area where Qutbuddin Aibak laid the foundation of the Delhi Sultanate *(see pp50–51)*. In 1193, he built the Quwwat-ul-Islam ("the might of Islam") Mosque and the Qutb Minar to announce the advent of the Muslim sultans. Later, Iltutmish, Alauddin Khilji and Feroze Shah Tughlaq added other buildings, bringing in a new architectural style *(see p26)*. The fusion of decorative Hindu panels and Islamic domes and arches shows the mingling of two cultures.

Iron Pillar
This 4th-century pillar, originally made as a flagstaff in Vishnu's honour, is a tribute to ancient Indian metallurgy.

Iltutmish's Tomb

Alauddin Khilji's Tomb

Qutb Minar
The five-storeyed Victory Tower started by Qutbuddin Aibak was completed by his successor, Iltutmish.

Carved Panels
Panels, carved with inscriptions from the Koran, embellish the gateway.

Alai Darwaza
This gateway to the complex, erected in 1311 by Alauddin Khilji, is one of the earliest buildings in India to employ the Islamic principles of arched construction (see p26).

Imam Zamin's Tomb

Dargah Qutb Sahib, shrine of the Sufi saint Qutbuddin Bakhtiyar "Kaki"

Iltutmish's Tomb
Built in 1235 by Iltutmish himself, its dome has vanished. The interior is carved with geometric and calligraphic patterns.

To Entrance

Quwwat-ul-Islam Mosque
Hindu motifs, such as tasselled ropes and bells, are clearly visible on the carved pillars of this mosque.

Exploring Mehrauli

Clustered round the *dargah* of Qutb Sahib, Mehrauli became a sylvan retreat for the later Mughals and top officials of the East India Company. Its medieval bazaar survives despite its recent conversion into boutiques and cafés, popular with Delhi's "smart set".

Medallion with calligraphy

🔲 Dargah Qutb Sahib

In the heart of the Mehrauli bazaar, lies the *dargah* of a Sufi saint called Qutbuddin Bakhtiyar or "Kaki", after the small sugared cakes (*kaki*) he was fed when he fasted. It has been rebuilt several times since his death in 1235, so that today many mosques, tanks and chambers surround it, among them the lovely Moti Masjid ("pearl mosque") built in 1709. A domed marble pavilion contains his grave, which women may only view through the marble *jaalis*. A royal necropolis in the same area has the graves of some later Mughal kings, such as Bahadur Shah I (1707–12) and Akbar II (1806–36). The *dargah* and the Jogmaya Temple are the starting point for the Phoolwalon ki Sair (*see p40*), the procession of flower-sellers which began in the 1720s as a floral tribute to the Mughal emperor. Revived by Nehru after 1947, it is now an important cultural event.

🔲 Adham Khan's Tomb

Near the bus terminus, at the approach to Mehrauli village, is an imposing, single-domed structure standing on a high platform. This is believed to be the last of the octagonal tombs built in Delhi and its shaded colonnades are much favoured by local youth for their siestas. Adham Khan, the son of Akbar's wet nurse, Maham Anga (*see p85*), was considered a foster-brother of the emperor. In 1562, Adham Khan killed a rival, Atgah Khan, the husband of another wet nurse (*see p82*). A furious Akbar ordered Adham Khan's execution, but was so moved by the death of his mother, Maham Anga, 40 days later, that he had a tomb built for both mother and son.

By far the largest building here, the tomb is locally known as the *bhulbhulaiyan* (maze) because of the narrow passages concealed within its walls. In the 1800s, the British used the tomb as a rest-house, police station and residence for minor officials.

A corridor in Adham Khan's Tomb

Sanskriti Museum

Sanskriti ㉑

Anandgram, Mehrauli-Gurgaon Rd.
Tel (011) 2650 1125. ⬜ 10am–5pm
Tue–Sun. ⬤ Mon & public hols.

This unusual museum is set
amidst beautifully land-
scaped spacious grounds
where exhibits are displayed
both in the garden and in
specially constructed rural
huts. The collection, too, is
equally unusual. It is devoted
to traditional objects of
everyday use, exquisitely
crafted by the unknown,
unsung, rural artisan. OP Jain,
whose personal collections
gave birth to this museum,
has donated exquisite combs,
nutcrackers, lamps, foot-
scrubbers and kitchenware.
Terracotta objects from all
over India are also on display.
The pots are especially
dazzling, particularly as their
production techniques have
not changed for centuries.

Sultan Ghari ㉒

Off Mahipalpur-Mehrauli Rd.

Sultan Ghari was the first
Islamic tomb to be built in
Delhi and among the earliest
in India. The Slave king,
Iltutmish erected this tomb in
1231 for his eldest son and
heir, Nasiruddin Muhammad,
who was killed in battle.
Today, its fortress-like exterior
appears out of place in the
midst of one of Delhi's largest
residential complexes, Vasant
Kunj. Inside is a raised
courtyard, and the tomb itself
is an octagonal platform,
forming the roof of the crypt
(ghar) below. Like many
monuments of this early
medieval period,
Sultan Ghari was
constructed from
pillars and stones
taken from
temples nearby.
Fragments of
these are visible
in the surround-
ing colonnades,
which may have
once housed a madrasa. The
mihrab on the west side has
some fine calligraphic
decoration and, interestingly,
there is a marble yonipatta,
the base of a Shiva linga (see
p319) embedded in the floor.
  The tomb, located on the
road from Andheria More to
Delhi Airport, is reached after
turning left from the Spinal
Injuries Centre and taking the
next left after that.

Tughlaqabad ㉓

Off Mehrauli-Badarpur Rd.

This spectacular fortress,
built by Ghiyasuddin
Tughlaq in the 14th century
(see p107), was completed in
just four years. The quality of
its construction was influenced
by building techniques in
Multan where Ghiyasuddin
had served as governor. It was
so sturdy that the rubble-built
walls clinging to the shape of
the hill, survive intact all along
the 6.5 km (4 mile) perimeter.
To the right of the main
entrance is the citadel from
which rise the ruins of the
Vijay Mandal ("tower of
victory"). To the left is a
rectangular area where
arches are all that
remain of a
complex of
palaces and
halls. Beyond
these, houses
were once laid
out in a neat
grid pattern.
Legend has it
that when Ghiyasuddin tried
to prevent the building of the
baoli at Hazrat Nizamuddin
Auliya's dargah (see p82), the
saint cursed him by saying that
one day only jackals and the
Gujjar tribe would inhabit his
capital. Perhaps the saint
forgot to add tourists and
monkeys to that list!
  A good view of the fort and
of the adjoining smaller one of
Adilabad is possible from the

**Ghiyasuddin Tughlaq's
Tomb**

The crumbling ramparts of Tughlaqabad Fort

The lotus-domed Baha'i House of Worship, one of Delhi's most spectacular sights

walls. Adilabad was built by Muhammad-bin-Tughlaq (r.1325–51), who is believed to have killed his father Ghiyasuddin by contriving to have a gateway collapse on him. They are both buried in Ghiyasuddin's Tomb, joined to the Tughlaqabad Fort by a causeway that crossed the dammed waters of a lake.

The tomb was the first in India to be built with sloping walls, a design that was repeated in all subsequent Tughlaq architecture. Its severe red sandstone walls, relieved by white marble inlay, are surmounted by a white marble dome. The red sandstone *kalasha* (urn) which crowns it and the lintel spanning the arched opening decorated with a lotus bud fringe, are both influenced by Hindu architecture.

Kalkaji Temple ㉔

Nehru Place. ⟨icon⟩ *Navaratri (Mar–Apr & Sep–Oct).*

This temple is a good place to see Hinduism in bustling, popular practice. It is approached through a narrow winding alley, lined with stalls selling laminated religious prints, bangles, *sindur* (vermilion powder) and fruit, while devotional hymns blast from rival cassette stalls. The 12-domed temple, with a heavily decorated pillared pavilion, was built in the mid-18th century on an older site by Raja Kedarnath, prime minister of Emperor Akbar II. Thereafter, many contemporary additions, financed by rich merchants, have been made. The goddess Kali or Kalka, draped in silks, sits under silver umbrellas and a marble canopy. Legend has it that a farmer, on discovering that his cow regularly offered her milk to the goddess, built this temple in her name.

Baha'i House of Worship ㉕

Bahapur, Kalkaji. **Tel** *(011) 2644 4029.* ⬜ *Apr–Sep: 9am–7pm; Oct–Mar: 9:30am–5:30pm Tue–Sun.* ⬛ *Mon & public hols.* **Prayer services** *10am, noon, 3pm & 5pm.*

Just opposite the Kalkaji Temple is the Baha'i House of Worship, a world where silence and order prevails. The arresting shape of its unfurling 27-petalled white marble lotus has given it its more popular name, the Lotus Temple. The edifice, circled by nine pools and 27 acres (92 ha) of green manicured lawns, is one of Delhi's most innovative modern structures.

The Baha'i sect originated in Persia and this temple was designed by Iranian architect, Fariburz Sahba. Construction began in 1980 and was completed in 1986. Inside, the lofty auditorium can seat 1,300 and all are welcome to meditate there and attend the daily 15-minute services. The temple looks spectacular after dark when the lighting gives the marble panels a luminous, ethereal quality.

Inside view of Kalkaji Temple

Day Trips from Delhi

If you want a break from the hustle and bustle of Delhi and wish to explore the surrounding countryside, there are several interesting sights to visit, all within a 50-km (30-mile) radius of the city. The lake at Sultanpur is a haven for migratory birds in winter, and in Pataudi is a beautiful palace which belongs to its cricket-loving nawabs, now open to tourists. Surajkund, with its vast medieval reservoir, is the venue of a popular crafts fair held every February. All these excursions take about eight hours. Since they are not particularly easy to reach by public transport, it is best to hire a car and driver for the day, which can be organized by your hotel or local taxi rank and is relatively inexpensive.

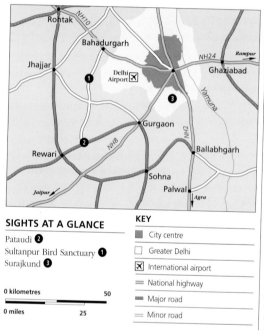

SIGHTS AT A GLANCE

Pataudi **2**
Sultanpur Bird Sanctuary **1**
Surajkund **3**

0 kilometres   50

0 miles   25

KEY

▮ City centre

☐ Greater Delhi

✕ International airport

— National highway

▬ Major road

═ Minor road

Sultanpur Bird Sanctuary **1**

46 km (27 miles) W of Delhi.
🛈 *Haryana Tourism, Chanderlok Building, Janpath, Delhi (011) 2332 4911.* ◯ *sunrise–sunset daily.*

This sanctuary, a two-hour drive from Delhi, has been developed around a low-lying marshy area that is dry in summer, but fills up during the monsoon to form a shallow lake *(jheel)*. Sultanpur is at its best in the winter when this shallow sheet of water provides a haven for migratory birds.

Several pleasant walks, including a paved pathway which runs around the small lake, allow one to explore the 35-km (22-mile) area, while the many hides or *machans*, mounted on stilts, provide a good view of the birdlife on the lake. The Sarus crane, the world's tallest flying bird, breeds in the mud spits covered with reeds that rise above the waters. Often, on late winter evenings, large, noisy flocks of demoiselle cranes descend on the lake. The other birds that visit the lake include egrets, herons, kingfishers, pelicans and painted storks.

The rolling tree-shaded lawns, home to herds of friendly deer, have beautifully sited picnic spots. The sanctuary shop has a good selection of books and posters on Indian birdlife.

Sultanpur, home to a variety of deer and many migratory birds

Pataudi ❷

60 km (37 miles) S of Delhi.
Ibrahim Kothi 🍴 *Advance
reservations are essential.* **Tel** *(011)
2301 3549.*

The approximately two hour
drive to Pataudi is a pleasant
one, particularly after crossing
Gurgaon when the road runs
through open wheat fields
and occasional villages.
Pataudi, a typical North
Indian town with a tangle of
narrow lanes and a congested
bazaar, is famous for its
cricket-playing nawabs who
claim descent from a 16th-
century Afghan noble.

The old palace, built about
200 years ago, is now derelict,
but still retains its romantic
charm. The new palace,
known as **Ibrahim Kothi**,
was built in 1939. The elegant
white, double-storeyed
building, set amidst 10 acres
(4 ha) of flowering gardens,
has deep, pillared verandahs
and is surmounted by a small
dome. The well-maintained
interior includes polished

Elegant interior of Ibrahim Kothi

parquet floors, pink Venetian
chandeliers and chintz
furnishings. The walls are
lined with portraits and sepia
photographs of the present
nawab's ancestors. One is of
his father as a member of the
famous "bodyline" English
cricket team which toured
Australia in the 1930s.

A section of this palace
has now been refurbished
and is run as a hotel by the
Neemrana group; perfect for
a truly royal holiday.

Ibrahim Kothi at Pataudi

SURAJKUND CRAFTS MELA

For two weeks in early February, Surajkund comes alive
with the sounds and colours of one of India's largest arts
and crafts fair. Craftsmen and artisans from every part of
the country sell their wares at a specially created village,
under thatched canopies decorated with *rangoli*. Here,
mirrorwork from Gujarat, painted puppets from Jaipur,
fanciful bell-metal beasts from Orissa and Madhubani
paintings from Bihar can be found at a wide range of
prices. There are balloon
sellers and food stalls to
give the *mela* a carnival
air, while folk dancers and
musicians in colourful
costumes weave in and
out of the crowds. The
evenings, given over to
folk theatre, dance and
music performances,
attract huge crowds.

A performance by folk singers at
the Surajkund Crafts Mela

Surajkund ❸

21 km (13 miles) S of Delhi.
ℹ️ *Haryana Tourism, Chanderlok
Building, Janpath, Delhi (011) 2332
4911.*

King Surajpal of the Rajput
Tomar dynasty *(see p48)*,
hero of many legends, built
this reservoir some time in
the late 10th or early 11th
century. An embankment of
stone terraces was built round
a pool which trapped rain
water running down from the
hills. A sun temple is thought
to have stood on the western
side. Tomar Rajputs trace their
descent from the sun, hence
the name: *suraj* (sun) *kund*
(pool). Today, the embankment is more or less intact,
though there is no trace of
the temple and the pool itself
is none too clean. The nearby
artificial lake is picturesque
and is best enjoyed from the
paddle or rowing boats on
hire. You might even glimpse
a pale green water snake
swimming alongside.

About 2 km (1.5 miles) to
the west is **Anangpur Dam**
built by the Tomar king,
Anangpal. A rather impressive
quartzite stone stucture, it
blocks a narrow ravine to
create an artificial lake. The
dam is reached on foot, but it
is an extremely brambly and
rocky walk and best avoided
in the rainy weather.

This area is a popular picnic
spot for Delhi's residents.
Haryana Tourism and the
Delhi Transport Corporation
run special daily buses to
Surajkund during the annual
crafts *mela (see p41).*

SHOPPING IN DELHI

The hallmark of shopping in Delhi is the fabulous variety of styles, merchandise and markets. Besides Connaught Place, almost every residential colony boasts a market. Old, established shops and bazaars co-exist happily with glitzy high-end boutiques and department stores, and one can buy

Logo of Dastkar

anything from seasonal vegetables, fruits and traditional handicrafts to designer clothes and the latest imported electronic items. Be prepared to bargain where required, even a small success will make your shopping spree in Delhi a complete and satisfying experience. For practical information, see page 264.

SHOPS AND MARKETS

New Delhi's main shopping centres are in Connaught Place and Janpath where the Central Cottage Industries offers an exciting and varied range of textiles, jewellery and souvenirs at fixed and reasonable prices. Indian handicrafts and handlooms are available at the state emporia on Baba Kharak Singh Marg, Dilli Haat and the Crafts Museum Shop *(see pp86–7)*. In the north is Chandni Chowk *(see p93)*, the traditional market, while to the south are Khan Market, Sundar Nagar and Santushti. The old urban villages of Hauz Khas, Shahpur Jat and Mehrauli have trendy boutiques where shoppers rub shoulders with loitering cows. The South Extension, Lajpat Nagar and Sarojini Nagar markets are popular with local shoppers. The five-star hotels, too, have shopping arcades that sell carefully-selected goods.

Silver fruit bowl

ANTIQUES, CARPETS AND SHAWLS

Genuine antiques are rare to come by and cannot be taken out of the country unless certified by the ASI *(see p279)*. However, hotel shops, Sundar Nagar and the **Crafts Museum Shop** stock excellent reproductions of miniature paintings, woodcarving and bronzes made by artisans today. Contemporary silverware is available at **Cooke & Kelvey** and **Ravissant**. For Afghan and Kashmiri carpets and shawls, such as the paisley jamawar and pashmina, the best outlets are **Cottage Industries** and **The Carpet Cellar**.

JEWELLERY

Superb pieces of traditional jewellery, such as *kundan* and *meenakari*, are available at **Bharany's**. The best places for silver jewellery are Dariba Kalan, in Chandni Chowk, and Sundar Nagar market.

Poster displaying a selection of cotton *dhurries* from Fabindia

TEXTILES AND QUILTS

Indian silks and cotton are famous throughout the world. Cottage Industries and the state emporia have a good selection of textiles from different parts of India. **Fabindia**, **The Shop**, **Tulsi** and **Anokhi** are fine places to shop for good quality readymade garments, linen and light cotton quilts, while **Shyam Ahuja** sells *dhurries* and linen. The best selection of designer clothes and accessories is available at **Abraham & Thakore**.

LEATHER

Leather goods, in particular shoes and bags, are found in most major shopping areas such as Connaught Place, Khan Market and South Extension. For quality handmade shoes and jackets, the Chinese-owned outlets such as **John Brothers**, still set the standards for comfort and durability. For trendier goods there is **Da Milano**, which has several branches.

Brass and copper vessels and other objects on sale, Sundar Nagar market

HANDICRAFTS AND GIFTS

Indian handicrafts are available at the state emporia, specifically **Kamala**, the Crafts Museum Shop and **Dilli Haat** on Aurobindro Marg. **Tibet House** has *thangkas*, carpets, woollen shawls and jackets. **The Neemrana Shop** and **Good Earth** have a good selection of gift items, such as candles, handmade paper products and artifacts in ceramics, wood and metal.

BOOKS, MUSIC AND NEWSPAPERS

Every local market has stalls selling newspapers, magazines, music cassettes and bestsellers. The largest number of books and music shops are in South Extension, Khan Market and Vasant Vihar. **The Book Shop**, **Bookworm** and **Full Circle** stock a wide variety of books by international publishing houses. **Motial Banarsidas** in Old Delhi specializes in books on Indology. Every

Embroidered textiles sold on Janpath

Sunday, a bazaar selling old and second-hand books is held on the pavements of Daryaganj where one can pick up interesting bargains.

SPECIALITY SHOPS

In Chandni Chowk's Dariba Kalan is **Gulab Singh Johari Mal**, a marvellous old-fashioned shop where one can test Indian perfumes from lovely cutglass bottles. Herbal cosmetics by **Kama** and **Forest Essentials** are found in their

outlets at Khan Market. Good Earth *(see Handicrafts and Gifts)* also sells Amritam, its own aromatheraphy brand.

Spices, dry and fresh seasonal fruit are found at INA Market while **Steakhouse** and the Gourmet Shoppe at The Oberoi *(see p235)* stock a wide variety of cheese, cold cuts, breads and pasteries. Indian tea, from the gardens of Assam and Darjeeling, can be found at various outlets in Khan Market and at **Aapki Pasand**.

DIRECTORY

ANTIQUES

Cooke & Kelvey
Janpath. **Map** 1 C5.
Tel (011) 2372 1081.

Cottage Industries
Janpath. **Map** 1 C5.
Tel (011) 2332 0439.

Crafts Museum Shop
Pragati Maidan.
Map 6 D2.
Tel (011) 2337 1887.

Ravissant
New Friends Colony.
Tel (011) 2683 7278.

The Carpet Cellar
1 Anand Lok.
Tel (011) 2626 1777.

JEWELLERY

Bharany's
Sundar Nagar Market.
Map 6 D3.
Tel (011) 2435 8528.

TEXTILES

Abraham & Thakore
31 Lodi Colony Main Mkt.
Tel (011) 2460 3455.

Anokhi
Khan Market. **Map** 5 B3.
Tel (011) 2460 3423.

Fabindia
Greater Kailash I.
Tel (011) 2621 2183.

Shyam Ahuja
Santushti. **Map** 4 E4.
Tel (011) 2467 0112.

The Shop
Connaught Place. **Map** 1 C5. **Tel** *(011) 2374 6050.*

Tulsi
Santushti. **Map** 4 E4.
Tel (011) 2687 0339.

LEATHER

Da Milano
Khan Market. **Map** 5 B3.
Tel (011) 4175 7155.

John Brothers
Connaught Place. **Map** 1 C4. **Tel** *(011) 2335 2812.*

HANDICRAFTS AND GIFTS

Good Earth
Santushti, **Map** 4 E4.
Tel (011) 2685 1757.

Kamala
Rajiv Gandhi Handicrafts Bhavan, Baba Kharak Singh Marg.
Map 1 B5
Tel (011) 2374 3322.

The Neemrana Shop
Khan Market. **Map** 5 B3.
Tel (011) 2462 0262.

Tibet House
Lodi Rd. **Map** 5 B5.
Tel (011) 2461 1515.

BOOKS AND MUSIC

Full Circle
Khan Market. **Map** 5 B3.
Tel (011) 2465 5641.

Motial Banarsidas
Jawahar Nagar.
Tel (011) 2391 1985.

The Bookshop
Khan Market.
Map 5 B3.
Tel (011) 2469 7102.

Bookworm
Jor Bagh Mkt.
Map 1 C4.
Tel (011) 4185 1113.

SPECIALITY SHOPS

Aapki Pasand
15, Netaji Subhash Marg.
Map 2 E3.
Tel (011) 2326 0373.

Gulab Singh Johri Mal
Dariba Kalan, Chandni Chowk. **Map** 2 E2.
Tel (011) 2327 1345.

Steakhouse
Jor Bagh Mkt.
Tel (011) 2461 1008.

ENTERTAINMENT IN DELHI

Logo of the
International Film
Festival of India

elhi, as the capital of India, has a rich and varied cultural life, mainly because the government has, over the last 50 years, consciously promoted a revival of traditional art forms. As a result, dancers, musicians and folk artistes from all over India deem it an honour to perform here before discerning audiences. Although Delhi is still a culturally conservative city, jazz, theatre and rock concerts are frequent, and there are several good bars and discotheques.

The city's cultural calendar livens up between October and March when the season is in full swing. The number of events multiply as all major festivals of music, dance, theatre and cinema are held at this time.

India International Centre, Delhi

ENTERTAINMENT GUIDES AND TICKETS

All newspapers list the day's entertainment on their engagements page. Other useful sources of information on events, restaurants, sports and related activities are the weekly *Delhi Diary* and the monthly magazine *First City*.

At several venues in the city, such as the India International Centre *(see Lectures and Discussions)*, entry is free. At others, such as the Indian Council for Cultural Relations, it is by invitation. Tickets for selected music festivals and theatre, however, are advertised and sold at certain bookshops or at the box office. A useful website is www.delhievents.com.

MUSIC AND DANCE

Delhi is the best place to experience the range and richness of classical dance and music. Performances by the best exponents of the

major dance styles of Bharata Natyam, Kathak, Odissi and Kathakali take place in the high season. The same is true of concerts of Hindustani and Carnatic music, the two major streams of classical music. During the season, shows are held mainly at **Siri Fort Auditorium** and **Kamani**. Some venues, such as **Triveni Kala Sangam** and the **India Habitat Centre**, have performances all the year round. The state-run **Indian Council for Cultural Relations** also organizes shows at Azad Bhavan and the FICCI auditorium.

Colourful folk dances from all over India can be seen during the annual Trade Fair at **Pragati Maidan** *(see p85)*.

City magazines

THEATRE

The main theatre repertory company is the **National School of Drama** which presents plays in its own open air auditorium and at Kamani Auditorium near by. In 1999, the company began a National Theatre Festival, to be held every May–Jun. Its performances are in Hindi and Urdu and include works by contemporary Indian and Western playwrights.

Several amateur theatre groups perform in both Hindi and English, contributing to a hectic theatre season in the winter. The main venues are **Shri Ram Centre**, Kamani, and the India Habitat Centre *(see Music and Dance)*.

FILMS

Delhi plays host to an international film festival which is held in the January of every even year at the Siri Fort complex. Tickets can be obtained from the box-office. Other film festivals, organized by the Directorate of Film Festivals, are held here as well. These are mainly regional Indian cinema and foreign films that are not usually screened on the commercial circuit. Documentary films, presenting the works of up-and-coming filmmakers, are screened at the India International Centre, **Max Mueller Bhavan** and the **British Council**. Many foreign cultural centres, like the Alliance Française and the **French Cultural Centre** also have regular film shows.

Popular Indian and foreign films are screened at the many cinema halls dotted all over

Shubha Mudgal, a well-known classical singer

the city. Among the better-equipped halls are **3Cs, PVR Anupam, Priya** and **Plaza**. All daily newspapers carry details of film shows. The tickets should be bought well in advance as cinema, both Indian and foreign, continues to be a major form of popular entertainment.

EXHIBITIONS

In the past five years the number of art galleries has grown in response to an increased interest in contemporary Indian art. Regular exhibitions present the work of painters, sculptors and photographers. Certain well known galleries such as **Art Heritage** and others located at Triveni Kala Sangam, India Habitat Centre, India International Centre and Max Mueller Bhavan are in the city

centre. Others, such as **Vadehra Art Gallery**, are in South Delhi. The **National Gallery of Modern Art** (see p71) and the **National Museum** (see pp72–5) both organize major exhibitions.

LECTURES AND DISCUSSIONS

Lectures, discussions and seminars covering a wide range of subjects, such as international and current affairs, wildlife and ecology, mountaineering and Indian culture are regularly held at the **India International Centre**. These are announced in the daily newspapers and are open to all. Other venues where such programmes are held are the **Indira Gandhi National Centre of the Arts** (IGNCA), British Council and the India Habitat Centre.

A popular bar in a five-star hotel

NIGHTLIFE

Delhi's nightlife is becoming livelier by the minute. The five-star hotels house most of the better bars and discotheques, such as **Club Lounge, Rick's, Dublin, Patiala Peg** and others. These are popular with the young crowd, especially on Saturday nights. Clubs are open only to their registered members.

DIRECTORY

MUSIC AND DANCE

India Habitat Centre
Lodi Rd. **Map** 5 B5.
Tel (011) 2468 2222.

Indian Council for Cultural Relations
Azad Bhavan, IP Estate.
Map 1 C4.
Tel (011) 2337 9199.

India Trade Promotion Org.
Pragati Maidan.
Map 6 D1.
Tel (011) 2331 4857.

Kamani Auditorium
Copernicus Marg.
Map 2 D5.
Tel (011) 2338 8084.

Siri Fort Auditorium
Asian Village Complex.
Tel (011) 2649 3370.

Triveni Kala Sangam
205 Tansen Marg.
Map 2 D5.
Tel (011) 2371 8833.

THEATRE

National School of Drama
Bhawalpur House.
Map 2 E5.
Tel (011) 2338 9402.

Shri Ram Centre
Mandi House. **Map** 2 D5.
Tel (011) 2371 4307.

FILMS

British Council
Kasturba Gandhi Marg.
Map 1 C5.
Tel (011) 2371 0111.

PVR Plaza
H Block, Connaught Place.
Map 1 C4.
Tel (011) 4151 6787

3 C's
Lajpat Nagar.
Tel (011) 2692 7846.

French Cultural Centre
Aurangzeb Rd.
Map 5 A3.
Tel (011) 2301 4682.

Max Mueller Bhavan
3 Kasturba Gandhi Marg.
Map 2 D5.
Tel (011) 2332 9506.

Priya Cinema
Vasant Vihar.
Tel (011) 2614 0048.

PVR Anupam
Community Centre, Saket.
Tel (011) 2686 5999.

EXHIBITIONS

Art Heritage
Triveni Kala Sangam.
Map 2 D5.
Tel (011) 2371 9470.

National Gallery of Modern Art
Jaipur House. **Map** 5 C2.
Tel (011) 2338 5378.

National Museum
Janpath. **Map** 5 A2.
Tel (011) 2301 9272.

Vadehra Art Gallery
D-178, Okhla Phase 1.
Tel (011) 6547 4005.

LECTURES AND DISCUSSIONS

India International Centre
40 Lodi Estate, Max Mueller Marg.
Map 5 A4.
Tel (011) 2461 9431.

Indira Gandhi National Centre for the Arts
Janpath. **Map** 5 A4.
Tel (011) 2338 9216.

NIGHTLIFE

Club Lounge
The Oberoi, Dr Zakir Hussain Marg. **Map** 6 D4.
Tel (011) 2436 3030.

Rick's
Taj Mahal Hotel.
Map 5 B3
Tel (011) 2302 6162.

Dublin
Maurya Sheraton.
Tel (011) 2611 2233.

Patiala Peg
Hotel Imperial, Janpath.
Map 5 A1.
Tel (011) 2334 5678.

Pegasus
Nirula's Hotel. **Map** 1 C4.
Tel (011) 2332 2419.

Someplace Else
The Park, Sansad Marg.
Map 1 C5.
Tel (011) 2374 3000.

Thugs
Hotel Broadway, **Map** 2 E3. *Tel (011) 2327 3821.*

DELHI STREET FINDER

Delhi is a confusing city to get around. New Delhi and the adjoining Nizamuddin to Purana Qila area are fairly well marked out, whereas Old Delhi is a maze of narrow lanes *(galis)* and bylanes. The city has extended far beyond the main city centre, in keeping with its burgeoning population, and the vast complexes of residential housing add to the confusion of getting around. Navigating the city's roads and streets *(margs)* is challenging. Signposts are

Ashokan lions

often hard to find and most of the names have changed in recent years or are known by more than one name. Connaught Place is now officially Rajiv Gandhi Chowk, Connaught Circus is Indira Gandhi Chowk and Sansad Marg is also known as Parliament Sztreet. The Street Finder covers the city centre area and lists the major sights, hotels, restaurants, shops and entertainment venues. The Further Afield map is on page 99 and covers the area north, west and south of the city centre.

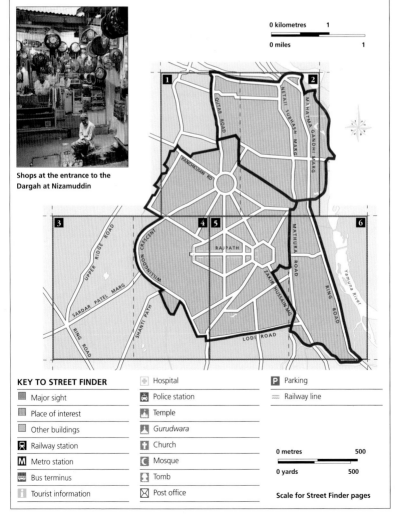

Shops at the entrance to the Dargah at Nizamuddin

0 kilometres 1

0 miles 1

KEY TO STREET FINDER

Major sight	Hospital	P Parking
Place of interest	Police station	Railway line
Other buildings	Temple	
Railway station	Gurudwara	
M Metro station	Church	0 metres 500
Bus terminus	C Mosque	0 yards 500
Tourist information	Tomb	
	Post office	**Scale for Street Finder pages**

◁ **The President's Bodyguard at the Republic Day Parade**

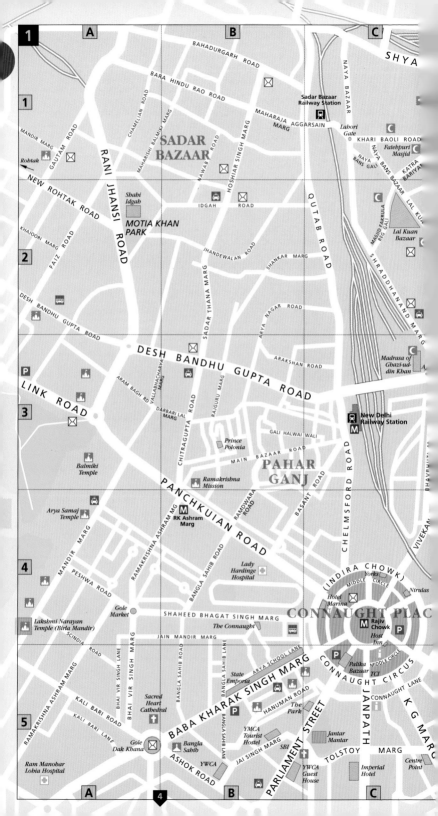

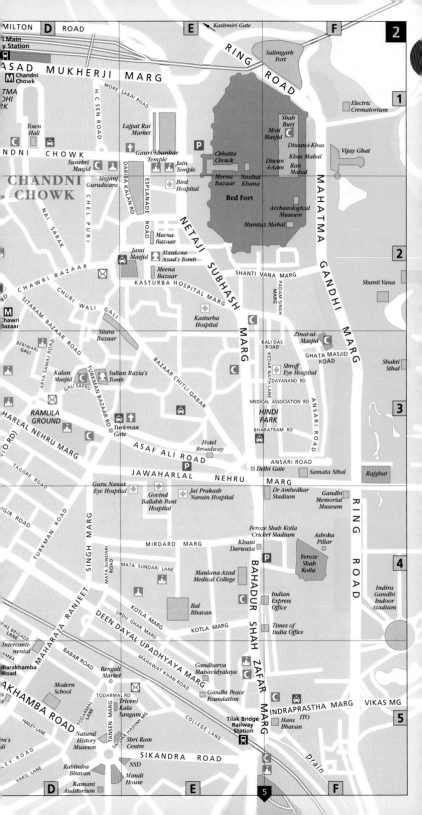

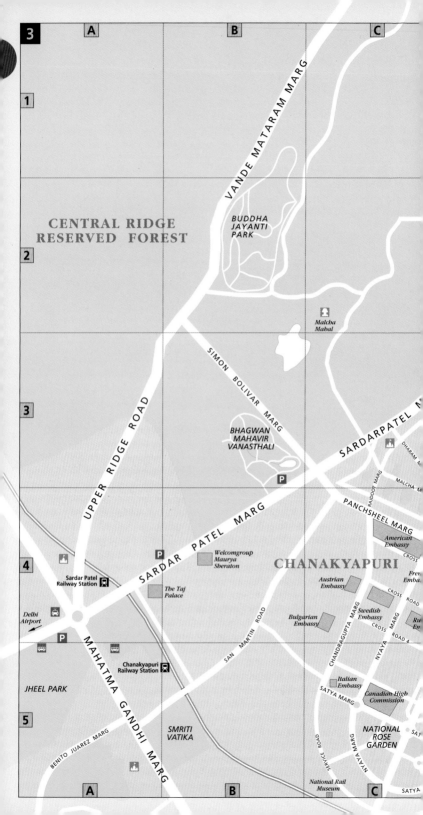

3

A · B · C

1

CENTRAL RIDGE
RESERVED FOREST

2

VANDE MATARAM MARG

BUDDHA
JAYANTI
PARK

Malcha
Mahal

3

SIMON BOLIVAR MARG

UPPER RIDGE ROAD

BHAGWAN
MAHAVIR
VANASTHALI

SARDARPATEL N

DHARAM M

MALCHA M

P

JAIDOOT MARG

PANCHSHEEL MARG

4

P

Welcomgroup
Maurya
Sheraton

SARDAR PATEL MARG

Sardar Patel
Railway Station

The Taj
Palace

CHANAKYAPURI

American
Embassy

CROSS

Austrian
Embassy

Fren
Emba

CROSS   ROAD

Swedish
Embassy

Ru
En

CHANDRAGUPTA MARG

CROSS   ROAD 4

Delhi
Airport

P

Bulgarian
Embassy

SAN MARTIN ROAD

NYAYA   MARG

Chanakyapuri
Railway Station

MAHATMA GANDHI MARG

JHEEL PARK

Italian
Embassy

SATYA MARG

Canadian High
Commission

5

SAT

NATIONAL
ROSE
GARDEN

SERVICE ROAD

NYAYA MARG

BENITO JUAREZ MARG

SMRITI
VATIKA

National Rail
Museum

SATYA

A · B · C

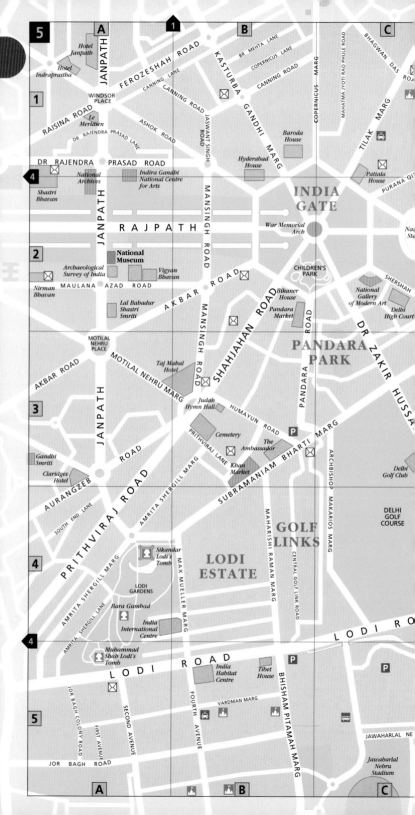

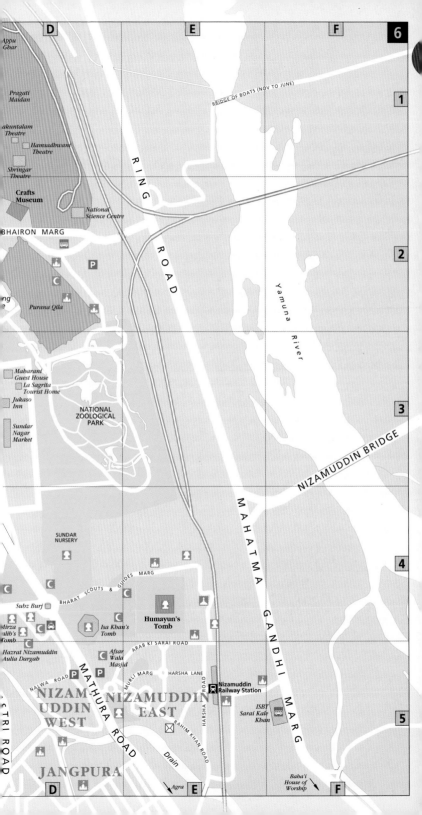

D **6**

Appu Ghar

Pragati Maidan

akuntalam Theatre

Hamsadhwam Theatre

Shringar Theatre

Crafts Museum

National Science Centre

1

BRIDGE OF BOATS (NOV TO JUNE)

R I N G

BHAIRON MARG

P

C

Purana Qila

2

Yamuna River

R O A D

Maharani Guest House

La Sagrita Tourist Home

Jukaso Inn

Sundar Nagar Market

NATIONAL ZOOLOGICAL PARK

3

NIZAMUDDIN BRIDGE

SUNDAR NURSERY

M A H A T M A

4

Subz Burj

BHARAT SCOUTS & GUIDES MARG

C

C

C

Isa Khan's Tomb

Humayun's Tomb

Mirza Galib's Tomb

C

C

Hazrat Nizamuddin Aulia Dargah

Afsar Wala Masjid

ARAB KI SARAI ROAD

G A N D H I

P P

NALWA ROAD

NIZAM-UDDIN WEST

M A T H U R A   R O A D

MURLI MARG

NIZAMUDDIN EAST

HARSHA LANE

HARSHA ROAD

Nizamuddin Railway Station

ISBT Sarai Kale Khan

M A R G

5

STRI ROAD

JANGPURA

RAHIM KHAN ROAD

Drain

Agra

Baha'i House of Worship

D **E** **F**

Street Finder Index

A

Afsar Wala Masjid	6 D5
Ajmeri Gate	1 C3
Ajmeri Gate Road	2 D2
Akbar Road	4 F3
continues	5 B2
American Embassy	3 C4
Amrita Shergill Lane	5 A4
Amrita Shergill Marg	5 A4
Ansari Road	2 F3
Appu Ghar	6 D1
Arab ki Sarai Road	6 E5
Arakshan Road	1 B3
Aram Bagh Road	1 A3
Archaeological Museum	2 F2
Archaeological Survey of India	5 A2
Archbishop Makarios Marg	5 C3
Arya Nagar Road	1 B3
Arya Samaj Road	2 D3
Arya Samaj Temple	1 A4
Arya School Lane	1 B5
Asaf Ali Road	2 E3
Ashok Hotel	4 D4
Ashok Road	1 B5
continues	5 A1
Ashoka Pillar	2 F4
Australian Embassy	4 D4
Austrian Embassy	3 C4
Aurangzeb Road	4 F4
continues	5 A4
Aurobindo Marg	4 F5

B

Baba Kharak Singh Marg	1 B5
Babar Road	2 D5
Bahadurgarh Road	1 B1
Bahadur Shah Zafar Marg	2 E4
Bal Bhavan	2 E4
Balli Maran	2 D1
Balmiki Temple	1 A3
Bangla Sahib Gurudwara	1 B5
Bangla Sahib Lane	1 B5
Bangla Sahib Road	1 B4
Bara Gumbad	5 A4
Bara Hindu Rao Road	1 B1
Barakhamba Lane	2 D5
Barakhamba Road	2 D5
Bardoloi Marg	4 D3
Baroda House	5 B1
Basant Road	1 B4
Bazaar Chitli Qabar	2 E3
Bengali Market	2 D5
Benito Juarez Marg	3 A5
Beriwari Gali	2 D3
Bhagwan Das Road	5 C1
Bhagwan Mahavir Vanasthali	3 B3
Bhai Vir Singh Lane	1 A5
Bhai Vir Singh Marg	1 A5
Bhairon Marg	6 D2
Bharat Scouts & Guides Marg	6 D4
Bharatram Road	2 F3
Bhavbhuti Marg	1 C3
Bhisham Pitamah Marg	5 B5
Bird Hospital	2 E2
Boating Lake	6 D2
BR Mehta Lane	5 B1
Brassey Avenue	4 E2
Bridge of Boats (Nov–June)	
British High Commission	4 D4
Buddha Jayanti Park	3 B2
Bulgarian Embassy	3 C4

C

Canadian High Commission	3 C5
Canning Lane	5 A1
Canning Road	5 B1
Cathedral Church of the Redemption	4 E1
Cemetery (Prithviraj Road)	5 B3
Central Golf Link Road	5 B4
Central Ridge Reserved Forest	3 A2
Central Secretariat	4 E2
Centre Point	1 C5
Chamelian Road	1 A1
Chanakyapuri	3 C4
Chanakyapuri Railway Station	3 A5
Chandni Chowk	2 D2
Chandni Chowk Road	2 D1
Chandragupta Marg	3 C5
Chawri Bazaar	2 D2
Chel Puri	2 D2
Chelmsford Road	1 C4
Chhatta Chowk	2 E1
Children's Park	5 B2
Chitragupta Road	1 B3
Church Mission Marg	1 C1
Church Road	4 E1
Churi Wali Gali	2 D2
Claridges Hotel	5 A3
College Lane	2 E5
Connaught Circus (Indira Chowk)	1 C5
Connaught Lane	1 C5
Connaught Place	1 C4
Copernicus Lane	5 B1
Copernicus Marg	5 C1
Crafts Museum	6 D2
Cross Road 2	3 C4
Cross Road 3	3 C4
Cross Road 4	3 C4

D

Dalhousie Road	4 E1
continues	4 F2
Dandi March Statue	4 D2
Dariba Kalan Road	2 E1
Darbari Lal Marg	1 B3
Dayanand Road	2 F3
Deen Dayal Upadhyaya Marg	2 D4
Delhi Flying Club	4 F5
Delhi Gate	2 E3
Delhi Golf Club	2 E3
Delhi Golf Course	5 C4
Delhi High Court	5 C2
Delhi Main Railway Station	2 D1
Delhi Riding Club	4 E4
Desh Bandhu Gupta Road	1 B3
continues	1 A2
Dharam Marg	3 C3
Diwan-i-Aam	2 F1
Diwan-i-Khas	2 F1
Dr Ambedkar Stadium	2 F4
Dr Rajendra Prasad Lane	5 A1
Dr Rajendra Prasad Road	5 A1
Dr Zakir Hussain Marg	5 C3
Dupleix Road	4 F3

E

Electric Crematorium	2 F1
Esplanade Road	2 E2

F

Faiz Road	1 A2
Fatehpuri Masjid	1 C1
Feroze Shah Kotla	2 F4
Feroze Shah Kotla Cricket Ground	2 F4
Fire Brigade Lane	2 D4
Ferozeshah Road	5 A1
First Avenue	5 A5
Fourth Avenue	5 B5
French Embassy	3 C4

G

Gali Halwai Wali	1 B3
Gali Safru	2 D3
Gandharva Mahavidyalaya	2 E5
Gandhi Memorial Museum	2 F4
Gandhi Peace Foundation	2 E5
Gandhi Smriti	4 F3
Gauri Shankar Temple	2 E1
Gautam Road	1 A1
German Embassy	3 C5
Ghata Masjid Road	2 F3
Gole Dak Khana	1 A5
Gole Market	1 A4
Golf Course	4 F5
Golf Links	5 B4
Govind Ballabh Pant Hospital	2 E4
Guru Nanak Eye Hospital	2 E4
Gurudwara Rakabganj Road	4 E1
continues	4 F1
Gymkhana Club	4 E4

H

Hailey Lane	2 D5
Hailey Road	2 D5
Hamilton Road	2 D1
Hamsadhwani Theatre	6 D1
Hans Bhavan	2 F5
Hans Plaza	2 D5
Hanuman Road	1 B5
Harsha Lane	6 E5
Harsha Road	6 E5
Hazrat Nizamuddin Aulia Dargah	6 D5
HC Sen Road	2 D1
Hindi Park	2 F3
Hoshiar Singh Marg	1 B1
Host Inn	1 C4
Hotel Broadway	2 E3
Hotel Diplomat	4 D3
Hotel Janpath	5 A1
Hotel Marina	1 C4
Humayun Road	5 B3
Humayun's Tomb	6 E4
Hyderabad House	5 B1

I

Idgah Road	1 B2
Imperial Hotel	1 C5
India Gate	5 B2
India Habitat Centre	5 B5
India International Centre	5 A4
Indian Airlines Office	2 F4
Indian Express Office	2 F1
Indira Chowk	1 C4
Indira Gandhi National Centre for Arts	5 A1
Indira Gandhi Smriti	4 F4
Indira Gandhi Sports Complex	2 F4
Indraprastha Hotel	5 A1
Indraprastha Marg	2 F5
Inner Circle (Rajiv Chowk)	1 C4
Intercontinental Hotel	2 D5
Irish Embassy	4 F5
Isa Khan's Tomb	6 D4
ISBT Sarai Kale Khan	6 F5
Italian Embassy	3 C5

J

Jahangir Road	2 D4
Jai Prakash Narain Hospital	2 E4
Jai Singh Marg	1 B5
Jain Mandir Marg	1 B4
Jain Temple	2 E1
Jami Masjid	2 E2
Jangpura	6 D5
Janpath	1 C5
continues	5 A1
Jantar Mantar	1 C5
Japanese Embassy	4 D5
Jaswant Singh Road	5 B1
Jawaharlal Nehru Marg	2 D3
Jawaharlal Nehru Stadium	5 C5
Jawaharlal Nehru Stadium Marg	5 C5
Jhandewalan Road	1 B2
Jheel Park	3 A5
Jor Bagh Colony Road	5 A5
Jor Bagh Road	5 A5
Judah Hymn Hall	5 B3
Jukaso Inn	6 D3

K

Kalan Masjid	2 D3
Kali Bari Lane	1 A5
Kali Bari Road	1 A5
Kali Das Road	2 F3
Kamal Ataturk Marg	4 E4
Kamani Auditorium	2 D5
Kamaraj Lane	4 F3
Kamaraj Road	4 F2
Kasturba Gandhi Marg	1 C5
continues	5 B1
Kasturba Hospital	2 E2
Kasturba Hospital Marg	2 E2
Katra Bariyan	1 C1
Kautilya Marg	4 D3
Kedar Nath Lane	2 F3
Khair-ul-Manazil	5 C2
Khajoori Marg	1 A2
Khan Market	5 B3
Khari Baoli Road	1 C1
Khas Mahal	2 F1
Khuni Darwaza	2 E4
Kotla Marg	2 E4
Krishi Bhavan	4 F2
Krishna Menon Lane	4 F3
Krishna Menon Marg	4 F3
Kushak Road	4 E3

L

Lady Hardinge Hospital	1 B4
Lahori Gate	1 C1
Lajpat Rai Market	2 E1
Lakshmi Narayan Temple (Birla Mandir)	1 A4
Lal Bahadur Shastri Marg	6 D5
Lal Bahadur Shastri Smriti	5 A2
Lal Kuan Bazaar	1 C2

Lal Kuan Bazaar Road 1 C2
Lambi Gali 1 C2
La Sagrita Tourist Home 6 D3
Le Meridien 5 A1
Link Road 1 A3
Lodi Estate 5 B4
Lodi Gardens 5 A4
Lodi Road 5 A5
continues 5 C4
Lok Sabha Marg 4 F1

M

Madrasa of Ghazi-ud-
din Khan 1 C3
Mahadev Road 4 F1
Maharaja Aggarsain Road 1 B1
Maharaja Ranjeet Singh
Marg 2 D4
Maharani Guest House 6 D3
Maharishi Balmiki Marg 1 A1
Maharishi Raman Marg 5 B4
Mahatma Gandhi Marg 2 F2
continues 3 A5
continues 6 E4
Mahatma Gandhi Park 2 D1
Mahatma Jyoti Rao
Phule Road 5 C1
Mahawat Khan Road 2 E5
Main Bazaar Road 1 B3
Malcha Mahal 3 C2
Malcha Marg 3 C3
Mandi House 2 E5
Mandir Marg 1 A1
Mandir Marg 1 A4
Mansingh Road 5 B2
Masjid Fakrula Beg Gali 1 C2
Mata Sundari Lane 2 E4
Mata Sundari Road 2 D4
Mathura Road 5 C1
continues 6 D3
Matka Pir 6 D2
Maulana Azad Medical
College 2 E4
Maulana Azad Road 5 A2
Maulana Azad's Tomb 2 E2
Max Mueller Marg 5 B4
Medical Association Road 2 F3
Meena Bazaar 2 E2
Middle Circle 1 C4
Minto Road 2 D3
Mirdard Marg 2 E4
Mirza Ghalib's Tomb 6 D4
More Sarai Road 2 D1
Moti Masjid 2 F1
Motia Khan Park 1 A2
Motilal Nehru Marg 5 A3
Motilal Nehru Place 5 A3
Mughal Gardens 4 D2
Muhammad Shah
Lodi's Tomb 5 A5
Mumtaz Mahal 2 F2
Murli Marg 6 E5

N

Nai Sarak 2 D2
Nalwa Road 6 D5
National Archives 5 A2
National Gallery of
Modern Art 5 C2
National Museum 5 A2
National Rail Museum 3 C5
National Rose Garden 3 C5
NSD (National School of
Drama) 2 E5
National Science Centre 6 D2
National Stadium 5 C2
National Zoological Park 6 D3

Natural History Museum 2 D5
Naubat Khana 2 E2
Nawab Road 1 B1
Naya Bans Bazaar 1 C1
Naya Bans Gali 1 C1
Naya Bazaar 1 C1
Nyaya Marg 3 C5
Nehru Memorial Museum
and Library 4 E3
Nehru Park 4 D5
Nehru Planetarium 4 E3
Netaji Subhash Marg 2 E2
New Delhi 4 E2
New Delhi Railway
Station 1 C3
New Rohtak Road 1 A2
Nirman Bhavan 5 A2
Nirulas 1 C4
Niti Marg 4 D4
continues 4 D5
Nizamuddin Bridge 6 F3
Nizamuddin East 6 E5
Nizamuddin Railway
Station 6 E5
Nizamuddin West 6 D5
North Avenue 4 E1
North Block 4 E2

P

Padam Singh Marg 2 F2
Pahar Ganj 1 B3
Palika Bazaar 1 C5
Panchkuian Road 1 B4
Panchsheel Marg 3 C4
continues 4 D4
Pandara Market 5 B2
Pandara Park 5 C3
Pandara Road 5 B3
Pandit Pant Marg 4 E1
Parliament House 4 F1
Parliament Street 1 B5
Patiala House 5 C1
Peshwa Road 1 A4
Polo Ground 4 E5
Pragati Maidan 6 D1
President's Estate 4 D2
Prince Polonia 1 B3
Prithviraj Lane 5 B3
Prithviraj Road 5 A4
PTI (Press Trust of India) 4 F1
Purana Qila 6 C2
Purana Qila Road 5 C2

Q

Qutab Road 1 C2

R

Rabindra Bhavan 2 D5
Race Course 4 E4
Race Course Road 4 E4
Rafi Ahmed Kidwai
Marg 4 F2
Rahim Khan Road 6 E5
Rail Bhavan 4 F2
Raisina Road 4 F1
continues 5 A1
Rajaji Marg 4 E3
Rajdoot Marg 3 C3
Rajghat 2 F3
Rajguru Marg 1 B3
Rajpath 5 A2
Rajya Sabha Marg 4 F1
Ram Manohar Lohia
Hospital 1 A5
Ramakrishna Ashram
Marg 1 A4

Ramakrishna Mission 1 B3
Ramdwara Road 1 B4
Ramlila Grounds 2 D3
Rang Mahal 2 F1
Rani Jhansi Road 1 A2
Rashtrapati Bhavan 4 E2
Red Cross Road 4 F1
Red Cross Society 4 F1
Red Fort 2 E2
Reserve Bank of India 4 F1
Ring Road 4 F5
continues 6 E2
Russian Embassy 3 C4

S

Sacred Heart Cathedral 1 A5
Sadar Bazaar 1 B1
Sadar Bazaar Railway
Station 1 C1
Sadar Thana Marg 1 B2
Safdar Hashmi Marg 2 E5
Safdarjung Aerodrome 4 E5
Safdarjung Lane 4 F4
Safdarjung Road 4 F4
Safdarjung's Tomb 4 F5
Salimgarh Fort 2 F1
Samata Sthal 2 F3
San Martin Road 3 B5
Sansad Marg 4 F1
Santushti Complex 4 E4
Sardar Patel Marg 3 C3
Sardar Patel Railway
Station 3 A4
Satya Marg 3 C5
continues 4 D5
Scindia Road 1 A4
Second Avenue 5 A5
Service Road 3 C5
Shah Burj 2 F1
Shah Jahan Road 5 B3
Shaheed Bhagat Singh
Marg 1 B4
Shahi Idgah 1 A2
Shakti Sthal 2 F3
Shakuntalam Theatre 6 D1
Shankar Marg 1 B2
Shanti Path 3 C5
continues 4 D4
Shanti Vana 2 F2
Shanti Vana Marg 2 E2
Shastri Bhavan 5 A2
Shershah Road 5 C2
Shraddhanand Marg 1 C2
Shringar Theatre 6 D1
Shroff Eye Hospital 2 F3
Shyama Prasad
Mukherji Marg 1 C1
Sikandar Lodi's Tomb 5 A4
Sikandra Road 2 E5
Simon Bolivar Marg 3 B3
Sisganj Gurudwara 2 D2
Sitaram Bazaar 2 D3
Sitaram Bazaar Road 2 D2
Smriti Vatika 3 B5
South Avenue 4 E3
South Block 4 E2
South End Lane 5 A4
Sri Ram Centre 2 E5
State Emporia
Complex 1 B5
Subz Burj 6 D4
Subramaniam Bharti
Marg 5 B3
Sultan Razia's Tomb 2 D3
Sundar Nagar Market 6 D3
Sundar Nursery 6 D4
Sunehri Bagh Road 4 F3
Sunehri Masjid 2 D1

Supreme Court 5 C1
Swedish Embassy 3 C4

T

Tagore Road 2 D3
Taj Mahal Hotel 5 B3
Taj Palace Hotel 3 A4
Talkatora Road 4 E1
Talkatora Gardens 4 D1
Tansen Marg 2 D5
Teen Murti Lane 4 E4
Teen Murti Marg 4 E3
The Ambassador 5 B3
The Connaught 1 B4
The Oberoi 6 D4
The Park 1 B5
Thyagaraja Marg 4 E2
Tibet House 5 B5
Tilak Bridge Railway
Station 2 E5
Tilak Marg 5 C1
Times of India Office 2 F4
Todarmal Lane 2 D5
Todarmal Road 2 E5
Tolstoy Marg 1 C5
Town Hall 2 D1
Triveni Kala Sangam 2 D5
Tughlaq Crescent 4 F4
Tughlaq Road 4 F4
Turkman Bazaar Road 2 D3
Turkman Gate 2 D3
Turkman Road 2 D4

U

Udyog Bhavan 4 F2
Ugrasen's Baoli 2 D5
Upper Ridge Road 3 A3
Urdu Ghar Marg 2 E4

V

Vakil Lane 2 D5
Vallabhacharya Marg 1 A3
Vande Mataram Marg 3 B1
Vardman Marg 5 B5
Vayu Bhavan 4 F2
Vigyan Bhavan 5 A2
Vijay Chowk 4 F2
Vijay Ghat 2 F1
Vikas Marg 2 F4
Vinay Marg 4 D5
Vishwa Yuvak Kendra 4 D3
Vivekanand Road 1 C4

W

War Memorial Arch 5 B2
Welcomgroup Maurya
Sheraton 3 B4
Willingdon Crescent 4 D1
continues 4 D3
Windsor Place 5 A1

Y

Yamuna River 6 F2
Yashwant Place 4 D5
Yorks 1 C4
YMCA Tourist Hostel 1 B5
YWCA 1 B5
YWCA Guest House 1 B5

Z

Zinat-ul-Masjid 2 F3

BEYOND DELHI
AREA BY AREA

BEYOND DELHI AT A GLANCE 134–135

NORTH OF DELHI 136–145

AGRA AND AROUND 146–177

JAIPUR AND ENVIRONS 178–225

Beyond Delhi at a Glance

Inlaid panel

The region beyond Delhi is bounded by the snow-capped Himalayas in the north and the ravines of the River Chambal in the south. The rich alluvial plains of the Ganges and Yamuna lie at its heart, and to the west are the Aravalli Range and Thar Desert.

The Rajputs and Mughals enriched the area with architectural gems of which the finest are in and around Agra and Jaipur. Mighty fortresses, luxurious palaces, mosques, tombs and temples are what draw tourists to the Delhi, Agra and Jaipur region. Away from the cities are wildlife sanctuaries, and to the north are rivers, ideal for white-water rafting and adventure sports.

Alwar (see pp206–7), *a former princely state, is dominated by a large hilltop fort, at the base of which lie elegant palaces, cenotaphs and gardens. Alwar is also a convenient base to explore forgotten forts and cities in and around the Sariska National Park.*

Ajmer (see pp218–19) *is best known for the shrine of the Sufi saint Khwaja Moinuddin Chishti and the ancient and stately Adhai Din ka Jhopra. The pilgrim city of Pushkar, where the annual camel fair is held, is a short distance away.*

DEL

JAIPUR AND ENVIRONS
(See pp178–225)

Jaipur (see pp182–99), *was built by Sawai Jai Singh II in the early 1700s. In 1949 it became the capital of Rajasthan. A popular tourist desti-nation, it is visited for its historic palaces, observatory, hilltop forts, palace-hotels and tempting markets.*

| 0 kilometres | 100 |
| 0 miles | 50 |

Haridwar (see p144), *one of North India's holiest cities, stands on the banks of the Ganges as it descends to the plains. The Kumbh Mela is held here every 12 years.*

NORTH OF DELHI
(See pp136–45)

Roorkee (see p143), *a small town on the way to Haridwar, lies in the heart of a rich horticultural belt. Its famous Engineering College, established in 1847, is housed in an elegant colonial building.*

AGRA AND AROUND
(See pp146–77)

Agra (see pp150–59), *the imperial Mughal capital during the 16th and 17th centuries, is best known for the Taj Mahal, built by Shah Jahan for his favourite wife, Mumtaz Mahal. Other Mughal monuments can be seen within and outside the city.*

Orchha (see pp176–7), *the early capital of the Bundela kings, is picturesquely situated on the banks of the Betwa. Its temples, palaces and cenotaphs are architectural gems.*

NORTH OF DELHI

L ying between the Ganges and Yamuna rivers, this agriculturally prosperous region is believed to be the cradle of Indian civilization. Its historical and mythological past extends from the ancient brick cities of the Indus Valley and the early Aryan settlements to the later Muslim and European forts and cities. Each culture has enriched the region and given it its remarkable diversity.

This vast plain, from about the second millennium on, has remained one of India's most densely populated areas. As time went on, ancient fortified city states developed into medieval walled towns which contained prosperous agricultural lands and flourishing markets. Many of these are today important industrial centres. Since the area had such a diverse history, its architectural remains are an eclectic mixture of styles so that ancient brick structures, Mughal monuments and colonial churches rub shoulders with modern factories.

To the north are the pilgrim towns of Haridwar and Rishikesh, where the Ganges, India's most holy river, enters the plains. With the splendid backdrop of the Shivalik Hills, this area, rich in flora and fauna, offers exciting places for adventure sports such as white-water rafting.

To most Indians, however, this is the sacred territory of the *Mahabharata (see p141)*, where gods and epic heroes fought a legendary battle at Kurukshetra and where Krishna *(see pp162–3)* expounded the famous *Bhagavad Gita*. The development of ideas that led to the later compilation of the *Vedas* and *Upanishads*, the bedrock of Hindu philosophy and ethics, are believed to have taken place here as well. Panipat, the site of three decisive battles that changed the history of North India, lies close by.

To the northeast and northwest lie the now forgotten towns of Narnaul, Hansi and Sardhana, associated with the medieval Tughlaq and Sur dynasties, and European freebooters and nabobs such as Skinner, Reinhardt and his wife, Begum Samroo. Meerut, the epicentre of the Indian Mutiny, is now a busy market and trading centre.

Roadside stalls selling religious paraphernalia, a common sight outside temples

◁ The famous Har-ki-Pauri ghat at Haridwar, seen from the Ganga Temple

Exploring North of Delhi

Beyond Delhi, the landscape changes dramatically. The way to Haridwar, at the foothills of the Himalayas, is lined with mango and litchi orchards. The canal network around Roorkee sustains an agriculturally prosperous rural region. On the other hand, the busy Grand Trunk Road that leads beyond Panipat and Kurukshetra all the way to the Punjab, has always been an important artery of trade and commerce. Rolling fields of paddy and wheat are dotted with electricity pylons that service this important industrial belt. Yet the odd *kos minar* and medieval fort recall another age when this was the scene of important battles and the road to the north.

St Andrew's Church at Roorkee

HARYANA

GETTING AROUND

This area is well served by roads, including the famous Grand Trunk Road (now National Highway 1). There are good tourist lay-bys with clean toilets and cafés along it. The high-speed Shatabdi Express between New Delhi railway station and Dehra Dun, as well as the overnight Mussoorie Express to Haridwar, are other ways to reach Haridwar. The New Delhi-Kalka Shatabdi Express stops at Ambala from where a taxi can be taken to Kurukshetra. Taxis and tourist buses also ply at regular intervals between New Delhi and Haridwar, and New Delhi and Chandigarh.

KEY

— Highway

— Major road

··· Minor road

—·— Railroad

— State border

SEE ALSO

• **Where to Stay** pp238–9

• **Where to Eat** pp259–60

Grazing sheep tended by Gujjar tribesmen near Panipat

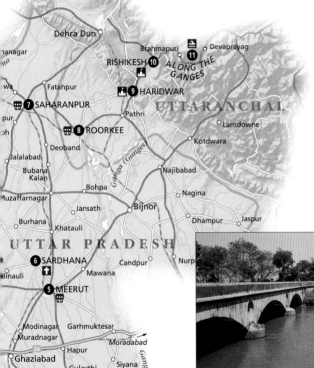

Dehra Dun

hanagar

Brahmapuri

Devaprayag

RISHIKESH 🔟 ALONG THE GANGES 🔟

Fatahpur

🎫 7 SAHARANPUR

HARIDWAR 9 🏃

Pathri

UTTARANCHAL

Lansdowne

🎫 8 ROORKEE

Deoband

Kotdwara

Jalalabad

Bubana
Kalan

Najibabad

Bohpa

Muzaffarnagar

Nagina

Jansath

Bijnor

Burhana

Khatauli

Dhampur

Jaspur

UTTAR PRADESH

Candpur

Nurp

Binauli

6 SARDHANA

Mawana

5 MEERUT 🎫

Modinagar

Garhmuktesar

Muradnagar

Moradabad

Hapur

Ghaziabad

Gulavthi

Siyana

Dadri

Sikandarabad

Bulandshahr

Anupshahr

idabad

labgarh

Khurja

Bareilly

val

Aligarh

dal

Agra

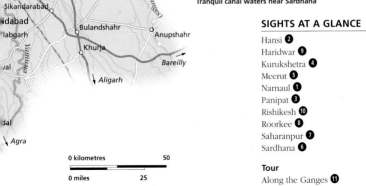

Tranquil canal waters near Sardhana

| 0 kilometres | 50 |
| 0 miles | 25 |

SIGHTS AT A GLANCE

Hansi ❷

Haridwar ❾

Kurukshetra ❹

Meerut ❺

Narnaul ❶

Panipat ❸

Rishikesh 🔟

Roorkee ❽

Saharanpur ❼

Sardhana ❻

Tour

Along the Ganges 🔟

Narnaul ❶

Narnaul district. 132 km (82 miles) W of Delhi. **Road map** C3.

Believed to have been founded by the Pandava Sahdev, the town of Narnaul is historically significant as the birthplace of the great ruler Sher Shah Sur *(see p84)* whose grandfather, Ibrahim Shah Sur, is buried here in a magnificent Afghan-style mausoleum. The Jal Mahal ("water palace"), situated in what was once an artificial lake built by Shah Quli Khan in 1591, is a Mughal-style structure; so is the Birbal ka Chatta, with its projecting balconies and pavilions. In the town's old section are some magnificent, but neglected *havelis* with murals in the Shekhawati style *(see p212)*.

Hansi ❷

Narnaul district. 137 km (85 miles) W of Delhi. **Road map** C2.

This nondescript town is associated with two soldiers of fortune. At the end of the 18th century, the Irish adventurer, George Thomas, repaired the city's defensive wall, remodelled the ruined fort and made it his headquarters. Some 30 years later, Colonel James Skinner *(see p101)* of Skinner's Horse, built a large mansion (now derelict) here where he spent his last years. The town is scattered with monuments dating to the 12th century, including the shrine called Char Qutbs, a Sufi *dargah* of the Chishtiya order, and the 19th-century tomb of Begum Skinner, one of Skinner's 12 Indian wives.

Memorial of the Third Battle of Panipat

Environs
Hissar, 26 km (16 miles) west of Hansi, was the favourite retreat of Feroze Shah Tughlaq *(see p97)*. He built palaces and forts here, now in ruins. An oddity from that time is an edifice called the Jahaz, so named as it resembles a ship.

Qalandar Shah's *dargah* at Panipat, built 700 years ago

Panipat ❸

Panipat district. 85 km (53 miles) N of Delhi on NH1. **Road map** C2. 🗓 *Urs of Qalander Shah (Jan–Feb).*

On the flat, dusty plains of Panipat, three decisive battles were fought that changed the course of Indian history. The Mughal empire *(see pp52–3)* was established in 1526 after Babur defeated the Delhi sultan, Ibrahim Lodi, and was consolidated 30 years later when his grandson Akbar triumphed over Sher Shah's general in 1556. Finally, in 1761, the Marathas, the Mughal emperor's military arm, were routed by Afghan invader, Ahmad Shah Abdali, paving the way for the British *(see pp54–5)*. Today, Panipat is a busy town well known for its furnishing fabrics and carpets. The 700-year-old Sufi *dargah* of Qalandar Shah is situated here. On its outskirts are *kos minars* (milestones) indicating that Panipat was part of the Grand Trunk Road *(see p160)*.

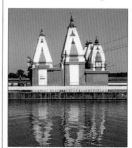

Sacred tank at Kurukshetra

Kurukshetra ❹

Kurukshetra district.175 km (109 miles) N of Delhi on NH1. **Road map** C1. 🗓 *Gita Jayanti (Nov–Dec).*

Linked with 360 legendary sites of the *Mahabharata*, this strategic plain was ruled by the Kuru tribe in the later Vedic period. The 18-day epic battle between the Pandavas and Kauravas was fought on this "field of righteousness". The town of Kurukshetra is also the start of a pilgrimage circuit of 128 km (80 miles) undertaken during the solar eclipse and at Gita Jayanti in November or December, when lighted clay lamps are set afloat on the sacred waters of the tanks during a ceremony called the *deepdan*.

The main bathing tanks are the Brahmasar, with a small temple on an island, and the smaller, more sacred Sannahit Sarovar, lined with ghats and temples. Hindus believe that a dip here during the solar eclipse is very sacred for it is when the twin planets, the malefic Rahu and Ketu, try to swallow the sun to spread terror in the world. However, the sun defeats their machinations, so, after a holy dip, pilgrims donate food equal to their body weight as thanksgiving. The last solar eclipse of the 20th century occurred in August 1999, and the first of the new millennium, was on 31 May 2003.

The Krishna Museum and Gita Research Centre in the town has a large collection that brings out the pervasiveness of the Krishna cult in Indian art down the ages.

The Mahabharata

Considered an inexhaustible fund of knowledge and ideas, the *Mahabharata* is about an eponymous battle between the Pandavas and Kauravas. Said to be first narrated by a sage, Ved Vyas, the epic was written down only between the 6th and 7th centuries BC. Eight times the length of the *Iliad* and *Odyssey* put together, the subtle moral subtext of its legends and stories codifies notions of theology and statecraft that inspired rulers down the ages.

The *Bhagavad Gita,* a later insertion of 700 stanzas, records the sermon

Ganjifa card of Arjuna

that was given by the divine charioteer, Lord Krishna, to the Pandava prince Arjuna on the epic battlefield of Kurukshetra. It extols the virtues of performing one's moral duty without seeking reward, and condones the use of violence against injustice. Its philosophy of righteous living and the importance of one's *dharma* (duty, calling) continues to guide the lives of millions of Indians. In the 1990s, a television serial on the *Mahabharata* became so popular that life came to a virtual standstill when it was transmitted.

The battle is an allegory for the war between right and wrong. The epic's didactic tone made it an authoritative manual on moral rules and righteous conduct.

Folk art often uses the epic as a theme. This *patachitra* from Eastern India is used as a visual aid by minstrels, while *ganjifa* playing cards similarly use Arjuna as the icon for a king.

Krishna is seen as the divine charioteer who steers the mind (chariot) and five senses (the five horses that pull Arjuna's chariot) to follow the right path through life.

THE BATTLE OF THE MAHABHARATA AT KURUKSHETRA
The kingdom of Hastinapur and Queen Draupadi were lost by the five Pandavas when their evil cousins, the Kauravas, tricked them in a game of dice. After a long exile, the Pandavas, though outnumbered by the hundred Kauravas, were led by Krishna to victory in the Battle of the Mahabharata.

Arjuna, *the skilled archer, shoots the eye of a fish reflected in water. This act won him the hand of Draupadi and the envy of the Kaurava princes.*

Lord Krishna *gives the sermon of the Gita to Arjuna on the battlefield of Kurukshetra. As the charioteer of the Pandavas in the war, this god plays a crucial role in the epic.*

A cantonment house in Meerut

Meerut **5**

Meerut district. 72 km (44 miles) NE of Delhi on NH24. **Road map** D2. ⚑ *1,074,000.* 🚉 Mon. 🎪 Nauchandi Mela (Mar).

An important commercial and administrative town, Meerut is better known as the place where the sepoys first mutinied on 10 May 1857 igniting the Indian Mutiny *(see pp54–5)*. Today, this bustling town swirls around architectural monuments dating to the 11th and 12th centuries, such as the Jami Masjid (1019), Salar Masa-ud Ghazi's *maqbara* (1194), the tomb of Makhdum Shah Wilayat and the *maqbara* of Shah Pir (1628). Meerut's colonial heritage is, however, preserved in its manicured cantonment to the north of the old city. This is one of the country's best-planned cantonments with a broad, tree-lined mall or main road and colonial bungalows *(see p25)* with sprawling gardens along its length. The cantonment's Neo-Classical St John's Church (1821), where British residents had gathered for refuge when the revolt broke out, was the scene of a bloody massacre that fateful May day. Memorial tablets with their names and histories lie inside. The old Central Jail, associated with the worst excesses of the Mutiny and its aftermath, is now converted into a public park.

Sardhana **6**

Meerut district. 85 km (57 miles) NE of Delhi. **Road map** D2. 🎪 Feast of Our Lady of Graces (2nd Sun of Nov). 🎨 (to Cathedral) 🎪

Surrounded by a network of canals, Sardhana's history is inextricably linked with two flamboyant European adventurers, Walter Reinhardt and George Thomas, who had come to India to seek their fortunes in the mid-18th century *(see pp54–5)*.

Reinhardt deserted the French army in 1750 and organized a band of fierce, well-trained mercenaries who fought for various local chiefs. Called "Sombre" or "Samroo" for his swarthy complexion, he settled in Sardhana on land gifted by Najaf Khan, a nobleman of Delhi. Reinhardt was succeeded by his wife, Begum Samroo, a formidable and wily lady who converted to Catholicism in 1781. She was known throughout the region as the only Roman Catholic "queen" in India, as she led her husband's troops until her death in 1836. Her military skills, matched by her piety and philanthropy, made her popular with the locals, who still respect her memory.

Begum Samroo's palace, the grand Dilkusha Kothi, with its impressive hallway, is situated within a garden of almost 75 acres (30 ha). It now houses a charity school and orphanage. The Cathedral nearby has a white marble altar inlaid with semi-precious stones and a Carrara marble monument to the Begum sculpted by Tadolini of Rome. Now raised to the status of a basilica, this is still an important centre for Catholics. Both the palace and cathedral, built between 1822 and 1834 in a hybrid colonial style, reflect the spirit of that adventurous era.

The classical façade of Dilkusha Kothi at Sardhana

Saharanpur ❼

Saharanpur district.165 km (103 miles) NE of Delhi on NH24. **Road map** D1. 🚇 *453,000.*

Saharanpur was founded in 1340 during the reign of Muhammad-bin-Tughlaq *(see p107)*. During the Mughal period it was a popular summer resort for nobles attracted by its cool climate and plentiful game. Many of the gardens that were laid out 200 years ago, such as the Company Bagh in the centre of town, were transformed into nurseries and botanical gardens in the 19th century, laying the foundation for the town's eventual growth into an important horticultural centre. Today, Saharanpur is one of North India's largest producers of luscious mangoes, while the sprawling Government Botanical Gardens, on its outskirts, is an important centre for research on the medicinal properties of plants.

Within the old city, highly skilled artisans craft items of intricately carved furniture, ornamental screens, panels and trays, brass-inlaid with traditional geometric and floral designs. Some of the finest examples of Saharanpur's woodcraft can be seen in St Thomas's Church. Also of interest are the old Jami Masjid (1530), Zabita Khan's Mosque (1779) and the old Rohilla Fort in Nawabganj.

Stone lion at the head of the aqueduct in Roorkee

Roorkee ❽

Haridwar district. 198 km (123 miles) from Delhi on Delhi-Haridwar Rd. **Road map** D1. 🏛 *Roorkee Flower Show (Mar).*

An important university and cantonment town, this was originally a sleepy village on the banks of the River Solani. It gained importance when the Ganga Canal Workshop was set up in 1843 as part of the massive Ganga Canal Irrigation Project. This transformed the surrounding arid region into the highly productive agricultural area of today. To the north of the town is a magnificent brick aqueduct, marked with two enormous stone lions. It was considered a major engineering feat of the 19th century, and carries the water of the Ganga Canal over the River Solani. The Thomson Civil Engineering College (now the University of Roorkee) was established in 1847 and is the oldest technical institution in the country. The pleasantly sited campus, located within extensive wooded areas, has several important research institutions. Some of the structures from the colonial period are exceptional, such as the Church of St John the Baptist (1852), with beautiful stained-glass windows. The town is also renowned for high quality replicas of 18th- and 19th-century engineering and survey equipment.

Interior of the Roorkee University

Saharanpur's Botanical Gardens, a repository of rare plants

MANGO

The mango or *aam* is the best-loved fruit of the country. The Mughal emperor Babur called it the "finest fruit of Hindostan." Hundreds of varieties, with exotic names and pedigrees, are available from May to July, before the monsoon arrives. Savoured most for the sweet pulp of the ripe fruit, the raw mango is also valued for its medicinal properties, as well as its sharp tang, and is made into pickles and chutneys eaten through the year. The popular design motif of the paisley is derived from the shape of its fruit, and mango leaves, considered auspicious, are used as buntings at festive occasions.

Langra **mangoes**

Pilgrims taking a dip in the holy Ganges at Haridwar

Haridwar ❾

Haridwar district. 214 km (133 miles) N of Delhi. **Road map** D1.
🚉 *175,000.* ℹ️ *GMVN Tourist Office, Rahi Motel (0133) 427 370.*
🚃 *Railway Rd.* 🎭 *Kumbh Mela (every 12 years; Feb–Mar); Ardh Kumbha Mela (every 6 years; Feb–Mar); Haridwar Festival (Oct); Dusshera (Oct–Nov).*

The Ganges, India's holiest river, descends from the Himalayas to the plains at Haridwar. This gives the town such a unique status that a pilgrimage to Haridwar is every devout Hindu's dream.

Remarkably bare of ancient monuments, Haridwar's most famous "sight" and a constant point of reference is the Ganges and its numerous bathing ghats, tanks and temples. These bustling sites

Chotiwala, a popular restaurant

of ritual Hindu practices, performed by pilgrims for the salvation of their ancestors and for their own expiation, demonstrate their deep faith in the power of the river. The main ghat, Har-ki-Pauri, is named after a supposed imprint of Vishnu's feet there. Hundreds attend the daily evening *aarti* at this ghat, when leaf boats are filled with flowers, lit with lamps and set adrift on the Ganges. Further south, a ropeway connects the town to the Mansa Devi Temple across the river with a panoramic view of Haridwar. South of the town, the famous Gurukul Kangri University is renowned as a centre of Vedic knowledge, where students are taught in the traditional oral style. It also has a section displaying archaeological exhibits.

A good way to experience Haridwar's ambience, which has changed little since ancient times, is to stroll along the riverside bazaar, lined with stalls full of ritual paraphernalia – small mounds of vermilion powder, coconuts wrapped in red and gold cloth, and brass idols. The most popular items with the pilgrims, however, are the jars and canisters sold here. These are used to carry back water from the Ganges *(Gangajal)*, a vital part of Hindu worship which, the faithful believe, remains ever fresh.

Rishikesh ❿

Haridwar district. 238 km (148 miles) N of Delhi. **Road map** D1.
🚉 *60,000.* ℹ️ *GMVN Tourist Office, Muni-ki-Reti (0135) 243 1793.*
🎭 *International Yoga Week (Feb).*

This twin city of Haridwar, situated at the confluence of the Chandrabhaga and the Ganges, is the start of the holy Char Dham pilgrim route to the Himalayas. Muni-ki-Reti (literally "sand of the sages"), lies upstream from the Triveni Ghat and is believed to be a blessed site since ancient sages meditated here. It has several famous ashrams, such as the Sivanand, Purnanand and Shanti Kunj ashrams, which offer courses to those interested in India's ancient knowledge systems. Maharishi Mahesh Yogi, a cult figure during the 1960s, when the Beatles were his followers, also has an ashram here.

KUMBH MELA

According to Hindu mythology, four drops of the immortal nectar *(amrit)* wrested by the gods from the demons, spilled over Haridwar, Allahabad, Ujjain and Nasik. A Kumbh Mela is held once every 12 years by rotation at these venues in Magh (Feb–Mar), when the sun transits from Pisces to Aries, and when Jupiter is in the sign of Aquarius *(Kumbh in Hindu astrology)*. Hindus believe that they can imbibe the immortal *amrit* and wash away their sins by bathing in the Ganges at this propitious time. The *mela* is regarded as the largest congregation of human beings in one place anywhere in the world, when millions come for a holy dip, and to attend the seminars, discourses and debates held in the camps of leading Hindu sages and theologians. Haridwar's last Kumbh Mela, held in 1998, attracted over ten million people. A smaller celebration, called the Ardh Kumbh (half-Kumbh), is held every six years.

Pilgrims thronging the ghats at the Kumbh Mela

River Tour along the Ganges ⑪

From September to April, the Ganges, swollen by the monsoon rains of the upper catchment areas, becomes a torrent gushing over the rocky boulders as it hurtles out of the mountains to the plains. This is the time when a few stretches of rapids, where the flow is rough but safe, become a popular circuit for enthusiasts of white-water rafting *(see p275).* Only organized tours, run by certified experts are allowed. For the less adventurous, a driving tour offers a panorama of this valley of the sages whose ashrams nestle in the surrounding forests along the holy river.

The Ganges flowing serenely through a forested valley

Kaudiyala ①
The starting point of the river tour, it has scenic camp sites on the river bank.

Marine Drive ②
This early camp site is named after a Bombay promenade famous for its views.

Devaprayag

The Wall

Three Blind Mice

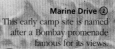

Golf Course

Shivpuri ③
The beautiful Glasshouse on the Ganges *(see p239)* offers a spectacular view of the river and the surrounding countryside.

Brahmapuri ④
An ashram, one of many along the Ganges, is located here.

KEY

■	Tour route
═	Roads
≈	River
☀	Viewpoint
🏔	Rapids
▲	Camping

Lakshman Jhula ⑤
A modern suspension bridge replaced the old rope bridge in 1929. This leads to the quieter east bank of Rishikesh where most ashrams are situated.

TIPS FOR RIVER RAFTERS

Length: 36 km (22 miles).
Stopping-off points: White-water rafting can be done in leisurely stages, over two days, with a night halt at the Kaudiyala Camp. Stopover points are provided at Marine Drive, Shivpuri and Brahmapuri. However, a shorter tour of the same stretch can also be covered in one day.

Rishikesh ⑥
An ancient spiritual centre, Rishikesh is serenely located on the banks of the Ganges amid lush, wooded hills.

0 kilometres   10

0 miles   5

AGRA AND AROUND

*A*gra was the imperial capital of the Mughal court during the 16th and 17th centuries before it was shifted to Delhi. The Mughals were prolific builders and nowhere is this more evident than in the picturesque riverine region along the Yamuna which is the backdrop for its palaces, tombs, forts and gardens. Three of these, the Taj Mahal, the Agra Fort and Akbar's abandoned capital of Fatehpur Sikri, have been declared World Heritage Sites by UNESCO.

The imperial Mughal highway which still runs along the Yamuna between Delhi and Agra is a link to the region's historical past. The rich pastoral and agricultural land around Brindavan, the supposed homeland of Krishna *(see p163)*, was the main axis of the Mughal empire. The outer fringes of this area, formed by Mathura, Bharatpur and Deeg, have wetlands that attract many rare migratory birds, such as the Siberian crane, who come each winter to the World Heritage Site of the Keoladeo Ghana National Park.

As one goes further west and south, the greens and gold of the Yamuna lands give way to the scrub and ravines along the River Chambal. This is the centre of the subcontinent: hot, dusty and vast. These awesome ravines were the preferred habitat of robbers, dacoits and bandits. After the decline of the Mughals, some of the more ambitious bandits declared themselves kings and built for themselves small, but powerful kingdoms with magnificent fortresses in this harsh area. Their architecture, that is a happy amalgam of traditional Hindu with Muslim building styles, can be seen in Datia, Orchha and Deeg.

Itinerant poets and musicians in this area still sing of daring kings and queens such as Laxmibai, the Rani of Jhansi. Her spirited resistance to the British forces during the Indian Mutiny of 1857, made her a popular icon during the Freedom Movement. Close by lies Gwalior. This important princely state has a magnificent fort that goes back to the 3rd century, and splendid palaces built by its Scindia rulers.

The three-domed mosque to the west of the Taj Mahal

◁ **Ablution tank in the *namazgah* of Fatehpur Sikri's Jami Masjid**

Exploring Agra and Around

Agra lies in the centre of a rich and varied cultural territory. At one end of this region are the pastoral fields around Yamuna, and at the other, the stark and awesome ravines of the Chambal River. Between these two rivers are a number of towns, monuments and sanctuaries, making this one of the most popular travel circuits in North India. In mythology, Mathura was the sacred territory of Krishna *(see p163)* while in history, it was the centre of an important Buddhist kingdom, and the imperial Mughal highway ran through it. Later, Jat and Rajput Bundela kings built forts and palaces in nearby Bharatpur, Deeg, Jhansi, Datia and Orchha. Thus, this region contains some of the best examples of Indian art and architecture, while the riverine wetlands around Bharatpur provide a natural habitat for a range of wildlife and migratory birds.

Cows near Brindavan, where they enjoy sacred status

A Mughal *kos minar* on the Grand Trunk Road

KEY

▬▬	Highway
▬	Major road
▭▭	Minor road
▭▭	Railroad
▬▬	State border

0 kilometres   50

0 miles   25

For additional map symbols *see back flap*

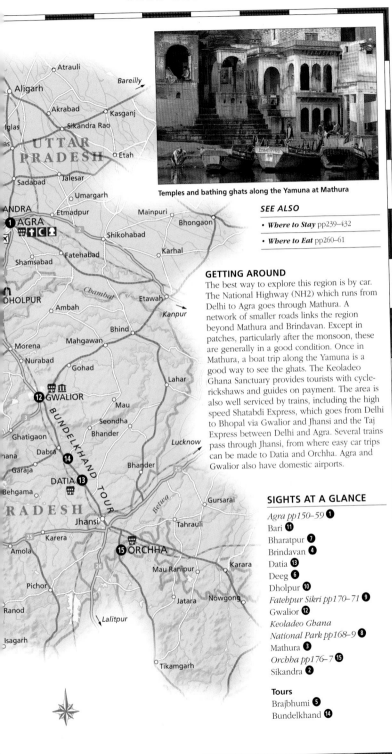

Temples and bathing ghats along the Yamuna at Mathura

SEE ALSO

- *Where to Stay* pp239–432
- *Where to Eat* pp260–61

GETTING AROUND

The best way to explore this region is by car. The National Highway (NH2) which runs from Delhi to Agra goes through Mathura. A network of smaller roads links the region beyond Mathura and Brindavan. Except in patches, particularly after the monsoon, these are generally in a good condition. Once in Mathura, a boat trip along the Yamuna is a good way to see the ghats. The Keoladeo Ghana Sanctuary provides tourists with cycle-rickshaws and guides on payment. The area is also well serviced by trains, including the high speed Shatabdi Express, which goes from Delhi to Bhopal via Gwalior and Jhansi and the Taj Express between Delhi and Agra. Several trains pass through Jhansi, from where easy car trips can be made to Datia and Orchha. Agra and Gwalior also have domestic airports.

SIGHTS AT A GLANCE

Agra pp150–59 **1**
Bari **11**
Bharatpur **7**
Brindavan **4**
Datia **13**
Deeg **6**
Dholpur **10**
Fatehpur Sikri pp170–71 **9**
Gwalior **12**
*Keoladeo Ghana
National Park pp168–9* **8**
Mathura **3**
Orchha pp176–7 **15**
Sikandra **2**

Tours

Brajbhumi **5**
Bundelkhand **14**

Agra ❶

Detail of *jaali*, Musamman Burj

Agra was the imperial Mughal capital during the 16th and 17th centuries. It was from here that the emperors Akbar, Jahangir and Shah Jahan governed their vast empire. The city flourished under their patronage, attracting artisans from Persia and Central Asia, and also from other parts of India, who built luxurious forts, mausoleums and gardens. Agra's strategic location on the banks of the Yamuna as well as on the Grand Trunk Road linking eastern India with the west, made it a trading station, visited by merchants and travellers from all over the world. With the decline of the Mughals, Agra was captured by the Jats, the Marathas, and finally the British.

A riverside view of the Jahangiri Mahal

🏛 Agra Fort

🕕 6am–6pm daily. 📷
🎭 **Son et Lumière** 7:30pm daily.

Situated on the west bank of the Yamuna, Agra Fort was built by Akbar between 1565 and 1573. Its imposing red sandstone ramparts form a crescent along the riverfront, and encompass an enormous complex of courtly buildings, ranging in style from the early eclecticism of Akbar to the sublime elegance of Shah Jahan. The barracks to the north are 19th-century British additions. A deep moat, once filled with water from the Yamuna, surrounds the fort.

The impressive **Amar Singh Gate** to the south leads into the fort. To its right is the so-called Jahangiri Mahal, the only major palace in the fort that dates to Akbar's reign. This complex arrangement of halls, courtyards and galleries with dungeons below was the zenana or main harem

building. In front of Jahangir Mahal is a large marble pool which, as legend says, in Nur Jahan's time used to be filled with thousands of rose petals so that the empress could bathe in its scented waters.

Along the riverfront are the **Khas Mahal**, an elegant marble hall with an exuberantly painted ceiling, characteristic of Shah Jahan's style of architecture, and two golden pavilions with typical *bangaldar* roofs (*see p319*). These pavilions were supposedly associated with the princesses Jahanara and Roshanara, and have narrow niches where jewels could be concealed. Facing them is **Anguri Bagh** ("grape garden") with its lily-pools and candle-niches. The **Sheesh Mahal** and royal baths are to the northeast near the gloriously

Musamman Burj

inlaid **Musamman Burj**, the double-storeyed octagonal tower with clear views of the Taj. This was where Shah Jahan, imprisoned by his son Aurangzeb, spent the last years of his life. **Mina Masjid** ("gem mosque"), probably the smallest in the world and the emperor's private mosque, is nearby. To the side of Musamman Burj is the **Diwan-i-Khas**, a lavishly decorated open hall where the emperor met his court. Two thrones, in white marble and black slate, were placed on the terrace for the emperor to watch elephant fights below. Opposite is the **Machchhi Bhavan** ("fish house"), once a magnificent water palace. To its west is the **Diwan-i-Aam**, an arcaded hall within a large courtyard. Its throne-alcove of inlaid marble provided a sumptuous setting for the fabled Peacock Throne. To the northwest is the graceful **Nagina Masjid** ("jewel mosque") built by Shah Jahan for his harem, and the **Moti Masjid** ("pearl mosque").

Beyond is the **Meena Bazaar**, the fort's shopping centre, overlooked by a fine marble balcony where, according to legend, the lovely Mumtaz Mahal first met Shah Jahan. The bazaar street led directly to Delhi Gate, the original entrance, and to the Jami Masjid in the old city. Both the gate and bazaar street are now closed to the general public.

Colonnaded arches of the Diwan-i-Aam

Jami Masjid, built by Shah Jahan's favourite daughter Jahanara

C Jami Masjid
○ *daily.*

A magnificently proportioned building in the heart of the medieval town, the "Friday Mosque" was sponsored by Shah Jahan's favourite daughter, Jahanara Begum, who also commissioned a number of other buildings and gardens, including the canal that once ran down Chandni Chowk in Delhi *(see pp90–91).* Built in 1648, the mosque's sandstone and marble domes with their

A detail of the minaret

distinctive zigzag chevron pattern dominate this section of the town. The eastern courtyard wing was demolished by the British in 1857 *(see pp54–5).* Of interest are the tank with its *shahi chirag* ("royal stove") for heating water within the courtyard, and the separate prayer chamber for ladies.

Environs
The area around Jami Masjid was a vibrant meeting place, famous for its kabab houses and lively bazaars. A stroll or

rickshaw ride through the captivating network of narrow alleys can be a rewarding experience, offering glimpses of a close-knit way of life reminiscent of Mughal Agra. This is also the city's crafts and trade centre, where a staggering array of products such as jewellery, *zari* embroidery, *dhurries*, dried fruit, sweets, shoes and kites are available.

Some of the main bazaars are Johri Bazaar, Kinari Bazaar, Kaserat Bazaar and Kashmiri Bazaar. The quieter back lanes such as Panni Gali have many fine buildings with decorative upper storeys and imposing gateways leading into secluded courtyards and thriving craft workshops.

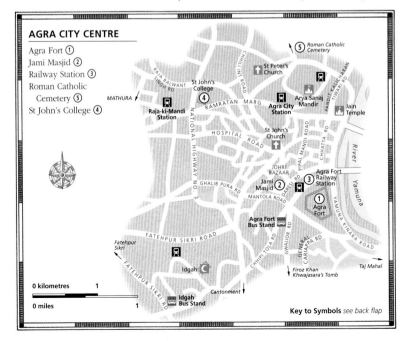

AGRA CITY CENTRE

Agra Fort ①
Jami Masjid ②
Railway Station ③
Roman Catholic Cemetery ⑤
St John's College ④

Key to Symbols *see back flap*

0 kilometres 1

0 miles 1

Exploring Agra: The Outer Sights

A pietra dura motif

Agra's European legacy dates to the reign of Akbar, when the first Jesuit missionaries from Portuguese-governed Goa visited his court to participate in religious debates. This marked the advent of Christianity in North India, and paved the way for future European traffic in the region. In the 18th and 19th centuries this was a great cosmopolitan centre where priests and scholars, merchants and mercenaries employed by the Scindias of Gwalior *(see p174)*, lived, traded or set up schools, colleges and impressive churches.

The monument in memory of John Hessing

🔲 Roman Catholic Cemetery

Opp Civil Courts. ⬭ *daily.*
Towards the north of the town is the Roman Catholic Cemetery, the oldest European graveyard in North India. It was established in the 17th century by an Armenian merchant, Khoja Mortenepus, on a piece of land purchased from the church as the burial ground for Agra's large Armenian trading community.

A number of Islamic-style gravestones, with inscriptions in Armenian, survive today, and include the graves of the cannon expert, Shah Nazar Khan, and Khoja Mortenepus himself. The cemetery also contains tombs of European missionaries, traders, and adventurers such as Walter Reinhardt *(see p140)*.

One of the oldest tombs belongs to the English merchant, John Mildenhall (d.1614), envoy of Elizabeth I, who arrived at the Mughal court in 1603 seeking permission to trade. Other interesting graves include those of the Venetian doctor,

Auto-rickshaws parked outside the Fort Railway Station

🚇 Fort Railway Station

Tel (0562) 132.
This memorable colonial building was constructed in 1891 as a stopover for colonial tourists visiting Agra's monuments. The octagonal bazaar *chowk* that originally connected the Delhi Gate and Agra Fort to the old city and the Jami Masjid was demolished and the many-towered station with its French château-style slate roofed platforms was built in its place. This is still one of Agra's most frequently-used stations; the other two are located in the cantonment and at Raja ki Mandi.

🚇 St John's College

NH2 (Drummond Rd/Mahatma Gandhi Rd). *Tel (0562) 252 0123.*
St John's College, started by the Church Missionary Society, has been described as "an astounding mixture of the antiquarian, the scholarly and the symbolic". It consists of a group of red sandstone buildings, including a hall and library, arranged around a quadrangle, all designed in a quasi-Fatehpur Sikri style by Sir Samuel Swinton Jacob *(see p194)*. The building was inaugurated in 1914 by the viceroy, Lord Hardinge, and it remains one of the region's highly lauded institutions.

St John's College, designed by Sir Samuel Swinton Jacob

St George's Church in Agra Cantonment

Bernardino Maffi, and Geronimo Veroneo (once wrongly regarded by some as the architect of the Taj).

Near the chapel is the tall obelisk marking the grave of the four children of General Perron, French commander of Scindia's forces. Another Frenchman, a member of the Bourbon family and kinsman of Henry IV of France, is also buried at this site.

The largest and most impressive grave is that of John Hessing (d.1803) who first ventured out East as a soldier with the Dutch East India Company at Kandy (Sri Lanka). He came to India in 1763 and joined the service of the Nizam of Hyderabad in the South, before moving northwards to be a mercenary with Scindia's forces. His red sandstone tombstone, interestingly modelled on the lines of the Taj Mahal, was built by a local architect.

One of the tombs, in memory of Father Santos, is enclosed by a trellis frame where Hindus and Muslims tie threads, praying for the fulfillment of their wishes.

To its south, on Wazirpura Road, is the **Roman Catholic Cathedral**, constructed in the 18th century at the expense of Walter Reinhardt. An old, derelict church from Akbar's time stands next to it.

🏛 Cantonment

Bounded by Mahatma Gandhi Rd, Grand Parade Rd and the Mall Rd. The pleasant, tree-shaded army cantonment area, with its own railway station and orderly avenues has many interesting public buildings,

churches, cemeteries and bungalows in a medley of styles dating from the British days. **St George's Church** (1826), a yellow ochre plastered building, visible even from the Taj, is a typical example of the North Indian cantonment style of architecture. JT Boileau, the architect, also built the Christ Church in Shimla.

Havelock Memorial Church (1873) constructed in a "trim Classical style" commemorates one of the British generals of the 1857 mutiny. **Queen Mary's Library** and the **Central Post Office** are other buildings in the area.

Structures such as the **Agra Club**, once the hub of British cantonment social life, and the hybrid Indo-Saracenic government Circuit House which used to accommodate officials of the Raj, are also located in the cantonment.

🏛 Firoz Khan Khwajasara's Tomb

S of Agra, on Gwalior Rd.
◻ *daily.*

A signpost on the Gwalior Road indicates the turning to this unusual 17th-century octagonal tomb, standing on the edge of a lake. This is where Firoz Khan, natural-born eunuch and custodian of Shah Jahan's palace harem, is buried. The red sandstone structure stands on a high plinth and has a gateway attached to the main building. Steps lead to the upper storey where a central pavilion containing the cenotaph is located. Highly stylized stone carvings decorate the surface. Interestingly, unlike other buildings of the period, there is an absence of calligraphic inscriptions. If the tomb is closed, the *chowkidar* from the village will open the gate.

The central pavilion where Firoz Khan is buried

GOLD THREAD AND BEAD ZARDOZI

Agra's flourishing local craft tradition of elaborate gold thread and bead embroidery is known as *zardozi*. This technique was Central Asian in origin and came to the region with the Mughal emperors. Local craftsmen in the old city added further refinements to create garments and accessories for the Imperial court. However, with the decline of court patronage, the skill languished and almost vanished. It owes its recent revival to encouragement from contemporary fashion designers. The delicate stitches and complicated patterns in genuine gold thread and coloured beads are now widely used for both traditional and contemporary garments and accessories, including shawls and scarves, bags and shoes.

Detail of a *zari*-embroidered textile

Taj Mahal

Carved dado on outer niches

One of the world's most famous buildings, the Taj Mahal commemorates both the Mughal emperor Shah Jahan, and Mumtaz Mahal, his favourite wife. Its perfect proportions and exquisite craftsmanship have been described as "a prayer, a vision, a dream, a poem, a wonder." This sublime garden-tomb, an image of the Islamic garden of paradise, cost nearly 41 million rupees and 500 kilos of gold. Around 20,000 workers laboured for almost 22 years to complete it in 1653.

The Dome
The 44-m (144-ft) double dome is capped with a finial.

★ Marble Screen
The filigree screen delicately carved from a single block of marble was meant to veil the area around the royal tombs.

Four minarets, each 40 m (131 ft) high and crowned by a *chhatri*, frame the tomb, highlighting the perfect symmetry of the complex.

Plinth

River Yamuna

★ Tomb Chamber
Mumtaz Mahal's cenotaph, raised on a platform, is placed next to Shah Jahan's. The actual graves, in a dark crypt below, are closed to the public.

STAR FEATURES

★ Marble Screen

★ Tomb Chamber

★ Pietra Dura

The Charbagh
was irrigated
by the waters
of the River
Jamuna.

**Main
entrance**

VISITORS' CHECKLIST

Tajganj. **Tel** (0562) 233 0498.
◻ 6am–7pm Sun–Thu
◻ Fri. 🈲 📷
🎫 Taj Mahotsav (Feb).
Museum ◻ 10am–5pm
Sun–Thu ◻ public hols. 🈲

The Lotus Pool
*Named after its lotus-shaped fountain spouts, the
pool reflects the tomb. Almost every visitor is
photographed sitting on the marble bench here.*

Pishtaq
*Recessed arches
provide depth while
their inlaid panels
reflect the changing
light to give the tomb
a mystical aura.*

★ Pietra Dura
*Inspired by the paradise garden,
intricately carved floral designs
inlaid with precious stones embellish
the austere white marble surface to
give it the look of a bejewelled casket.*

Calligraphic Panels
*The size of the Koranic verses
increases as the arch gets higher,
creating the subtle optical illusion
of a uniformly flowing script.*

TAJ MAHAL

1 Main Tomb
2 *Masjid* (mosque)
3 *Mehmankhana*
   (guesthouse)
4 *Charbagh*
5 Gateway

KEY

◻ Central illustration
◻ Charbagh

Decorative Elements of the Taj

Stylized floral motif

It is widely believed that the Taj Mahal was designed to represent an earthly replica of one of the houses of paradise. Its impeccable marble facing, embellished by a remarkable use of exquisite surface design, is a splendid showcase for the refined aesthetic that reached its height during Shah Jahan's reign. Described as "one of the most elegant and harmonious buildings in the world", the Taj indeed manifests the wealth and luxury of Mughal art as seen in architecture and garden design, painting, jewellery, calligraphy, textiles, carpet-weaving and furniture.

Detail of the marble screen with an inlaid chrysanthemum

PIETRA DURA

The Mughals were great naturalists who believed that flowers were the "symbols of the divine realm". In the Taj, *pietra dura* has been extensively used to translate naturalistic forms into decorative patterns that complement the majesty of its architecture.

Flowers *such as the tulip, lily, iris, poppy and narcissus were depicted as sprays or arabesque patterns. Stones of varying degrees of colour were used to create the shaded effects.*

Inlaid marble above the mosque's central arch

White marble, black slate and yellow, red and grey sandstone are used for decoration

PIETRA DURA

The Florentine technique of *pietra dura* is said to have been imported by Jahangir and developed in Agra as *pachikari*. Minute slivers of precious and semi-precious stones, such as carnelian, lapis lazuli, turquoise and malachite, were arranged in complex stylized floral designs into a marble base. Even today, artisans in the old city maintain pattern books containing the intricate motifs used on the Taj and can still re-create 17th-century designs in contemporary pieces.

A contemporary inlaid marble platter

A single flower often had more than 35 variations of carnelian

CARVED RELIEF WORK

Decorative panels of flowering plants, foliage and vases are realistically carved on the lower portions of the walls. While the *pietra dura* adds colour to the pristine white marble these highlight the texture of the polished marble and sandstone surface.

Floral sprays, *carved in relief on the marble and sandstone dado levels, are framed with pietra dura and stone inlay borders. The profusion of floral motifs in the Taj symbolizes the central paradise theme.*

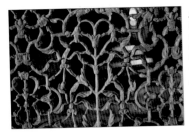

Jaali patterns *on the octagonal perforated screen surrounding the cenotaphs are a complex combination of the floral and geometric. The filtered light captures the intricate designs and casts mosaic-like shadows on the tombs.*

CALLIGRAPHY

Inlaid calligraphy in black marble was used as a form of ornamentation on undecorated surfaces. The exquisitely detailed panels of inscriptions of Koranic passages, that line the recessed arches like banners, were designed by the Persian calligrapher, Amanat Khan.

Exploring the East Bank

The picturesque east bank of the Yamuna is dotted with the remains of gardens, palaces, pavilions and the exquisite tomb of **Itimad-ud-Daulah**. North of Itimad-ud-Daulah is **Chini ka Rauza**, (literally, "China tomb" after its tiled exterior) built by Afzal Khan, a poet-scholar from Shiraz who was Shah Jahan's finance minister. This large square structure is Persian in style, and at one time its surface was covered with glazed tiles from Lahore and Multan, interspersed with calligraphic panels in graceful Naskh characters. The burial chamber within has painted stucco plaster design that once must have comple-mented the tiled exterior.

Further upriver is the quiet, tree-shaded **Rambagh** or Aram Bagh ("garden of rest"). This is said to be the first Mughal garden laid out by Babur in 1526 (see p167), and his temporary burial place before his body was taken to Kabul to be interred. The spacious walled garden, divided by walkways leading to a raised terrace with open pavilions overlooking the river, was further developed by Nur Jahan.

Chini ka Rauza
1 km (less than a mile) N of Itimad-ud-Daulah. ☐ daily. 📷

Rambagh
3 km (2 miles) N of Itimad-ud-Daulah. ☐ daily. 📷

Riverside pavilion at Rambagh

Itimad-ud-Daulah's Tomb

A stylized floral motif

Lyrically described as a "jewel box in marble", the small, elegant garden tomb of Itimad-ud-Daulah, the "Lord Treasurer" of the Mughal empire, was built over a period of six years from 1622 by his daughter Nur Jahan, Jahangir's favourite wife. This tomb is a brilliant combination of white marble, coloured mosaic, stone inlay and lattice work. Stylistically too, this is the most innovative 17th-century Mughal building and marks the transition from the robust, red sandstone architecture of Akbar to the sensuous refinement of Shah Jahan's Taj Mahal.

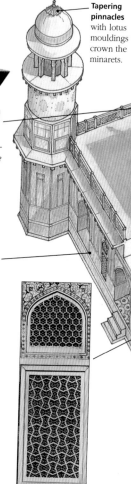

Tapering pinnacles with lotus mouldings crown the minarets.

Upper Pavilion
The replica tombs of Itimad-ud-Daulah and his wife are placed in the marble-screened upper pavilion.

Mosaic Patterns
Panels of geometric designs created by inlaid coloured stones decorate the dado level of the tomb.

STAR FEATURES
★ Pietra Dura

★ Tomb Chamber

★ Marble Screens

★ **Marble Screens**
Perforated marble screens with complex ornamental patterns are carved out of a single slab of marble.

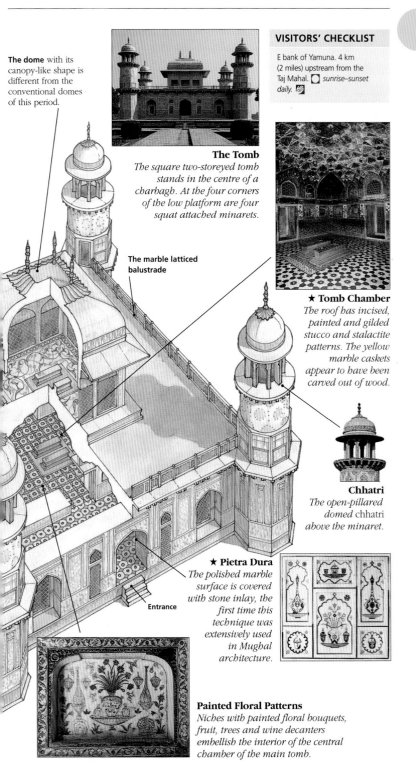

The dome with its canopy-like shape is different from the conventional domes of this period.

The Tomb
The square two-storeyed tomb stands in the centre of a charbagh. At the four corners of the low platform are four squat attached minarets.

The marble latticed balustrade

★ **Tomb Chamber**
The roof has incised, painted and gilded stucco and stalactite patterns. The yellow marble caskets appear to have been carved out of wood.

Chhatri
The open-pillared domed chhatri above the minaret.

★ **Pietra Dura**
The polished marble surface is covered with stone inlay, the first time this technique was extensively used in Mughal architecture.

Entrance

Painted Floral Patterns
Niches with painted floral bouquets, fruit, trees and wine decanters embellish the interior of the central chamber of the main tomb.

The entrance to Akbar's mausoleum at Sikandra

Sikandra ❷

Agra district. 8 km (5 miles) NW of Agra on NH2. **Road map** D2. 🚗
Akbar's Mausoleum *Tel* (0562) 237 1230 . ⊙ 7am–5:15pm daily.
🏞️ 📷 🚻 🎫
🎪 Urs at Akbar's tomb (mid-Oct).

The Mughal Emperor, Akbar, is buried in this small village on the outskirts of Agra. Named after Sikander Lodi, one of the last of the Delhi sultans (see pp50–51), this was a pleasant garden suburb during Agra's golden age. It is widely believed that Akbar designed and started the construction of his own mausoleum which, after his death, was modified and completed by his son and successor, Jahangir. The result is this impressive, perfectly symmetrical complex with the tomb, located in the centre of a vast, walled garden.

The main gateway (see p25) to the south is a magnificent red sandstone structure with a colossal central arch, finished with an exuberant poly-chrome mosaic of inlaid white marble, black slate and coloured stones. On each corner of the gateway are four graceful marble minarets, considered to be forerunners of those found later on the Taj Mahal (see pp154–5).

The garden, where deer and monkeys frolic, is a typical *charbagh (see p167)*. The wide sweep of stone causeways leading to the tomb divides the area into four quadrants, each with its own fountain and sunken pond, fruit trees and bushes, now a derelict tangle.

The main tomb is a distinct departure from the conventional domed structure of the tomb of Akbar's father, the second Mughal emperor, Humayun, at Delhi (see p83). The first three storeys of this majestic, four-tiered compo-sition, comprise red sand-stone pavilions. Above them is an exquisite marble-screened terrace enclosing the replica tomb, which is pro-fusely carved with floral and arabesque designs, Chinese cloud patterns, and the 99 names of Allah. The upper levels, earlier accessible through special permission, are now closed due to security reasons.

The actual tomb is within a domed sepulchre in the heart of the building, illumi-nated by shafts of light from an arched window. A low door at the end of the ramp

Detail of a panel on the entrance gateway at Sikandra

ensures that every visitor bows his head with respect on entry. Just outside the complex is the **Kanch Mahal**, a double-storeyed red sandstone mansion with an ornamented façade and fretted balconies. Further down, on Mathura Road, is **Mariam Zamani's Tomb**, where one of Akbar's wives is buried in a square building set on a high plinth within a small garden. It was used as an orphanage by the Church Missionary Society in 1812. A church has been constructed in the compound. Further along the Agra-Delhi highway is **Guru-ka-Tal**, a unique example of the many tanks constructed by Jahangir for collecting rain-water. Broad flights of steps lead down to the water. The reservoir is now part of a *guru-dwara* complex dedicated to the ninth Sikh guru, Tegh Bahadur (see p90).

Environs
About 4 km (2 miles) south of Sikandra stands a lifesize red sandstone horse on the spot where Akbar's favourite steed supposedly died. Located opposite, is the gateway of **Kachi-ki-Sarai**, a historic rest house along this route.

THE GRAND TRUNK ROAD

A roadside *dhaba*

The Grand Trunk Road, Rudyard Kipling's "stately corridor" that linked Calcutta in the east with Kabul in the northwest, was laid out by Sher Shah Sur (see p84) in the 16th century. In those days, it resounded with the movement of armies on campaign, and in times of peace, with the pomp and pageantry that accompanied the Mughal emperors as their court moved from Agra to Delhi.

This is still one of Asia's great roads and North India's premier highway. Some of the ancient shade-giving trees still stand, but the old caravanserais are now in ruins. Instead, at frequent intervals along the highway, there are *dhabas* for long-distance travellers, especially lorry-drivers, to stop for a cheap and filling meal of dal and *roti*, washed down with glasses of hot tea or cooling *lassi*, and to snatch a quick nap on string cots thoughtfully provided by the owner.

Vishram Ghat at Mathura where every evening at sunset oil lamps are floated on the river

Mathura ❸

Mathura district. 62 km (39 miles)
from Agra on NH2.
Road map D3. 🏠 300,000.
🚉 🚌 🛈 *Old Bus Stand, Mathura.*
🎎 *Hariyali Teej (July), Janmashtami
(Aug–Sep), Annakut (Sep–Oct), Kansa
Vadha (Sep), Holi (Feb–Mar).*

Mathura, on the west bank
of the Yamuna, is where the
story of Krishna begins. A
dark, cell-like room in the
complex of the rather modern
Sri Krishna Janmabhoomi
Temple on the periphery of
the city, is revered as the
birthplace of one of India's
most popular gods. Further
away, along the riverfront, the
city's 25 ghats form a splendid network of temples,
pavilions, trees and steps
leading to the water. Teeming
with colourful shops selling
traditional items, such as its
delicious *pedas* (milk sweets),
this is the heart of the town.
   The evening *aarti*, when
small oil lamps are floated on
the river, is performed at
Vishram Ghat, where legend
says Krishna rested after he
killed the tyrant Kamsa. Close
by is the **Sati Burj**, a red sandstone pavilion built in the
1570s, and **Kans Qila**, the site
of the old fort where Sawai
Jai Singh II of Jaipur
constructed one of his five
observatories *(see pp192–3)*.
   The **Jami Masjid**, with its
striking tile-work, and a
number of other interesting
buildings with elaborately
carved façades, lie behind the
riverfront. A charming oddity
is the Roman Catholic Church

of the Sacred Heart, built in
1860 in the army cantonment.
It combines Western elements
with details taken from local
temple architecture.
   Mathura's ancient history
predates the better known
legend of Krishna. From
about the 5th century
BC until the 4th
century AD, the city
prospered as a major
centre of Buddhism.
Under the powerful
Kushana and Gupta
dynasties, it was
renowned throughout
the ancient world as
North India's cultural
capital. During this
period the Mathura
School of Art flourished
(see pp46–7), and
superb pieces of
sculpture, made from   **A religious icon**
the distinctive local   **from Mathura**
white-flecked red sandstone,
were carved by artisans in
workshops here and exported
to far off places.
   The **Government Museum**
collection highlights the
Mathura School of Art and

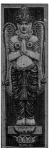

has some exquisite pieces.
These include a perfectly
preserved Standing Buddha,
the famous headless statue of
the great Kushana king
Kanishka, as well as a huge
collection of carved columns,
railings and fragments of
narrative panels, exca-
vated from nearby
archaeological sites,
depicting court scenes
and religious imagery.
   Also on view are
artifacts from the other
centres of Buddhist art,
such as Gandhara (now
in Pakistan), showing
Graeco-Roman influ-
ences after Alexander's
invasion of the north-
west. There are also
sections on terracotta
pottery and figurines
dating from the
2nd–1st centuries BC,
coins and medieval stone,
brass and metal objects.

🏛 **Government Museum**
Dampier Nagar. **Tel** *(0565) 250 0847.*
⬜ *10:30am–4:30pm Tue–Sun.* ⬤
Mon & public hols. 📷 *extra charges.*

A boat carrying pilgrims along the Yamuna

Brindavan ➍

Mathura district. 68 km (42 miles)
N of Agra off NH2. **Road map** D3.
🏠 *57,000.* 🚌 ℹ️ *Old Bus Stand,
Mathura.* 📷 *Holi (Feb–Mar), Rath ka
Mela (Mar), Hariyali Teej (Jul),
Janmashtami (Aug–Sep).* 🕉️ *daily.*

Situated along the River
Yamuna, Brindavan (literally,
"forest of fragrant basil")
became an important pilgrim
centre after the early 16th
century when Chaitanya
Mahaprabhu, a Vaishnava
saint from Bengal, revived the
Krishna cult. He encouraged
Bengali devotees, especially
widows, to settle here in
ashrams endowed by wealthy
Hindu merchants. However,
the town's mythic origins are
much older, as devout Hindus
believe that the young Lord
Krishna once lived here as a
humble cowherd with his
foster parents. So "his" cows
still have the run of the streets
and his name is continuously
chanted in prayer halls. Stalls

Pilgrims on the *chaurasi kos ki yatra*

outside temples sell elaborate
flower garlands and milk
sweets called *pedas*, believed
to have been loved by
Krishna. All this gives the
feeling that the people of
Brindavan live in an
enchanted time warp.

This charming phenomenon
is best seen in Brindavan's
numerous temples and ghats,
built by the Hindu kings of
Amber, Bharatpur and Orchha
and by rich merchants. The

edge of the old town has the
historic **Govindeoji Temple**,
originally a seven-storeyed
structure built in 1590 by Raja
Man Singh I of Amber. The
presiding deity is now in
Jaipur *(see p182)*. Across this
temple is the 19th-century **Sri
Ranganathji**, an imposing
Dravidian-style temple with a
gold-plated ritual pillar and a
fascinating museum of temple
treasures. Beyond these, and
within the narrow streets of

Brajbhumi Driving Tour ➎

Devotees believe that the area around
Braj is composed of sacred *mandalas*
(circuits) that map the idyllic pastoral
landscape of Krishna's early life. Divided
by the Yamuna, this tour partly follows
the *chaurasi kos ki yatra*, a traditional
pilgrimage of about 300 km (112 miles),
undertaken around Janmashtami.

Kosi ➅
This was the
treasure-house of
Krishna's foster
father, Nand.

DELHI

NH2

Barsana ➃
With its 17th-century
Ladliji temple, Barsana is
believed to be the home
of Radha.

Nandgaon ➄
Krishna lived here
with foster parents
Nand and Yashoda
after his escape
from Gokul and
the evil Kamsa.

Govardhan ➂
This pilgrim town has grown
around the hill that legend says
Krishna lifted on his finger to shield
the people of Braj from torrential
rain. Nearby is Kusum Sarovar.

the old town, are the sacred walled groves of Seva Kunj, linked with the Raslila dance of the region (see p28).

The **Shahji Temple** with its spiral columns, lies on the way to Nidhivana where Swami Haridas, the guru of Tansen (see p174), developed the classic musical tradition of Dhrupad in the 16th century.

Other notable temples are the **Madan Mohan Temple**, built in 1580 with local red sandstone, on a hill next to the river. A little further are the popular **Banke Bihari Temple**, which can be approached from the main bazaar street, and the 16th-century **Jugal Kishore Temple**, adjoining the main pilgrim route to the ghats. The **Gopinath** and **Radha Raman** temples are located close to each other near Keshi

Gopuram of the South Indian-style Ranganathji Temple

Ghat. The ISKCON Temple and the Brindavan Research Institute, on the outskirts of the town, are recent additions to the town's skyline.

At Holi and Janmashtami (see pp36–7), Brindavan is a riot of colour and dance as people celebrate the god who still enchants them and where his *lila* (divine sport) is still a living presence.

A Vaishanavite *sadhu*

Deeg ❻

Bharatpur district. 98 km (61 miles) N of Agra on NH2. **Road map** D3. 🛈 *RTDC Hotel Saras, Agra Rd, Bharatpur (05644) 22 3700.* 🎑 *Holi (Feb-Mar), Rath ka Mela (Mar).*

Once the capital of the Jat kings of Bharatpur (see p166), Deeg rose to prominence after the decline of the Mughal empire in the 18th century. Its square fort, a massive edifice, has mud and rubble walls which are buttressed by 12 bastions and a shallow moat. The fortified town outside the fort once had grand mansions, lush gardens and pools, that now lie unkempt and forlorn. Deeg's Raja Suraj Mal and his son, Jawahir Singh, were also builders of lavish pleasure palaces. Of these, the most remarkable is the **Water Palace** (see pp164–5), built in celebration of the monsoon. This was a favourite summer retreat of the Bharatpur kings.

Radhakund ②
Said to be Radha's personal bathing pool, it has a special sanctity for her devotees.

KEY

■	Tour route
═	Roads
≋	Rivers

0 kilometres 5

0 miles 2

Brindavan ①
An important pilgrim centre, it is separated from Mathura by the River Yamuna.

TIPS FOR DRIVERS

Length: 105 km (65 miles).
Stopping-off points: Brindavan has good hotels and restaurants and is the ideal base for the tour. Both Radhakund and Barsana have UPSTDC tourist bungalows, and Govardhan and Kosi have petrol stations. However, private transport will be a more convenient way to explore this region.

THE KRISHNA CULT

Sanjhi, Brindavan's paper stencil craft

A peacock feather, a flute and the colour blue announce the presence of Krishna. Named after his dark skin, this most human of gods still haunts the glades and forests along the Yamuna. A naughty child who was passionately fond of milk and butter, Krishna is also the charming flute-player whose flirtatious dalliance with Radha is a metaphor for the complex metaphysics of temporal and spiritual love, widely celebrated in art and literature.

Deeg Water Palace

Sandstone carving on Singh Pol

The magic of the monsoon and the traditions of music and dance associated with it inspired the Bharatpur kings to build a romantic "water palace" at their summer capital, Deeg. A lyrical composition of sandstone and marble pavilions, gardens and pools, this late 18th-century marvel, built by Raja Suraj Mal, used a number of innovative special effects that simulated monsoon showers, even producing rainbows. The skilful cooling system drew water from a huge reservoir that originally took two days to fill. The coloured fountain-jets are now played only during the Jawahar Mela.

Nand Bhavan
Huge terracotta water pitchers placed inside its innovative double roof insulated its interior against the heat of summer.

The main entrance, Singh Pol, is named after the two lions *(singh)* sculpted on its front arch.

★ Sawan Pavilion
Shaped like an upturned boat, its ingenious water system created a semi-circle of falling water.

Gopal Sagar Tank

Mughal Marble Swing
This was a part of Suraj Mal's war booty, now placed in front of Gopal Bhavan.

Bhadon Pavilion

★ Gopal Bhavan
This elegant complex is flanked by the boat-shaped Sawan-Bhadon pavilions. Its numerous overhanging kiosks and balconies are reflected in Gopal Sagar from which it seems to rise. The interior still retains the original furnishings and objets d'art of this palace.

VISITORS' CHECKLIST

Bharatpur district. 95 km (59 miles) NW of Agra. **Road map** D3. 🚌 🚗 *8am–5pm daily.* ⚫ *the day after Holi (Mar).* 📷 *Jawahar Mela (Aug).* 🏛 *Mon.* 📷

★ **Keshav Bhavan**
Heavy lithic balls were placed on the roof here. When water gushed up the hollow pillars and pipes inside the arches, the balls rolled on the roof to produce "thunder".

Lotus Quoins
Placed at each corner of the plinth, these urns were inspired by Mughal designs.

Rup Sagar Tank

Suraj Bhavan
A pillared, secluded pavilion with a splendid view of the charbagh, *it was part of the zenana enclosure.*

Kishan Bhavan

The roof-level reservoir had water drawn to it from four wells. Pipes led from holes in its sides to supply the chutes and fountains with a continuous stream of water.

Charbagh

MONSOON ARCHITECTURE

In the dry areas of North India, light and wind direction guided architecture. Underground rooms, water channels, fountains, latticed screens, terrazzo floors and open courtyards were devices to keep homes cool before the advent of electricity. The Sawan-Bhadon pavilions at Deeg, named after the months of the monsoon (July–August), are an architectural style inspired by the rainy season. Built to savour the thunder and rain of the monsoon, such pavilions adorned forts and palaces.

Coloured water fountains at Deeg

STAR FEATURES

★ Gopal Bhavan

★ Sawan Pavilion

★ Keshav Bhavan

Bharatpur ❼

Bharatpur district. 55 km (34 miles)
from Agra. **Road map** D3.
🏛 204,500. ℹ️ opp RTDC Hotel
Saras, Agra Rd (05644) 22 3700. 🚍
🎭 Jaswant Mela (Oct).

Most famous for its bird
sanctuary, the kingdom of
Bharatpur, on the eastern
edge of Rajasthan, came into
prominence during the
declining years of the Mughal
Empire. It was founded by
the fearless Jats, a community
of landowners. Their most
remarkable leader was Raja
Suraj Mal (r.1724–63), who in
1733 captured and fortified
the city of Bharatpur, thereby
laying the foundations of his
capital. This powerful ruler
defied the reigning Mughal
emperor, stormed Delhi and
Agra and brought home the
massive gates of Agra Fort
and installed them at his own
fort at Deeg's Water Palace
(see pp164–5), near Bharatpur. A prolific builder as well,
he used the loot from Mughal
buildings, including a swing
(now in Deeg), to embellish
the forts and palaces he built
throughout his kingdom.

In the centre of the town is
Lohagarh ("iron fort"), which
withstood repeated attacks by
the Marathas and the British
until it was finally captured
by Lord Lake in 1805. When
built, it was a masterpiece of
construction with massive
double ramparts of
solid packed mud and rubble
that were surrounded by
impressive moats. Most of the

The State Museum at Lohagarh Fort, Bharatpur

outermost ramparts have
disintegrated, but the inner
ones are intact and are
distinguished by two towers,
the Jawahar Burj and Fateh
Burj, built to mark successive
Jat victories over the Mughals
and British. The Victory
Column at Jawahar Burj
carries an inscription
with the genealogy
of the Jat kings.
Both its north and
south gates were
part of the loot from
the imperial Mughal
capital at Delhi.

Three palaces
were built in the
fort by the rustic
Jats in a surprisingly
fine mix of Mughal
and Rajput stylistic
detail. The royal apartments,
in Mahal Khas, had unusual
octagonal chambers in the
corners with colourful painted
walls, but these are now the
site of a pharmaceutical
college. The other two

palaces were located around
the Katcheri (court) Bagh,
and now house the **State
Museum**, where a rare
collection of 1st- and 2nd-
century stone carvings and
terracotta toys from nearby
excavations can be seen. An
interesting sunken
hamam is close by.

In 1818, Bharatpur
became the first
Rajput state to sign
a treaty of alliance
with the British East
India Company. A
later maharaja was
a keen collector of
Rolls Royce cars,
which he converted
for use on tiger and
duck shoots.

**Figure of Krishna,
State Museum**

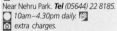
🏛 **State Museum**
Near Nehru Park. *Tel* (05644) 22 8185.
🕙 10am–4.30pm daily. 📷
⚹ extra charges.

Keoladeo Ghana National Park ❽

See pp 168-9.

Fatehpur Sikri ❾

See pp 170-71.

Dholpur ❿

Dholpur district. 54 km (34 miles)
S of Agra. **Road map** D3. 🏛 92,000.
ℹ️ Bharatpur, (05644) 22 3700. 🚍

Situated on the banks of the
River Chambal, the small
town of Dholpur was
strategically located on the

The moat and ramparts of Lohagarh

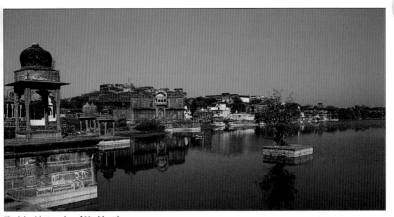

The lakeside temples of Machkund

route from Delhi to the Deccan, making it the target of invading armies. In 1504, Sikandar Lodi *(see pp50–51)* set up camp here for a month on his march against Gwalior. Some 20 years later, Babur made this a royal domain of his new empire. The ruined Shergarh Fort, said to be 1,000 years old, is in Dholpur and so is a modest 19th-century palace (closed to the public) which can only be seen through an ironwork railing. The palace has a number of art deco rooms covered with European tiles. Dholpur is today associated with the beige-coloured sandstone quarried nearby, used in buildings all over Rajasthan and made famous by Lutyens, who used it for the building of New Delhi *(see pp68–9).*

Environs

Dholpur town is a convenient base to explore a number of fascinating neighbouring sites. **Machkund** (3 km/2 miles west), has over 100 temples along its lake. Its waters are said to heal all skin diseases. **Damoh**, a popular picnic spot, has 76 waterfalls. **Talab Shahi** (40 km/25 miles) has the remains of hunting lodges developed by the Jat rulers of Dholpur for their numerous European guests. Off the beaten track is **Jhor** (16km/10 miles), where in 1978, Babur's 400-year-old Lotus Garden was discovered.

Bari ⑪

Dholpur district. 84 km (68 miles) SW of Agra. **Road map** D4.
🛈 *Bharatpur, (05644) 22 3700.* 🚉.

Shah Jahan's palace gate, Bari

The site of an old 100-acre garden once so dense that sunlight could not reach the ground, Bari was where Emperor Shah Jahan built a number of pleasure pavilions. Located nearby is the Vana Vihar Ram Sagar Wildlife Reserve, home to crocodiles, sambhar, wild boar and several species of migratory bird. Remains of an old fort built by Feroze Shah Tughlaq *(see p97)* can also be seen here.

BABUR AND THE PARADISE GARDEN

The Garden of Fidelity in the *Babur Nama*

The concept of the Paradise Garden, the hallmark of Mughal landscape design, was introduced by the first Great Mughal, Babur. Yearning for the natural beauty of Ferghana, his homeland in Central Asia, he recreated the Persian paradise garden based on Islamic geometric and metaphysical concepts of design.

The *charbagh* was an enclosed garden divided into four quarters, representing the four quarters of life, by a system of raised walkways, sunken groves and water channels. Water was the central element, for it was regarded by the rulers of Central Asian desert kingdoms as the source of life. The intersecting water channels met at a focal point which contained a pavilion for the emperor, seen as a representative of God on earth.

The Mughals used their gardens as living spaces, and also as settings for their garden tombs *(see p27).* The Jhor garden of paradise, sometimes referred to as the Lotus Garden, was laid out in 1527, barely a year after Babur invaded India. Three water channels, Babur's hot bath, a tank and a pavilion are all that remain of the original garden, which once covered several acres.

Keoladeo Ghana National Park ❽

A World Heritage Site regarded as one of the world's most important bird sanctuaries, Keoladeo Ghana derives its name from a Shiva temple (Keoladeo) within a dense *(ghana)* forest. This once-arid scrubland was first developed by the Bharatpur rulers in the mid-18th century by diverting the waters of a nearby irrigation canal to create a private duck reserve. Extravagant shooting parties for viceroys and other royal guests were held here, and horrifying numbers of birds were shot in a single day. Today, the park spreads over 29 sq km (11 sq miles) of wetlands, and attracts a wide variety of migrant and water birds who fly in each winter from places as distant as Siberia. Keoladeo's dry area has a mixed deciduous and scrub vegetation and is home to many mammals such as the nilgai.

Bharatpur's wetlands, which hold one of the world's finest heronries

Around the Park
Expert boatmen navigate the wetlands and point out bird colonies. Bicycles and cycle-rickshaws are also available for touring the forest paths.

Dry scrubland provides good grazing for many species of deer and cattle.

BIRDS, RESIDENT AND MIGRANT

The male Sarus crane dances to attract his mate

The park attracts over 375 bird species belonging to 56 families. Egrets, darter cormorants, grey herons and storks hatch nearly 30,000 chicks every year. The park's most eagerly awaited visitor, the Siberian crane, is now an endangered species. Other birds include the peregrine falcon, steppe eagle, garganey teal, snake bird and the white ibis. Among the large variety of storks are the open-bill stork, the painted stork and the black-necked stork, considered to be the world's tallest stork. When standing on its coral-coloured legs, the bird rises to a height of 2 m (6 ft), with a wing spread of 2.5 m (8 ft). The Sarus crane, a symbol of fidelity in Indian mythology, woos its partner for life with an elaborate mating dance.

Baby cormorants

Map labels

JAIPUR

NH11

Forest Lodg

Shan
Kuti

Mrig
Tal

Sa

Ramnagar

Lala
ka K

Chiksana Canal

Aghapu

KEY

- ▬ Main road
- ═ Minor road
- ‑ · Park boundary
- ▬ Walk/cycle trail
- ▦ Marshland
- ☀ Viewpoint
- ◘ Jetty
- ⬇ Boating area
- ▣ Police station
- ⛩ Temple

BHARATPUR CITY

NH11

• Jatoli

AGRA

0 kilometres 1

0 miles 1

Painted Storks
Between July and October, the trees become nesting sites for nearly 5,000 pairs of these birds named after their colourful beaks and plumage which is "painted" with black bands.

Turtle
Other living species include turtles, otters, foxes and reptiles such as the rock python.

Nilgai (Blue Bull)
The largest of all Asiatic antelopes, these avid crop grazers are protected against hunting because of their resemblance to the holy cow. Their broad backs offer comfortable resting places to birds.

Kadam Kunj

• Ghasola

Madeo ple an ovar

hon int Hans Sarovar

White-Throated Kingfisher
One of the most commonly sighted birds in the park, the vividly-coloured kingfisher is usually found near the ponds, lakes and marsh-lands, perched on branches of trees, waiting for its prey.

Koladahar

• Bahnera

Chiksana Canal

Naswaria

• Darapur

A stone plaque near the temple records figures of past bird shoots.

Nesting
With the arrival of the monsoon (late June), thousands of birds set up nesting colonies. As many as 60 noisy nests on one tree may be seen during this season.

Fatehpur Sikri ◑

Fretwork *jaali*

Built by Mughal Emperor Akbar in 1571 in honour of the famous Sufi saint, Salim Chishti, Fatehpur Sikri was the Mughal capital for 14 years. An example of a Mughal walled city with defined private and public areas and imposing gateways, its architecture, a blend of Hindu and Islamic styles, reflects Akbar's secular vision as well as his style of governance. After the city was abandoned, some say for lack of water, many of its treasures were plundered *(see pp54–5)*. It owes its present state of preservation to the initial efforts of Lord Curzon *(see pp56–7)*, a legendary conservationist.

Pillar in the Diwan-i-Khas
The central axis of Akbar's court, supported by carved brackets, was inspired by Gujarat buildings.

Haran com

Jami Masjid

Khwabgah
The emperor's private sleeping quarters, this "chamber of dreams" with murals and Persian calligraphy has an ingenious ventilating shaft near his bed.

Anoop Talao or pool is associated with Akbar's legendary court musician Tansen who, it is said, could light oil lamps with the magic of his voice.

Abdar
Khana

Entrance

★ Turkish Sultana's House
The elaborate dado panels and delicately sculpted walls of this ornate sandstone pavilion make the stone seem like wood. It is topped with an unusual stone roof with imitation clay tiles.

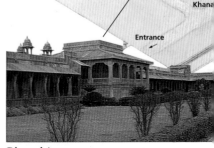

Diwan-i-Aam
This large courtyard with an elaborate pavilion was originally draped with rich tapestries and use for public hearings, receptions and celebrations.

★ Panch Mahal
A five-storeyed open sandstone pavilion, it overlooks the Pachisi Court, where Akbar's queens savoured the cool evening breezes. Its decorative screens were probably stolen after the city was abandoned.

VISITORS' CHECKLIST

Agra district. 37 km (23 miles) W of Agra. **Road map** D3.
🛈 UPTDC, 64 Taj Rd, Agra (0562) 222 6431. ◻ 7am–7pm daily. 🎫 📷 🚻

Jodha Bai's Palace

Maryam's House

Birbal's House

★ Diwan-i-Khas
Perhaps a debating chamber, the real function of this unique structure is still unknown.

Ankh Michauli
Sometimes identified as the treasury, this building has mythical guardian beasts carved on its stone struts. Its name means "blind man's buff".

Pachisi Court is named after a ludo-like game played here by the ladies of the harem.

PLAN OF FATEHPUR SIKRI

Fatehpur Sikri's royal complex contains the private and public spaces of Akbar's court, which included the harem and the treasury. The adjoining sacred complex containing the Jami Masjid, Salim Chishti's tomb and the Buland Darwaza, are separated from the royal quarters by the Badshahi Darwaza, an exclusive royal gateway.

KEY
◻ Area illustrated above
◻ Other buildings
◼ Sacred complex (Jami Masjid)

STAR FEATURES
★ Diwan-i-Khas
★ Panch Mahal
★ Turkish Sultana's House

Exploring Fatehpur Sikri

Detail of a carved panel

The principal buildings of the imperial palace complex, clustered on a series of terraces along the sandstone ridge, formed the core of Akbar's city. Stylistically, they marked the absorption of Gujarat into the Mughal Empire and reveal a successful synthesis of pre-Islamic, Hindu and Jain architecture (as in the carved brackets) with the elegant domes and arches of Islamic buildings. The concentric terraces clearly divide the public spaces from the private royal quarters. The buildings, mostly in Akbar's favourite red sandstone, were quarried from the ridge on which they stand.

Stone "tusks" at the Hiran Minar

Aerial view of Fatehpur Sikri

Even today, the access to the city that was Akbar's capital is provided by a straight road he built, then lined with exotic bazaars. It leads visitors through the Agra Gate to the triple-arched **Naubat Khana**, where the emperor's entry used to be announced by a roll of drums. The imperial palace complex is entered from the west through the Naubat Khana and opens into the spacious cloistered courtyard of the **Diwan-i-Aam**, where Akbar gave public audiences. A passage behind it leads into the so-called "inner citadel" which contains the **Diwan-i-Khas, Khwabgah** and **Anoop Talao**, along with the the treasuries and the **Abdar Khana** where water and fruit for the royal household were stored. It also contains the curiously named **Turkish Sultana's House**. Though probably built for one of Akbar's wives, the identity of the "Turkish Sultana" is

unclear. The great courtyard in front of the Diwan-i-Khas is the **Pachisi Court**, named after the central open space that resembles the board game of *pachisi*, similar to ludo.

The **Haram Sara**, or harem complex, was a maze of interconnected buildings beyond Maryam's House or **Sunehra Makan** ("golden house"), named after its rich frescoes and gilding. The massive and austere exterior of the harem leads to **Jodha Bai's Palace**, a large inner courtyard, surrounded by pavilions decorated with azure glazed tiles on the roof. A screened viaduct, presumably for privacy, connected the palace to the **Hawa Mahal** facing a small formal garden. The **Nagina Masjid**, adjoining the garden, was the royal ladies' private mosque. The two-storeyed pavilion popularly said to be

Birbal's House, situated to the east of Jodha Bai's palace, has spectacular carving on the exterior and interior of its unusual layout. Beyond this lies a large colonnaded enclosure surrounded by cells, meant probably for the servants of the harem, and the royal stables.

The **Hathi Pol** and **Sangin Burj**, the original gateways to the harem, lead to the outermost periphery of the palace complex. This was laid out in concentric circles around the inner citadel and is made up of ancillary structures, such as the caravanserais, the domed *hamams* and waterworks. The **Hiran Minar** ("deer tower"), believed to be a memorial to Akbar's favourite elephant, was probably an *akash deep* ("heavenly light") with lamps suspended from stone "tusks" to guide visitors.

Entrance to Birbal's House

Jami Masjid

An inlaid panel

This grand open mosque towers over the city of Fatehpur Sikri and was the model for several Mughal mosques. Flanked by arched cloisters, its vast *namazgah* has monumental gates to the east and south. However, the spiritual focus of the complex is the tomb and hermitage of the Sufi mystic, Salim Chishti, as popular today as it was in the days of its Mughal patrons.

Tomb of Sheikh Salim Chishti
Exquisite marble serpentine brackets and almost transparent screens surround the inner tomb which has a mother-of-pearl canopy inlaid with sandalwood.

Hujra
Symmetrically flanking the main mosque, this pair of identical cloistered prayer rooms has flat-roofed pillared galleries that run round the complex.

Badshahi Darwaza
Akbar used the steep steps of this royal gateway to enter the complex. The view of the sacred mosque directly across, greeted his entry.

Corridors

Buland Darwaza
Erected by Akbar, the huge 54 m (177 ft) gateway later inspired other lofty gates. Young boys dive from its ramparts into the pool below to fish for coins.

MAKING A WISH IN CHISHTI'S TOMB

Ever since Akbar's childlessness was ended by the remarkable prediction of Salim Chishti in 1568, the saint's tomb has become the haunt of those in search of a miracle. The dargah, lavishly endowed by both Akbar and his son Jahangir, attracts crowds of supplicants who make a wish, tie a small cotton thread on the screen around the tomb, and go back confident that the saint will make it come true.

A thread tied to a screen in Chishti's tomb

The strikingly ornamental façade of Gwalior Fort

Gwalior ⑫

Gwalior district. 118km (73 miles) S
of Agra on NH3. **Road map** D4.
🏯 827,000. ℹ *TO Hotel Tansen,
M G Rd (0751) 223 4557.* 🚌 🚉
🎵 *Tansen Music Festival (Oct–Nov).*

This royal seat of the Scindias
is dominated by the massive
Gwalior Fort. The interior
owes some of its finest
features to the Tomar
musician-king, Man
Singh (r.1486–1517).
Near the ornate
Hindola Gate, one of
three gateways located
near the old city, is the
romantic Gujari Mahal
(1510) built by Man
Singh for his tribal
wife, the beautiful
Mrignayani, and it now
houses the outstanding
Archaeological Museum. His
main palace, the Man Mandir,
with an amazing variety of

Frieze in
Gwalior fort

ornamental glazed tile
patterns, is considered the
most remarkable example of
an early Hindu palace. In the
city below the fort, the 19th-
century Italian palazzo-style
Jai Vilas Palace houses the
Scindia Museum. Famous for a
magnificent crystal staircase
and furniture, its vast Durbar
Hall has Venetian chandeliers
that weigh three tons. A silver
model train, laden with
brandy and cigars, once
used to serve guests at
the spectacular royal
feasts held here.

Other notable sights
are the tombs of Tansen
and Muhammad Ghaus,
as well as early temples
such as Teli ka Mandir
(see p24) and the Sas-
Bahu ka Mandir.

🏛 **Gwalior Fort**
🕐 sunrise–sunset.
Son et Lumière daily. 📷

🏛 **Archaeological Museum**
🕐 10am–5pm Sun–Thu.
🔴 Fri & public hols. 📷
🏛 **Jai Vilas Palace**
S of Fort. 🕐 9am–5pm Tue–Sun.
🔴 Wed & public hols. 📷 🚫

Datia Palace

Datia ⑬

Datia district. 187 km (116 miles) S
of Agra. **Road map** D4. 🏯 83,000.
ℹ *UPTDC, Hotel Veerangana, Shivpuri
Rd, Jhansi (0517) 244 2406.* 🚌

The main focus of this
ghostly town is the five-
storeyed Datia Palace, an
outstanding building of great
structural complexity. Built by
the Bundela king Bir Singh
Deo in 1620, its sinister
underground chambers still
exude an eerie ambience. The
finely painted royal
apartments within the main
courtyard are connected to
the galleries around them by
double-storeyed bridges.

Another important historic
building is the later Rajgarh
Palace, which offers a panoramic view of the entire
walled town.

GWALIOR GHARANA OF MUSIC

Akbar, Tansen and Guru Ramdas

The Gwalior Gharana is one
of the oldest schools of
North Indian classical music.
Its greatest achievement was
the adaptation of folk music
into the orthodox Dhrupad
mode, a contribution of Raja
Man Singh and Mrignayani,
whose tribal music wove a
spell on the king. This form
was given lively expression
by Gwalior-born Tansen, Akbar's court musician, who
developed a range of lyrical new *ragas (see p28).*

A Tour of Bundelkhand ⑭

Gwalior and the adjoining region of Bundelkhand, named after the Bundela Rajputs, make up a culturally distinctive area in Central India. Innumerable forts and monuments, situated in a boulder-strewn landscape of great beauty, still echo with stories of the valour and pageantry of the Bundela Rajput courts, and warriors such as the Rani of Jhansi. The area's glorious history and refined cultural traditions are reflected in the architectural treasures of Gwalior, the magical, medieval town of Orchha, and the hilltop temples of Sonagiri.

Gwalior ①
The capital city of many great dynasties since its origins in the 1st century AD, Gwalior is the most splendid of the "gateways" to the Bundelkhand region.

Pawaya ②
The remains of an ancient fort can be seen in this capital of the Nag kings (3rd century AD) from the highway at Dabra.

AGRA

Dabra

Sind

Sonagiri ③
This impeccably maintained complex of 77 Jain temples is approached through a thriving pilgrim settlement.

Datia ④
This erstwhile Bundela capital surrounded by numerous small lakes, has scenically located palaces on hillocks.

B U N D E L K H A N D

Betwa

LALITPUR

Jhansi ⑤
The town is best known for its impressive fort and the heroic Rani Laxmi Bai, who died leading her troops in the 1857 Indian Mutiny.

KEY

▦ Tour route
═ Other roads
▨ Rivers

0 kilometres 20
0 miles 10

Orchha ⑥
The temples, cenotaphs and tiered palaces here are perfect examples of Bundelkhand architecture *(see pp176–7)*.

TIPS FOR DRIVERS

Length: 120 km (75 miles).
Stopping-off points: Gwalior, Sonagiri, Datia, Jhansi, Taragram, Orchha. After Gwalior, there is a petrol pump at Dabra on NH3. Accommodation in the form of state tourism hotel and guest-houses is available at Gwalior, Jhansi and Orchha. Local buses run between the major stops.

Taragram ⑦
Its fascinating handmade paper factory is an interesting experimental centre aimed at upgrading local craftsmanship.

The 16th-century Chaturbhuj Temple at Orchha

Orchha ⑭

Tikamgarh district. 238 km (148 miles) S of Agra. **Road map** E5. 🛈 *MPTDC, Sheesh Mahal.* 🎭 *Ramnavami (Mar–Apr), Dussehra (Sep–Oct).*

Orchha is dramatically positioned on a rocky island, enclosed by a loop of the River Betwa. Founded in 1531, it was the capital of the Bundela kings until 1738, when it was abandoned in favour of Tikamgarh.

Crumbling palaces, pavilions, *hamams*, walls and gates connected to the town with an impressive 14-arched causeway, are all that remain today. Three main palaces, **Raj Mahal** (1560), **Jahangiri Mahal** (1626) and **Rai Praveen Mahal** are massed symmetrically together. Rai Praveen Mahal was named after a royal paramour and Jahangiri Mahal after the Mughal prince who spent a mere night here.

There are three beautiful temples in the old town, the Ram Raja, the Chaturbhuj and the Laxminarayan. A unique blend of fort and temple styles, the **Chaturbhuj Temple**, dedicated to Vishnu, has huge arcaded halls for massed singing and a soaring spire towering over the area.

Lying along the Kanchana Ghat of the Betwa are 14 hauntingly beautiful *chhatris* of the Orchha rulers. Along with the many *sati* pillars in Jahangiri Mahal's museum, these are reminders of Orchha's feudal past when *sati* queens jumped into their husband's funeral pyres.

Jahangiri Mahal

Flower motif in turquoise stone

Named after the Mughal emperor Jahangir who spent one night here with his Bundela ally Bir Singh Deo, this is an excellent example of Rajput Bundela architecture. The many-layered palace has 132 chambers off and above the central courtyard and an almost equal number of subterranean rooms. The square sandstone palace is extravagantly embellished with lapis lazuli tiles, graceful *chhatris* and ornate *jaali* screens. The palace also has a modest museum.

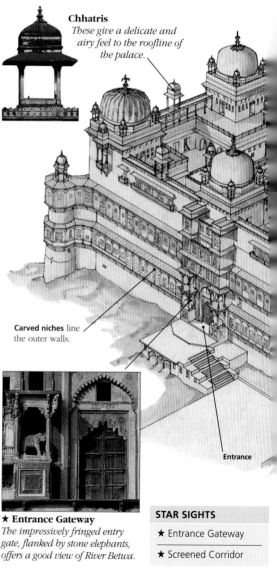

Chhatris
These give a delicate and airy feel to the roofline of the palace.

Carved niches line the outer walls.

Entrance

★ **Entrance Gateway**
The impressively fringed entry gate, flanked by stone elephants, offers a good view of River Betwa.

STAR SIGHTS

★ Entrance Gateway

★ Screened Corridor

★ Screened Corridor
A screened corridor runs round the fourth level which has eight pavilions with lavishly painted interiors, separated by courts.

VISITORS' CHECKLIST

Palace Complex. ◯ *8am–6pm daily.* ◉ *public hols.* 🛈 *MPTDC, Sheesh Mahal.* 🖼 📷 🍴 📷 👥 **Museum** ◯ *10am–5pm.*

Glazed Tilework
Geometric lapis motifs decorate the outer façade at the upper levels.

Jahangir's bedroom

Fortified bastions
protect the palace.

PLAN OF ORCHHA
The fortified town of Orchha encloses three major palaces and ruined ancillary structures.

1 Jahangiri Mahal
2 Sheesh Mahal
3 Raj Mahal
4 Rai Praveen Mahal
5 *Hamam*
6 Stable

KEY

☐ Area illustrated above

The central courtyard can be viewed from each part of the palace and has a small museum in a set of rooms that run along it.

JAIPUR AND ENVIRONS

The Jaipur region of Rajasthan lies on the eastern fringes of the Thar Desert, a semi-arid land cut southwest to northeast by the craggy Aravalli Hills. Studded by hilltop and jungle forts, its valleys and plains glitter with palaces and pavilions, pleasure gardens and temples. Once ruled by proud Rajput princes, this territory is still sustained by memories of a feudal past that is kept alive by its splendid architectural remains and deep-rooted traditional culture.

At the end of the 11th century, the Kachhawahas of Jaipur established their kingdom at Amber. In the region around it lay other Rajput kingdoms – the Chauhan stronghold of Ajmer that would soon fall to Muslim forces, and the massive Rathore jungle fort of Ranthambhore, which would later become a Mughal preserve. By the 18th century the fierce feudal lords of Shekhawati would become vassals of Amber-Jaipur, while Jat kings would rule over Bharatpur, the only non-Rajput kingdom in the area.

The early Rajput states engaged in bitter internecine clan wars, but with the rise of the Delhi sultans *(see pp50–51)*, their energies were directed at keeping their lands safe from the marauding Muslim troops. Finally, under the Mughal emperor Akbar, military and matrimonial alliances paved the way for peace in the region. The result was a cultural and social synthesis which produced some outstanding art and architecture. The British also followed this policy of appeasement and offered the princes military protection in return for their loyalty. The rule of the princely states ended when, after Independence, they were incorporated into the modern Indian state of Rajasthan, with Jaipur as the administrative capital.

But despite democracy, the Rajput feudal tradition, with its code of loyalty to the local chieftain, and immense pride in their past, remains alive. This is perhaps what has preserved the extraordinary culture of the region, so that for many it still remains the romantic land of forts, palaces and kings it was in medieval times.

Devotees thronging the sacred ghats at Pushkar during Kartik Purnima

◁ Jaipur's signature building, the fanciful Hawa Mahal or "Palace of Winds"

Exploring Jaipur and Environs

This historically rich territory is centred around the old capital of Amber and the "newer" city of Jaipur with its palace, observatory, temples and bazaars and impressive modern buildings. To Jaipur's north are the attractive Samode palace and Shekhawati areas, while to its northeast is the wooded area of the Aravallis, where Alwar, a former princely state, and the Sariska National Park are situated. To the southwest, past the textile towns of Sanganer and Bagru, are the religious sites of Ajmer and Pushkar. Southeast of Jaipur lies Chaksu, a pilgrim centre, and the important medieval kingdom of Tonk, beyond which is the spectacular tiger sanctuary of Ranthambhore, nestling beneath the grand ramparts of a historic medieval fort.

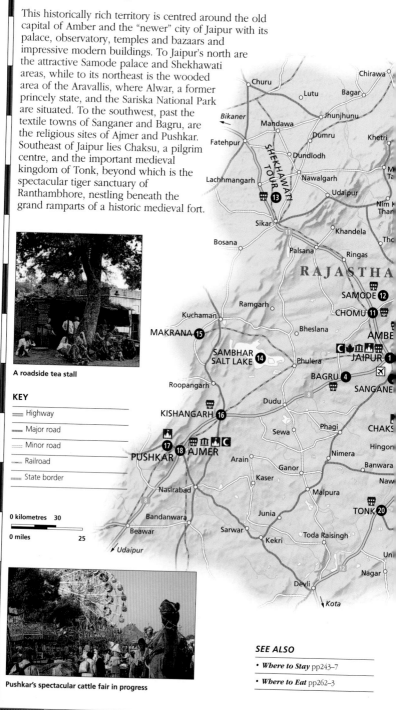

A roadside tea stall

KEY

▬▬	Highway
▬▬	Major road
▬▬	Minor road
▬▬	Railroad
▬▬	State border

0 kilometres   30

0 miles   25

Pushkar's spectacular cattle fair in progress

SEE ALSO

- *Where to Stay* pp243–7
- *Where to Eat* pp262–3

For additional map symbols *see back flap*

GETTING AROUND

Jaipur's airport is at Sanganer (*see p204*), and two superfast trains (the Pink City Express and Shatabdi Express) connect the city to Delhi. Air-conditioned luxury coaches from Delhi to Jaipur are run by Rajasthan Tourism. The rest of the region is best explored by road. The Palace on Wheels (*see p295*), a luxury rail tour through the region, is for the well-heeled tourist who wishes to savour the trip through the desert in royal comfort.

A sacred tank at Galta

Sagar Lake in front of Amber Fort

Printed textiles drying in the sun at Sanganer

SIGHTS AT A GLANCE

Ajmer (see pp218–21) 🔟8
Alwar (see pp206–7) ❺
Amber (see pp200–203) ❷
Bagru ❹
Bairat ❾
Bhangarh 🔟0
Chaksu 🔟9
Chomu 🔟1
Indergarh ㉓
Jaipur (see pp182–99) ❶
Kishangarh 🔟6
Makrana 🔟5
Pushkar (see pp216–17) 🔟7
Rajgarh ❼
Ranthambhore National Park (see pp224–5) ㉒
Sambhar Salt Lake 🔟4
Samode 🔟2
Sanganer ❸
Sariska National Park (see pp210–11) ❽
Sawai Madhopur ㉑
Siliserh ❻
Tonk ㉐

Tours

Shekhawati 🔟3

Jaipur ❶

Stone guardian at Hawa Mahal

A labyrinth of fascinating bazaars, opulent palaces and historic sights, Jaipur offers a chance to see the medieval alongside the modern. On its colourful streets camels jostle for space with motorbikes, and turbaned village elders rub shoulders with youngsters in blue jeans. Often called the Pink City because its prominent buildings are washed with this colour, Jaipur's old walled area has the City Palace Museum, a medieval astronomical observatory and bazaars that sell everything from precious jewellery to camel skin shoes. Recent additions include a multi-arts centre, yet the city's focal point is still the myriad-windowed pink Hawa Mahal, the Palace of Winds.

Govind Dev Temple, dedicated to Krishna

charbagh, it has features such as water channels and fountains. Towards the north is the **Badal Mahal**, a five-arched hunting pavilion on the banks of the Talkatora. Its ceilings still bear faint traces of the cloud (*badal*) patterns.

🏛 City Palace Museum
See pp188–91.

🕌 Govind Dev Temple
Jaleb Chowk, behind City Palace.
◯ 5–11am, 6–8pm daily. 🎭 Holi (Mar), Janmashtami (Jul–Aug), Annakut (Oct–Nov).
The presiding deity of this unusual temple is the flute-playing Krishna (also known as Govind Dev). This image, originally from the Govindeoji Temple in Brindavan (*see p162*), was brought to Amber in the late 17th century to save it from the iconoclastic zeal of Aurangzeb. It is believed that this temple was once a garden pavilion called Suraj Mahal where Sawai Jai Singh II lived while his dream-city Jaipur was being built. Legend has it that one night, the king awoke from his sleep to find himself in the presence of Krishna who demanded that his *devasthan*

("divine residence") be returned to him. Jai Singh then moved to the Chandra Mahal, at the opposite end of the garden, and installed the image as the guardian deity of Jaipur's rulers. Devotees are allowed only a brief glimpse of their god seven times a day, and on special festivals such as Janmashtami (*see p39*).

🌿 Jai Niwas Bagh
◯ 6am–10pm daily.
Just behind the temple is the 18th-century Jai Niwas Bagh, planned as a private leisure ground for the ladies of the royal household. Inspired by the classic Mughal

A view of the walled city of Jaipur

SIGHTS AT A GLANCE

Chaugan Stadium ⑤
City Palace Museum ①
Govt Central Museum ⑨
Govind Dev Temple ②
Hawa Mahal ⑧
Jai Niwas Bagh ③
Jantar Mantar ⑦
Talkatora ④
Tripolia Bazaar ⑥

♣ Talkatora

N of Jai Niwas Bagh. ⬭ *daily.*
The Talkatora is an artificial
tank that existed before Jaipur
was built. This may have
been one of the reasons why
this site was chosen for the
new city. When excavated, it
was surrounded on three
sides by a lake known as
Rajamal ka Talab, making it
look like a *tal-katora*, literally
a "bowl in a lake". Sawai Jai
Singh II was particularly fond
of this rather secluded spot
and used to breed crocodiles
here. The original lake was

later filled in and developed
as a residential area.

Chaugan Stadium

Brahmpuri. ⬭ *5am–8pm daily.*
This large open area near the
City Palace derives its name
from *chaugan*, an ancient
Persian form of polo played
with a curved stick. In the
past, this area was used for
festival processions, wrestling
matches, as well as elephant
and lion fights. The maharajas

VISITORS' CHECKLIST

*261 km (162 miles) from Delhi on
NH8.* 🚉 *2,324,000.*
✈ *Sanganer.* 🚌 🚌 *Sindhi
Camp.* ℹ *RTDC, Swagatam
Complex (0141) 220 3531.
Paryatan Bhavan, MI Rd
(0141) 511 0595.* 🏦 *Mon–Sat.*
🎉 *Gangaur (Mar–Apr), Elephant
Festival (Feb–Mar), Teej (Jul–Aug),
Kite Flying (mid-Jan).*

and nobility watched from the
pavilions of Chini ki Burj
(which still retains some of
the old blue and white
tilework), Moti Burj, Chatar ki
Burj and Shyam ki Burj, all
located here. *Chaugan* is not
played any more, but the
stadium is the venue for the
famous Elephant Festival held
at the time of Holi *(see p38)*.

Caparisoned elephant at a festival

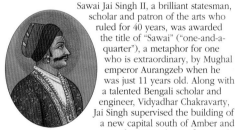

KEY

🟦 Street-by-Street area

Key to Symbols *see back flap*

THE BUILDING OF JAIPUR

**Sawai Jai Singh II
(r.1700–43)**

Sawai Jai Singh II, a brilliant statesman,
scholar and patron of the arts who
ruled for 40 years, was awarded
the title of "Sawai" ("one-and-a-
quarter"), a metaphor for one
who is extraordinary, by Mughal
emperor Aurangzeb when he
was just 11 years old. Along with
a talented Bengali scholar and
engineer, Vidyadhar Chakravarty,
Jai Singh supervised the building of
a new capital south of Amber and
named it Jaipur ("city of victory").
Work started in 1727 and took six
years to complete. Surrounded by
a crenellated wall pierced by seven gates, Jaipur is one of
North India's finest examples of a planned urban city. Its
grid of nine rectangular sectors, believed to represent the
nine cosmic divisions of the universe, is actually based on
a geometric and pragmatic plan with a system of main
streets, intersected by spacious market squares. Jai Singh
encouraged traders and artists to settle here, giving tax
incentives to merchants to ensure its economic prosperity.

Street-by-Street: Around Badi Chaupar

The Badi Chaupar ("large square") is at one end of the colourful Tripolia Bazaar. There have been few changes to the original 18th-century plan of streets and squares. Narrow pedestrian lanes branch out of the main streets where artisans fashion puppets, silver jewellery, and other local crafts in tiny workshops. Behind are the *havelis* of eminent citizens, some used as schools, shops and offices. The area is a hub of activity, rich with pungent smells and vibrant colours, with temple bells adding to the cacophony of street sounds.

Gangaur Festival
A colourful procession of bullock carts marks Gangaur festivities.

Ishwar Lat
Ishwari Singh built this tower in 1749 to commemorate his victory over his stepbrother, Madho Singh I.

City Palace

★ **Jantar Mantar**
Jai Singh II's observatory of astronomical instruments looks like a set of futuristic sculptures (see pp192–3).

Tripolia Gate

TRIPOLIA

MANIHARON KA RASTA

Chandpol

Chhoti Chaupar ("small square") leads to Kishanpol Bazaar, famous for its shops selling rose-, saffron-, almond- and vetiver-flavoured sherbets.

NATANIYON KA RASTA

KISHANPOL BAZAAR

Maharaja Arts College

Flower Sellers
Marigolds and other flowers made into garlands, sell briskly as offerings to beloved deities in temples and roadside shrines.

Lac Bangles
Maniharon ka Rasta is full of tiny workshops of lac bangle-makers.

★ Hawa Mahal
An unfamiliar rear view of the Hawa Mahal, seen from the City Palace.

★ Johari Bazaar
Vegetable sellers sit at one end of this street where the big gem dealers also have their offices and shops.

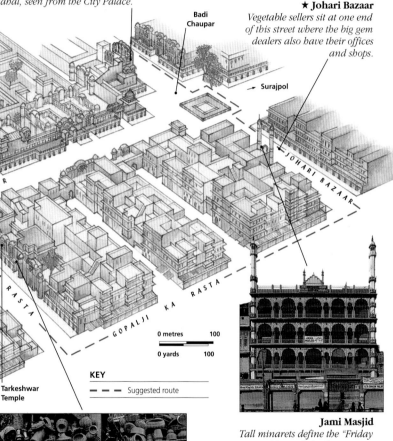

Badi Chaupar

Surajpol

JOHARI BAZAAR

ZAAR

HAURA RASTA

GOPALJI KA RASTA

| 0 metres | 100 |
| 0 yards | 100 |

KEY

– – – Suggested route

Tarkeshwar Temple

Jami Masjid
Tall minarets define the "Friday Mosque", its three storeys fronted by arched screens.

Pottery Shop
Large terracotta urns, pots of all sizes, bells, statues, foot-scrapers and oil lamps made by traditional craftsmen are sold here.

STAR SIGHTS

★ Jantar Mantar

★ Hawa Mahal

★ Johari Bazaar

⛩ Hawa Mahal

Sireh Deori Bazaar. **Tel** *(0141) 261 8862.* ◯ *9am–4:30pm.* ● *Holi & public hols.* 📷 ◎ *extra charges.*

A whimsical addition to Rajasthan's rich architectural vocabulary, the fanciful Hawa Mahal or "Palace of Winds" was erected in 1799 by the aesthete Sawai Pratap Singh (r.1778–1803). Its ornate façade has become an icon for the city, a tiered baroque-like composition of projecting windows and balconies with perforated screens. Though five storeys high it is just one room deep, with walls no thicker than 20 cm (8 inches). Built of lime and mortar and painted pink, this structure was so designed to enable the purdahed ladies of the harem to watch unnoticed the colourful street scenes and state processions on Sireh Deori Bazaar below. Visitors are permitted to climb up the winding ramp to the top.

Pratap Singh was a poet, composer and patron of the arts. A devotee of Krishna, he dedicated the Hawa Mahal to him, and many believe that when seen from afar, the building looks like the *mukut* (crown) that often adorns Lord Krishna's head.

A gateway towards the west leads into the complex and to

Façade of Hawa Mahal

the administrative offices and **Archaeological Museum**.

🏛 Archaeological Museum

Tripolia Bazaar. ◯ *9am–5pm.* ● *Fri & public hols.*

⛩ Tripolia Bazaar

To the south of the City Palace is one of the walled city's busiest streets and bazaars. The shops here mainly sell an enormous range of metal goods and kitchenware. The pavements outside the shops attractively display utensils in brass, copper, aluminium and steel as well as crowbars, chisels and other assorted hardware. Sometimes, handicrafts, plastic and paper products, such as the traditional red cloth-bound *bahi khathas* (account books) still used by merchants and moneylenders, are also available. At Badi Chaupar, towards the end of the street, are flower-sellers with baskets full of fragrant roses, marigolds, tuberoses and jasmine, and shops selling silver jewellery, hand-embroidered *jootis* (slippers) and feather-light cotton quilts.

Detail of a painted gate

In the centre of this lively commercial artery stands the majestic Tripolia ("triple-arched") Gate. Constructed in 1734, this was once the main entrance to the palace and on festive occasions, crowds watched the royal entourage of the maharaja and his nobles *(thakurs)*, clad in ceremonial robes, seated on elephants and horses, pass through this impressive gate. Today, its use is confined to members of the royal family and their special guests, and a guard on duty reminds visitors that this is not a public thoroughfare.

A short distance from Tripolia Gate, towards the east, is the well-maintained **Nawab Saheb ki Haveli**, named after Nawab Faiz Ali Khan, Ram Singh II's *(see p194)* prime minister. This 18th-century mansion was once the residence of Vidyadhar Chakravarty *(see p183)*, who is believed to have chosen this site to supervise the building of the new city of Jaipur. Its enclosed terrace offers some marvellous views of the city. Other *havelis* of eminent citizens can be seen in the narrow alleys off the main street. Some of these gracious old buildings are still occupied by descendants of the original owners, others have been rented out to schools, shops and offices.

⛩ Nawab Saheb ki Haveli

◯ *10am–6pm daily.* 📷

A view of Tripolia Gate with Ishwari Singh's victory tower seen in the distance

Jewellery

Be it the fabulous emeralds and rubies sported by former maharajas and their queens or the splendid silver and bone ornaments worn by peasants, jewellery is an integral part of Rajasthani culture. Even camels, horses and elephants are adorned with specially designed anklets and necklaces. Jaipur is one of the largest ornament-making centres in India, and *meenakari* (enamelling) and *kundankari* are two traditional

A kundankari pendant

techniques for which it is most famous. In the 16th century, Man Singh I *(see p49)*, influenced by the prevailing fashions of the Mughal court, brought the first five Sikh enamel workers from Lahore to his state. Since then, generations of highly skilled jewellers have lived and worked here. Jaipur caters to every taste, from chunky silver ornaments to elegant designs intricately set in gold with precious stones.

A jewelled trinket box *with a kundankari lid, the lower portion of this box is worked in fine meenakari and has traditional floral patterns in red, blue, green and white.*

Sarpech, *the cypress-shaped turban ornament, was a fashion statement introduced by the Mughal emperors in the early 17th century to display their finest gems. Rajput rulers, impressed by Mughal flamboyance, sported dazzling ornaments like this piece of enamelled gold set with emeralds, rubies, diamonds and sapphires with a pearl drop.*

The skill of setting stones *can be seen in the crowded alleys of Haldiyon ka Raasta, Jadiyon ka Raasta and Gopalji ka Raasta. An inherited art, the trade of jewellery is in the hands of artisans' guilds.*

Meenakari *embellishes the obverse side of* kundan *jewellery, for the Rajasthani love of adornment decrees that even the non-visible back of a piece of jewellery, which touches the wearer's skin, must be as beautiful as the front.*

Kundankari *uses a highly refined gold as the base, which is then inlaid with lac and set with precious and semi-precious stones to provide the colour and design. Purified gold wire outlines the design and also conceals the lac background.*

Jaipur *is now a centre of lapidary, specializing in the cutting of emeralds and diamonds that come from Africa, South America, and parts of India. Gem-cutters learn their skill by cutting garnets.*

City Palace Museum

Jaipur's coat-of-arms

Occupying the heart of Jai Singh II's city, the City Palace has been home to the rulers of Jaipur since the first half of the 18th century. The sprawling complex is a superb blend of Rajput and Mughal architecture, with open, airy Mughal-style public buildings leading to private apartments. The opulence and exquisite craftsmanship is a tribute both to the wealth of the former maharajas and their lavish patronage of the arts. Today, part of the complex is open to the public as the Maharaja Sawai Man Singh II Museum, popularly known as the City Palace Museum, but the beautiful Chandra Mahal remains the residence of the erstwhile maharaja.

★ Pritam Chowk
The "Court of the Beloved" has four delicately painted doorways representing the seasons.

Sileh Khana
The erstwhile armoury houses the museum's collection of weapons, some lavishly decorated, and is considered among the finest in India.

Crafts demonstration area

★ Mubarak Mahal
This sandstone "Welcome Palace" was built in 1900 by Madho Singh II to receive guests, hence the name. It is now the costume and textile gallery.

★ Rajendra Pol
Flanking the gateway are two large elephants, each carved from a single block of marble.

STAR FEATURES

★ Pritam Chowk

★ Mubarak Mahal

★ Rajendra Pol

★ Silver Urns

Chandra Mahal

Each floor of this seven-storeyed palace is extravagantly decorated and has a specific name according to its function. The palace is closed to the public.

VISITORS' CHECKLIST

City Palace Complex. ***Tel*** (0141) 260 8055. ☐ 9:30am–4.45pm daily. ● public hols. ☑ ◎ extra charges. ☑ ☑ **Director's permission needed to see Ram Singh II's Reserve Collection of photos.**

★ Silver Urns
Two giant silver urns in the Diwan-i-Khas, listed in the Guinness Book as the largest silver objects in the world, carried sacred Ganges water for Madho Singh II's visit to London in 1901.

Riddhi-Siddhi Pol

Shops

Transport gallery

Entrance   Ticket counter

Diwan-i-Aam
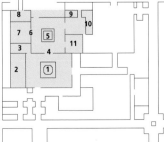
In the Art Gallery is this "golden throne" (Takht-e-Rawan) on which the maharaja sat when he appeared in public. It was either put on an elephant's back or carried by palanquin bearers.

THE CITY PALACE

1 Mubarak Mahal
2 Crafts Demonstration Area
3 Sileh Khana
4 Rajendra Pol
5 Diwan-i-Khas
6 Riddhi-Siddhi Pol
7 Pritam Chowk
8 Chandra Mahal
9 Shops
10 Transport Gallery
11 Diwan-i-Aam

KEY

☐ Building area

0 metres   200

0 yards   200

Exploring the City Palace Museum

Archery ring

The Maharaja Sawai Man Singh II Museum provides a splendid introduction to the arts and crafts and the courtly pomp and ceremony of Jaipur in the old days. In their long reign, which spanned almost a thousand years, the Kachhawaha rulers amassed a fabulous collection of treasures – rare manuscripts, miniature paintings, carpets, textiles, costumes and weaponry, palanquins and chariots. These are some of the royal and historical memorabilia displayed here. Initially a private collection open only to select visitors and dignitaries, in 1959 it was formally declared a state museum that is open to the public.

A detail of a gold-embroidered skirt belonging to one of the queens

TEXTILES AND COSTUMES GALLERY

A glittering collection of textiles and costumes from the royal *toshakhana* is displayed on the first floor of **Mubarak Mahal**. On view are rich, gorgeous brocades, known as *kimkhabs*, from Surat, Aurangabad and Varanasi, exquisitely embroidered and handloom-woven shawls from Kashmir, embroidered silks, embossed velvets and light, gossamer muslins typical of Dhaka (today in Bangladesh), which collectively represent India's great textile tradition. The expert and refined craftsmanship that existed in Jaipur almost three centuries ago is visible in the wide variety of hand blockprinted textiles from nearby Sanganer and tie-and-dye *(bandhini)* pieces specially produced by the printers and dyers from the palace workshops. Equally breathtaking is the

A tissue *ghaghara*, early 20th century

incredible range of well-preserved royal garments. Dazzling gathered skirts and long, flowing veils *(odhnis)*, decorated with delicate *zari* (gold thread embroidery) and *gota* (gold or silver frill), worn by the ladies of the court, vie for attention with the brocaded robes, waistbands *(patkas)*, pyjamas and turbans that comprised the male attire. The most striking of these royal robes is the enormous pale pink *atamsukh* ("comfort of the soul") of Sawai Madho Singh I (r.1750–68), who was 2 m (7 ft) tall and 1.23 m (4 ft) in girth, and weighed about 230 kg (500 lbs)! This long, quilted cloak-like robe, worn usually by men in winter, is embossed with gold work.

Other exhibits include a range of royal paraphernalia including rich tent hangings, curtains, carriage and dish covers dating back to the 17th century. Among these is a rare gold brocaded velvet throne cover bearing seal marks that date to 1605, and an intricately woven gold and silk circular *thal-posh* (dish-cover).

The lattice screens that run round the balcony here once enabled royal ladies to view the hall without being seen.

ART GALLERY

The Diwan-i-Aam or Sabha Niwas, built on a raised, pillared platform, was once used by the maharajas for formal durbars, ceremonies and receptions. This has now been converted into an art gallery, displaying some of the museum's greatest treasures. Exhibits include an excellent collection of 17th-century Mughal and Indo-Persian floral carpets, woven in Lahore, Herat and Agra during the reign of Emperor Shah Jahan. Also displayed here are the maharajas' valuable and fine collection of miniatures from the late Mughal, Rajput and Deccani courts, depicting both religious and secular themes. Some of the treasures include *Krishna Playing Holi* (Amber-Jaipur, 1737), *Lord Krishna's Cosmic Dance* (Jaipur, late 18th century), *Allah-Wirdi Khan with Attendants in a Garden* (Deccan, early 18th century), *Madho Singh I on a Boat* (Jaipur, 18th century) and *Nari Kunjar* (Jaipur, 18th century), an unusual compostion of female figures entwined imaginatively to

One of the rare Mughal miniatures in the Art Gallery

create an elephant. There is also a large selection of *Ragamala* and *Baramasa* sets depicting the seasons, as well as some superb paintings from Kishangarh *(see p215)* by Nihal Chand.

This gallery also has rare palm leaf manuscripts and books bound with painted wood covers, and scrolls of religious texts. Of particular interest are the two priceless Persian manuscripts of the Hindu epics, the *Ramayana* and the *Mahabharata*. The latter, known as *Razmnama*, was specially prepared, at huge cost, for Emperor Akbar by Abu'l Fazl, his biographer, and profusely illustrated by his court painters. Sadly, this unique manuscript is never displayed. Sawai Jai Singh II's large personal collection of astronomy books in Arabic, Persian, Latin and Sanskrit, which formed the basis for his study and understanding of the movement of the planets, is also kept in the art gallery.

Other interesting items are an ivory howdah, a silver mobile throne and a selection of old cameras and black and white prints dating to the reign of Ram Singh II (1835–80), a versatile ruler and passionate photographer.

Manuscript of the *Geet Govinda* in the Art Gallery

ARMS GALLERY

This gallery known as the Sileh Khana is located near the Mubarak Mahal. Some of the exhibits, displayed under exuberantly painted ceilings, are reputed to be the finest examples of weapons used in medieval India and are a tribute to the Rajput warrior's worship of arms. Whether specially commissioned, or acquired by the maharajas, the weapons in the royal armoury were both lethal and exquisitely crafted. On view are a range of swords, daggers and *katars*, a two-sided blade with a grip handle. Some are of green or white jade and are carved, while others are studded with jewels. Hilts are engraved with hunting

Diamond-studded dagger with pistols

Mughal helmet

scenes, images of gods and goddesses, or topped with the heads of exotic birds and animals. Among the swords on display is one belonging to Raja Man Singh I (r.1590–1619) weighing about 5 kg (11 lbs). Another, made by Abdullah Isfahani, bears the emblem of the Shah of Persia. There are two swords of Jahangir and Shah Jahan and also Akbar's gold-encrusted helmet, shaped like a turban. A fascinating section displays gunpowder containers, some made of ivory, others decorated with mother-of-pearl inlay on shell.

The gallery's collection also contains such gut-wrenching exhibits as a lotus-shaped steel mace belonging to Jai Singh I. When rammed into the enemy's stomach, it would spring into a deadly fan of sharp spikes and disembowel the victim.

TRANSPORT GALLERY

A comparatively recent addition is the Transport Gallery situated near the Art Gallery. It exhibits a selection of palanquins, chariots, *ikkas*, buggies and carriages from the old Buggi Khana which fell into disuse after the motor car became popular with the maharajas. Don't miss the gigantic Indra Vamaa carriage, which used to be pulled by four elephants. Until it was installed here, it was used only for ceremonial occasions. Now it conjures up some of the pomp of a bygone era.

Fragment of a 16th-century Persian carpet

Jantar Mantar

Kantivrita Yantra

Of the five observatories built by Sawai Jai Singh II, the one in Jaipur is the largest and best preserved; the others are in Delhi *(see p77)*, Ujjain, Mathura and Varanasi. A keen astronomer himself, Jai Singh was aware of the latest astronomical studies in the world, and was most inspired by the work of Mirza Ulugh Beg, the astronomer-king of Samarkand. Built between 1728 and 1734, this observatory resembles a giant sculptural composition of 16 instruments and has been described as "the most realistic and logical landscape in stone". Some of the instruments are still used to forecast how hot the summer months will be, the expected date of arrival, duration and intensity of the monsoon, and the possibility of floods and famine.

Narivalaya Yantra
Inclined at 27°, these represent the two hemispheres and are sundials that calculate time by following the solar cycle.

Unnatansha Yantra was used to determine the positions of stars and planets at any time of day or night.

Laghu Samrat Yantra
This "small sundial" is constructed on Latitude 27° North (Jaipur's latitude) and calculates Jaipur's local time up to an accuracy of 20 seconds.

City Palace Museum

Entrance

Chakra Yantra
A brass tube passes through the centre of two circular metal instruments through which the angle of stars and planets from the equator can be observed.

★ Ram Yantra
Vertical columns support an equal number of horizontal slabs in two identical stone structures that comprise this instrument. The readings from these determine the celestial arc from horizon to zenith, as well as the altitude of the sun.

Jantar Mantar
The complex of stone and metal instruments was repaired with the addition of marble inlay by Madho Singh II in 1901.

★ Samrat Yantra
Jai Singh believed that gigantic instruments would give more accurate results. This 23-m (75-ft) high sundial forecasts the crop prospects for the year.

Hawa Mahal

Rashivalaya Yantra
This is composed of 12 pieces, each of which represents a sign of the zodiac and so faces a different angle and constellation. This unique yantra is used by astrologers to make accurate horoscopes.

★ Jai Prakash Yantra
Two sunken hemispheres map out the heavens. This instrument is believed by some historians to have been invented by Jai Singh himself to verify the accuracy of all the others in the observatory.

STAR FEATURES

★ Ram Yantra

★ Samrat Yantra

★ Jai Prakash Yantra

South of the Walled City

Jaali detail

By the end of the 19th century, Jaipur had spread far beyond the boundaries established by Sawai Jai Singh II. Much of the area outside the walled city was developed by the enlightened ruler, Sawai Ram Singh II (r.1835–80). This able administrator also modernized the city by adding many civic amenities such as good roads, street lighting and running water. As Jaipur expanded, it incorporated the pleasure palaces and hunting lodges existing on its outskirts. The still-gracious city we see today is a harmonious blend of the old and the new.

The Indo-Saracenic-style Government Central Museum (Albert Hall)

🏛 Government Central Museum

Ram Niwas Bagh. **Tel** *(0141) 257 0099.* ⬜ *10am–4:30pm daily.* 📷 Ø

Designed by Sir Samuel Swinton Jacob, Albert Hall or the Government Central Museum was commissioned by Sawai Ram Singh II to honour the visit of Albert, the Prince of Wales, in 1876. Swinton Jacob had perfected the Indo-Saracenic style of architecture *(see p25)*, a hybrid form that combined modern European with traditional Indian elements to create a highly ornamental style used for many public buildings during the Raj.

This grand multi-layered building, with its domes, parapets and balustrades, is located in the centre of the Ram Niwas Gardens. Its ground floor displays decorative shields and embossed salvers in Jaipur's famed metalware, life-sized models of rural scenes, good examples of Jaipur's glazed pottery, and even an Egyptian mummy. A 30-ft (9-m) long *phad* (painted cloth scroll), depicts the life of Pabuji, a 14th-century Rajasthani folk hero. The first floor has a fine collection of Mughal and Rajput miniature paintings.

The museum's greatest treasure, one of the world's largest Persian garden carpets (1632) housed in the Durbar Hall, can be seen on request.

🏛 Museum of Indology

Nilambara, Prachaya Vidya Path, 24 Gangwal Park. **Tel** *(0141) 260 7455.* ⬜ *8am–6pm, daily.* 📷 🚫 Ø

The large mansion of the reputed scholar, Acharya RC Sharma "Vyakul", is now home to a privately owned museum that displays his unusual personal collection. Among the exhibits are impressive displays of maps and coins, manuscripts, textiles and jewellery, fossils, gems and clocks. The museum's

charm, however, lies in its idiosyncrasies, such as a map of India painted on a grain of rice, a copy of Rajasthan's oldest newspaper (1856), and letters written, incredibly, on a single strand of hair.

🏛 Moti Doongri

Jawaharlal Nehru Marg. ⬤ *to the public.*

Moti Doongri owes its florid exterior to Sawai Man Singh II who converted the old fort of Shankargarh into a palace, and added turrets in the style of a Scottish castle. In 1940 he married the beautiful Princess Gayatri Devi of Cooch Behar, and this palace with its modernized interior became the venue for glittering parties hosted by the glamorous couple for their wide circle of friends. After his death in 1970, the maharani, by then a Member of Parliament, lived here for some years to keep in touch with her constituency. The palace, a private property, is perched on a low hillock, with only its ramparts and the tall spire of an ancient Shiva temple visible from the road.

At the foot of Moti Doongri is the white marble **Lakshmi Narayan Temple**. This generously endowed building was erected in 1979 on a piece of land sold by the Jaipur royal family for a token sum to the Birlas, an important industrial family. Though the sale was disputed and created a huge uproar in the local press, the temple is now a popular place of worship, admired for its carvings.

Lakshmi Narayan Temple, a white marble addition to the Pink City

The luxurious interior of Rambagh Palace

✦ Statue Circle

Bhagwan Das Rd.

This popular landmark is a traffic roundabout, circling an imposing white marble statue of Sawai Jai Singh II, commissioned by the Sawai Jai Singh Benevolent Trust. It was installed in 1968 and is now a lunch-hour recreation spot for office workers and for evening joggers.

Facing the statue to the left is the **Birla Planetarium**. The complex comprises two modern buildings: the science museum with an auditorium, and the main planetarium. The main entrance of the building is a replica of Amber Fort's Ganesh Pol *(see pp200–201)*. Exhibitions and sales of Rajasthani handicrafts are held here periodically.

Statue of Sawai Jai Singh II

🏛 Birla Planetarium

Statue Circle, Prithviraj Rd.
⏰ 11am–8pm daily. **Tel** (0141) 238 3536. 📷 🚫

✦ Rambagh Palace

Bhawani Singh Rd. **Tel** (0141) 221 1919. 🍴 open to non-residents.

The Rambagh Palace, now a splendid hotel *(see p245)*, has had a colourful past. From its modest origins in 1835 as a small, four-roomed garden pavilion for Ram Singh II's wet nurse, it was used as a hunting lodge after she died in 1856. Later, when Ram Singh II's son, Madho Singh II returned from England, he transformed it with the help of Swinton Jacob into a royal playground with squash and tennis courts, a polo field and indoor swimming pool. In 1933 it was selected as the official residence of Madho Singh's adopted son and heir, Man Singh II, who invited Hammonds of London to re-do the interiors, adding a red and gold Chinese room, black marble bathrooms and fabulous Lalique crystal chandeliers, fountains and an illuminated dining table. Surrounded by fairy-tale gardens, this was the perfect setting for Man Singh and his lovely wife. Rambagh became the official residence of the Head of State of the new Rajasthan Union in 1949, and a hotel in 1957.

✦ Raj Mahal Palace

Sardar Patel Marg. **Tel** (0141) 510 5665. 🍴 open to non-residents.

Now a grand heritage hotel *(see p244)*, this 18th-century palace, less opulent than the Rambagh Palace, occupies a special place in the history of Jaipur. Built in 1739 for Sawai Jai Singh II's favourite queen, Chandra Kumari Ranawatji, it was used as a summer resort by the ladies of the court. In 1821, it was then declared the official home of the British Resident in Jaipur. However, the most glamorous and memorable phase of its colourful history dates to the time when Man Singh II and Gayatri Devi moved here from Rambagh Palace in 1956. Among the celebrities they entertained were Prince Philip, a polo player like Man Singh, and Jackie Kennedy.

Jawahar Kala Kendra

🏛 Jawahar Kala Kendra

Jawaharlal Nehru Marg. **Tel** (0141) 270 5879. ⏰ 10am–5pm. 🖥 📷

Designed by Indian architect Charles Correa in 1993, this remarkable building offers tribute to contemporary Indian design. Imaginatively patterned after the famous grid system of the city, each of the nine squares or courts houses a *mahal* named after a planet. Each *mahal* displays selected exhibits of textiles, handicrafts and weaponry, while in the centre there is a grand open air plaza where performances of traditional Rajasthani music and dance are also held.

POLO – THE GAME OF KINGS

Polo, said to be Central Asian in origin, was brought to India by the Muslim conquerors. Its requirement of superior cavalry skills made it a popular sport among Rajput royalty and the army. Man Singh II was a dashing polo player and formed the Jaipur polo team and club in the 1930s. Ironically, he died in England in 1970, playing the game he loved so well. Jaipur is still a well-known venue, and international figures such as Prince Philip and Prince Charles have played polo here.

A Jaipur polo player in action

Beyond Jaipur: East

Wall painting

Enclosing a narrow valley, a parallel range of hills runs along Jaipur's eastern periphery from Sanganer in the south up to Amber and beyond. This combination of rocky terrain and thickly wooded slopes provided an attractive environment for the rulers and nobility who built temples, garden pavilions and palaces here for themselves. The area is also known for its wildlife, particularly monkeys, after whom the valley is fittingly named the Valley of Monkeys.

One of Galta's sacred tanks

🛕 Galta

10 km (6 miles) E of Jaipur on Agra Rd.

The picturesque Galta gorge plunges down the hillside to join the Jaipur-Agra road. A great sage, called Galav, is supposed to have lived and performed penance here. Deep within the gorge is Galta Kund, an 18th-century religious site with two main temples dedicated to Ram and Vishnu; the Achariyon ki Haveli; and a number of smaller shrines and now derelict buildings. High on the ridge is the Surya Temple. At different levels are seven sacred tanks, fed throughout the year by natural spring water flowing from a rock resembling a cow's mouth. The water is said to have curative powers. The two *baradaris* on either side of the complex have fairly well preserved frescoes depicting legends from Krishna's life, including a ceiling profusely painted with gorgeous lotus blooms. From the summit there are spectacular views of Jaipur, but do beware of monkeys in search of food.

🌸 Sisodia Rani ka Bagh

Purana Ghat. 6 km (4 miles) E of Jaipur on Agra Rd. **Tel** (0141) 268 0494. ☐ 8am–6pm daily. 📷

This terraced garden was laid out in the 18th century for Sawai Jai Singh II's second wife, a Sisodia princess from Udaipur. The marriage was one of convenience, to foster better relations between the two powerful princely states, and one of the conditions was that the new queen's son would succeed to the Jaipur throne. To escape the ensuing and inevitable palace intrigues, the queen decided to shift to a more private home outside the walled city.

Her little double-storeyed palace is surrounded by beautiful gardens artfully planted with fragrant bushes of jasmine, where peacocks dance amid the spray of fountains and gurgling water channels. The interiors are decorated with lively murals depicting episodes from Krishna's life, hunting scenes and polo matches, mythical beasts and heroic events. Not surprisingly, this enchanting place has become a popular location for Indian films.

Environs

Opposite Sisodia Rani ka Bagh is **Vidyadhar ka Bagh**, a small and once beautiful 18th-century garden dedicated to the courtier traditionally credited with designing Jaipur *(see p183)*.

🛕 Ghat ke Balaji

1 km (4 miles) N of Sisodia Rani ka Bagh towards Galta.

Behind Sisodia gardens a double flight of steps ends in a pair of tall gateways leading to a small temple dedicated to the monkey-god Hanuman (also known as Balaji). This endearing deity is cherished by the local people who treat him with tender care, and in winter wrap his image in a muffler and quilt to keep him warm. The monkeys that inhabit the area are equally well looked after. Every evening at 4pm, a charming ritual takes place when, to the call of the priests, hordes of silver grey langurs with black faces and long tails descend on the temple for a meal specially cooked for them. Then, swishing their tails, they head back to the valley that bears their name.

🛕 Ghat ki Guni

6 km (4 miles) E of Jaipur on Agra Rd.

In the 18th and 19th centuries the ministers and dignitaries of the Jaipur court created a tranquil summer retreat in this valley, when the area would bustle with the constant to and fro of aristocracy. Now, the deserted *havelis*, temples

Sisodia Rani ka Bagh, laid out as a formal Mughal *charbagh*

Elegant *chhatris* of deserted buildings lining the Ghat ki Guni road

and bathing ghats are all that remain of this once exclusive resort. On either side of the road today, are dense rows of niched façades perforated by tiny windows and arched *chhatris*, elegant eaves and domes, while among the ruins and winding alleys, a number of tea-stalls and little shops selling trinkets and souvenirs have sprung up.

🛕 Ramgarh

40 km (25 miles) E of Jaipur.
Ramgarh, on the banks of a man-made lake, is the site of one of the earliest fortresses of the Kachhawahas. It was built by the dynasty's founder, Duleh Rai (r.1093–1135), after he defeated the local Meenas by attacking them on a Diwali night when they were for-bidden to carry weapons. A temple dedicated to the goddess Jamvai Mata, whose divine intervention is said to have led to his victory, was also constructed by him. This temple is visited by thousands of devotees all through the year. The lake itself was created in the late 19th century when Sir Samuel Swinton Jacob planned the con-struction of a dam across the Banganga River, and was, until recently, Jaipur's main source of drinking water. On its northern bank is Ramgarh Lodge, an elegant French villa-style hunting lodge built in 1931 for the Jaipur royal family, and now a pleasing heritage hotel *(see p245)*. Ramgarh is a tranquil retreat for those who wish to escape from the city and its Polo Club is one of the best in the country.

The man-made Ramgarh Lake

HANUMAN – THE MONKEY GOD

A much loved figure in the pantheon of Hindu gods *(see pp24–5)*, Hanuman appears wherever Rama is worshipped. In the *Ramayana (see p37)*, this loyal trooper and his monkey army play a crucial role in the defeat of Ravana and the rescue of Sita. To this day, warriors, acrobats and wrestlers regard him as their patron deity. The cult of Hanuman as a martial god and protector is so widespread that even a simple stone daubed with orange vermilion paste *(sindur)* signals his presence.

Yet, he has another more loveable side which widens the circle of his devotees. They believe this fearless warrior, who set Lanka afire and decimated Ravana's army, is ignorant of his own miraculous powers. Not only can he cure disease and exorcise evil spirits; he can cure infertility because his celibacy gives him that power. Others believe he also knows the secrets of yoga and the finer points of music and Sanskrit grammar. By combining the might of a martial god with the endearing qualities of the monkey he resembles, Hanuman becomes a link between warrior princes and simple peasants.

Hanuman statue

Beyond Jaipur: North

Mural motif

Towering above Jaipur are the two dramatic fortresses of Nahargarh and Jaigarh that guard the approach from the north to both Amber and the new capital of Jaipur. Today, they recall a bygone age when warrior clans fought for supremacy. The surrounding rocky terrain also has the remains of fortified walls, temples and shrines, *havelis* and the ornate marble cenotaphs of the Kachhawaha kings.

🏛 Nahargarh

9 km (5 miles) NW of Jaipur on Amber Rd. **Tel** (0141) 514 8044.
⏱ 10am–10pm daily. ⬤ public hols.
📷 🏛 🎨

The forbidding hill-top fort of Nahargarh ("tiger fort") stands in what was once a densely forested area. The fierce Meena tribe ruled this region until they were defeated by the Kachhawahas. Legend says that this was the site of the cenotaph of Nahar Singh, a martyred Rathore warrior, and when Sawai Jai Singh II ordered that its fortifications be strengthened to defend the newly-built Jaipur, the warrior's spirit resisted all construction until a priest performed tantric rites. Successive rulers further expanded the fort. Madho Singh II added a lavish palace called Madhavendra Bhavan for his nine queens. Laid out in a maze of terraces and courtyards, it has a cool, airy upper chamber from which the ladies of the court could view the city. Its walls and pillars are an outstanding example of *arayish*, a plaster-work technique that is hand-polished with a piece of agate to produce a marble finish.

🏛 Pundarik ki Haveli

Shastri Chowk, Brahmpuri.
Tel (0141) 241 1534.
⏱ 8am–5pm daily.
🎨 🚫

Lying to the east of Nahargarh, on the way to Gaitor, is the Brahmpuri area where the grand *havelis* of the pundits and scholars of the Jaipur court once stood. One mansion was the residence of Pandit Ratnakar Pundarik, a Brahmin courtier during the reign of Sawai Jai Singh II who, it is said, conducted the *puja* that appeased the spirit of Nahar Singh. Fortunately, this *haveli* has survived the ravages of time and is partly occupied. A portion is now a protected monument to preserve the superb frescoes decorating the walls and ceilings of the living rooms. These lively paintings depict gods and goddesses, courtly scenes and festival processions. One also portrays life on the different floors of the seven-storeyed Chandra Mahal (*see pp188–9*).

🏛 Gaitor

Brahmpuri. ⏱ 9am–4:30pm.
⬤ public hols.

The marble cenotaphs of the Kachhawaha kings are enclosed in a walled garden just below Nahargarh Fort. Sawai Jai Singh II chose this to be the new cremation site after Amber was abandoned (*see p203*). Ornate, carved pillars support the marble *chhatris* erected over the plat-forms where the maharajas were cremated. One of the most impressive cenotaphs is that of Jai Singh II himself. It has 20 marble pillars, carved with mythological scenes and

Maharani ki Chhatri

One of the exquisite, well preserved murals at Pundarik ki Haveli

The picturesque Jal Mahal seemingly afloat in the monsoon

topped by a white marble dome. Another is that of Sawai Ram Singh II, with stone pillars and dome panels carved with images of Hindu deities and scenes from Krishna's life. There is another sandstone and marble *chhatri* in memory of Madho Singh II. The most recent cenotaph was erected in 1997 in memory of Jagat Singh, the only son of Sawai Man Singh II and Gayatri Devi.

Environs
The *chhatris* of the official wives of the Jaipur kings are located in a separate enclosure called **Maharani ki Chhatri**, outside the Jorawar Singh Gate of the walled city, on the road to Amber. Set in a pleasant garden, the complex with its cupolas and carved pillars was restored in 1995.

🚩 Maharani ki Chhatri
Amber Rd. 🕘 *9am–4:30pm daily.*
● *public hols.* 📷

🚩 Jal Mahal
Amber Rd, opp Trident Hotel.
🕘 *restricted entry.*
During the monsoon when water fills the Man Sagar, the Jal Mahal or "water palace" seems to float serenely on the calm waters of the lake. Built in the mid-18th century by Madho Singh I, it was based on the Lake Palace at Udaipur where the king spent his childhood. Later it was used as a lodge for duck shooting parties, and even today, a large number of waterbirds can be sighted here. A terrace garden is enclosed by arched passages, and at each corner is a semi-octagonal tower capped by an elegant cupola.

Environs
Sawai Jai Singh II performed a number of Vedic *yagnas* on the western banks of Man Sagar. Dating to that period are traces of a **Yagna Stambha** ("pillar") where he performed a horse sacrifice, and the **Kala Hanumanji**, a temple dedicated to the well-known monkey god.

To the north of Jal Mahal is the splendidly restored **Kanak Vrindavan Temple** dedicated to Krishna, where the image of Govind Dev *(see p182)* was lodged before it was taken to the City Palace. This picturesque complex with its well-landscaped gardens, fountains and pavilions, makes a popular picnic spot.

🚩 Jaigarh
Amber Rd. **Tel** *(0141) 267 1848.*
🕘 *9am–4.30pm.* ● *public hols.* 📷
Legendary Jaigarh, the "victory fort", watches over the old capital of Amber, its great, crenellated outer walls delineating the edge of a sharp ridge for 3 km (2 miles)

from north to south. Located within the fort is one of the world's few surviving cannon foundries. Its most prized possession is the monumental Jai Van, cast in 1726 and believed to be the world's largest cannon on wheels. Its 6-m (20-ft) long barrel has fine carvings of elephants, birds and flowers. Ironically, despite its impressive size, the cannon remained a work of art and was never fired.

An interesting sight is the massive Diva Burj, a tower on whose uppermost seventh storey a huge oil lamp would be lit on the king's birthday and during Diwali, until the top two storeys were struck down by lightning. The fort has two temples and a large palace complex built over 200 years by different rulers. Located here are the Subhat Niwas (audience hall), the profusely painted Aram Mandir (an airy pleasure pavilion), the residential Laxmi Niwas with baths, and a small theatre for music, dance and puppet shows. The fort's intricate system of collecting and storing rainwater in huge tanks located in the courtyard is unique. Legend has it that Man Singh I's vast treasure, amassed during his military campaigns, was hidden within these tanks. In 1976, the government carried out a massive but unsuccessful hunt, even to the extent of draining the water tanks to locate this legendary trove.

The famous Jai Van

The ramparts of Jaigarh Fort, a feat of military engineering

Amber Fort ❷

Detail of door at Shila Devi

The fort palace of Amber was the Kachhawaha citadel until 1727, when their capital moved to Jaipur. However, successive rulers continued to come here on all important occasions to seek the blessings of the family deity, Shila Devi. The citadel was established in 1592 by Man Singh I on the remains of an earlier 11th-century fort, but various buildings added by Jai Singh I (r.1621–67) constitute its magnificent centrepiece.

Elephant ride on the cobbled pathway to the fort

Aram Bagh, the pleasure garden.

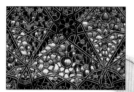

★ Sheesh Mahal
The flame of a single candle, reflected in the tiny mirrors embedded in this chamber, transforms it into a starlit sky.

Jas Mandir
This hall of private audience has latticed windows, a floral ceiling of elegant alabaster relief work and glass inlay. A marble screen here overlooks the Maota Lake and wafts in cool air.

Jai Mandir

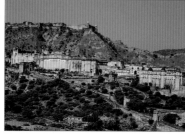

Location of Amber Fort
Protected by Jaigarh Fort, the massive ramparts of Amber Fort follow the contours of a natural ridge.

STAR FEATURES

★ Sheesh Mahal

★ Ganesh Pol

★ Shila Devi Temple

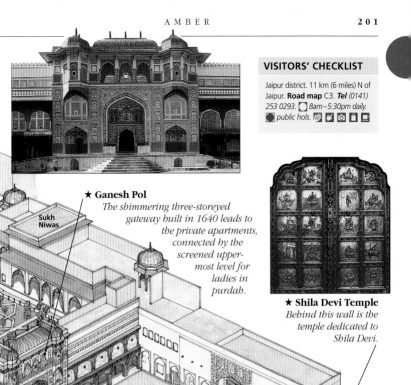

VISITORS' CHECKLIST

Jaipur district. 11 km (6 miles) N of Jaipur. **Road map** C3. **Tel** (0141) 253 0293. ⬤ 8am–5:30pm daily. ⬤ public hols. 🎟️ 📷 ⬤ ⬤ ⬤

★ **Ganesh Pol**
The shimmering three-storeyed gateway built in 1640 leads to the private apartments, connected by the screened upper-most level for ladies in purdah.

Sukh Niwas

★ **Shila Devi Temple**
Behind this wall is the temple dedicated to Shila Devi.

Sattais Katcheri

Diwan-i-Aam

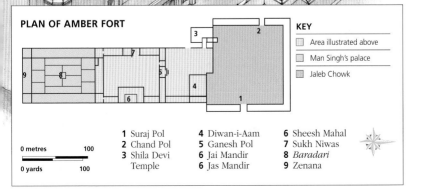

PLAN OF AMBER FORT

KEY

☐ Area illustrated above

☐ Man Singh's palace

☐ Jaleb Chowk

1 Suraj Pol	**4** Diwan-i-Aam	**6** Sheesh Mahal
2 Chand Pol	**5** Ganesh Pol	**7** Sukh Niwas
3 Shila Devi Temple	**6** Jai Mandir	**8** *Baradari*
	6 Jas Mandir	**9** Zenana

0 metres 100

0 yards 100

Exploring Amber (the Old Capital)

Painting detail on Ganesh Pol

Crowning the crest of a hill, Amber Fort offers a view of Maota Lake, two formal gardens, and the historic old town at the base of the hill, dotted with the remains of an older capital before it shifted to the precincts of the fort. Some of the old *havelis* and numerous temples here are well-preserved, while stepwells and lakes point to the existence of a self sufficient township where the Mughal emperor Akbar stopped on his annual pilgrimage.

Sattais Katcheri, where the revenue records were written

The Fort Complex

The main entrance to the historic Amber Fort is through the imposing **Suraj Pol** ("sun gate"), so called because it faces the direction of the rising sun, the Kachhawaha family emblem. This gate leads into a huge flagged courtyard, **Jaleb Chowk**, literally, "the square where elephants and horses are tethered". Originally the fort's parade ground, its central area is surrounded on three sides by guard rooms, now souvenir and refreshment shops. A flight of steps leads to the **Shila Devi Temple**, which contains the image of the Kachhawaha family deity, a stone (*shila*) goddess Kali, brought here by Man Singh I from Bengal in 1604. The temple has ornately carved silver doors presented by the second wife of the last maharaja in 1939, silver oil lamps and grand pillars of green marble carved to look like banana trees.

The next courtyard has the **Diwan-i-Aam**, the space for public audience. Near it are 27 (*sattais*) airy colonnades, called the **Sattais Katcheri**, where scribes once sat to record revenue petitions.

The magnificent **Ganesh Pol** is the gateway to three private palaces built around a Mughal-style garden (*see p167*), **Aram Bagh**. Each of these pleasure-palaces has some special feature. Sukh Niwas has doors carved from fragrant sandalwood, and water cascades over marble chutes to cool the interior. The marble Jai Mandir, at the other end of the garden, has the superb **Sheesh Mahal** studded with mirrors. The adjoining **Jas Mandir** has a marble screen across its eastern façade that overlooks the Maota Lake.

The lake, which provided water to the fort, is surrounded by two exquisite gardens. The **Kesar Kyari Bagh** has star-shaped flower beds once planted with saffron (*kesar*) flowers, while **Dilaram Bagh**, built in 1568 as a resting place for Emperor Akbar on his way to Ajmer, is a clever pun on the name of its architect, Dilaram ("heart's ease"). A small archaeological museum is located near Dilaram Bagh.

The furthermost end of the fort, which was also its oldest section, was converted into the **Zenana** ("women's quarters") by Man Singh I to house his 12 wives and concubines. The apartments bear the distinct stamp of Mughal zenana architecture, with screens and covered balconies for the protection and purdah of the royal ladies. Faint traces of frescoes are still visible on the walls. In the centre of the courtyard is a colonnaded pavilion called the **Baradari**.

Kesar Kyari Bagh, named after rare saffron flowers once planted in its star-shaped flower beds

Bharmal ki Chhatri, the old cenotaphs of the Kachhawaha rulers

The Township

The **Chand Pol** ("moon gate"), directly opposite Suraj Pol, leads to the old town outside the fort. The **Narsimha Temple**, built in the early 15th century by the Kachhawaha king Narsingh Dev, is the first of many on this route. The temple itself is only a small part of a derelict palace complex which was the site of past coronations before the Amber rulers abandoned it for the fort.

East of this lies the beautiful **Jagat Shiromani Temple**, erected in the early 17th century by Man Singh I in memory of his eldest son, Jagat Singh. A remarkable *toran* (carved lintel) adorns the doorway of the temple which has images of Vishnu, Radha and Krishna. Legend says that the Krishna image was brought here in the 16th century by the saint-poetess Mira Bai, famous for her devotion to Lord Krishna, from Chittorgarh, her home in southern Rajasthan.

Moving further east is the **Sanghi Jutharam Temple** which at one time had a beautiful 12-sided well, a small garden and several chambers. It is now protected by the Archaeological Survey of India (ASI). To its northeast lies the **Ambikeshwar Mahadev Temple**, dedicated

Marble carving in Narsimha Temple

to a manifestation of Shiva. One of the oldest temples here, it now stands 3 m (10 ft) below ground level and is said to be slowly sinking.

North of the Ambikeshwar Temple is **Panna Mian ka Kund**, built in the 17th century by a eunuch Panna Mian, a leading figure at the court of Raja Jai Singh I. From here, there is a cobbled path winding eastwards past further ruins and out through **Kheri Gate**, one of the old gates of Amber, leading to a popular picnic spot called **Sagar**, with its two terraced lakes. These were once important sources of water supply during times of siege. Located in a depression formed by the surrounding hills, just behind Jaigarh Fort, the site still bears traces of an elaborate water transport system in which elephants were used to carry water up to the fort.

These monuments lie to the west of the main Jaipur-Delhi highway that cuts across the town. The main market and the Amber bus stand are also located along this road, which is

now almost entirely occupied by tiny wayside eateries and souvenir shops. Further along this road, to the north, stands the **Akbari Mosque**, built by Emperor Akbar in 1569 at one of the spots where he stopped to pray on his way to Ajmer *(see pp218–19)*. The basic structure of the mosque remains intact even though it has been often repaired.

Further westwards down this road is **Bharmal ki Chhatri**, a walled enclosure containing a group of memorials. This was the old cremation site for the rulers of Amber until a new spot was established at Gaitor *(see pp198–9)* after the capital moved from Amber to Jaipur.

Steps criss-crossing down to the water in the partly restored Panna Mian ka Kund

Marble statue of a Jain *tirthankara* at Sanganer's Sanghiji Temple

Sanganer ❸

Jaipur district. 16 km (10 miles) SW of Jaipur. **Road map** C3. ✈ 🏠 *daily.*

Two ornate triple-arched gateways lead into Sanganer, a colourful town renowned for its blockprinted cotton textiles. According to local lore this tradition of blockprinting goes back to the 16th century when Sanga, one of the 18 sons of Prithviraj, the Kachhawaha ruler of Amber, re-established the town. Printers from nearby villages were asked to migrate to this new settlement to develop a range of textiles for the Jaipur court. It was Sanganer's river with its mineral powers of fixing the colours of the dyes that gave this printing village its fame and wealth. Today, the town resounds with the thud of printing, as craftsmen work in their sheds amidst bolts of cloth, dye-soaked pads and wooden blocks. Most of the printers and dyers in the town belong to a guild with retail outlets that sell reasonably priced fabric, tailored linen and accessories.

Sanganer is also a centre of handmade paper, a spin-off from textile printing, and Jaipur's famous Blue Pottery *(see p266)*. Raja Man Singh I of Amber *(see p49)* set up the first workshops here to produce this special type of hand-painted pottery inspired by Persian and Chinese blue and white tiles so popular at the Mughal court.

Frieze at Sanghiji Temple

Tucked away in the old walled town is an impressive 11th-century Jain temple. The **Sanghiji Temple** was probably built by a Jain trader with additional donations from the town's other wealthy merchants. Like other Jain temples found elsewhere in Rajasthan, this too is lavishly decorated with ornate stone carvings that include images of all the 24 Jain *tirthankaras* (saints) and a beautiful statue of Mahavira, the founder of Jainism, in the innermost sanctuary.

Sanganer is now a busy suburb of Jaipur city and the location of its airport.

Bagru ❹

Jaipur district. 32 km (20 miles) SW of Jaipur past Sanganer on Ajmer Rd. **Road map** C3. 🚌 🏠 *daily.*

The small village of Bagru is yet another traditional textile printing centre. Unlike the refined prints of Sanganer, Bagru's are bolder and more earthy, and originally had a limited colour palette of red and black. The indigo, yellow and green that we see today are later additions. The origins of blockprinting in Bagru date back some 300 years, when the first few printing families were brought to this village by the then *thakur* of Bagru, an important fiefdom of the Jaipur kings. Over time, more printers settled here, lured by state patronage as well as the abundant supply of water, so essential for printing.

Bagru's printers *(chhipas)* supplied the fabric that was used by the local farming communities as both stitched and unstitched garments. As the demand for blockprinted textiles increased, their clientele became more varied and their range of products more diversified. Yet, in many ways, little has changed and this is one of the few places to see the printing process at work. Craftsmen still follow the traditional methods of resist-printing, blockprinting and bleaching, and though the use of synthetic dyes has crept in, some colours, such as black and yellow, are still extracted from vegetable and mineral matter.

Faded wall paintings outside the palace at Bagru

Blockprinted Textiles

Delicate flowers and foliage, paisleys, birds and animals on a white background are Sanganer's typical motifs. Handed down from father to son, these designs were inspired by the flower studies of miniature paintings *(see pp30–31)* and Mughal *pietra dura* motifs *(see pp156–7)*. Blockprinting can be seen in the workshops of the city's Chhipa Mohalla, where each stage of this ancient technique, from

An intricate paisley motif

chiselling intricate patterns on wooden blocks, to dyeing the fabric in huge copper vats on wood-fed fires, and printing, is all done by hand. In the more complex designs, a single motif may use up to ten different colours with as many blocks, each with a different design. In the final stage, swathes of printed cloth are spread on riverbanks or hung on huge frames to dry under the sky.

Sanganeri motifs *of stylized flowers* (phool) *and leaves* (buti) *in soft colours re-create a field of dainty flowers.*

Textile printing *is done with wooden blocks. These are dipped in dye to print the cloth stretched across a low stool. Earlier, colours were extracted from vegetable and mineral matter. Pomegranate rinds, saffron, madder root, turmeric and the indigo plant were some natural sources. Chemicals have now replaced natural dyes.*

Wooden printing blocks *are carved by hand with popular design motifs. Traditional designs have today been enlivened by inputs from modern Indian fashion designers.*

Bagru's *floral, figurative and geometric motifs are printed on a coarse cotton cloth that is made into blouses and gathered skirts worn by local women. However, in recent years, these earthy prints have become popular in urban centres too.*

HANDMADE PAPER

The Kagazi Mohalla, the colony of papermakers, recycles scraps of cloth and silk thread to produce an impressive range of decorative and functional paper products. Fabric is first converted into pulp and then flattened on a wire mesh. The thin sheets of paper are finally peeled off and hung up to dry. These craftsmen jealously preserve their trade secrets and seldom marry outsiders.

Sheets of handmade paper hung to dry

Alwar

Gate of Fateh Jang's Tomb

Situated between Mughal and Rajput territories, Alwar's place in history was manipulated by its rulers who made shrewd alliances to gain political leverage. Alwar's growth from a vassal state of the Kachhawaha kings to a significant Rajput state came about after Pratap Singh captured the fort of Bala Qila in 1775. Later, as the British cultivated it as a friendly base in Rajputana, there followed a burst of architectural extravagance that went along with a lavish round of tiger shoots, as its rulers tried to rival the glittering lifestyle of their cousins in Jaipur. Today, Alwar is a dusty provincial town with some remarkable monuments, mostly visited by tourists on their way to the Sariska National Park.

From the *Gulistan*, an 18th-century Mughal manuscript

City Palace

Near Collectorate. ☐ 10am–4:30pm.
A stunning profusion of architectural features marks this palace, with Rajput *bangaldar* eaves and elegant *chhatris* alongside Mughal floral tracery and *jaalis*. Built in 1793, the District Collectorate and Police Headquarters now occupy most of the palace, so it is best viewed from the large central courtyard. A stairway flanked by two marble kiosks leads from here to the gorgeous Durbar Hall and Sheesh Mahal, to see which special permission is needed.

A door on the right of the courtyard leads to the **City Palace Museum**, spread over three halls of the upper storey. These contain some treasures of the erstwhile rulers, such as their famed collection of miniature paintings of the Alwar, Jaipur and Mughal schools. The 7,000 rare manuscripts in Persian, Arabic,

Dagger, City Palace Museum

Urdu and Sanskrit include an illuminated Koran, a version of the rare and precious *Gulistan* of the great Persian poet Sa'adi, as well as the *Babur Nama* or "Memoirs of Babur" (1530). The awesome armoury display includes the swords of Mohammed Ghori, Akbar and Aurangzeb, and a macabre coil called *nagphas*, used for strangling enemies. The first room contains a silver dining table with dividers, through which moving metal shoals of swimming fish can be seen. Behind the palace, across a magnificent *kund*, is the cenotaph of Maharaja Bakhtawar Singh (r.1790–1815). It is locally known as **Moosi Maharani ki Chhatri** after his mistress who performed *sati* here when he died. One of Rajasthan's most elegant monuments, blending brown sandstone and white marble, its carved pavilion has domed arches with exquisite

floral tracery, and ceilings adorned with fading gold leaf paintings of mythological characters and courtly scenes.

🏛 City Palace Museum
☐ 10am–4:30pm. ● Fri & public hols. 🎫 📷

� Moosi Maharani ki Chhatri
☐ 10am–4:30pm. ● Fri & public hols. 🎫 *Shoes not allowed.*

♘ Bala Qila
☐ *daily. Written permission is needed from the office of the Superintendent of Police, City Palace.*
Perched on a steep hill above the city, easily accessible by car, the Bala Qila was originally a 10th-century mud fort. Several additions were made to it by the Jats and Mughals (Babur is said to have spent a night here) until it was finally captured in 1775 by Pratap Singh of Alwar. Now a police wireless station, this sprawling fort was defended by 66 large and small towers. The frescoed palace within, the Nikumbh Mahal, was named after its first occupants, the Nikumbh Rajputs. The entire city can be seen from the fort's extensive ramparts, which give an idea of its scale and of the engineering skills that went into its building. Also visible are the ruins of Salim Mahal, named after Jahangir (Salim), who was exiled here after he plotted to kill Abu'l Fazl, Akbar's official biographer and one of the "nine gems" of his court.

The elegant marble pavilion at Moosi Maharani ki Chhatri

The aqueduct which brought water from Siliserh to the Company Bagh

VISITORS' CHECKLIST

Alwar district. 150 km (93 miles) NE of Jaipur. **Road map** C3. 🏘 260,000. 🚌 Nehru Marg. 🚍 Manu Marg. 🛈 TRC, near Railway Station, Alwar (0144) 234 7348; Paryatan Bhavan, MI Road, Jaipur (0141) 511 0595. 🏬 daily. 🎭 Jagannathji Fair (Mar–Apr), Laldas Mela (May), Sawan Teej (Jul–Aug), Diwali (Oct–Nov).

♣ Company Bagh

Vivekanand Marg. ◷ 6am–6pm.
A lovely garden when it was laid out in 1868, the Company Bagh is now a shadow of its former self. It was originally named after Alwar's British ally and protector, the East India Company. Later, it was christened Purjan Vihar by Maharaja Jai Singh. An enchanting greenhouse here is named "Simla", because it reminded the maharaja of the British summer capital in North India. A three-km (two-mile) long aqueduct, made of solid stone masonry, brought water from a reservoir at Siliserh to this garden.

🛈 Fateh Jang's Tomb

Near Railway Station.
◷ 9:30am–4:30pm.
The tomb of Fateh Jang, one of Shah Jahan's ministers, is a five-storeyed monument, constructed in 1647. Dominated by an enormous dome, its walls and ceiling have raised plaster reliefs, and fine calligraphic inscriptions can be seen on the first floor. A school now occupies the tomb's compound.

Environs
To the north of Alwar, located at the edge of Vijay Sagar Lake, is the 105-roomed **Vijay Mandir Palace**, built to look like an anchored ship by Jai Singh (r.1892–1937). A great builder of palaces, the eccentric Jai Singh had the famous 100-roomed Moti Doongri palace-fortress to the south of the Company Bagh blown up because it offended his sensibilities. Vijay Mandir was his last official residence and he lived here for many years. The former ruling family still occupies it and reserves the right of admission to it.

Alwar is full of apocryphal stories of Jai Singh's strange tastes. His Bugatti cars were "buried" after he tired of them, and he once ordered a custom-made gold Lancaster car that resembled the King of England's coronation coach, minus the horses!

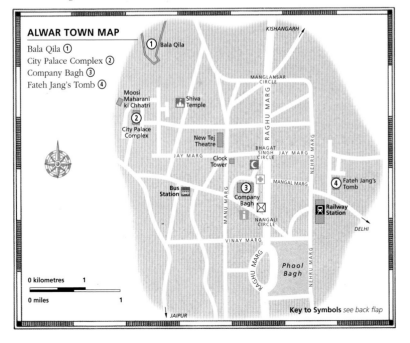

ALWAR TOWN MAP

Bala Qila ①
City Palace Complex ②
Company Bagh ③
Fateh Jang's Tomb ④

KISHANGARH

① Bala Qila

MANGLANSAR CIRCLE

Moosi Maharani ki Chhatri

Shiva Temple

② City Palace Complex

RAGHU MARG

New Tej Theatre

JAY MARG

Clock Tower

BHAGAT SINGH JAY MARG CIRCLE

NEHRU MARG

Bus Station

③ Company Bagh

MANGAL MARG

④ Fateh Jang's Tomb

NANGALI CIRCLE

Railway Station

MANU MARG

VINAY MARG

DELHI

RAGHU MARG

Phool Bagh

NEHRU MARG

0 kilometres 1
0 miles 1

↑ JAIPUR

Key to Symbols see back flap

Siliserh ⑥

Alwar district. 13 km (8 miles) SW of Alwar. **Road map** C3. 🛈 *TRC, near Railway Station, Alwar (0144) 234 7348.* 🌐

This enchanting spot is midway between Alwar and Sariska National Park *(see pp210–11)*. The 10.5 sq km (4 sq miles) Siliserh Lake, in a valley bounded by low forested hills, is still the main reservoir supplying water to Alwar and the surrounding area. Perched on a hillock overlooking the lake is the water palace built in the mid-19th century by the king of Alwar, Vinay Singh, for his beautiful wife, a local village girl, so that she could be near her family home. This once-grand palace is now a hotel and an ideal place for a quiet getaway, as the only sounds one hears are those made by cormorants, ducks and other waterbirds. Pathways lead up the foothills and around the lake where the remains of old cenotaphs still stand. From the palace's open terrace there are wonderful views of the sun setting over the lake.

Rajgarh Fort, once the capital of the Alwar kings

Rajgarh ⑦

Alwar district. 35 km (22 miles) S of Alwar. Road map C3. 🛈 *TRC, near Railway Station, Alwar (0144) 234 7348.* 🌐

Overlooking a picturesque valley, with green fields and citrus groves, is the grand hilltop fort of Rajgarh, the old capital of the Alwar rulers. Built by the founder of the dynasty, Pratap Singh, in the mid-18th century, its status as the capital was brief, and in 1775, when Pratap Singh captured Bala Qila *(see p206)*, the court moved to Alwar. The fort, however, with its once beautiful Sheesh Mahal, frescoed walls and secret passages, was maintained as a summer residence, but over time it fell into disuse until finally it was abandoned. The town, too, at the foot of the hill, wears a desolate look.

Sariska National Park ⑧

See pp210–11.

Bairat ⑨

Alwar district. 64 km (40 miles) SW of Alwar. **Road map** C3. 🛈 *TRC, near Railway Station, Alwar (0144) 234 7348.* 🌐

Nowhere is the age and majesty of the Aravalli Hills as apparent in the region as it is at Bairat. The striking topography of giant rocks, variously textured and shaped, provides a dramatic backdrop for an excavated, ancient archaeological site that dates back to the 3rd century BC. One of the cities along the main north-south trade route, this was a major Buddhist centre. A rock edict of Emperor Ashoka (273–232 BC) was found here, and at one end of the village, off a dirt track, high on a hillock locally known as Bijak ki Pahadi, are the remnants of a Buddhist monastery and circular temple. It is believed to be India's oldest free-standing structure. Historians have identified it as a *chaitya* hall or chapel which was once supported by 26 octagonal wooden columns.

Siliserh Palace, built on a hillock overlooking the lake

Bairat's history, however, goes back to the time of the *Mahabharata* (around the 9th century BC), when this land formed part of a kingdom comprising much of eastern Rajasthan, and was ruled by King Virat from his capital of Viratnagar (present Bairat). It was here that the Pandavas *(see p141)* spent the 13th year of their exile. Locals believe that one of the Pandava brothers, the mighty Bhim, lived at **Bhim ki Doongri** ("Bhim's hillock"), and that Arjuna created the River Banganga when he struck an arrow into the earth. King Virat joined the Pandavas in the battle at Kurukshetra, and his daughter married Arjuna's son, Abhimanyu.

On the other side of town, near the rock edict, is an early 17th-century garden mansion dating to Jahangir's reign. Within the compound is a Jain temple, and just outside is the charming 16th-century hunting lodge where Akbar camped on his way to Ajmer. Locally known as the Chhatri, it was built on a raised platform, with five well-sculpted pavilions.

Remains of the circular temple dating to the Buddhist period, Bairat

Bhangarh ❿

Alwar district. 56 km (35 miles) S of Sariska via Thana Gazi. **Road map** C3. ⓘ *TRC, near Railway Station, Alwar (0144) 234 7348.* 🚍

A bumpy ride from Sariska will take you to the abandoned city of Bhangarh, a fascinating site said to be a Kachhawaha clan citadel before Amber. Local legend says that the place was deserted when cursed by an evil magician, and many of its structures were transported to the new capital, Ajabgarh.

Built in the early 17th century by Madho Singh, the younger brother of Amber's Raja Man Singh I *(see p49)*, Bhangarh, also known as the "City of Ten Thousand Homes", exemplifies the hierarchy of traditional town planning.

A stone colonnaded pathway lined with market kiosks, stables or residences leads to the inner sanctum at the foot of the hills where a ruined palace, derisively called Randiyon ka Mahal ("palace of the prostitutes") remains, overlooking the Someshwar Temple, still in use. Three other temples dot the sprawling site, of which the Mangala Devi Temple, with a corbelled dome and finely carved exterior, is by far the most imposing.

Environs
On the road to Bhangarh is Ajabgarh, built by Madho Singh's grandson as a new settlement for the people of Bhangarh. Part of the old town is under water, but a fort and some ruins may still be seen.

Carved bracket from the Mangala Devi Temple, Bhangarh

THE PANDAVAS IN EXILE

The great epic, the *Mahabharata (see p141)*, describes how, after losing the Pandava kingdom and wife Draupadi to the wicked Kauravas at a game of dice, Prince Yudhishthira, along with his brothers, Bhim, Arjuna, Nakul and Sahdev, were banished to 13 years of exile. The last year was the most crucial and had to be spent in complete anonymity for, if recognized, it meant another 12 years of exile. Forced to accept these rigid terms, the Pandavas roamed the country, spending their 13th year in disguise at the court of King Virat. The story of the Pandavas, their exile and the final battle are important components of the land's folklore, while sites such as Kurukshetra *(see p140)*, associated with their adventures, are venerated pilgrim spots.

The five Pandava brothers, from a popular TV serial

Sariska National Park

Silk cotton flower

Designated a tiger reserve under Project Tiger *(see p223)* in 1979, the park sprawls over 800 sq km (308 sq miles) with a core area of 480 sq km (185 sq miles). The Aravallis branch out at Sariska, forming low plateaux and valleys that harbour a wide spectrum of wildlife in the dry jungles. Formerly the private hunting ground of Alwar State, Sariska owes a debt to the strict game and protection laws laid down by its conservation-conscious rulers, which preserved its natural habitat and wildlife. A 17th-century fortress and several ancient temple ruins, such as the Pandupol Temple, also lie within the park.

Langur Monkeys
These black-faced primates with long tails are known as Hanuman langurs.

Sariska Palace
An elegant 19th-century hunting lodge of the Alwar rulers, this palace, now a luxury hotel, has a collection of vintage photographs of past hunts, and period furnishings.

Endangered Species
Rampant poaching in recent years has resulted in the depletion of the park's tiger population.

Water Holes
To combat the chronic shortage of water in the region, the Forest Department has laid out a series of water holes at Pandupol, Bandipol, Slopka, Kalighati and Talvriksha. These make good vantage points to view wildlife, especially at sunset, when herds of animals flock to them to quench their thirst.

JAIPUR

Thanaghazi

Bandipol

Sariska

Bha

Kar

Entrance

Udainath Kankwadi

Kalighat

Te

Flora

The dry deciduous forests of Sariska come to life during the brief spring and early summer when the flowering dhak *(Butea monosperma) and laburnum bloom. The date palm begins to bear fruit, while berries, locally known as* kair *(Capparis decidua) appear on the bushes.*

Jackal

Jackals and hyenas often lead trackers to a tiger kill. Along with panthers and jungle cats, these carnivores feed on the many species of deer, nilgai or blue bull, wild boar and porcupine in the forest.

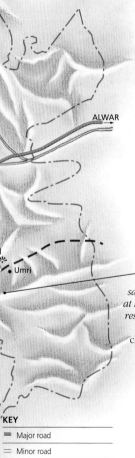

ALWAR

0 kilometres 5

0 miles 2

Umri

Cheetal

The gentle cheetal or spotted deer, like the sambar, is commonly seen at the park's water holes, or resting under the trees. The other deer species, the chowsingha *(four-horned antelope), is specific to Sariska and can be seen around Pandupol.*

KEY

🟰	Major road
═	Minor road
─	Park border
🔆	Viewpoint
─	Trails
⋔	Archaeological sight, ruin
🏠	Palace
🛕	Temple
ℹ️	Information centre

Grey Partridge

The hides at Kalighati and Slopka are ideal for observing the park's birdlife, such as the crested serpent eagle, the great Indian horned owl, woodpeckers, kingfishers and partridge.

Chomu ⓫

Jaipur district. 32 km (20 miles) NW
of Jaipur. **Road map** C3. *TRC
Govt Hostel, MI Rd, Jaipur (0141) 511
0598.* daily.

The small town of Chomu
links Jaipur with the
Shekhawati region. Traces of
a grander past are visible in
its once impressive fort,
handsome *havelis* and stepwells. But Chomu's charm lies
in its rural ambience, where
bullocks and camels plough
the fields, and the unique
four-pillared well is the main
source of water. In the
market, tractor spare parts
and tubewell pump-sets vie
for attention with hand-carts
spilling over with mounds of
cucumbers and *ber (Zizyphus
mauritiana)*, a berry for
which the region is famous.

Samode ⓬

Jaipur district. 42 km (26 miles) NW
of Jaipur. **Road map** C3. *TRC
Govt Hostel, MI Road, Jaipur (0141)
511 0598.* daily. *Gangaur
festival (Mar–Apr).*

Samode's romantic palace,
immortalized in films such
as *The Far Pavilions*, is the
main reason why this minor
Rajput hamlet is now a

The fairy tale Samode Palace, a luxurious retreat set amidst rugged hills

luxurious tourist destination.
Erected in the late 19th
century by a powerful noble
of the Jaipur state, this jewel-
like palace nestles among the
hills below an older hill fort.

A flight of stairs leads up to
a massive gateway and into
the palace. Its simple exterior
is highly deceptive for, surrounding the vast central
courtyard, are spacious rooms
on three levels. Of these, the
chambers on the uppermost
level are the most opulent.
The Durbar Hall, Sheesh
Mahal and Sultan Mahal are
embellished with dazzling
mirrorwork and elaborate
murals that depict courtly life,
hunting scenes and religious
themes, along with floral and
geometric motifs. The murals

represent the best of the
Jaipur style and are said to
rival those at Jaipur's Chandra
Mahal *(see pp188–9)* and
Tonk's Sùnehri Kothi *(see
p222)*. However, entrance is
restricted since it is now a
luxury hotel *(see p247)*.

A short distance away is
Samode Bagh *(see p246)*
where the more adventurous
can stay in one of the 50
deluxe tents pitched in the
formal garden. Other points
of interest are the abandoned
old fort at the end of a
strenuous walk up 376 steps,
and the quaint little village
where a wide variety of local
handicrafts such as hand-
woven *dhurries*, tie-and-dye
fabric, lac bangles and *jootis*
(slippers) are available.

THE PAINTED HAVELIS OF SHEKHAWATI

In the many little towns of Shekhawati are the ancestral
homes of some of India's leading industrialist families, such
as the Birlas, Dalmias and Goenkas. These sprawling old
havelis with their exuberantly frescoed walls *(see p27)* were
built between the late 18th and early 20th centuries by the

A "pop art" view of Rajput
chieftains

local Marwari merchants who
had migrated to the port-cities
of Bombay and Calcutta to seek
their fortunes. Their interaction
with the British and exposure to
modern urban and industrial
trends influenced their lifestyles, and their homes reflected the
new ideas they brought back with them, as well as their new-
found wealth and social status.

The entrance to Biyani
Haveli, Sikar

The style and content of the Shekhawati frescoes are a telling
comment on the urbanization of a traditional genre. The local
artists still followed the one-dimensional realism of traditional
Indian painting *(see pp30–31)*, but juxtaposed among the gods,
goddesses and martial heroes are images from a changing world.
In their celebration of contemporary "pop" themes, the frescoes
of British ladies, top-hatted gentlemen, brass bands and soldiers,
trains, motor cars, aeroplanes, gramophones and telephones,
symbolize the emerging industrial society of the late 19th century.

A Tour of Shekhawati ⑬

Northeast of Jaipur, situated along the old camel caravan trade route, lies Shekhawati, or the "garden of Shekha", named after Rao Shekha, a fiercely independent ruler who consolidated the region in the 15th century. Today, the region resembles a vast open-air museum full of frescoed mansions. A network of excellent roads through semi-arid scrubland connects most towns and villages where the painted *havelis* of India's leading merchant families stand today in ghostly splendour.

Gods and goddesses frolic on the wall of Biyani Haveli, Sikar

Mandawa ④
The fort-palace is now a charming hotel and a convenient base from which to visit the neighbouring towns.

Dundlod ⑤
Its fort-palace and two splendid Goenka *havelis* are worth a visit.

Fatehpur ③
This picturesque mid-15th century town is best known for the Singhania, Goenka and Jalan *havelis*.

JHUNJHUNU

Mukundgarh

KEY
- Tour route
- Roads
- Rivers

0 kilometres 20

0 miles 10

Lachhmangarh ②
This 19th-century town is based on Jaipur's grid plan. The Char Chowk ("four coutyards") Haveli, owned by the Ganeriwala family, is said to be the grandest in the region.

Nawalgarh ⑥
The Poddar and the Aath ("eight") *havelis* are renowned for their frescoes.

NAGAUR

JAIPUR

TIPS FOR DRIVERS

Length: 111 km (69 miles).
Stopping-off points: Mandawa, Dundlod, Mukundgarh, Fatehpur and Nawalgarh have good hotels. Petrol pumps are at regular intervals on the main road. Apart from NH11, the lesser roads towards Jhunjhunu are poor, but there are roadside eateries at intervals selling mineral water, hot and cold drinks and snacks.

Sikar ①
Sikar's charm lies in its *havelis*, bazaars and rural ambience.

Sambhar Salt Lake ⑭

Jaipur district. 70 km (44 miles) NE of Ajmer. **Road map** B3. 🚌 🏛
Sambhrai Mata Mela (Oct).

Sambhar Lake is among the six important sites in India designated by the World Wide Fund for Nature (WWF) as a wetland of international importance. This vast inland saline lake spreads over an area of roughly 230 sq km (89 sq miles) and is fed by five rivers. During November and December, several species of migratory bird, especially flamingoes, can be seen here. A number of local legends are connected with the lake's origin, and a Shiva temple and two sacred tanks dedicated to mythological princesses are an indication of the lake's antiquity. The place, however, came into prominence after it was noticed by Babur in the 16th century. Since then, it has been a major source of salt for the country. One of the reasons for this is that after a good monsoon, the water level can rise by up to 3 ft (1 m), but over winter, the lake turns brackish due to capillary action caused by evaporation, drawing up salt from underground deposits. The little township that has

Flamingoes in flight over Sambhar Lake

grown around the lake survives on the extraction and packaging of salt. Men, women and even children can be seen working away at the countless trenches and mounds that are spread across the ghostly-white terrain. This has now become a highly commercial business, and though only one state-owned company has the monopoly, there has been an unprecedented growth in the numbers of private manufacturers. Many *bunds* (small dams) have been illegally constructed in the catchment area to retain rainwater for small-scale operations. This has affected not only the flow of water into the lake but has also put a considerable strain on its ecosystem.

Makrana ⑮

Nagaur district. 80 km (50 miles) N of Ajmer. **Road map** B3. 🏠 *83,000.*
🏨 *Khadim Hotel, Ajmer.* 🛒 *daily.*

Great slabs of hewn marble indicate that Makrana is a highly commercial stone-quarrying centre. The quarries stretch over a distance of

Marble quarrying at Makrana

20 km (12 miles) and produce the highly-prized luminous white marble that was used to build the Taj Mahal *(see pp154–5).* Quarrying began several centuries ago, and traditional open-pit methods are still used to excavate the stone. The demand for good quality marble has not lessened, and nearly 50,000 tons are mined annually and transported throughout the country. The town is also a good place to pick up gifts and souvenirs. Many small workshops have sprung up where artisans carve statues, pillars, vases, lamps and other objects for local sale and export. Objects are also sent to Agra where marble inlayers recreate the same delicate floral patterns as seen in the Taj Mahal *(see pp156–7).*

Salt packaging at Sambhar Salt Lake

Phool Mahal Palace in a picturesque setting

Kishangarh ⑯

Ajmer district. 30 km (19 miles) NE of Ajmer on NH 8. **Road map** B4. 🚉 116,000. 🏨 Khadim Hotel, Ajmer.

Of all Rajputana's princely states, this was the smallest. It was established in the early 17th century by Kishan Singh, a Rathore prince from Jodhpur, on lands near Ajmer. The king's sister was one of Jahangir's wives *(see pp52–3)*, a privilege that gave him a special status at the Mughal court. An obvious outcome of this proximity was that the Kishangarh kings tried to emulate the cultured lifestyle of the Mughal emperors, and when the arts lost imperial patronage under the leadership of the austere

Aurangzeb, this tiny state became a haven for several migrant miniature painters.

The old city is certainly worth exploring as it remains much as it was in the past. The narrow streets are lined with *havelis*, some of which have been converted into shops, and on the pavements

Roopangarh Fort

are vendors selling all kinds of merchandise, including red chillies for which the region is famous. The **Phool Mahal**, a privately-owned palace which is now a heritage hotel, has an idyllic setting on the banks of a lake that attracts a variety of waterbirds. Shady balconies, courtyard gardens and brass doors flanked by paintings hint at its past glory.

🏨 **Phool Mahal**
Tel (01463) 24 7405.

Environs
The 17th-century Roopangarh Fort, 25 km (15 miles) from Kishangarh, was once the capital of the state. Among the riches of this splendid heritage hotel is a rare collection of the famous Kishangarh miniatures.

THE KISHANGARH SCHOOL (1735–70)

In the mid-17th century, many miniature painters left the imperial atelier and moved to the Rajput, Central Indian and Punjab hill states, where each court evolved its own distinct regional style. Kishangarh's School of Painting flourished under the reign of Raja Sawant Singh (r.1748–64) who was a mystic, poet and Krishna devotee. His talented court painter, Nihal Chand, immortalized the love story of the king and his court singer in lyrical, romantic paintings where they are portrayed as Radha and Krishna. They are often surrounded by animals and birds, also in pairs, celebrating the union of the gods. The most famous painting is the portrait of Bani Thani, as the court singer was known. She is depicted in profile with a sharp nose and very elongated eyes and tapering wrist and fingers. This highly stylized form of portraiture became the hallmark of the Kishangarh School.

Portrait of Bani Thani

Street-by-Street: Pushkar 🅐

A turtle shrine

A peaceful pilgrim town of lakes and 400 temples, Pushkar derives its name from *pushpa* (flower) and *kar* (hand) after a legend that says that its lakes were created from the petals that fell from the divine hands of Brahma, the Creator *(see pp22–3)*. Today, life revolves around its lakeside ghats, temples and vibrant, colourful bazaars, and it is this harmonious mix of the spiritual and commercial that draws people to Pushkar.

Villagers at the Fair
Hundreds of thousands of people, camels and cattle attend the annual fair, said to be one of Asia's largest.

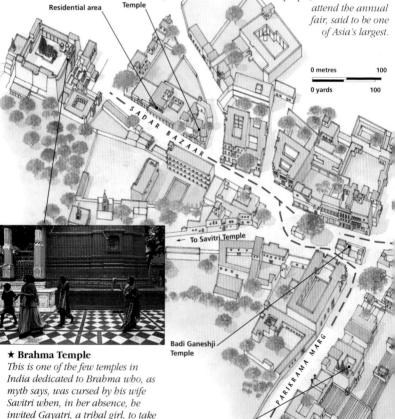

Residential area

Dhanna Bhagat Temple

SADAR BAZAAR

← To Savitri Temple

| 0 metres | 100 |
| 0 yards | 100 |

Badi Ganeshji Temple

PARIKRAMA MARG

★ **Brahma Temple**
This is one of the few temples in India dedicated to Brahma who, as myth says, was cursed by his wife Savitri when, in her absence, he invited Gayatri, a tribal girl, to take her place in an important ritual.

Parshuram Temple

KEY

– – – Suggested route

STAR SIGHTS

★ Brahma Temple

★ Ghats

Pushkar Lake
On top of a hill, by the sacred lake at Puskhar, is the temple of Savitri. Across the lake, on another hill, is the Gayatri Temple.

Rangaji Temple
This temple is conspicuous for its South Indian style of architecture. Its gopuram *(pagoda), intricately carved with over 360 images of deities, towers over the area.*

VISITORS' CHECKLIST

Ajmer district. 144 km (89 miles) SW of Jaipur. Road map B4. ⌂ 15,000. ⎕ ℹ RTDC, Hotel Sarovar (0145) 277 2040. ⌚ 9am–8pm daily. 🎪 Pushkar fair (Oct–Nov). **No eggs, meat or alcohol available/allowed.**

Women at Sadar Bazaar

gambar Jain
naramshala   **Mosque**

← To the fair ground

SADAR BAZAAR

To Ajmer bus stop →

Rangaji Temple

Chhatri

Camel race at the Pushkar fair

Pushkar Mela
In the Hindu month of Kartik (Oct–Nov), ten days after Diwali, this quiet town and its environs come alive as the much-anticipated annual cattle fair gets going. Temporary tents and campsites suddenly appear to accommodate the thousands of pilgrims, tourists and villagers who come here with herds of cattle, horses and camels to participate in this spectacular event.

Pushkar has always been the region's main cattle market for local herdsmen and farmers buying and selling camels and indigenous breeds of cattle. Over the years, this trade in livestock has increased in volume and has become one of Asia's largest cattle fairs.

In the vast, specially-built amphitheatre on the outskirts of the town, camel, horse and donkey races and contests take place amid lusty cheers from a huge audience.

A festive funfair atmosphere prevails over Pushkar during the Mela's two-week duration. Giant Ferris wheels and open air theatres offer amusement, while food and souvenir stalls do brisk business. In the evenings, people huddle round camp-fires, listening to the haunting strains of Rajasthani folk ballads.

The fair reaches a crescendo on the night of the full moon *(purnima)*, when pilgrims take a dip in the holy lake. At dusk, during the beautiful *deepdan* ceremony, hundreds of clay lamps on leaf boats are lit and set afloat in a magical tableau.

★ Ghats
Pushkar has 52 ghats. Devout Hindus make at least one pilgrimage to Pushkar and bathe at the holy ghats to wash away their sins and thereby earn themselves salvation.

Ajmer ⑱

Calligraphy, Adhai Din ka Jhonpra

Famous throughout the subcontinent as the holiest Muslim pilgrim centre after Mecca, Ajmer's prominence in history is connected to the *dargah* of a Sufi saint, Khwaja Moinuddin Chishti. The Mughals made Ajmer the provincial capital of their territories in Rajputana, and it was here that Sir Thomas Roe, the first British ambassador, presented his credentials to Jahangir in 1615. Although the *dargah* is still its most important landmark, Ajmer is also known for its proximity to another famous pilgrim centre, Pushkar. The town is framed by undulating hillocks dotted with interesting ruins. The picturesque environs of Anasagar Lake with charming pavilions, are popular with picnickers.

⛩ Taragarh Fort
◻ 9:30am–4:30pm.
This rugged, sprawling 7th-century "Star Fort" occupies the summit of Beetli Hill. A series of five gateways lead into this once-impregnable citadel, said to be the earliest hill fort in the country. Many ruined buildings lie within it, among which are a mosque, still in use, and the shrine of Miran Sayyid Hussain, a 12th-century governor of the fort. The later structures were added by the British whose troops occupied the fort in the 19th century.

🕌 Dargah Sharif
See pp220–21.

⛩ Adhai Din ka Jhonpra
N of Dargah Sharif, Nalla Bazaar.
◻ 9:30am–4:30pm.
This impressive complex of pillared cloisters is all that remains of a mosque built around AD 1200 by the Slave king, Qutbuddin Aibak. Some say that the mosque's name, which means "a hut of two-and-a-half days", indicates the time taken to build it.

The Dargah Sharif dome rising above the surrounding houses

However, it is more likely that it refers to the duration of a religious fair held during the Urs in the 18th century. Like the Quwwat-ul-Islam mosque at Delhi's Qutb complex (see *p112*), also built at the same time, pillars and fragments from nearby Hindu and Jain temples were used for its construction. The mosque itself, said to have been built over a demolished Jain college, stands on a platform cut out of the hillside, with ten shallow domes supported by 124 columns. The glory of the structure is an exquisite seven-arched screen in front of the many-pillared hall. Each arch is different from the next, and every column is ornamented with delicate engravings and calligraphic inscriptions in both Kufic and Tughra (early Arabic scripts). The sheer exuberance of the decoration and ingenious use of materials led Cunningham, the first Director-General of the Archaeological Survey of India, to describe it as "one of the noblest buildings the world has produced".

🏛 Government Museum Ajmer
Near bus stand. **Tel** (0145) 262 0637.
◻ 9:30am–4:30pm daily. ◕ public hols. 🎟
Akbar's fort and palace was the first seat of Mughal power in Rajasthan and was later used by the British as an arsenal. On the orders of Viceroy Lord Curzon, it was converted into a museum in 1908. Formerly known as the Rajputana Museum, its varied collection highlights sculpture and other antiquities gathered from sites all over Rajasthan. The most impressive exhibits are the sculptures dating from the 4th to 12th centuries, of which the most remarkable are the four-armed Vishnu seated on Garuda, and a door-frame from the ancient site of Baghera, depicting the ten *avatars* of Vishnu. Other important displays include antique coins, inscriptions, copper plates, paintings and weapons.

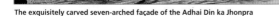

The exquisitely carved seven-arched façade of the Adhai Din ka Jhonpra

The Aravalli Range, picturesquely framing the Anasagar Lake

Nasiyan Temple.

Anok Chowk, Seth Moolchand Soni Marg. □ summer: 8am–5pm; winter: 8:30am–5pm daily.

Built in the 19th century, the "Red Temple" in the heart of Ajmer is a fine example of a Jain religious building. Just behind the main temple (closed to non-Jains) is the double-storeyed Svarna Nagari Hall. It is elaborately decorated with coloured glass mosaics, and large gilded wooden figures re-create scenes from Jain mythology, such as the birth and life of Rishabhdeva, the first Jain *tirthankar* (saint).

Anasagar Lake

Circular Rd. □ 7am–10pm.

This tranquil lake to the north of the city is named after Anaji (r.1135–50), the grandfather of Prithviraj Chauhan. Charmed by its scenic beauty, Jahangir laid out a garden, Daulat Bagh, and Shah Jahan built the marble pleasure pavilions.

Overlooking this popular picnic spot is a grand colonial building, now the Circuit House, where the British Resident once lived.

Mayo College

Can visit with Principal's permission.

Set up in 1875 by Lord Mayo as an "Eton of the East" for Rajput princes, the school's main building, designed by Charles Mant, is a jewel of Indo-Saracenic architecture *(see p25)*. Its early students were allowed to live in their individual "houses" with English private tutors and family retainers. Some, such as the prince of Alwar, would ride to school after vacations on an elephant. After 1947, commoners were allowed entry, and today, along with its girls' section, Mayo is rated as one of India's best public schools.

Lord Mayo

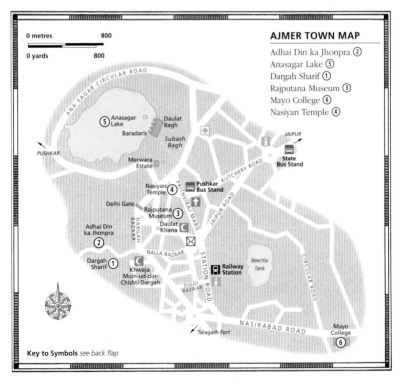

AJMER TOWN MAP

Adhai Din ka Jhonpra ②
Anasagar Lake ⑤
Dargah Sharif ①
Rajputana Museum ③
Mayo College ⑥
Nasiyan Temple ④

Key to Symbols see back flap

Dargah Sharif

Shahjahani Gate

A revered Muslim pilgrim centre since the 12th century, the Dargah Sharif contains the tomb of the famous Sufi saint Khwaja Moinuddin Chishti (1143–1236), popularly called Garib Nawaz, or "protector of the poor". Reputed to possess miraculous powers, the saint draws people of every faith to his *dargah* to seek favours and blessings. It is said that the saint entered his cell to pray in seclusion until his death on the sixth day. Each year, six days in the seventh lunar month (October) are marked as his Urs (death anniversary celebrations). Over the years, the saint's royal devotees built grand extensions to the tomb, so that today the *dargah* complex, teeming with pilgrims and tourists, is virtually a township in itself.

★ Mehfil Khana
Built in 1888 by the fabulously wealthy Nizam of Hyderabad, this is the venue for all-night qawwalis.

★ Shahjahani Masjid
Emperor Shah Jahan built this marble mosque. The Mughals made many such generous endowments.

Qawwali Singers
Qawwalis (see p28), always sung by a group, are specially composed to sing the saint's praises in front of his tomb.

Ibadat Khana, (prayer hall)

★ Mazar Sharif
Chishti's tomb, begun during the saint's lifetime by Iltutmish, was completed in the 16th century by Emperor Humayun. Later Mughal princes added to it. A marble dome surmounts the simple brick tomb, enclosed by a silver railing and a marble lattice screen.

STAR FEATURES

★ Mazar Sharif

★ Shahjahani Masjid

★ Mehfil Khana

Akbar's Mosque

Akbar, Chishti's most illustrious devotee, walked from Agra to Ajmer twice: once for enabling his conquest of Chittor, and again after the birth of his heir, Prince Salim, the future Jahangir.

VISITORS' CHECKLIST

Ajmer district. 141 km (87 miles) SW of Jaipur. **Road map** B4.
🛈 *RTDC TO Hotel Khadim* (0145) 262 7426. ⬜ daily.
📷 Urs (July). 🏳

Pilgrims

People of every faith come to seek favours and bring flowers and chadors *as thanksgiving offerings.*

Nizam Gate

Dargah Bazaar

Shahjahani Gate

Buland Darwaza

This imposing entrance doorway was erected by one of the Khilji rulers. A flag is hoisted over its ramparts to mark the start of the Urs ceremony held each October.

Degs

Two enormous degs *(iron cauldrons), one nearly 10 ft (3 m) in diameter, are used during the Urs for cooking a special rice pudding,* tabarrukh. *After they have been emptied, professional divers "loot" the* degs *by jumping in and scooping out the dregs.*

Dargah Bazaar

The long road that lies outside the Nizam Gate, the main entrance to the complex, is the location of a bustling market. Colourful stalls and kiosks sell baskets of rose petals as well as chadors *for devotees to offer at the* dargah.

A 15th-century manuscript, Arabic and Persian Research Institute, Tonk

Chaksu ⑲

Jaipur district. 43 km (27 miles) S of Jaipur on NH12. **Road map** C4. 🏠 17,000. 🚌 🔔 Shitala Ashtami (Mar–Apr).

This sleepy little village on the road from Jaipur towards Sawai Madhopur is known for its small white temple dedicated to Shitala Mata, the goddess who wards off disease, especially smallpox. A hundred steps lead to the shrine, around which devotees gather for a gossip session after propitiating the deity. Shitala Mata is much venerated in parts of rural Rajasthan where many diseases are still fatal. Every year in March or April a fair is held here, which attracts a large number of pilgrims. Food is cooked a day before Ashtami, the eighth and most auspicious day after the new moon, and offered cold to the goddess to ensure her protection.

Tonk ⑳

Tonk district. 96 km (60 miles) S of Jaipur on NH12. **Road map** C4. 🏠 1,211,000. 🚌 🔔 daily. 🔔 Id (Feb–Mar).

The small principality of Tonk, the only Muslim kingdom in Rajasthan, was created by the British in the early 19th century to appease the powerful Pathan warlord, Amir Khan. The legacy of its nawabs is evident throughout the old city. They constructed the imposing Jami Masjid, as well as a number of fine painted mansions, of which the **Sunehri Kothi** ("golden mansion"), built in 1824 by Amir Khan in the old palace complex, is the most spectacular. Magnificent enamelled mirrorwork and gilded stucco cover the walls and ceilings of its jewel-like interior, the windows are fitted with stained-glass and the floors beautifully painted.

The old city also has many Raj-style bungalows that were once the homes of the British Resident and his entourage.

The nawabs were dedicated patrons of art and literature. In the late 19th century, the third ruler established a grand centre of Islamic art, now known as the **Maulana Abul Kalam Azad Arabic and Persian Research Institute**. Its collection of rare Arabic and Persian manuscripts includes several illuminated Korans, such as Aurangzeb's *Alamgiri Koran Sharif* and the *Koran-e-Kamal*, prepared on the orders of Shah Jahan. There are also translations of the epics, the *Ramayana* and the *Mahabharata* inscribed in exquisite Persian as well as Arabic calligraphy.

🏛 **Sunehri Kothi**
Partially operational. Enquire at MAKA Arabic & Persian Research Institute.

🏛 **MAKA Arabic and Persian Research Institute**
Near new bus stand. 🕙 10am–5pm. ● Sun. **Tel** (01432) 24 7389.

Sawai Madhopur ㉑

Sawai Madhopur district. 172 km (107 miles) SE of Jaipur. **Road map** C4. 🏠 97,500. 🚉 🚌 🔔 Mon–Sat. 🔔 Shivaratri (Feb), Ganesha Chaturthi (Aug–Sep).

An important railway junction and entry point to the Ranthambhore National Park, Sawai Madhopur is named after its founder Sawai Madho Singh I (r.1750–68). The historic 10th-century

A cart stands outside a village hut on the outskirts of Sawai Madhopur

A rooftop view of the distant Indergarh Fort

Ranthambhore Fort (now in the park), a strategic point on the main route to Central India, was the scene of many terrible battles between its Rajput chieftains and the invading armies from Delhi and Agra. The fort was attacked by Alauddin Khilji *(see pp50–51)* and later by Akbar in 1569. This battle has been glorified in Mughal miniatures and bards have sung about the heroic deeds of its Rajput defenders. The fort was eventually handed over to the Amber kings *(see pp200–203)*. This jungle fort, despite its ruined state, looks daunting. Its massive gateways, ramparts and bastions make entry a tricky affair. Within it is an 8th-century temple dedicated to Ganesha, whose priest receives sacks of letters, sometimes addressed simply to "Shri Ganesha, Ranthambhore", especially during the marriage season, in order to invoke the deity's blessings. Clumps of grass, tied together by newlyweds for luck, are also seen along the way to the fort temple.

Environs
About 37 km (24 miles) west of Sawai Madhopur is the sprawling **Uniara Palace**. Further towards Tonk, past **Hathi Bhata**, a life-sized elephant carved out of a single rock, is the picturesque **Kakod Fort**. East of Sawai Madhopur, is the vast **Mansarovar Lake**.

Ranthambhore National Park ㉒

See pp224–5.

Indergarh ㉓

Kota district. 52 km (33 miles) S of Sawai Madhopur. **Road map** C4. **Indergarh Fort** ☐ *8am–5pm daily, on request to the caretaker who lives below the fort. Donation optional.*

This small town, founded by Raja Indrasal in 1605, lies huddled beneath the ramparts of a picturesque hill fort which is clearly visible from the flat rooftops of houses where, in summer, people sleep at night. Though dilapidated, some fort areas still bear traces of exquisite murals depicting colourful court scenes and legends. Indergarh's two main temples, one dedicated to Bijasan Mata (a form of Durga) and the other to Kuanwalji (Lord Shiva), are popular places of worship for pilgrims.

TALE OF THE TIGER

The tiger plays a major role in Indian myth as a symbol of supreme power, kingship and manhood. In Puranic legend it is Durga, the fearsome goddess with ten arms, who rides a tiger and defeats the invincible buffalo-headed demon, Mahishasura. Yet, for all its aura of strength and power the tiger is a vulnerable creature today.

Durga riding a tiger, detail of a miniature painting

Statistics claim that at the turn of the 20th century India's tiger population was about 40,000, but by 1972, the figure had dropped to roughly 1,800. This was when a special Task Force of the Indian Board for Wildlife constituted Project Tiger to address the alarming issue of dwindling tiger populations across the country. In the first year of Project Tiger, nine wildlife sanctuaries were declared tiger reserves, one of them being Ranthambhore.

There are now 27 Project Tiger Reserves, and the number of tigers has grown substantially, though persistent habitat destruction, illegal poaching and trading of tiger parts for medicinal and other derivatives in many Far Eastern countries continue to threaten the life of this supreme predator.

Ranthambhore National Park ㉒

Park sign

This park lies in the shadow of the Aravalli and Vindhya mountain ranges and covers a core area of 400 sq km (155 sq miles). Its razor-sharp ridges, deep boulder-filled gorges, lakes and jungle are the habitat of carnivores such as the caracal, panther, jackal and hyena, species of deer, and a rich variety of resident and migratory birds. The most famous resident, however, is the endangered tiger, and it is a unique experience to catch glimpses of this majestic and fascinating animal. Like other parks in the region, this was originally the Jaipur state's hunting grounds and became a Project Tiger Reserve in 1973.

Rajbagh
Ruined pavilions stand on the banks of Rajbagh Talao, one of the three lakes in the park.

Ranthambhore Fort
The park derives its name from this great Rajput jungle fort that is 1,000 years old and stands at a height of 215 m (705 ft).

Sambar Stag
Large herds of sambar are seen around the lakes, wallowing in the water, swimming and feeding on aquatic plants, unperturbed by jeeps and visitors.

JAIPUR

TONK

Sawai Madhopur

MUMBAI

Malik Talao
Padam Talao
Rajbagh Tal
Ranthambhore Fort
Jogi Mahal

Nalghati Valley

Lahapur

Man Sarovar

Banyan Tree
India's second-largest banyan tree (Ficus bengalensis) lies in the grounds of Jogi Mahal. Its several spreading branches are all supported by roots.

0 kilometres   5

0 miles   2

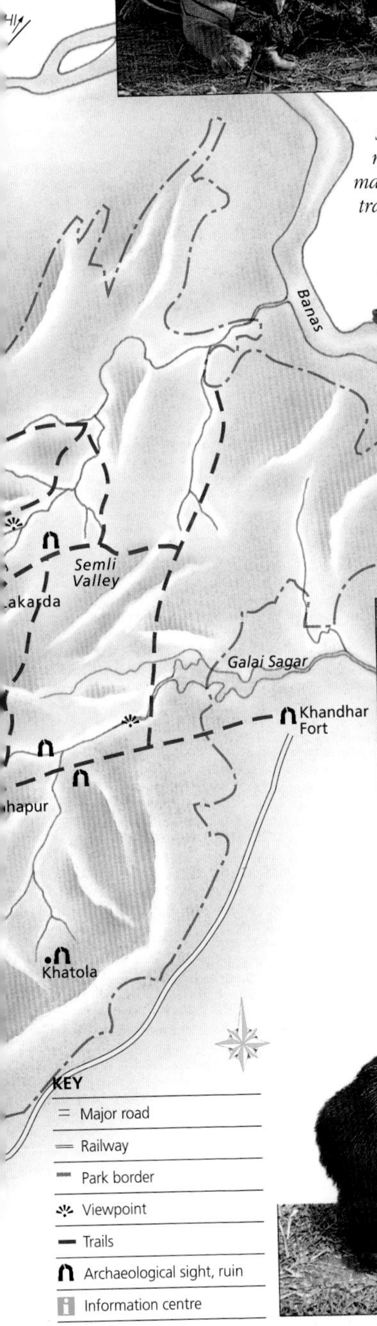

Tiger

Sighting the park's main predator is a matter of chance, but traces of its activities are often seen.

VISITORS' CHECKLIST

Sawai Madhopur district. 180 km (112 miles) SE of Jaipur. **Road map** C4. *Sawai Madhopur.* *RTDC Hotel Vinayak, Sawai Madhopur* (07462) 22 1333. *Oct–Jun: 7–10am & 3–6pm.* *Jul–Sep.* The Dastkari Kendra, opp Kutalpura village on way to Kundera. **Tel** (07462) 25 2049. **No walking** only jeeps hired from the TO at Hotel Vinayak (which gives permits) are allowed inside the park. **Tel** (07462) 22 0223.

Indian Roller Bird

This is one of the many bird species found in the park. The others include birds of prey such as the crested serpent eagle and Bonelli's eagle, and many species of pigeons, flycatchers, storks and waterbirds.

Marsh Crocodiles

Muggers, or marsh crocodiles, are commonly seen submerged in water or basking on the shores of the lakes. Ungulates are their main prey, and sometimes one can glimpse a crocodile dragging the carcass of a deer into the water. The monitor lizard and python are some of the other reptiles found in the park.

Sloth Bear

This shaggy bear with short hind legs and a long muzzle emerges at dusk to feed. During the day it shelters in the rocky outcrops and is difficult to sight.

Banas
Semli Valley
akarda
Galai Sagar
Khandhar Fort
hapur
Khatola
KEY
Major road
Railway
Park border
Viewpoint
Trails
Archaeological sight, ruin
Information centre

TRAVELLERS' NEEDS

WHERE TO STAY 228–247

WHERE TO EAT 248–263

SHOPS AND MARKETS 264–269

ENTERTAINMENT 270–271

SPECIAL INTERESTS AND
OUTDOOR ACTIVITIES 272–275

Popularly known as the Golden Triangle, the Delhi, Agra and Jaipur region receives the largest number of tourists in India, so this area is well-equipped with places to stay. The choice of accommodation ranges from up-market luxury hotels run by international or leading Indian chains, to small guesthouses and youth hostels. In addition, there are state-run tourist hotels in several towns, with comfortable board and lodging at reasonable rates. On the more exotic

Palace doorman

side are the grand old palaces and *havelis* of the Jaipur region which re-create the lavish lifestyles of former rulers and aristocracy *(see pp232–3)*. For the budget traveller, on the other hand, there is a choice of ashrams and small guesthouses, sometimes with extremely basic facilities. Tented accommodation is as yet rare, as is self-catering. Rooms are usually cheaper during the off-season (Apr–Sep). For more information on places to stay in this region, refer to the detailed listings on pages 234–47.

HOTEL CHAINS, GRADING AND FACILITIES

At the top end of the range are the five-star deluxe hotels which provide luxurious accommodation for the international visitor. Many of these are part of national chains, such as the **Ashok Group**, or of international groups such as the **Sheraton** and **Radisson** *(see p231)*. Below them are the four- and three-star hotels, guesthouses and tourist lodges, some of which may offer additional facilities, such as a pool or tennis court. International television channels are now shown on most hotel room sets. In Agra and Jaipur, palaces, bungalows and *havelis* have been converted into heritage hotels, which carry the flavour of erstwhile grandeur

and graciousness. Except in some of the lower priced hotels, the bathrooms, even in older properties, are in Western style. Room service, safe deposits and daily laundry are standard in more expensive places. The reception desk can advise on tours, and large hotels have travel agencies on the premises.

Traditional huts, Desert Resort, Mandawa

LUXURY HOTELS

India's top luxury hotels match the best in the world in their elegance, professional services, and wide range of facilities. Architecturally, many of them have cleverly combined traditional Indian and modern

Five-star hotel logo

design, while their interiors are sumptuously decorated with the best of Indian crafts and textiles. The hotels run by the large international and national chains are fully air-conditioned and offer a wide range of conveniences such as a resident doctor, shopping arcades and patisseries, banqueting halls, a 24-hour coffee shop, bars and gourmet restaurants. For the business traveller there are business and conference centres equipped with computers for personal use with facilities for access to the Internet. Desk jacks and modems are provided for personal computers and laptops. Additional facilities include beauty parlours and fitness centres, swimming pools and tennis courts. The front desk can often make bookings for golf and other activities. Some hotels even have a regular palmist, tarot card reader or astrologer.

Agra's Mughal Sheraton, renowned for its innovative architecture

◁ **Vegetables temptingly stacked in a roadside stall**

HERITAGE HOTELS

Several palaces and stately homes, particularly in Rajasthan, have been restored and converted into hotels. These come under the banner of **Heritage Hotels Association of India**. A private agency, **WelcomHeritage** *(see p231)* specializes in booking accommodation in these hotels which have been classified as Grand, Classic and Ordinary, and are priced accordingly. However, most travel agents can also make bookings at these places.

MIDDLE-RANGE HOTELS

These are four- and three-star establishments that may lack the stylish decor, slickness and range of facilities of five-star hotels. Though smaller in size they are always comfortable, clean and well-serviced. The rooms are generally air-conditioned with attached baths that have hot and cold running water. Some are surrounded by extensive gardens and may even have cafés and business centres.

Logo of the Welcomgroup chain

BUDGET HOTELS AND TOURIST LODGES

Budget hotels are usually found in the older sections of cities, near the railway and bus stations. The accommodation is mostly simple and varies from very basic to homely guesthouses. Ceiling fans, mosquito nets and private, Indian- or Western-style bathrooms are generally provided. The rates in Delhi are higher than in the rest of the region.

The wide network of tourist "bungalows" or lodges established by state tourism departments, and the national India Tourism Development Corporation's (ITDC) Ashok Group *(see p297)*, make travelling to lesser-known places easier. The rates are reasonable, and there is a choice of dormitories as well as double rooms with attached bathrooms.

GUESTHOUSES

The term "guesthouse" can be a misnomer. Both mid-range and budget hotels can have "guesthouse" appended to their name, and so the prices and the services can vary enormously. If you opt for a lower priced one, do make it a point to inspect the room before checking in, especially the bathroom, which may contain an Indian-style toilet. The better guesthouses all have air-conditioning and attached baths with Western toilets. In Jaipur, some families have converted all or part of their large *havelis* into guesthouses, providing meals on order.

A *dharamshala* in Haridwar

PAYING GUESTS

You can find short-term paying guest accommodation in Delhi through the **Government of India Tourist Office** *(see p279)* or your travel agent. In Agra, the tourist information counter at the railway station can supply addresses, and in Jaipur, **Rajasthan Tourism (RTDC)** *(see p291)* has an official and comprehensive list of families under a good Paying Guest Scheme administered by them. **Munjeeta Travel**, based in the United Kingdom *(see p231)* can organize Homestay Tours across India.

DHARAMSHALAS AND ASHRAMS

Rest houses for pilgrims known as *dharamshalas* are run by religious trusts, but anyone can stay, as in the **International Rest House** in Brindavan, or **Ramakrishna Mission** and **Sri Aurobindo Ashram** in Delhi *(see p231),* provided the rules of the place are strictly followed. They charge absurdly low rates. In cities, *dharamshalas* in the older sections may have dubious standards of hygiene, and the facilities can amount to a bare room with no bedding, shared with others along with the bathroom. Some temples and ashrams also rent out rooms to guests seeking a religious retreat. The amenities here are basic, though clean, and guests are expected to respect the rules of the community.

A luxurious deluxe room in a five-star hotel

YOUTH HOSTELS

There is a network of youth hostels across India, including the YMCA *(see p281)*. They offer unbelievably low rates, although the YMCA's are pricier with better facilities and are found only in selected cities. Though it is not necessary to be a member of Youth Hostel International to gain entry, during the busy season its members do get priority and always get lower rates. Rooms and dormitories are both usually available, and the rules of the hostel must be respected.

NATIONAL PARKS AND CAMPING SITES

The national parks have several places to stay in, but no dedicated camping sites. At the Pushkar fair grounds, Rajasthan Tourism sets up a **Tourist Village** on a large campsite. A few hotels in Rajasthan, such as Samode Bagh or **Sawai Madhopur Lodge** also offer some tent accommodation, and in Uttar Pradesh, apart from private operators, such as **Outdoor Adventures** and **Milestones**, the state government has a river rafting campsite on the River Ganges at Rishikesh.

PRICES AND DISCOUNTS

Rates vary between cities, with Delhi being the most expensive, and the small town hotels being very cheap at times. The five-star luxury

A view of the main swimming pool at the Rajvilas Hotel in Jaipur

and the palace or heritage hotels are at the top end of the scale. Those run by the state tourism develop-ment corporations can vary from state to state with Delhi again being the most expensive. Prices at the so-called guesthouses swing from high to low. Most hotels offer discounts during the low season from April to September. This can bring the original rates down by almost 50 per cent at times.

RAJVILĀS

Logo of an Oberoi luxury hotel

Every October, hotels raise their rates by a nominal percentage. Various taxes are charged, over and above the listed rates, as notified by the government from time to time. Foreigners have to pay the dollar room rate, plus any additional taxes on the listed price. This is payable in foreign currency or in Indian rupees.

TAXES

Although the government has abolished the 10 per cent hotel expenditure tax on rooms, it does levy a luxury tax which varies state to state, from 5 to 20 per cent. Expect to pay luxury tax on the published tariff for fare on discounted rooms. VAT, about 12.5 per cent in most states, has replaced the sales tax on food and beverages.

HIDDEN EXTRAS

Services for which you may be charged extra could include bottles of mineral water, breakfast, laundry, extra bedding, telephone calls, e-mails and faxes, the mini bar in your room, and special pay channels on television (you should read the screen or your room service folder before pressing the remote). Hotels usually charge extra for transport to and from the hotel. When telephoning, it is cheaper to use the pay phones in the lobby or at outside STD booths *(see p291)*. At small town hotels with no running hot water, the hotel will give you a bucket of hot water once a day at a nominal cost.

BOOKING, CHECKING IN AND OUT

It is a good idea to make your hotel bookings well in advance, especially for the peak October to March tourist

The Glass House on the Ganges in Rishikesh

season when many conferences and cultural festivals take place. You can fax or telephone your requirements, but do insist that you are sent a written confirmation.

Check out time is usually at 12 noon, though at smaller establishments they are not so particular and calculate by the day. Before checking out, do study your bills carefully and retain all the receipts.

TOUTS

At the airport or railway station you may be besieged by touts *(see p265)*, many of whom also operate as taxi and three-wheeler drivers, who insist on taking you to hotels where they get a commission. The best solution is to have prior bookings. Failing this, the tourism counter at the airport or station will help you find a place suitable to your needs. However, if there is no other option, you should be firm about how much you are willing to spend and check out the tout's commission. You should also ask for choices, and when you reach the hotel, be sure it is acceptable to you before dismissing the driver. If touts continue to pester you, speak to the nearest policeman.

Samode Bagh's exquisite tents, recreating a royal Mughal ambience

FACILITIES FOR CHILDREN

The staff at hotels are usually very good with children. Many hotels will willingly add an extra bed in your room for a child for a small extra charge. Very few provide baby-sitting services, and you should check at the front desk, but usually parents are expected to look after their children. Most hotels do not have any special facilities for children.

DISABLED TRAVELLERS

Only the newer and fancier hotels make an effort to provide ramps, special lifts and wheelchairs for disabled travellers. However, you can always seek the help of the staff. Many of the older hotels, especially in Rajasthan, which are converted from palaces and private mansions, have several levels within them, with no ramp or lifts for easy movement. Do check out these facilities before making your bookings.

TIPPING

Tips are expected even though there may be a service charge on bills. The amounts are at the discretion of the guest, starting with Rs10 for car parking attendants, slightly more for a porter, and 10 per cent of the total bill for waiters.

DIRECTORY

HOTEL CHAINS

Ashok Group
3 Jeevan Vihar, Parliament Street, Delhi. **Map** 4 F9.
Tel (011) 237 4557.

Oberoi Group
7 Shamnath Marg, Delhi.
Tel (011) 2389 0606.
www.oberoihotels.com

Radisson Hotels
National Highway 8, Mahipalpur Rd, Delhi.
Tel (011) 2677 9191.

Taj Group
Taj Mahal, Mansingh Rd, Delhi.
Map 5 B3.
Tel (011) 2302 6162.
www.tajhotels.com

Welcomgroup Maurya Sheraton
Maurya Sheraton, Sardar Patel Marg, Delhi.
Tel (011) 2611 2233.

HERITAGE HOTELS

Heritage Hotels Association of India
Mandawa Haveli, Sansar Chandra Rd, Jaipur.
Tel (0141) 237 1194.

WelcomHeritage
31, FF Siri Fort Rd, Delhi.
Tel (011) 2626 6650.

PAYING GUEST ACCOMMODATION

Munjeeta Travel
12 Cavendish Rd, Woking, Surrey GU22 OEP, UK.
Tel (01483) 77 3331.

RTDC, Jaipur
Govt Hostel, MI Rd.
Tel (0141) 511 0598.
Swagatam Tourist Campus.
Tel (0141) 220 2586.

DHARAMSHALAS AND ASHRAMS

International Rest House
Shri Krishna-Balaram Temple, Brindavan.
Tel (0565) 254 0021.

Ramakrishna Mission
Ramakrishna Ashram Marg, Delhi.
Tel (011) 2358 7110.

Sri Aurobindo Ashram
Aurobindo Marg, Delhi.
Tel (011) 2656 9225.

NATIONAL PARKS AND CAMPING SITES

Milestones
C-426 Chittaranjan Park, Delhi. *Tel (011) 2627 8529.*
www.milestones.net

Outdoor Adventures
S–234 Panchsheel Park, Delhi.
Tel 986813518 (Mobile).

Sawai Madhopur Lodge
National Park Rd, Sawai Madhopur.
Tel (07462) 22 0541.

Tourist Village (RTDC)
Pushkar.
Tel (0145) 262 7426.

Heritage Hotels

The title "heritage hotel" is given to some palaces and *havelis* that have been discreetly modernized to meet the needs of international travellers and run as high-class hotels. Fitted with modern plumbing and air-conditioning and with facilities such as swimming pools and tennis courts, such hotels take care that their history, architecture and innate elegance are suitably highlighted. The interiors display old sepia photographs, memorabilia and exquisite furniture tended by a caring staff, often old family retainers. The high tariffs of such hotels are compensated for by their special ambience.

Castle Mandawa, Mandawa
This mid-18th century fortress is now a charming heritage hotel and an ideal base to explore the painted havelis of Shekhawati. Live entertainment by Rajasthani folk dancers and musicians, and camel rides are some of its attractions (see p245).

Samode Palace, Samode
All the grandeur of royal Rajasthan is visible in this opulent painted palace. Its magnificent Durbar Hall and Sheesh Mahal are now reception areas where guests can dine (see p247).

JAIPUR AND ENVIRONS

Hotel Pushkar Palace, Pushkar
The lake-side palace, once the property of the Maharaja of Kishangarh, is now a popular hotel in this temple town. Its location is ideal for views of the bathing ghats, the rugged Aravalli Hills and the town's 400 temples (see p246).

Narain Niwas Palace, Jaipur
Surrounded by sprawling gardens and mango orchards, this traditional palace was built in 1928 (see p244).

Neemrana Fort Palace, Neemrana
Built in 1464, this fort was one of India's first heritage hotels. Meticulously restored to re-create the original plan and architecture, its interior is an eclectic blend of traditional design and its modern interpretations (see p246).

0 kilometres   100

0 miles   50

DELHI

The Hill Fort, Kesroli
This seven-turreted fort is believed to be 600 years old. Built on top of a small hillock, it commands a splendid view from its high ramparts and is a perfect base from which to visit neighbouring sites and sanctuaries (see p243).

AGRA AND AROUND

Laxmi Vilas Palace, Bharatpur
Located near the Keoladeo National Park, the palace was built in 1899 for the women of the royal family. The architecture is a mix of Mughal and Rajput styles. Spacious airy rooms are furnished with period furniture and the courtyards are decorated with colourful frescoes *(see p241).*

Sawai Madhopur Lodge, Sawai Madhopur A colonial building furnished in the 1930s style, on the outskirts of the Ranthambhore National Park, this was a hunting lodge of the Maharaja of Jaipur *(see p247).*

Usha Kiran Palace, Gwalior
The Maharaja of Gwalior's official guesthouse is now a pleasant hotel with an old-world charm (see p242).

Choosing a Hotel

The hotels in this guide have been carefully selected across a wide price range for various facilities provided, good value for money, excellent services, comfort or style and location. They have been listed according to region for your convenience. Map references refer to the Delhi Street Finder maps on pages 124–131.

DELHI

NEW DELHI Prince Polonia

2325-26, Tilak Gali, Paharganj **Tel** 011 2358 1930 **Fax** 011 2358 7026 **Rooms** 27   **Map** 1 B3

Located amidst the hustle and bustle of Paharganj it is among the better choices from the low-budget hotels in the vicinity. Relax in their swimming pool or the neat and cosy rooms. Ideal for tourists and backpackers. Connaught Place, the city's business and shopping centre, is right next door. **www.princepolonia.com**

NEW DELHI Master Guest House

R-500, New Rajinder Nagar **Tel** 011 2874 1089 **Fax** 011 6547 9947 **Rooms** 4

The Master Guest House is situated in a peaceful, quiet corner of Delhi. Each of its four rooms has a special theme evident in the names given to them (Mogul, Ganesh, Krishna and Lucky) and the rates are very affordable. It ensures a quiet, peaceful time in the city. **www.master-guesthouse.com**

NEW DELHI YMCA Tourist Hostel

Jai Singh Road **Tel** 011 2336 1915 **Fax** 011 2374 6023 **Rooms** 106   **Map** 1 B5

A great budget hotel situated at the heart of the city. Frequented by international students and budget travellers. Rooms are clean and the food is excellent for its price. However, the decor could be improved keeping non-students in mind. Rooms offer views of Jantar Mantar, the 18th-century astrological observatory. **www.delhiymca.com**

NEW DELHI YWCA of Delhi Blue Triangle Family Hostel

YWCA of Delhi, Ashoka Road **Tel** 011 2336 2975 **Fax** 011 2336 0202 **Rooms** 45   **Map** 1 B5

The Blue Triangle Family Hostel serves the travelling woman's need for safety and comfort. The rooms are neat and the restaurant serves reasonably good food. A popular hotel among international students and tourists since it has an excellent location and affordable rates. **www.ywcaindia.org**

NEW DELHI YWCA International Guest House

10 Sansad Street, Sansad Marg **Tel** 011 2336 1662 **Fax** 011 2334 1763 **Rooms** 24   **Map** 1 B5

Popular among female students and women travelling alone or with children, the YWCA offers good services at a low cost. With a prime location near Delhi's main business and shopping area, the rooms are simple yet comfortable. Free breakfast from 8–10am. Beverages are available round the clock. **www.ywcaindia.org**

NEW DELHI Ahuja Residency

193 Golf Links **Tel** 011 2462 2255 **Fax** 011 2464 9008 **Rooms** 12   **Map** 5 B4

Each apartment at the Golf Links Apartments, run by Ahuja Residency, has three neatly furnished bedrooms, a bathroom and a well-equipped kitchen. The cost includes an attendant's services as well. The peaceful green environs of the golf links make it a much sought-after alternative accommodation. **www.ahujaresidency.com**

NEW DELHI Hotel Centre Point

13 Kasturba Gandhi Marg **Tel** 011 2335 4304 **Fax** 011 2332 9138 **Rooms** 55   **Map** 1 C5

A Colonial residence converted into a hotel with a host of excellent services, keeping budget in mind. The rooms have an air of luxury of days gone by. The Centre Point is strategically located near important business and media centres. One of the best mid-price range accomodations for the travelling businessman or tourist.

NEW DELHI The Connaught

37 Shaheed Bhagat Singh Marg **Tel** 011 2336 4225 **Fax** 011 2334 0757 **Rooms** 80   **Map** 1 B4

This no frills hotel is suitable for bed and breakfast. Avoid rooms on the third floor as they don't offer very exciting views. Centrally located next to major shopping malls. Rooms are neat but some require urgent renovation. Offers all the services of a typical four-star hotel such as speciality restaurants and a 24-hour coffee shop.

NEW DELHI Hotel York

K-10 Connaught Circus **Tel** 011 2341 5769 **Fax** 011 2341 4419 **Rooms** 80   **Map** 1 C4

Located at the hub of Delhi's commercial area, York is one of the oldest three-star hotels of the capital, with friendly staff and a helpful travel desk. Neat and comfortable, the rooms offer basic amenities. Great for a stay amidst the Colonial architecture of Lutyens's Delhi. **www.indiamart.com/hotelyork**

Key to Symbols see back cover flap

NEW DELHI Jor Bagh '27' Guesthouse

27 Jor Bagh **Tel** *011 2469 4430* **Fax** *011 2469 8647* **Rooms** *18*

Modest yet capable of providing the kind of comfort that other mid-price range hotels fail to offer. Conveniently located and connected to the bustle of the city, although it is surprisingly calm and peaceful with cosy rooms that are neatly furnished. The staff provide friendly service and the facilities are good value for money. **www.jorbagh27.com**

NEW DELHI The Hans Plaza

15 Barakhamba Road **Tel** *011 2331 6868* **Fax** *011 2331 4830* **Rooms** *67*   **Map** *2 D5*

Picture luxury and comfort, add a dash of history and the gorgeous architecture of Delhi's Colonial past. Situated on one of the busiest streets, this hotel is close to popular tourist locations. Stately rooms are not too loud in terms of decor. Services could be improved however, considering the rates. **www.hanshotels.com**

NEW DELHI Hotel Janpath

Janpath Road **Tel** *011 2334 0070* **Fax** *011 2334 68618* **Rooms** *213*   **Map** *5 A1*

One of the oldest mid-budget hotels, this charming place has seen better days. The exterior needs renovation, although the larger rooms each have a private balcony and are comfortable and clean. Sagar Ratna is the popular in-house South-Indian restaurant. **www.theashokgroup.com**

NEW DELHI Ramada Plaza

19 Ashok Road, Connaught Place **Tel** *011 000 0000* **Rooms** *448*   **Map** *5 A1*

The Ramada Plaza is the newest hotel in town, strategically located on the site of the former Ashok Niwas Yatri. Luxurious rooms offer space and a blend of contemporary and classic decor. It boasts of being the biggest mid-market hotel of the parent Ramada chain of hotels. **www.ramada.com**

NEW DELHI The Taj Ambassador

Sujan Singh Park, Cornwallis Road **Tel** *011 2463 2600* **Fax** *011 2463 2252* **Rooms** *88*   **Map** *5 B3*

Ideal for the connoisseur of art, the hotel's colonnaded building exudes a certain old-world charm. If you are looking for a peaceful and relaxed stay, then their simple yet elegant rooms are the right choice. Take a walk to Lodi Gardens or shop at Khan Market, a treasure trove of boutiques and restaurants. **www.tajhotels.com**

NEW DELHI Claridges

Aurangzeb Road **Tel** *011 4133 5133* **Fax** *011 2301 0625* **Rooms** *138*   **Map** *5 A3*

Situated in the quiet of the diplomatic avenues, this stylish hotel blends the classic and contemporary to perfection. The rooms are luxurious and tastefully furnished, with most having lovely views of the pool or the surrounding greenery. It offers facilities ideal for a relaxed and peaceful stay. **www.claridges-hotels.com**

NEW DELHI The Imperial

Janpath **Tel** *011 2334 1234* **Fax** *011 2334 2255* **Rooms** *263*   **Map** *1 C5*

Considered to be among Asia's finest hotels, The Imperial offers visitors a unique Colonial experience blended with shades of Indian history. Luxurious rooms have modern facilities hidden behind a vintage feel. Next to Janpath, it is conveniently situated to explore colourful contemporary citylife. **www.theimperialindia.com**

NEW DELHI Intercontinental The Grand

Barakhamba Avenue, Connaught place **Tel** *011 2341 1001* **Fax** *011 2341 2233* **Rooms** *444*   **Map** *2 D5*

A popular choice for the travelling business executive, this hotel provides a mix of sophistication, comfort and style. Rooms are stately, spacious and contemporary in their decor. The Law Club, the first of its kind, is a popular place for the city's top legal fraternity. Its in-house restaurants and bars are superb. **www.thegrandhotels.net**

NEW DELHI Jaypee Sidharth

3 Rajendra Place **Tel** *011 2576 2501* **Fax** *011 2578 1016* **Rooms** *98*

Tucked away about 20 minutes from the city centre, this is a pleasant hotel. Rooms have a modern decor and are well equipped with all basic amenities. Apart from good restaurants and bars, it also has a great health club, Ananda, which has a well-equipped gym and other facilities. **www.jaypeehotels.com**

NEW DELHI Le Meridien

Windsor Place **Tel** *011 2371 0101* **Fax** *011 2371 4545* **Rooms** *355*   **Map** *5 A1*

Situated at the heart of Central Delhi, this is a lovely atrium hotel with the highest rooftop nightclub in the city, among other popular bars and speciality restaurants. The luxurious rooms are equipped to provide you comfort. The recently renovated lobby is modern but lacks the hotel's earlier warmth. **www.lemeridien-newdelhi.com**

NEW DELHI The Metropolitan Hotel Nikko

Bangla Sahib Road **Tel** *011 4250 0200* **Fax** *011 4250 0300* **Rooms** *176*   **Map** *1 B5*

This hotel houses world-class facilities and is a perfect blend of the Orient and the West. Lavish, spacious rooms have a classic, elegant decor. Their beautifully designed craft shop is great for souvenirs. Indulge in luxury at their Zen Health Club with relaxing spas and therapeutic massages. **www.hotelnikkodelhi.com**

NEW DELHI The Oberoi

Dr. Zakhir Hussain Marg **Tel** *011 2436 3030* **Fax** *011 2436 0484* **Rooms** *300*   **Map** *6 D4*

Awarded "Best five star hotel in India" recently, The Oberoi assures you of a comfortable, luxurious and exciting stay. The rooms are the finest in the city, with glamorous and stylish interiors. A must-try for lovers of quality and excellence. Be sure to check out Baan Thai, their speciality Thai restaurant. **www.oberoidelhi.com**

NEW DELHI The Park

15 Parliament Street **Tel** *011 2374 3000* **Fax** *011 2374 4000* **Rooms** *224*   **Map** *1 C5*

Stay in this hotel for unadulterated luxury and privacy. The rooms have a progressive, avant-garde look and offer state-of-the-art services. A popular gift shop in the shopping arcade, The Box, offers unique handicrafts and accessories. Restaurants provide world-class cuisines. **www.theparkhotels.com**

NEW DELHI Shangri La

19 Ashok Road, Connaught Place **Tel** *011 4119 1919* **Fax** *011 4119 1988* **Rooms** *323*   **Map** *5 A1*

The hotel lobby is adorned with paintings by world-renowned painter, M.F.Hussain. Rooms are lavishly furnished and offer a spectacular view of the city. Janpath, the popular shopping arcade, is just a walk away. Overall, this newly-built luxury hotel is popular with the travelling businessman and tourist alike. **www.shangri-la.com**

NEW DELHI The Taj Mahal Hotel

1 Mansingh Road **Tel** *011 2302 6162* **Fax** *011 2302 6070* **Rooms** *296*   **Map** *5 B3*

A home from home, the Taj offers lavish rooms, created especially for the discerning traveller who appreciates quality and sophistication. The Mughal decor and hospitable service are truly royal. The Taj Mahal hotel boasts of Machan, their ever popular coffee shop, and Ricks, a lively lounge bar. **www.tajhotels.com**

NIZAMUDDIN La Sagrita Tourist House

14 Sunder Nagar **Tel** *011 2435 9541* **Fax** *011 2435 6956* **Rooms** *25*   **Map** *6 D3*

Tucked away in a peaceful street lined with trees, La Sagrita offers a refreshing respite from the concrete jungle. The interiors are cool, clean and contemporary. Some rooms offer a lovely view and the garden terrace is good for unwinding after a hectic day of sightseeing. Very affordable rates and quality service. **www.lasagrita.com**

NIZAMUDDIN Jukaso Inn

50 Sundar Nagar **Tel** *011 2435 1249* **Fax** *011 2435 4402* **Rooms** *19*   **Map** *6 D3*

Built in a quiet residential area, this is an upmarket guesthouse with a friendly atmosphere. The accommodation offered ranges from standard single rooms to luxury double suites. Conveniently located close to Pragati Maidan, one of the country's largest exhibition areas, which is the venue of many colourful trade fairs and concerts.

OLD DELHI Hotel Broadway

4/15A Asaf Ali Road **Tel** *011 2327 3821* **Fax** *011 2327 9966* **Rooms** *26*   **Map** *2 E3*

This is one of the city's oldest economy hotels and the first skyscraper built 50 years ago. The rooms overlook the busy Asaf Ali Road and also offer a view of the spectacular Mughal environs of Old Delhi. Comfortable rooms, friendly staff and two speciality restaurants make this a popular tourist refuge. **www.oldworldhospitality.com**

FURTHER AFIELD (EAST) The Mosaic Hotel

C-1 Sector 18, Noida **Tel** *0120 4025 000* **Rooms** *48*

Opened in August 2006 and situated in suburban Delhi, the Mosaic Hotel is driven to meet the needs of the corporate traveller. The Cycle Menu at Lattitude, their speciality restaurant, offers an interesting dining experience. The rooms have an elegant artistic design much in sync with the name of the hotel.

FURTHER AFIELD (EAST) Radisson Hotel Noida

L-2 Sector 18, Noida **Tel** *0120 430 0000* **Fax** *0120 430 3000* **Rooms** *114*

Noida's first five-star hotel, Radisson Hotel Noida offers a range of excellent services. S-18, the 24-hour brasserie, offers world-class cuisines with a difference. The best part is that the guests get to use the gym and sauna as part of the hotel's complimentary service during their stay. **www.radisson.com/noidain**

FURTHER AFIELD (NORTH) Hotel Clark

5/47 W.E.A, Saraswati Marg, Karol Bagh **Tel** *011 2575 6552* **Fax** *011 2575 8080* **Rooms** *32*

Though a little out of the way, the area is nonetheless, flooded with guesthouses. Hotel Clark is still one of the better hotels of the lot. Rooms have an elegant interior, the staff are friendly and their restaurant is worth a visit. This budget hotel is decent value for money. **www.hotelclarkdelhi.com**

FURTHER AFIELD (NORTH) Oberoi Maiden's

7 Sham Nath Marg **Tel** *011 2397 5464* **Fax** *011 2398 0771* **Rooms** *53*

One of the oldest hotels in the city, the classic architecture of this building could have been the inspiration for Lutyens who stayed here on his first visit to India more than a century ago. With spectacular views of the lush green Delhi Ridge, this heritage hotel exudes an air of serenity and quiet beauty. **www.maidenshotel.com**

FURTHER AFIELD (SOUTH) Hotel Corporate World

B-495 New Friends Colony **Tel** *011 2684 7053* **Fax** *011 5162 7166* **Rooms** *25*

Swiss and U.S.A trained staff offer pleasant and helpful service. The rooms are decent with a neat, basic decor. The hotel also provides apartment facilities at nominal rates. They have a modest café and their in-house chef prepares multi-cuisine dishes for guests. Overall, a charming budget hotel. **www.hotelcorporateworld.com**

FURTHER AFIELD (SOUTH) The Qutab Hotel

Shaheed Jeet Singh Marg **Tel** *011 2652 1010* **Fax** *011 2696 8287* **Rooms** *60*

This hotel is named after the beautiful 13th-century minaret, Qutb Minar, that stands close by. The rooms are comfortable and chic, catering to guests with an array of state-of-the-art services. It also has a wide variety of sports facilities and even a bowling alley to keep guests entertained.

Key to Price Guide *see p234* **Key to Symbols** *see back cover flap*

FURTHER AFIELD (SOUTH) Crowne Plaza

New Friends Colony **Tel** *011 2683 5070* **Fax** *011 2683 7758* **Rooms** *229*

This luxury hotel is housed in a beautiful white marble building with lavish restaurants and cafés that make a stay truly enjoyable. Stroll over to the adjoining community centre for a host of notable eateries and boutiques. Guests may find the hotel travel desk slow. **www.ichotelsgroup.com**

FURTHER AFIELD (SOUTH) Jaypee Vasant Continental

Vasant Vihar **Tel** *011 2614 8800* **Fax** *011 2614 5959* **Rooms** *119*

A popular business hotel adjoining South Delhi's favourite shopping arcade, Priya Complex. It offers three speciality restaurants and a coffee shop with mouthwatering desserts. The rooms are lavish and well equipped with world-class facilities after their recent renovation. The poolside is ideal for a romantic dinner. **www.jaypeehotels.com**

FURTHER AFIELD (SOUTH) The Manor

77 Friends Colony (West) **Tel** *011 2692 5151* **Fax** *011 2692 7510* **Rooms** *10*

Built in the late 1950s, The Manor is set against a lovely residential backdrop. It is a friendly stopover for a stay away from home. The rooms have stately queen-sized beds and other modest facilities. For a relaxing experience, lounge at their roof terrace, which overlooks a pretty and quiet garden. **www.themanordelhi.com**

FURTHER AFIELD (SOUTH) Uppal's Orchid

NH-8. Near Indira Gandhi International Airport **Tel** *011 2506 1515* **Fax** *011 2506 1516* **Rooms** *84*

India's first eco-friendly hotel, Uppal's Orchid is a peaceful, modern five-star hotel. Elegant accommodation merges sophistication with personalised service. Rooms overlook lush green surroundings. A host of speciality restaurants serve contemporary Continental and Indian cuisine. **www.uppalsorchidhotel.com**

FURTHER AFIELD (SOUTH) WelcomHotel

District Centre, Saket **Tel** *011 4266 1122* **Fax** *011 4266 2112* **Rooms** *220*

A great, friendly staff assists a visitors' every need and a wide selection of restaurants offers excellent food quality. The downside is exorbitant beverage rates and a whopping 25 per cent tax on wines, so keep an eye on your bill. From a stately reception hall to spacious, elegant rooms, this hotel has it all.

FURTHER AFIELD (SOUTH) The Grand

Nelson Mandela Road, Vasant Kunj **Tel** *011 2677 1234* **Fax** *011 2670 5891* **Rooms** *444*

The Grand stands out for its style and decor. It has stunning interiors and a stylish coffee shop. The rooms have beautiful wooden panels and are exquisitely furnished to ensure a grand and luxurious stay. Also enjoy a host of amazing speciality restaurants and pubs. **www.thegrandnewdelhi.com**

FURTHER AFIELD (SOUTH) Hyatt Regency

Bhikaji Cama Place **Tel** *011 2679 1234* **Fax** *011 2679 1122* **Rooms** *508*

Majestic and grand, the rooms at the Hyatt Regency exude sheer luxury. Modern furnishing, wooden floors and exquisite glasswork portray a chic, avant-garde look. La Piazza undoubtedly serves the city's best Italian cuisine and TK's Oriental Grill offers an interactive cooking and dining experience. **http://delhi.regency.hyatt.com**

FURTHER AFIELD (SOUTH) InterContinental Eros

Nehru Place **Tel** *011 4122 3344* **Fax** *011 2622 4288* **Rooms** *224*

Opulent in every aspect, from the elegant rooms to the location next to Delhi's silicon valley, Nehru Place. Many popular restaurants and shopping complexes are minutes away. Visit the in-house restaurant, Empress of China for authentic Oriental cuisine or indulge yourself at their luxury spa. **www.ichotelsgroup.com**

FURTHER AFIELD (SOUTH) Radisson Hotel

Sikandarpur, National Highway No. 8 **Tel** *011 2677 9191* **Fax** *011 2677 9090* **Rooms** *256*

Part of the worldwide chain of 350 hotels, the Radisson is conveniently located close to the airport. The hotel endeavours to exceed their guests' expectations by providing world-class rooms and sheer luxury. It houses many popular restaurants and bars although be wary of unexpectedly steep taxes. **www.radisson.com**

FURTHER AFIELD (WEST) The Ashok

50-B Chanakyapuri **Tel** *011 2611 0101* **Fax** *011 2687 3216* **Rooms** *550*

The Ashok's dramatic and palatial Mughal architecture along with sweeping views and impeccable staff make it a grand holiday treat. The rooms are lavish, spacious and luxurious. Visitors can spend their days lazing by the sun-drenched poolside or at the spa, Amatra City. Their pub, Soho, hosts many music events. **www.theashok.com**

FURTHER AFIELD (WEST) Hotel Samrat

Kautilya Marg, Chanakyapuri **Tel** *011 2611 0606* **Fax** *011 2467 9056* **Rooms** *247*

Hotel Samrat is a decent stopover, though not really advisable for a longer stay. The upper floors are occupied by important government offices. The rooms are neat and comfortable. However, the services offered are moderate and need to be improved. The plus points are its location and popular health club. **www.theashokgroup.com**

FURTHER AFIELD (WEST) Maurya Sheraton

Diplomatic Enclave, Sardar Patel Marg **Tel** *011 2611 2233* **Fax** *011 2611 3333* **Rooms** *484*   **Map**

This exclusive hotel offers luxury, privacy and style along with a range of world-class facilities. Its list of leisure activities extends from tarot readings to a round of golf at a 27-hole Jack Nicklaus signature course. It also houses Bukhara and Dum Pukht (see p.259), two of the city's top restaurants. **www.itcwelcomgroup.in**

FURTHER AFIELD (WEST) The Taj Palace Hotel
Sardar Patel Marg, Diplomatic Enclave **Tel** 011 2611 0202 **Fax** 011 2611 0808 **Rooms** 422

Overlooking the Delhi Ridge, this majestic hotel merges ultra-modern facilities with age-old traditions. Popular with travelling VIPs. The building faces the pool and their spa services are excellent. Avoid driving in or out of the hotel in the evening as there is usually a traffic jam in the nearby roads. **www.tajhotels.com**

FURTHER AFIELD (SOUTH OF DELHI) Ibrahim Kothi
District Pataudi, Haryana **Tel** 011 2301 3794 **Fax** 011 2301 7834 **Rooms** 15

Designed by the famous architect Heinz in the early 20th century, Ibrahim Kothi, also known as The Pataudi Palace, has served as the prime location for many popular Bollywood movies. Spread over 10 ha (25 acres) of lush green gardens, the rooms are fit for royalty. **www.neemranahotels.com**

FURTHER AFIELD (SOUTH OF DELHI) Heritage Village
NH-8, Manesar, Gurgaon **Tel** 0124 229 0305 **Fax** 0124 229 0345 **Rooms** 82

Showcasing the opulence of historic India, this hotel offers visitors a touch of ethnic Indian culture and palatial luxury close to the metropolis. Each cluster of rooms is surrounded by trees, the interiors are shaded with soothing peach tones and equipped with traditional furnishings and modern amenities. **www.selecthotels.co.in**

FURTHER AFIELD (SOUTH OF DELHI) The Bristol
Adjacent to DLF Qutab Enclave Phase1, Gurgaon **Tel** 0124 435 1111 **Fax** 0124 405 4444 **Rooms** 83

Charming hotel strategically located within DLF, the popular business destination. From the brightly lit lobby to the swanky rooms, the place has European-style decor. They offer a number of recreational services including a gym, swimming pool and spa. It gained popularity especially after its recent renovation. **www.thebristolhotel.com**

FURTHER AFIELD (SOUTH OF DELHI) Tikli Bottom
Manendar Farm, Gairatpur Bas, PO Tikli, Gurgaon Tel 0124 276 6556 *Rooms* 4

The beauty and traditions of Colonial India come alive at Tikli Bottom. This lovely Lutyens-style building offers four luxurious rooms with breathtaking views of the surrounding Aravalli Hills. Room tariffs include all meals and drinks. Indulge in a stay at this mansion for complete and sublime relaxation. **www.tiklibottom.com**

FURTHER AFIELD (SOUTH OF DELHI) Trident-Hilton Gurgaon
443 Udyog Vihar, Phase V, Gurgaon **Tel** 0124 245 0505 **Fax** 0124 245 0606 **Rooms** 136

Voted "India's Leading Business Hotel for 2005", the Trident-Hilton is the latest buzzword among the swanky hotels that have sprung up around the city. Their lavish rooms are equipped with ultra-modern facilities to suit the travellers comfort needs. Cilantro, their multi-cuisine restaurant, is popular. **www.trident-hilton.com**

NORTH OF DELHI

HARIDWAR Sagar Ganga Resorts
Niranjan Akhara Road, Mayapur **Tel** 01334 222 115 **Rooms** 7

This exclusive property once belonged to the Nepalese royal family, and has large, luxurious rooms and an Art Deco ambience. It is situated on the banks of the Ganges and even has its own private *ghat* (steps leading to the water). Each room has its own balcony offering lovely river views. **www.sagarresort.com**

HARIDWAR Teerth
Har Ki Pauri, Subhash Ghat **Tel** 01334 225 311 **Fax** 01334 225 111 **Rooms** 36

Athough the surrounding area is crowded, the hotel is situated on the banks of the Ganges. Each room has a balcony with a great view of the river and Har-ki-Pauri, the busy and colourful main *ghat* in Haridwar. The hotel also provides tourist information. **www.hotelteerth.com**

HARIDWAR Classic Residency
Jwalapur Road **Tel** 01334 228 005-07 **Fax** 01334 220 374 **Rooms** 47

The rooms at the Classic are basic but comfortable. The hotel offers some interesting adventure activities, has a swimming pool and health club and serves good vegetarian food at the in-house restaurant. There is also a pleasant lawn and garden. **www.classichotelsindia.com**

RISHIKESH Bhandari Swiss Cottage
Laxman Jhula, By Pass Road **Tel** 0135 243 2939 **Rooms** 29

An old establishment with great charm and character. This guesthouse has two halls for yoga, meditation, Reiki, ayurveda and Pranic healing under the guidance of experts. The accommodation also includes tents for camping during fine weather.

RISHIKESH GMVN Tourist Bungalow
Muni-Ki-Reti **Tel** 0135 243 0373 **Fax** 0135 243 1793 **Rooms** 40

Pleasant and roomy cottages set in a quiet and pretty garden, located a short distance away from the city centre. Offering basic accommodation with the added bonus of river views. The complex has no restaurant; however, meals can be delivered to the room. It is advisable to book rooms in advance. **www.gmvnl.com**

Key to Price Guide *see p234* **Key to Symbols** *see back cover flap*

RISHIKESH New Bhandari Swiss Cottage

After Ram Jhula **Tel** *0135 243 5322* **Rooms** *22*

The rooms are basic and simple, with a common bath. The main attraction here is the in-house bakery which offers fresh breads, delicious muffins and pies every morning. Located in the forest, it offers a range of accommodation. The rooftop suite has airconditioning, TV and a bathtub.

RISHIKESH Ganga View

63 Haridwar Road **Tel** *0135 243 0781* **Fax** *0135 243 6146* **Rooms** *27*

Great views of the Ganges and the surrounding mountain ranges come with this modern hotel. The amenities are meant to suit tourists who want comfort as well as peace. Pilgrimage and wildlife tours, trekking, boating and river rafting are organised. Also offers yoga classes. **www.uttrakhandhotels.com**

RISHIKESH High Bank Peasants Cottage

Upper Tapovan **Tel** *0135 243 3478* **Fax** *0135 243 1654* **Rooms** *9*

This cosy place is attractively located high above the Ganges and has a pretty flower and vegetable garden. Good discounts are given for stays extending over a week. They arrange rappelling, kayaking and rock climbing for kids, expert yoga teachers conduct classes, and ayurvedic massages can also be organised. **www.rishikesh.org**

RISHIKESH Ganga Kinare

16 Veerabhadra Road **Tel** *0135 243 1658* **Fax** *0135 243 5243* **Rooms** *38*

This riverside hotel has a panoramic view of the hills, a lovely riverside lawn and private *ghat*. It offers yoga and meditation classes and ayurvedic massages are also arranged. Boating and white-water rafting tours are organised by the in-house travel desk. **www.uttrakhandhotels.com**

RISHIKESH The Glasshouse on the Ganges

23rd Milestone, Rishikesh-Badrinath Road **Tel** *01378 269 224* **Fax** *011 2435 1112* **Rooms** *15*

Set in a royal fruit orchard with a garden of tropical plants and rare birds, this exclusive resort has a private spring and sand beach. The six cottages overlook the Ganges and the mountains beyond. The hotel organises walks, river rafting, water-skiing in Dak Pathar near Dehra Dun and winter sports in Auli. **www.neemranahotels.com**

RISHIKESH Ananda In The Himalayas, Rishikesh

The Palace Estate, Narendra Nagar **Tel** *01378 227 500* **Fax** *01378 227 550* **Rooms** *70*

Set in a 40-ha (100-acre) estate, this is one of India's most luxurious spa-resorts. Focusing on traditional Indian sciences of yoga and ayurveda, it combines modern facilities with age-old traditions. It offers meditation, yogic and ayurvedic treatments and other forms of holistic healing in various special spa packages. **www.anandaspa.com**

AGRA AND AROUND

AGRA Lauries Hotel

Mahatma Gandhi Road **Tel** *0562 242 1433* **Fax** *0562 226 8045* **Rooms** *28*

One of Agra's oldest hotels, its lack of air conditioning keep the rates low. It is conveniently located on Mahatma Gandhi Road and offers comfortable accommodation and good service. With its very basic amenities, it is popular with backpackers. Lauries also offers camping and money changing facilities.

AGRA Amar Yatri Niwas

Tourist Complex Area, Fatehabad Road **Tel** *0562 223 3030* **Fax** *0562 223 3035* **Rooms** *41*

Though the decor is slightly garish, the hotel is popular and has a range of rooms equipped with all essential facilities. It is conveniently located on the main road of the city's tourist complex, and is close to the Taj Mahal, the railway station and bus stand. **www.amaryatriniwas.com**

AGRA Ganga Ratan

Fatehabad Road **Tel** *0562 223 2660* **Fax** *0562 233 0193* **Rooms** *66*

This hotel is known for its friendly service and clean, comfortable rooms. All basic amenities are provided and the in-house restaurant serves Indian, Chinese and Continental food. It is conveniently located near the state emporia and is a few yards away from the Taj Mahal. **www.hotelgangaratan.com**

AGRA Mayur Tourist Complex

Fatehabad Road **Tel** *0562 233 2302* **Fax** *0562 233 2907* **Rooms** *24*

A mid-range, well-managed hotel with cottages set within an extensive lawn. Each cottage has a private garden. Very popular and often full, it has a good garden resturant, Bage-E-Bahar, with an efficient and courteous staff. It also has a children's park and camping facilities. **www.mayurcomplex.com**

AGRA Taj Khema (UPSTDC)

Eastern Gate, Taj Mahal **Tel** *0562 233 0140* **Fax** *0562 223 0001* **Rooms** *6*

A small government-run hotel near the Taj with simple, good value standard rooms. Its restaurant offers Indian, Chinese and Continental meals. Photographers wil appreciate the superb views of the monument from the raised garden. This is a highly affordable, clean and fun place to stay. **www.up-tourism.com**

AGRA Tourist Bungalow (UPSTDC)

Raja Ki Mandi, Delhi Gate **Tel** *0562 285 0120* **Fax** *0562 285 3472* **Rooms** *35*

A small, clean and cheerful hotel with a pleasant courtyard. Good food and a clean environment are coupled with thoughtful and friendly staff. This budget hotel offers a range of accommodation that includes deluxe rooms with air conditioning. **www.up-tourism.com**

AGRA Clarks Shiraz

54 Taj Road **Tel** *0562 222 6121* **Fax** *0562 222 6128* **Rooms** *237*

Pleasantly located amidst extensive manicured gardens, this was India's first five-star hotel and has recently been given an attractive face-lift. The rooms have beautiful views of the Taj as does the rooftop restaurant. It has a large number of good in-house restaurants and bars, a coffee shop and confectionaries. **www.hotelclarksshiraz.com**

AGRA Hotel Yamuna View

6-B The Mall **Tel** *0562 236 1223* **Fax** *0562 236 1620* **Rooms** *58*

Located close to the railway station, this well-managed hotel offers traditional hospitality, comfortable rooms and friendly staff. Its in-house restaurants serve a variety of Chinese, Indian and Continental meals while the bar offers domestic and imported alcohol. **www.hotelyamunaviewagra.com**

AGRA Howard Park Plaza International

Taj Ganj, Fatehabad Road **Tel** *0562 233 1870* **Fax** *0562 233 0408* **Rooms** *84*

An elegant hotel with a rooftop viewing gallery. The hotel's cuisine is renowned, especially that of the poolside restaurant which serves delicious Indian food. The hotel has a shopping arcade, perfect for gifts and souvenirs. Classical music concerts take place at the open-air Oriental restaurant every evening. **http://howardindia.com**

AGRA Mansingh Palace

Fatehabad Road **Tel** *0562 233 1771* **Fax** *0562 233 0202* **Rooms** *97*

This luxurious hotel, named after a famous Rajput king, has some rooms overlooking the Taj. The bar, Jacuzzi and swimming pool with a water-slide are special attractions. Live *ghazal* concerts take place at the Sheesh Mahal restaurant which overlooks the pool. The hotel has a good coffee shop and bar. **www.mansinghhotels.com**

AGRA Holiday Inn

Sanjay Place, M G Road **Tel** *0562 252 3460* **Fax** *0562 252 3591* **Rooms** *145*

A relatively new hotel owned by a well-known international chain, it is sensitively designed and serviced in the best traditions of Indian hospitality. The facilities are modern, clean and well-maintained. The buffet breakfasts and lunches are especially popular and are served by friendly and efficient staff. **www.ichotelgroup.com**

AGRA Jaypee Palace Hotels

Tora Village, Fatehabad Road **Tel** *0562 233 0800* **Fax** *0562 233 0850* **Rooms** *350*

Luxurious rooms set around a series of impressive terraced courts in 10 ha (25 acres) of lush gardens and ponds, make this an attractive place for a longer stay. Live Bharat Natyam performances and *ghazals* are regular entertainment features in the evening. Also popular is the ayurvedic spa. **www.jaypeehotels.com**

AGRA Taj View

Taj Ganj, Fatehabad Road **Tel** *0562 223 2400* **Fax** *0562 223 2420* **Rooms** *100*

This magnificent hotel nestles amongst four ha (nine acres) of beautiful gardens. The rooms are stylish and luxurious with most commanding a view of the Taj; some open onto meticulous lawns and the poolside. They offer a wide range of activities including sports, magic shows, cookery classes and puppet shows. **www.tajhotels.com**

AGRA The Trident

Taj Nagari Scheme, Fatehabad Road **Tel** *0562 233 1818* **Fax** *0562 223 1516* **Rooms** *138*

This hotel's impressive decor is Mughal-inspired. Considered Agra's most superior accommodation, its range of luxurious rooms are pleasing and modern. They offer special "Discover India" winter packages which include sightseeing at promotional rates, available at all Trident hotels in the country. **www.hilton.com**

AGRA Amar Vilas

Taj East Gate Road **Tel** *0562 223 1515* **Fax** *0562 223 1516* **Rooms** *102*

Set in elegant Mughal gardens with fountains, pavilions and pools, every room in this spa-hotel offers glorious views of the Taj Mahal. It is built in a style inspired by Moorish and Mughal architecture and the rich interiors are reflective of the opulence of the age of emperors. **www.oberoiamarvilas.com**

AGRA Welcomgroup Mughal Sheraton

Fatehabad Road **Tel** *0562 233 1701* **Fax** *0562 233 1730* **Rooms** *287*

This spectacular hotel won the Aga Khan Award for excellence in Mughal architecture. Set in 16 ha (39 acres) of glorious gardens and lavishly furnished, this is one of India's best hotels. A wide array of leisure activities includes a sauna, buggy rides and live music every evening at their restaurant, Bagh-e-Bahar. **www.welcomgroup.com**

BHARATPUR Hotel Saras (RTDC)

Agra Road **Tel** *05644 223 700* **Rooms** *28*

A government-run tourist hotel, the main advantage of Hotel Saras is that it is walking distance from Keoladeo National Park. This budget hotel, offering basic service and standard rooms, does get filled up rather quickly, so it is advisable to book well in advance. **www.rajasthan-tourism.com**

Key to Price Guide *see p234* **Key to Symbols** *see back cover flap*

BHARATPUR Chandra Mahal Haveli

Peharsar, Nadbai tehsil, Jaipur Agra Road **Tel** *05643 264 336* **Fax** *011 404 4657* **Rooms** *22*

This 19th-century heritage *haveli* is tucked away in Peharsar, a short distance from Bharatpur town. It is surrounded by sunshine-yellow mustard fields in winter. The building showcases exquisite Mughal architecture, complete with central courtyard, marble fountain and numerous airy balconies. **www.chandramahalhaveli.com**

BHARATPUR Eagle's Nest

Bird Sanctuary Road **Tel** *05644 225 144* **Fax** *05644 222 310* **Rooms** *12*

This is one of several little guesthouses located in close proximity to the Bharatpur bird sanctuary. Very friendly and welcoming, its hospitality makes up for the lack of sophistication and luxurious rooms. It also has a beautiful lawn, perfect for relaxing under the sun or in the evening after a day of bird-watching.

BHARATPUR Bharatpur Forest Lodge (ITDC)

Keoladeo National Park **Tel** *05644 222 760* **Fax** *05644 222 864* **Rooms** *17*

Although comparatively expensive, this eco-friendly hotel located inside the Bharatpur bird sanctuary, is the best place to stay. Its restaurant is open to non-residents. The rooms are air conditioned, with attached bathrooms. Cycle rickshaws and bicycles are arranged for park trips and tour guides for bird-watching.

BHARATPUR Laxmi Vilas Palace

Kakaji Ki Kothi, Agra Road **Tel** *05644 223 523* **Fax** *05644 225 259* **Rooms** *30*

This heritage hotel built in 1887 is an eclectic and lively fusion of Rajput and Mughal architecture, set in 20 ha (50 acres) of secluded land. The rooms are elegantly furnished and the decor fit for royalty. The inner courtyard is perfect for a romantic dinner under the stars. Special jeep safaris can be arranged. **http://laxmivilas.com**

BRINDAVAN Bhaktivedanta Ashrama & MVT Guest House

Behind ISKON Temple, Raman Reti **Tel** *0565 254 0050* **Rooms** *29*

Definitely the nicest place to stay in Brindavan, this guesthouse, part of the Bhaktivedanta Ashram, is meticulously clean. Set amongst mango trees, in neat lawns that are home to peacocks and parrots. Some rooms have attached kitchenettes and bathrooms. They also offer tourist information for pilgrimage tours. **www.mvtindia.com**

BRINDAVAN Sri Krishna Balaram International Guest House

Raman Reti **Tel** *0565 254 0020* **Fax** *0565 254 0023* **Rooms** *32*

Adjacent to the ISKCON temple, this guesthouse offers basic, clean rooms, open to its members and their guests at a discounted fare. Non-members can also book rooms depending on availability. A small, recently-built restaurant serves purely vegetarian meals. Try a variety of Indian sweets at Bhoga Bhandar. **www.iskonvrindavan.info**

DEEG Midway Hotel

District Bharatpur **Tel** *05641 221 000* **Rooms**

A tiny guesthouse located 24 kms (15 miles) from Bharatpur on the Alwar State Highway and close to the Deeg bus stand, this government hotel is walking distance from Deeg Palace. Rooms come with attached bath and running hot and cold water. The lounge contains the hotel's sole television.

DHOLPUR Raj Niwas Palace

Dholpur **Tel** *011 2643 6572* **Fax** *011 4162 3448* **Rooms** *8*

This beautiful heritage hotel offers its visitors a wealth of facilities and luxurious interiors inspired by traditional royal designs. The rooms are opulent with beautiful high ceilings. Leisure activities include a movie theatre, swimming pool, library, or evening walks in the manicured gardens. **www.dholpurpalace.com**

FATEHPUR SIKRI The Archaeological Survey Dak Bungalow

The Mall **Tel** *05613 282 248* **Rooms** *6*

This spacious old Colonial-style resthouse adjoining the historic complex of Fathepur Sikri must be booked through the Archaeological Survey of India (ASI) office. It is, however, usually reserved for government guests only. Meals are cooked by the staff only on request.

FATEHPUR SIKRI Gulistan Tourist Complex

Agra Road **Tel** *05613 282 490* **Rooms** *24*

Surprisingly attractive for a small town hotel run by the government, Gulistan is conveniently located close to the bus stand. This comfortable mid-range place offers a small discount from April to September. A pleasant place in a peaceful location, it is built around a courtyard and has a reasonably good restaurant. **www.up-tourism.com**

GWALIOR Gwalior Regency

Link Road **Tel** *0751 234 0670* **Fax** *0751 234 3520* **Rooms** *48*

A well-appointed hotel in the centre of town with rooms ranging from good-value economy to the super deluxe. Set in pleasant grounds, it offers a range of leisure and sporting activities. It also has a discotheque, a bar and an excellent multi-cuisine restaurant.

GWALIOR Shelter

Padav, Near Indian Airlines Office **Tel** *0751 232 6209* **Fax** *0751 232 6212* **Rooms** *54*

A newish hotel, typical of many small towns, it is close to all major tourist sites, the bus and railway stations. The multi-cuisine restaurant offers a standard range of Indian, Chinese, Mughlai and Continental food. It offers assistance with travel bookings and tourist information as well as a 24-hour taxi service. It also has a 24-hour café.

GWALIOR Tansen Gwalior (MPSTDC)
6-A Gandhi Road, Civil Lines **Tel** *0751 234 0370* **Fax** *0751 234 0371* **Rooms** *36*

Located in a pleasant area, this hotel is popular with business travellers. The rooms are clean and comfortable with all the basic amenities provided. It also has a large conference room and an in-house restaurant. Rooms fill up rather quickly so advance booking is advised. **www.mptourism.com**

GWALIOR Usha Kiran Palace
Jayendraganj, Lashkar **Tel** *0751 244 4000* **Fax** *0751 244 4018* **Rooms** *40*

This glamorous and luxurious hotel was once the maharaja's guesthouse. Snooker, croquet, yoga, cookery classes and badminton facilities are available on the premises while outside recreational activities can be arranged on prior notice. The spa, located in the royal *zenana* chambers, offers massages and aromatherapy. **www.tajhotels.com**

MATHURA Agra Hotel
Bengali Ghat **Tel** *0565 240 3318* **Rooms** *11*

Overlooking the river, this small, clean 80-year-old hotel has maintained its standards and offers all essential facilities. The rooms are fairly decent; the ones with hot water and a view of the Yamuna come for an extra charge. It is about a six-minute walk to Vishram Ghat.

MATHURA Abhinandan
Govardhan Chauraha, Near Railway Station **Tel** *0565 242 2290* **Fax** *0565 242 3213* **Rooms** *30*

This warm and friendly boutique hotel, fitted with pleasant contemporary decor, is located in the heart of the city. The rooms are luxurious with a range of amenities and are favoured by business travellers and corporate guests. They also offer tourist information at their travel desk. **www.hotelabhinandan.com**

MATHURA Brijwasi Royal Hotel
State Bank Crossing, Station Road **Tel** *0565 240 1224* **Fax** *0565 240 1227* **Rooms** *40*

This large hotel is conveniently located close to the railway station and the main bus stand. It is also near the Dwarkadhish Temple. The rooms are clean and comfortable with essential amenities provided. The in-house restaurant serves multi-cuisine meals and there is also a bar. **www.brijwasiroyal.com**

MATHURA Madhuvan
Krishna Nagar **Tel** *0565 242 0064* **Fax** *0565 242 0684* **Rooms** *27*

One of the fancier hotels in town, it has a swimming pool and health centre. Rooms come with attractive garden-views and all basic amenities. Mayur, their in-house restaurant, serves Indian, Chinese and Continental cuisine enlivened by live music performances. The outdoor bar is a good place to unwind in the evenings.

MATHURA Sheetal Regency
Deeg Gate, near Sri Krishna Janam Bhoomi **Tel** *0565 240 4597* **Fax** *0565 240 0106* **Rooms** *28*

This clean, friendly hotel is located close to the train and bus stations. It organizes guides and vehicles for sightseeing as well as games to keep children busy. It offers tourist information and a "Jewels of Brij Bhoomi" package. They provide adequate parking space. **www.hotelsheetalregency.com**

MATHURA Best Western Radha Ashok
P O GTB, Masani Bypass Road **Tel** *0565 253 0395* **Fax** *0565 253 0396* **Rooms** *25*

This ritzy hotel, run by a reputable hotel group, is popular with international clientele. Surrounded by lush lawns, it is reasonably close to tourist attractions in Agra and Mathura. They have money changing facilities and a travel help-desk that arranges car hires and offers tourist information. **www.mathura-vrindavan.com**

ORCHHA Betwa Cottages (MPSTDC)
Orchha, Dist Tikamgarh **Tel** *07680 252 618* **Fax** *07680 252 624* **Rooms** *24*

Charming individual cottages are set in a garden near the banks of the River Betwa. The complex is walking distance from the superb Orcha cenotaphs. Its serene environment is recommended for a relaxing, peaceful time. They organise river rafting tours and have camping facilities. **www.mptourism.com**

ORCHHA Sheesh Mahal (MPSTDC)
Orchha, Dist Tikamgarh **Tel** *07680 252 624* **Rooms** *8*

A newer wing of the historic early 17th-century Jahangiri Mahal, this heritage property is now a charming state-run hotel wedged between Jahangiri Mahal and Raj Mahal. The rooms, redolent with history, offer visitors a romantic ambience and range from economy rooms to the grand maharani suites. **www.mptourism.com**

ORCHHA Bundhelkhand Riverside
Orchha, Dist Tikamgarh **Tel** *7680 252 612* **Fax** *7680 252 333* **Rooms** *29*

Once the royal retreat of the Maharaja of Orchha, this exclusive hotel is set in sprawling grounds on the banks of the River Betwa. The rooms are large and luxurious, furnished by beautiful hand-crafted furniture. Enjoy spectacular full moon nights on the turretted terrace that overlooks the river. **www.bundelkhandriverside.com**

ORCHHA The Orchha Resort
Kanchana Ghat, Dist Tikamgarh **Tel** *07680 252 222* **Fax** *07680 285 677* **Rooms** *45*

This resort is popular with tourist groups as it is one of the few options available in Orchha and offers standard comforts. Located on the banks of the River Betwa, they have tent accommodation, available also in the winter season. They serve only vegetarian food in their restaurant. **www.orchharesort.com**

Key to Price Guide *see p234* **Key to Symbols** *see back cover flap*

JAIPUR AND ENVIRONS

AJMER KHADIM (RTDC)

Near Savitri Girls College, Civil Lines **Tel** *0145 262 7490* **Fax** *0145 243 1330* **Rooms** *57*

A standard state-run tourism hotel which is well-maintained and offers a range of accommodation from dormitories to air-cooled rooms. Centrally located, close to the railway station and bus stand, they also arrange air and rail tickets. They have a decent in-house restaurant and bar. **www.rajasthantourism.gov.in**

AJMER Fort Baghera

PO & Village Baghera **Tel** *01467 281 231* **Rooms** *5*

This historic 17th-century fort, converted into a heritage hotel, stands on the Ajmer-Sawai Madhopur bus route. It offers a chance to enjoy folk music and dances in beautiful surroundings. They also offer boating and yachting on the river and Varah Sagar Lake. The fort has five double rooms and a charming, medieval ambience.

AJMER Mansingh Palace

Near Anasagar Lake, Vaishali Nagar **Tel** *0145 242 5702* **Fax** *0145 242 5858* **Rooms** *54*

In spite of its wonderful location near the lake, its spacious rooms and its good facilities, services could be improved to justify the hotel's comparatively high rates. Their in-house restaurant overlooks the Ana Sagar lake. Book in advance during the annual *Urs* (Sufi festival). **www.mansinghhotels.com**

ALWAR Hotel Aravali

1 CEB, near railway station **Tel** *0144 233 2316* **Fax** *0144 233 2011* **Rooms** *36*

Though small, this is without doubt the best place to stay in Alwar, although some rooms can be noisy. The hotel is conveniently located close to the railway station. It is equipped with most facilities and the owners help to organise treks and tours. Delicious home-cooked *thali* meals are on offer in their restaurant. **www.hotelaravali.com**

ALWAR Hotel Alwar

25 Manu Marg **Tel** *0144 270 0012* **Fax** *0144 233 9501* **Rooms** *18*

The hotel is economical, clean and quiet with comfortable, good-sized rooms. Situated within pleasant green lawns and pretty flowerbeds where they claim you have only the birds for company. Jeep safaris to Sariska National Park, golf and fishing trips can be arranged, while their in-house activities include snooker. **www.hotel-alwar.com**

ALWAR Hill Fort Kesroli

Village Kesroli, via MIA, PO Bahala **Tel** *01468 289 352* **Fax** *01468 289 352* **Rooms** *21*

This seven-turretted heritage site is one of the oldest in India. Sited atop a cluster of dark rocks just outside Alwar, it commands spectacular views from its ramparts. Its rooms are elegant, the decor befitting royalty. They arrange village safaris, camel cart rides and visits to nearby historical tourist sites. **www.neemranahotels.com**

DUNDLOD Dundlod Fort

Dundlod, Dist Jhunjhunu, Shekhawati **Tel** *01594 252 199* **Fax** *01594 252 519* **Rooms** *24*

An 18th-century heritage hotel where a royal welcome, with folk music, camels and garlands, can be arranged on request. The rooms are decorated in typical Rajput style, the rooftop restaurant lit by rustic oil lamps in the evenings. They arrange horse safaris, cycle polo and cultural programmes. **www.dundlod.com**

FATEHPUR Hotel Haveli (RTDC)

NH-11, Fathepur, Dist Sikar **Tel** *01571 230 293* **Fax** *01571 232 831* **Rooms** *8*

For those who wish to spend a few days in the Shekhawati area, this clean, reasonably-priced, old-fashioned place offers both air-cooled rooms and dormitories. Tourist information and car rental services are available at the travel desk. They can arrange camel rides and village visits on request. **www.rajasthantourism.gov.in**

JAIPUR Bissau Palace Hotel

Near Saroj Cinema, outside Chandpol **Tel** *0141 230 4371* **Fax** *0141 230 4628* **Rooms** *48*

A charming heritage hotel, this oasis in the heart of the Pink City nestles within orange and lemon orchards. It has a fascinating collection of rare books, old silver and armour. They arrange camel and cart tours and their lunch and dinner buffets are accompanied by live folk music and *sitar* recitals. **www.bissaupalace.com**

JAIPUR Diggi Palace

Diggi House, S.M.S Hospital Road **Tel** *0141 237 3091* **Fax** *0141 237 0359* **Rooms** *45*

This is a small and attractive *haveli*-turned-guesthouse. The modest charges here may suit the budget traveller in search of traditional hospitality. Situated amidst 7 ha (18 acres) of beautiful gardens, the rooms range from the simple to the luxurious. They arrange camel safaris, yoga and cultural programmes. **www.hoteldiggipalace.com**

JAIPUR Gangaur (RTDC)

Mirza Ismail Road **Tel** *0141 237 1642* **Fax** *0141 237 1647* **Rooms** *63*

Located in the quiet bylanes of a busy road, this popular hotel has three good restaurants serving Indian and Chinese cuisines. On certain days, it also serves a special Rajasthani menu. It has a convenient souvenir shop and arranges city tours and transport on request. **www.rajasthantourism.gov.in**

JAIPUR Jai Mahal Palace

Jacob Road, Civil Lines **Tel** *0141 222 3636* **Fax** *0141 222 0707* **Rooms** *100*

Designed by Sir Swinton Jacob, this 18th-century building is now a luxurious heritage hotel. It is situated within walking distance of the boutiques in Civil Lines. Spacious grounds, solar-heated pool, elegant interiors with antique furniture, barbeque dinners and exceptional service make this a much-recommended hotel. **www.tajhotels.com**

JAIPUR Jaipur Ashok (ITDC)

Jai Singh Circle, Bani Park **Tel** *0141 220 4491* **Fax** *0141 220 4498* **Rooms** *97*

The tourism department manages this well-designed hotel located near the railway station. Set in a garden, it is well-appointed with most modern facilities. Popular with both tourists and businessmen, it has money-changing facilities and a travel desk that makes travel arrangements and organises sightseeing tours. **www.theashokgroup.com**

JAIPUR Karauli House

New Sanganer Road **Tel** *0141 229 0763* **Fax** *0141 229 2633* **Rooms** *4*

This old family home has been converted to a small guesthouse. It has a lovely garden and a warm, friendly atmosphere. A popular homestay option is offered, delicious meals served on request while sightseeing and pick-ups and drops are arranged from the airport, bus terminal and railway station. **www.karauli.com**

JAIPUR Khasa Kothi

MI Road **Tel** *0141 237 5151* **Fax** *0141 237 4040* **Rooms** *36*

Literally a "special mansion", this old heritage hotel, run by RTDC, was once a state guesthouse 100 years ago and is, unfortunately, a bit scruffy. However, it is centrally located and has large rooms surrounded by cool lawns. Tours are arranged at the Government of India tourist counter. **www.rajasthantourism.gov.in**

JAIPUR L.M.B Hotel

Johri Bazaar **Tel** *0141 256 5844* **Rooms** *33*

With small well-maintained rooms, this three-star hotel's main attraction is its location above a famous vegetarian restaurant, LMB (*see p.262*), in the centre of one of Jaipur's most popular *bazaars*. Its in-house restaurant and shop come highly recommended. They arrange sightseeing tours and transport at their travel desk. **www.hotellmb.com**

JAIPUR Alsisar Haveli

Near Sindhi bus stand, Sansar Chandra Road **Tel** *0141 236 4685* **Fax** *0141 236 4652* **Rooms** *47*

This beautiful 19th-century heritage *haveli* has retained its medieval look with large courtyards, arched corridors and a spacious terrace. It is centrally located although well secluded in a huge garden. The service is excellent. Nightly puppet shows and cultural programmes are arranged while guests dine. **www.alsisar.com**

JAIPUR Narain Niwas Palace Hotel

Kanota Bagh, Narian Singh Road **Tel** *0141 256 1291* **Fax** *1041 256 3448* **Rooms** *37*

Built in 1928, this popular heritage hotel was the royal Kanota family's country residence. It is surrounded by mango orchards and its traditional Rajasthani interior has been carefully preserved. It is equipped with a pool, a bar, two restaurants and a well-stocked reading hall. Sightseeing and transport can be arranged on request.

JAIPUR Raj Mahal Palace

Sardar Patel Marg, C-Scheme **Tel** *0141 5105 665* **Fax** *0141 222 1787* **Rooms** *31*

Prince Philip and Jacqueline Kennedy Onassis are among the hotel's famous visitors. Run as a hotel by the royal family, this palace has luxurious rooms and vast grounds where peacocks call through the day. Its rosewood-panelled library, billiard room and collection of memorabilia adds to its exclusivity (*see p195*). **www.royalfamilyjaipur.com**

JAIPUR Royal Castle Kanota

Kanota Bagh, Narian Singh Road **Tel** *0141 256 1291* **Fax** *0141 256 3448* **Rooms** *10*

Built in 1872, this fortified castle is private and exclusive. Situated amidst three ha (eight acres) of colourful fruit orchards, the rooms are lavish. It has a library with a collection of over 10,000 rare books. Village safaris and sightseeing trips are arranged as well as horse and camel rides. Evenings are enlivened with various cultural shows.

JAIPUR Chokhi Dhani

12th Mile, Tonk Road **Tel** *0141 277 0555* **Fax** *0141 277 0558* **Rooms** *65*

Designed to look like a Rajasthani village complex, this hotel offers accommodation in air-cooled cottages and *havelis*. It has a restaurant and bar, an entertainment centre and an open courtyard for meals and entertainment. Although some might find it kitschy, it continues to be one of Jaipur's top attractions. **www.chokhidhani.com**

JAIPUR Clarks Amer

P.O.Box 222, Jawaharlal Nehru Marg **Tel** *0141 255 0616* **Fax** *0141 255 0319* **Rooms** *211*

This hotel is located conveniently close to the airport and the textile town of Sanganer is also within easy reach. There is a rooftop restaurant and a café and bar. They recently launched the "Jaipur Pride Project", a homestay scheme in which home-cooked meals can also be arranged on request. **www.hotelclarks.com**

JAIPUR Holiday Inn Jaipur

Opp Ramgarh Modh bus stand, Amer Road **Tel** *0141 267 2000* **Fax** *0141 267 2335* **Rooms** *72*

This fine hotel has views of the beautiful Nahargarh Fort. The rooms are comfortable and spacious while the decor is contemporary and pleasing. Their ethnic outdoor "village" restaurant, which serves traditional Indian fare is open only for dinner and is enlivened by folk dancers, fortune-tellers fire-eaters. **www.holidayinnjaipur.com**

Key to Price Guide *see p234* **Key to Symbols** *see back cover flap*

JAIPUR Hotel Mansingh

Sansar Chandra Road **Tel** *0141 237 8771* **Fax** *0141 237 7582* **Rooms** *95*

Equipped with a range of modern conveniences, this hotel has a wonderful feeling of space. There are large windows set within well-decorated rooms that are very comfortable. Popular with business travellers, it has a health club, a rooftop restaurant, lounge bar and 24-hour money exchange counter. **www.mansinghhotels.com**

JAIPUR Hotel Mansingh Towers

Sansar Chandra Road **Tel** *0141 237 8771* **Fax** *0141 237 7582* **Rooms** *45*

This is the elegant and well-appointed new wing of Hotel Mansingh with which it shares some of its facilities. All essential amenities are provided in the rooms and each suite has its own private Jacuzzi. Their multi-cuisine restaurant serves good food and also has live music performances in the evening. **www.mansinghhotels.com**

JAIPUR Rajputana Palace Sheraton

Palace Road **Tel** *0141 510 0100* **Fax** *0141 510 2102* **Rooms** *216*

A large, elegantly designed hotel, with high standards of service. Various cultural programmes held in the evenings add to its attractions. It has a health club, a discotheque, a small theatre, shopping arcade and beauty parlour within its interiors. An open-air courtyard is enlivened by music and dance performances. **www.welcomgroup.com**

JAIPUR Ramgarh Lodge

Ramgarh lake, Jamwa **Tel** *01426 252 078* **Fax** *01426 252 079* **Rooms** *11*

This former royal hunting lodge *(see p197)* is set amidst beautiful gardens, exuding an old-world charm mingled with rustic earthiness. Polo, tennis, fishing and boating are on offer. Apart from elegant rooms they also offer camping facilities. Try to book a suite overlooking the glorious Ramgarh Lake. **www.tajhotels.com**

JAIPUR Samode Haveli

Samode House, Gangapol **Tel** *0141 263 2407* **Fax** *0141 263 1397* **Rooms** *29*

This graceful mansion offers stunning rooms with original wall paintings, exquisite antiques and mirrorwork. Their restaurant venues include an airy verandah and an outdoor back garden perfect for romantic evenings. They also arrange puppet shows, folk dances and live music performances in the central courtyard. **www.samode.com**

JAIPUR Trident Hilton Jaipur

Amber Road **Tel** *0141 267 0101* **Fax** *0141 267 0303* **Rooms** *137*

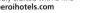

Apart from high standards of service and decor, the hotel's most attractive quality is its location directly opposite the Jal Mahal. The rooms are airy and luxuriously equipped, with some having garden or grand hill views. The Mansagar bar overlooks the swimming pool, the Aravalli Hills and the Man Sagar Lake beyond. **www.hilton.com**

JAIPUR Rajvilas

Goner Road **Tel** *0141 268 0101* **Fax** *0141 268 0202* **Rooms** *71*

A spectacular boutique hotel of the Oberoi chain, with impeccable service. Set in beautifully landscaped gardens recreating the magnificence of the Rajput age. Each room, luxury tent and villa is superbly crafted with a fine attention to detail. Their luxurious spa is adorned with frescoes on the walls. **www.oberoihotels.com**

JAIPUR Rambagh Palace Hotel

Near Ram Bagh Circle, Bhawani Singh Road **Tel** *0141 221 1919* **Fax** *0141 238 5098* **Rooms** *89*

This hotel retains much of the original and splendid decor from the time it was home to the Jaipur royal family *(see p195)*. It offers a taste of fine royal living, from the grand lobby to their "historical" suites. The decor is extravagant yet tasteful. A complimentary tour of the hotel is offered with champagne to round it off. **www.tajhotels.com**

JHUNJHUNU Hotel Jamuna Resort

Nathji ka Tila, Khemsati Road **Tel** *01592 232 871* **Fax** *01592 234 070* **Rooms** *14*

The resort is close to Hotel Shiv Shekhawati and run by the same owner. It comprises thatched cottages set amidst pleasant lawns, shady trees and flowerbeds. Various programmes are offered to instruct visitors on Indian arts, culinary delights and yoga. Bicycle tours and massages are arranged on request. **www.shivshekhawati.com**

JHUNJHUNU Hotel Shiv Shekhawati

Near Muni Ashram, Khemsati Road **Tel** *01592 512 695* **Fax** *01592 234 070* **Rooms** *18*

A clean, *haveli*-style lodge, whose owner is a storehouse of information on the history and architecture of the Shekhawati area, and happy to share the knowledge with his guests. This hotel offers basic, comfortable rooms and good set-price meals. They offer full- and half-day town tours in cars or jeeps. **www.shivshekhawati.com**

KISHANGARH Phool Mahal Palace

Near Kishangarh Fort **Tel** *01463 247 405* **Fax** *01463 247 505* **Rooms** *21*

This recently restored heritage property has the massive Kishangarh Fort as its backdrop. It has lovely deluxe rooms that are luxurious and fitted with modern facilities. Sightseeing can be arranged as well as visits to local artisans and artists and stone-cutting factories. **www.royalkishangarh.com**

MANDAWA Castle Mandawa

Mandawa, Dist Jhunjhnu **Tel** *01592 223 124* **Fax** *01592 223 171* **Rooms** *74*

One of the oldest and most popular heritage hotels in the region, its medieval charm blends with excellent service and modern amenities. Some rooms have marble fountains and arched windows offering splendid views. Sightseeing can be arranged on request; they also have a relaxing massage centre. **www.castlemandawa.com**

MANDAWA The Desert Resort

Mandawa, Dist Jhunjhunu **Tel** *01592 223245/514* **Fax** *01592-223151* **Rooms** *70*

A lovely resort built on a sand dune and designed to look like a traditional village, this is an ideal take-off point from Mandawa into the desert. Accommodation includes distinctively styled rooms and cottages with exteriors decorated by lime-paste and interiors adorned with mirrorwork and glass beads. **www.mandawahotels.com**

MUKUNDGARH Mukundgarh Fort

Mukundgarh, Dist Jhunjhunu, **Tel** *01594 252 397* **Fax** *01594 252 395* **Rooms** *49*

Located in the heart of the Shekhawati area, this heritage hotel has seen better days and could do with a face-lift. It is, however, set in a pleasant lawn. The interiors are reasonably clean. Sightseeing tours and camel rides can be arranged on request. **www.crosscountry.co.in**

NAWALGARH Apni Dhani

Jhnujhunu Road **Tel** *01594 222 239* **Fax** *01594 224 061* **Rooms** *8*

The owner of this "eco-conscious" resort is also one of the best guides in the region. The resort comprises imaginatively-designed mud huts, equipped with baths and solar panel heating. Delicious meals are served. Guided tours can be arranged along with camel cart rides and visits to workshops where local artisans display their skills.

NAWALGARH Roop Niwas Palace

PO Village Nawalgarh **Tel** *01594 222 008* **Fax** *01594 223 388* **Rooms** *23*

This heritage hotel is a charming blend of European and Rajput style architecture. Well-mannered staff add to its gracious atmosphere. Cart rides and horse and camel tours are a regular feature. Situated in a lovely garden that is perfect for relaxed evening strolls. Other leisure activities include billiards, swimming and sightseeing tours.

NEEMRANA Neemrana Fort Palace

PO Neemrana, Dist Alwar **Tel** *01494 246 006* **Fax** *01494 246 005* **Rooms** *44*

Immaculate hospitality and service awaits guests in this beautiful fort palace. This heritage hotel is highly recommended for its architectural splendor, exquisite interiors and its unique location, concealed within the Aravelli Hills. Rising to over ten storeys, it commands magnificent views. **www.neemranahotels.com**

PUSHKAR Hotel Sarovar

Pushkar, Dist Ajmer **Tel** *0145 277 2040* **Fax** *0145 277 2040* **Rooms** *40*

Located near the Pushkar Palace and the Rangji and Brahma temples, this state tourism hotel offers rooms and dormitories with pleasant views of the lake. One of the few places in town that can organise camel, horse and jeep safaris. They can also make transport arrangements on request. **www.rajasthantourism.gov.in**

PUSHKAR Peacock Holiday Resort

Panchkund Road **Tel** *0145 277 2093* **Fax** *0145 277 2516* **Rooms** *32*

A large, shaded courtyard adds to the tranquil atmosphere of this temple town hotel. The rooms have attached baths. Special prices are offered during the Pushkar Mela. It has three in-house restaurants, a water-slide and treadmill. Kerala massages, horse riding and camel safaris can be arranged. **www.peacock-pushkar.com**

PUSHKAR Tourist Village (RTDC)

Ganehra-Nagaur Road **Tel** *0145 277 2074* **Fax** *0145 277 2040* **Rooms** *30*

During the annual camel fair, the government sets up a tented village of 300 single and double tents at different price ranges that include meals. A few huts kept open all year are subject to price variations according to season. They provide an ideal setting amidst the hustle of the town. **www.rajasthantourism.gov.in**

PUSHKAR Pushkar Palace

Pushkar Lake, Chhoti Basti **Tel** *0145 277 3001* **Fax** *0145 277 2226* **Rooms** *53*

With a beautiful location on the banks of the Pushkar Lake, this 400-year-old palace hotel commands a panoramic view. The rooms are tastefully furnished with simple, elegant decor. The restaurant serves Indian, Chinese and Continental cuisine. During the annual camel fair, tented lodging is also available. **www.pushkarpalace.com**

PUSHKAR Pushkar Resorts

Village Ganhera, Motisar Road **Tel** *0145 277 2944* **Fax** *0145 277 2946* **Rooms** *40*

Consisting of clusters of luxury cottages with private lawns this resort recreates an oasis space. Set in lovely grounds amidst fruit orchards, with a pool and golf driving range, the hotel also offers sand volleyball, a library and croquet. An added attraction is the town's only bar and non-vegetarian restaurant. **www.pushkarresorts.com**

ROOPANGARH Roopangarh Fort

Roopangarh Fort, Dist Ajmer **Tel** *01497 220 444* **Fax** *01497 220 217* **Rooms** *22*

This fortress-turned-hotel is ideally situated for excursions to nearby historic sites. Beautifully furnished with antique pieces, the decor reflects the sense of history that surrounds this building. The cuisine is inspired by centuries-old family recipes. Visitors can explore the fort's secret passages and underground tank. **www.royalkishangarh.com**

SAMODE Samode Bagh

Vill Fatehpura, Bansa **Tel** *01423 240 235* **Fax** *01423 240 014* **Rooms** *44 tents*

Associated with the Samode Palace hotel, the Bagh has luxury tents with attached baths situated in an idyllic garden. A 61-metre-long (200-feet) row of fountains fed by natural springs also adorns the lawns. It offers the ambience of a royal desert camp. Leisure activities include massages, tennis, crafts and bird-watching. **www.samode.com**

Key to Price Guide *see p234* **Key to Symbols** *see back cover flap*

SAMODE Samode Palace

Samode Village **Tel** *01423 240 014* **Fax** *01423 240 014* **Rooms** *41*

This 400-year-old palace *(see p212)* has exquisite interiors and modern facilities. Charming and romantic, it offers elegant, luxurious rooms. The marble and mosaic pool is set against the Aravalli Hills while cultural shows are organized in the outdoor courtyard. Undeniably the region's finest heritage hotel. **www.samode.com**

SARISKA Tiger's Den (RTDC)

Sariska Road, via Thana Gazi **Tel** *0144 284 1342* **Rooms** *30*

Adjacent to the Sariska sanctuary, this is the only budget option for visitors to the park. The dormitories, rooms and services have fairly acceptable standards of comfort and efficiency. They can make transport arrangements while also offering tourist information and organised sightseeing tours. **www.rajasthantourism.gov.in**

SARISKA Sariska Palace

Sariska Road **Tel** *0144 284 1371* **Fax** *011 2615 4390* **Rooms** *100*

After a tiring day at the sanctuary, the comforts of this former royal hunting lodge are most welcome. The decor is opulent and the rooms are comfortable. There is an ayurvedic health centre as well as a health club. Folk songs, dances and a campfire are arranged in the evenings for groups. Sariska safaris also be arranged.

SARISKA Hotel Amanbagh

Village Ajaibgarh, Tehsil Thana Gazi **Tel** *01465 223 333* **Fax** *01465 223 335* **Rooms** *38*

This famed resort, rated by *Condé Nast Traveler* as one of the best in the country, is set within a walled oasis and reflects the region's architectural style. It has *haveli* suites, pool pavilions and a luxurious spa. The hotel arranges safaris and sightseeing tours. It is a good base from which to explore the Alwar area. **www.amanresorts.com**

SAWAI MADHOPUR Castle Jhoomar Bari (RTDC)

Ranthambhore Road **Tel** *07462 220 495* **Fax** *07462 220 495* **Rooms** *12*

This charming old royal jungle lodge, situated on top of a hill, has superb views of the forested countryside and is rich in atmosphere. You can even hear tigers roar at night in the nearby sanctuary. Very much in demand, so book in advance. Safaris into the sanctuary can be arranged. **www.rajasthantourism.gov.in**

SAWAI MADHOPUR Ranthambhore Regency

Ranthambhore Road **Tel** *07462 223 456* **Fax** *07462 223 500* **Rooms** *60*

A comparatively new hotel which offers decent service for surprisingly good rates. The building is set within pleasant lawns and the air-cooled rooms are quietly plush with traditional decor. The staff are welcoming and the two in-house restaurants serve good food, with bread freshly baked in their outdoor clay oven. **www.ranthambhor.com**

SAWAI MADHOPUR Aman-i-Khas

Sherpur, Khiljipur **Tel** *07462 252 052* **Fax** *07462 252 172* **Rooms** *10*

Set on the fringes of the Ranthambore National Park, and surrounded by rugged countryside, this wilderness retreat has luxury accommodation tents and a spa. The resort arranges safaris and camel rides. Aman-i-Khas is only open for seven months a year, from October until the end of April. **www.amanresorts.com**

SAWAI MADHOPUR Sawai Madhopur Lodge

Ranthambhore Road **Tel** *07462 220 541* **Fax** *07462 220 718* **Rooms** *32*

Built in the 1930s, this lovely lodge, once owned by the maharaja of Jaipur, combines modern comforts with elegant, classic style. The building is compact and set amidst beautifully manicured lawns. Jungle safaris are offered on request as well as nature talks, air pistol shooting, kite flying and bird-watching. **www.tajhotels.com**

SAWAI MADHOPUR Sher Bagh

Village Sherpur, Khiljipur **Tel** *07462 252 119* **Fax** *07462 220 811* **Rooms** *12*

This forest-friendly tented camp, open from October to March, organises interesting forest excursions. The accommodation is luxurious with attached verandahs and bathrooms. Special talks are held with expert conservationists. Great food, wonderful atmosphere and excellent service are on offer. **www.sherbagh.com**

SAWAI MADHOPUR Vanya Vilas

Ranthambhore Road **Tel** *07462 223 999* **Fax** *07462 252 042* **Rooms** *25*

The tents in this secluded forest resort have teak floors, sun-drenched private decks and marble bathrooms. The restaurant is gorgeously decorated with hand-painted frescoes and serves a delicious multi-cuisine menu. The spa has views of the lake and is set in a lovely fountained courtyard. **www.oberoihotels.com**

SILISERH Lake Palace (RTDC)

Siliserh **Tel** *0144 288 6322* **Rooms** *10*

Overlooking the lake, this fairytale summer palace is best suited for a quiet retreat, with the promise of glorious sunsets over tranquil waters. Built in 1845 by Maharaja Vinay Singh for his queen Shila, the building offers luxurious and regal rooms. Leisure activities include boating, walks and bird-watching. **www.rajasthantourism.gov.in**

UNIARA Sardar Fort Uniara

Tonk-Uniara Highway **Tel** *1234 56 789* **Fax** *1234 56789* **Rooms**

This sprawling old Uniara palace en route to Sawai Madhopur has been renovated by the sons of the former raja. The fort, set inside the walled city, offers breathtaking views while its rooms offer royal luxury. Highly recommended for its peaceful and evocative atmosphere. They also arrange jeep, camel and horse safaris.

WHERE TO EAT

The unique flavours of Indian food depend heavily on the imaginative blend of spices and use of fresh ingredients. Once, seasonal fruits and vegetables dictated menus in restaurants, so the standard restaurant offered a choice of Mughlai preparations and a sprinkling of colonial fare, such as roast lamb with mint sauce, fried fish, and vegetables *au gratin*. Today, eating habits, especially in Delhi, have become much more sophisticated, and most Indians, when they dine out, prefer food that is quite different from what is

Chief chef of a five-star Delhi hotel

cooked at home. The search for new culinary experiences has led to the proliferation of excellent speciality restaurants, fast food and pizza parlours to satisfy all tastes. These newer, fancier, and more cosmopolitan establishments have added to the eating-out scene, but good Indian food, such as succulent kababs, rich aromatic curries, or even the simple dal and *roti* served at *dhabas* still remain popular. The listings of restaurants on pages 256–63 are organized by area to help you choose where and what kind of food you wish to eat.

The stylish Polo Bar at Rambagh Palace Hotel, Jaipur

RESTAURANTS

There is a wide choice of places to eat in Delhi, from snack bars in markets to speciality restaurants in luxury hotels. Every commercial area has a large number of eateries, starting with mobile vans which offer low priced sandwiches, burgers and Indian-style Chinese chowmein and soups. South Indian eating places are widespread and good value for money with a wide choice of dishes. Others specialize in the North Indian barbecued and tandoori meats and fish. Most places, however, offer standard Indian breads and curries. Many of the American fast food giants, such as Pizza Hut, McDonalds and Dominos, have already made their appearance in the

Sign of an Indian restaurant

bigger cities, and are hot favourites with both children and an older crowd. Agra and Jaipur also have a wide range of restaurants, though good Western food is found mainly in the five-star hotels. Here, too, you will find the tempting lunch buffet where you can feast in luxury.

Most restaurants are open from 11am to midnight. It is a good idea to book in advance for the popular gourmet places. Late hour or early meals are best had at the 24-hour coffee shops at hotels.

SPECIALITY RESTAURANTS

Up-market restaurants specializing in authentic foods from different parts of the world have become very popular, particularly in Delhi, where you have a choice of

cuisines from China and Thailand, Japan, Mexico or Italy, prepared by chefs from these countries. Most of these restaurants tend to be in the luxury hotels, though a few independent ones have been opened in places like the Hauz Khas Village in Delhi. Prices may be a bit steep, but the food and stylish decor are worth it. Afghan and Middle Eastern, Kashmiri as well as Tibetan food are also found in selected places.

For Indian specialities, most of the good hotels in the Jaipur region make it a point to include traditional Rajasthani dishes on the menu, while in Delhi and Agra, almost all places will treat you to a delicious Mughal or Punjabi meal prepared from recipes handed down through generations of cooks.

Barbecued foods, a speciality at Bukhara, Maurya Sheraton

Breakfast on the ramparts of Kesroli Fort

COFFEE SHOPS

All the bigger hotels have 24-hour coffee shops where you can get snacks and even light meals. At busy market places, there are coffee shop-like cafés that are open from 10am to midnight offering a menu of refreshments and simple multi-cuisine dishes that may range from Indian to Indianized Western and Chinese. The quality of food is average. It is safer to stick to the more common dishes, and to avoid fish and prawns here.

ROADSIDE AND MARKET FOOD STALLS

If you are adventurous, the roadside food stalls or *dhabas* offer a typically Indian meal with a choice of a couple of basic curries, more often than not vegetarian, and *rotis* hot from the fire. However, do remember that the dishes are made to suit an Indian palate that prefers hot spicy food, and when ordering, insist that your meal is made with a minimum of spices. It is also advisable to eat at stalls which appear to have a rapid turnover as the food will be freshly cooked. For health precautions see page 286.

You could also try the Indian-style savoury- and sweet shops. The choice of sweets is overwhelming; syrupy at times, but delicious. The snacks are often deep-fried such as potato and flour fingerlings, or a variety of spiced nuts. Indian-style

Chinese fried chowmein is a great favourite in these places. Indian cities are fast becoming tourist savvy, with market food stalls offering a greater variety of Western-style soups, salads, as well as bakery products, and with the menus almost always in English.

VEGETARIANS

There is a superb tradition of vegetarian cooking in India. Most of the roadside food stalls are strictly vegetarian, and all three cities have good vegetarian restaurants, which include the ubiquitous South Indian eateries that also offer vegetarian *thalis.* Some of them display a sign that says: "Cooked in pure ghee", or "Cooked in ghee made from cow's milk" which is meant to reassure hardcore vegetarians.

A special salad buffet

WINE AND DRINKS

There are strict restrictions on serving alcohol in the Delhi, Agra, Jaipur region, and only some restaurants and hotels with a liquor permit are allowed to serve alcoholic drinks, though there are liquor shops in all cities. A few places are licensed to serve only beer. Most larger hotels have their own bars and serve both "Indian Made Foreign Liquor" (whisky, rum, gin, vodka and beer), as well as many foreign brands, at a price. Indian wines are few, but some excellent foreign wines are available. Drinking your own liquor in a restaurant is not permitted. The 1st and 7th of each month, national holidays and notified election days are "dry days".

PRICES AND TIPPING

Prices are fixed everywhere, even at the roadside stalls. At luxury hotels the rates are high and there will be added taxes, but eating at most restaurants and coffee shops in the city is generally affordable, and at the roadside stalls, it is positively cheap. The prices are always listed on the menu and you should check that the figures are right on your bill. Waiters do expect to be tipped, and ten per cent of the bill is appropriate.

A roadside tea stall in Rajasthan

The Flavours of Delhi, Agra and Jaipur

This region's traditional food is renowned for its range. Delhi's finest flavours are preserved in Mughlai cuisine and a long heritage of vegetarian fare. Jaipur and Agra are famous for spicy snack foods, made fragrant with cloves, cardamom and pepper, with spice levels toned down for the faint-hearted. Tandoori food *(see pp252–3)*, still considered a culinary upstart by traditionalists, is increasingly popular today. The wide variety of delicately flavoured milk sweets must also be tasted to experience the full talents of the region's cooks.

Bayleaves, cinnamon, cardamom, cumin, cloves and turmeric

Fresh local produce on a stall in a Delhi vegetable market

DELHI

Delhi, with its wide variety of Indian and foreign residents, offers food from virtually every part of India, as well as abroad. However, its unique culinary heritage is preserved in ancient recipes, handed down through generations of chefs and served in the Old City's eateries. Even prime ministers are known to have made their way here to savour the authentic Mughlai dishes, still cooked in huge brass pots over wood fires. Often tucked away in smoky warrens, these modest places are an essential part of the authentic Delhi culinary experience. Spices are ground fresh each day and their heady smells float out as they are lovingly cooked. Stuffed bread *(paratha)*, is another Old Delhi speciality – it even has a lane named after it. No visitor to Delhi should miss the colours and smells of its fruit and vegetable markets. Vendors sing out bargain prices to tempt buyers, while keeping a sharp eye out for the ever-lurking cows. For centuries, the Indian street stalls have provided the raw materials for its gifted cooks. Spices are an integral part of the culinary tradition and each region has its own secret combinations and recipes.

Missi Roti   Naan   Lecha Paratha   Poori
Garlic Naan

Bhatura

Lecha Paratha Pudina (with mint)

A small selection from the vast range of Indian breads

REGIONAL DISHES AND SPECIALITIES

Most of the food in this region is classified as vegetarian or non-vegetarian and, broadly, it reflects the traditional Hindu and Muslim culinary styles. Curried or dry vegetables are served with a range of breads. Found throughout the region, the *aloo poori*, along with the *paratha*, appears at breakfast or a main meal. Mutton (which can mean goat meat too in India) and chicken form the core of Mughlai food, often served in curried stews such as *korma* and *rogan josh*. Stewed lentils, called dal, are the staple comfort food throughout North India and are eaten with rice or bread. Milk is the main ingredient of desserts, often dressed temptingly with delicate silver sheets and slivers of nuts.

Mint and chillies

Poori *are puffy, deep-fried breads, served with spicy potato (aloo) or other vegetable, curried or dry.*

Fiery red chillies being dried before being ground into powder

AGRA

In Agra, almost every neigh-bourhood or market has a *halwai* shop. This is the Indian version of a deli, except that you will only find vegetarian food and sweets here. It is possible to get a full meal, served on a *thali*, or just a savoury snack.

A typical *thali* meal will include dal, curried potatoes, pumpkin and other seasonal vegetables. *Pooris* and rice are eaten with the curried or dry vegetables, along with raita, chutneys and pickles, served in small bowls. *Thalis* are modestly priced.

Halwai shops are rather sophisticated now: levels of hygiene have improved, and bottled water is available. Service is prompt and orders are yelled across to the kitchen, usually at the back.

JAIPUR

Be prepared to have your palate tickeld with robust flavours when you eat in Jaipur. Rajasthani food, vegetarian or not, is robust and highly spiced. Fresh

Bazaar vendor cooking samosas in a *tawa* (wok)

batches of the round onion *masala kachauri* are fried in huge woks from morning to night and served on leaf plates. *Lal maas*, a rich, red mutton dish, is the region's signature offering, along with the vegetarian *gutta* curry. Millet breads *(bajra rotis)*, served with chutneys, local vegetables and berries, are another speciality. Curds, set overnight in clay vessels, are churned with sugar and cardamom to make a frothy drink called *lassi*. This is often served in delicate terracotta cups which, like leaf plates, reflect ancient practices that helped to conserve precious water in a desert region.

BAZAAR FOOD

The sizzle of ghee on hot griddles, the sputter of spices as they are added and the aromas of food cooked lovingly in huge vats and pans are traditional bazaar wiles to tempt customers. As for curries, there is a bewildering variety to choose from: from the rich red of the mutton korma, served with a range of breads, to the turmeric based *karhi* with yellow dumplings, served with rice. Food courts with a range of regional and traditional cuisines have sprung up close to these bazaars and attract customers all day. Food may be washed down with hot, sweet, milky *masala chai* (tea flavoured with cinnamon, cardamom and ginger).

Korma *is fragrant with cardamom and cloves. This rich curry is eaten with either Indian bread or rice.*

Dal *combines lentils with a heady mix of onions, garlic and spices. It is considered India's "soul food".*

Gulab Jamun *may be served hot or cold. These syrupy little dough balls are often topped with ice cream.*

The Flavours of the Tandoor

A wood-fired clay oven, the tandoor is used all over Western Asia. Its entry into the mainstream of Indian cooking began with the arrival of Punjabi refugees at the time of Partition (see pp58–9). Meats or vegetables are marinated in a spiced yoghurt mixture, then speared onto long skewers and slowly cooked in the tandoor until the outer skin is crisp and smoky. Tandoori breads are rolled by hand, flung up in the air to stretch, deftly caught and then fired in the tandoor. Tandoori cuisine is undoubtedly the most popular "finger food" of this region.

Raita, a cooling yoghurt salad

Murg Tikka *is a spicy cube* (tikka) *of chargrilled boneless chicken*

Barra Kebab *features robustly flavoured lamb chop*

Mughlai Kebab *is minced lamb spiced in the Mughlai style*

Seekh Kebab, *uses spicy minced lamb, and is named after the skewer* (seekh)

Tandoori Murgh, *a whole spring chicken* (murgh), *is the original tandoori delicacy*

Reshmi Kebab, *made with minced chicken, gets its name from being as smooth as silk* (resham)

ON THE TANDOORI MENU

Achari Murg: chicken kebabs in a strong pickle *(achar)* marinade.

Achari Paneer Tikka: cottage cheese *(paneer)* chunks in a sharp pickle *(achar)* marinade go well with a chilled beer.

Afghani Murg: grilled chicken basted with butter and spices.

Bharwan Tamatar: tomatoes *(tamatar)* stuffed with a spicy potato filling. This squishy dish must be eaten in one bite.

Boti Kebab: chunks of mutton, grilled medium-rare.

Dahi ka Kebab: the base of this delectable melt-in-the-mouth kebab is strained curds *(dahi)*.

Galouti Kebab: richly spiced, finely minced mutton patties that melt in the mouth. However, the pepper in them has a slow fuse so take care.

Hariyali Murg: grilled spring chicken in a green marinade, often featuring coriander.

Kakori Kebab: cardamom-flavoured soft kebabs originally devised for a toothless nawab by the royal chef of Kakori.

Kalmi Kebab: chicken twists with soft buttery marinade.

Kathal Kebab: often called a vegetarian lamb substitute, this jackfruit kebab tastes like a mutton shami kebab.

Lehsuni Murg Tikka: garlicky *(lehsun)* chicken kebabs.

Machli Tikka Ajwani: fish *(machi)* kebab flavoured with the oregano-like herb *ajwain*.

Malai Makai Seekh: creamy sweetcorn *(makai)* kebabs, served char-grilled on skewers.

Mutton Chop Adrakhi: ginger *(adrak)* features in this dish.

Paneer Pudina Tikka: cottage cheese kebab flavoured with mint *(pudina)*.

Pasanda: boneless, flattened lamb in a cardamom-based marinade. Garnished with roasted almonds and sultanas.

PICKLES AND CHUTNEYS

No Indian meal is complete without accompanying relishes, set in small bowls alongside the main meal. Raw mango pickle is a favourite, the tender fruit mixed with spices and mustard oil. Raw mango is also a base for spicy chutneys with fresh coriander, mint and chillies. Among other popular chutney bases are red tomatoes and garlic. Pickled shallots are often served with tandoori platters. Shredded ginger, pickled in lime juice, turns pink with time and aids digestion. Sweet pickles are flavoured with cloves.

Mango, mint and tomato chutneys, among the many varieties that accompany a meal

Tandoori Gobhi *is spiced florets of cauliflower* (gobhi) *lightly grilled in the tandoor*

Paneer Tikka *or delicately grilled chunks of cottage cheese* (paneer)

Tandoori Sabzi *feature assorted skewered, grilled vegetables* (sabzi)

Bharwan Simla Mirch *are barbecued green and red peppers* (simla mirch) *with a spicy potato stuffing*

Bharwan Aloo *are potatoes* (aloo) *that are scooped out and stuffed with a spicy filling, then grilled*

Hariyali Kebabs *are green* (hara) *kebabs made of lentils and spinach*

Tandoori chef with a whole leg of lamb (raan) for the oven

Sabzi Seekh Kebab: served on skewers, this is a vegetarian *(sabzi)* variation of the popular seekh kebab.

Seekh Kebab Roll: A soft *rumali* (handkerchief) bread is rolled round a seekh kebab, spiced with mint chutney and onion rings.

Shami Kebab: finely minced meat, stuffed with chopped onions, ginger and fresh coriander. Raisins may be added.

Tandoori Bater: marinated quails *(bater)* skewered and chargrilled.

Tandoori Bhindi: tender whole okra *(bhindi)*, smeared in tandoori marinade and grilled to a crunchy finish.

Tandoori Jhinga: marinated jumbo prawns *(jhinga)* garnished with pomegranate seeds.

Tangri Kebab: chicken drumstick kebabs.

Tandoori Khumb: Kashmiri mushrooms *(khumb)* are spiced and grilled to a creamy bite.

Tandoori Pomfret: a whole marinated fish, served with onion rings, lemon and mint chutney.

Tandoori Raan: grilled leg of lamb, marinated in spiced yoghurt dressing.

Tandoori Salad: features seasonal vegetables such as peppers, tomatoes and lotus root.

A Glossary of Typical Indian Food

Jamuns, a monsoon fruit

The essence of traditional Indian food lies in the infinite variations in the blending and combination of a variety of spices. Chillies need not be used and, in fact, are often regarded as the inputs of a poor cook who uses them to camouflage the lack of subtlety in his seasonings. A typical menu in the region includes meat, lentils, vegetables and *tandoori* dishes, accompanied by rice and *rotis*. Street food is extremely popular with locals, and consists of savoury snacks, eaten through the day.

SNACKS

Sweet and savoury snacks are an important part of the Indian diet.

Aloo Tikki
Stuffed potato cutlet cooked on a griddle.

Chaat
The most popular items are *papri*, made of fritters, chickpeas, potatoes, yoghurt and spicy sauces; and *gol-guppas*, puffed flour crisps filled with cumin spiced water and chickpeas.

Idli and **Dosa**
Popular South Indian steamed rice cakes and crisp pancakes, served with coconut curry and a spicy lentil curry are a national breakfast favourite.

Skewered tikkis

Jalebi
Crisp golden coils of flour batter dipped in a rose-flavoured syrup.

Pakora
Vegetables or cottage cheese fried in gramflour batter.

Samosa
Deep-fried pastry triangles filled with spiced potato and peas.

Tikkas
Marinated and char-grilled small chunks of chicken, mutton, fish and cottage cheese. The *burra* kebab is meat with bone from the rib, prepared in the same way.

MAIN NON-VEGETARIAN DISHES

Often spicy and rich, these are among the most delicious examples of Indian cuisine.

Bhuna Gosht
A dry meat curry, stir-fried slowly till tender.

Butter Chicken
Tandoori chicken with a rich tomato and butter sauce.

Dal Gosht
Meat with lentils.

Dil Bahar Dopiaza
A spicy mutton stew in a thick sauce made with onions.

Kadhai Murg
Chicken curry stir-fried in a wok.

Kofta
Meatballs in broth.

Lal maas
A Rajasthani mutton dish cooked with red chillies. A variation is *safed maas*, a "white" curry with almonds and cashew nuts.

Nargisi Kofta
The Mughlai version of Scotch Eggs – hard-boiled eggs covered in minced meat and served in a spicy sauce.

Murg Mussallan
A masala roast chicken, sometimes stuffed with hard-boiled eggs.

Rogan josh, a meat dish

Korma
Braised meat or chicken cooked on a slow fire with yoghurt and spices.

Nihari
Stewed lamb shanks, usually cooked all night over embers. It is eaten for breakfast during the month of Ramadan.

Rogan Josh
Cubes of mutton cooked with red chillies and spices.

Saag Gosht
Meat cooked with spinach.

Red chilli

Curry leaves and masur dal

VEGETARIAN DISHES

Traditionally, only seasonal vegetables (*sabzi*) were used, limiting the choice of dishes.

Aloo Gobhi
Potatoes (*aloo*) cooked with cauliflower (*gobhi*) and ginger.

Aloo Methi
Browned potatoes and fenugreek (*methi*) leaves.

Baingan ka Bharta
Smoked aubergine puréed with onions and tomatoes.

Bhindi Piaz
Okra and onions (seasonal).

Dum Aloo
Potatoes with yoghurt and spices cooked over low heat.

Gatta Curry
Gramflour dumplings in a delicate, aromatic sauce.

The *chaat-wallah's* variety of savouries served in mouth-watering combinations

A streetside restaurant specializing in *parathas*

SWEETS

Sweets are mainly milk-based.
Gajar ka Halwa
Grated carrots cooked in milk and sugar and browned with pistachios and almonds.
Gulab Jamun
Deep-fried milk and flour dumplings in a thick syrup.
Kulfi
Hand-churned ice-cream flavoured with pistachios.
Phirni
A Mughlai riceflour pudding, flavoured with saffron (*kesar*).
Rabri
Thickened milk and sugar garnished with nuts.
Rasmalai
A flatter version of the *rasgulla* (*paneer* balls in a thin syrup) in a mildly flavoured creamy sauce.

Gajar ka Halwa

Kadhi
Fried gramflour dumplings cooked in a yoghurt and gramflour-thickened sauce.
Kair Sangri
Small local berries cooked with spinach-like leaves.
Khumb-matar Curry
A mushroom and pea curry.
Malai Kofta
Cottage cheese dumplings in a thick tomato gravy.
Masala Baingan
Stuffed aubergines (eggplants) braised in oil.
Paneer
Paneer (cottage cheese), an all time favourite, is cooked in a variety of combinations. *Palak paneer* is with spinach, and *matar paneer* with peas.
Paneer Makhani
Cottage cheese in a tomato and butter sauce.
Sarson ka Saag
Mustard leaves cooked in milk and served in a puréed form with butter.

LENTILS

Dal, a lentil curry, is the staple meal. *Masur* and *moong* are two varieties.
Chhola Bhatura

Chhola Bhatura

Chickpeas thickly coated with a spicy sauce eaten with a puffed, deep-fried bread.
Dal Makhani
Unhulled dal cooked in cream and butter.
Rajma Curry
A red kidney-bean curry.
Sambhar
A South Indian speciality made with *arhar* dal and a special curry powder.

BREADS

Common breads cooked on a griddle are the *chapati*, paper-thin *roomali roti* and *paratha*. *Pooris* are deep fried, while *tandoori* breads include the *tandoori* and *khastha roti* and *naan*.

RICE

Biryanis and *pulaos* are eaten with *raitas* (whipped yoghurt mixed with onions, tomatoes, coriander and green chillies), and a wide range of pickles and chutneys.
Biryani
Mutton or chicken korma is layered with rice, cooked on a slow charcoal fire, and flavoured with saffron.
Navratan Pulao
Rice cooked with nine types of vegetables.
Yakhni Pulao
Rice and mutton cooked in stock flavoured with aniseed and whole spices.

DRINKS

Elaichi Chai
Flavoured cardamom tea.
Lassi
Whipped yoghurt shake.
Nimbu Pani
Fresh, sweetened or salted lime juice with water or soda.
Panna
Peeled raw mango boiled, puréed, and mixed in water with salt, sugar and cumin.
Sherbet
A flavoured sweet drink.

PAAN

Betel leaf packed with areca nut, lime (*catechu*) paste, and other ingredients such as cardamoms and cloves.

Paan, a good digestive, can be made to suit individual tastes

Choosing a Restaurant

The restaurants in this guide have been selected to suit a wide price range and many are located in recommended hotels. They are chosen for their exceptional food, good value for money and convenient or interesting locations. The restaurants are listed by area. For map references, see pages 124–131.

PRICE CATEGORIES
The price ranges are for a meal for one, including tax and service charges but not alcohol.

Rs. Under 100 Rs.
Rs. Rs. Rs.100–Rs.200
Rs. Rs. Rs. Rs.200–Rs.400
Rs. Rs. Rs. Rs. Rs.400–Rs.700
Rs. Rs. Rs. Rs. Rs. Over Rs.700

DELHI

NEW DELHI Triveni Tea Terrace

Triveni Kala Sangam, 205 Tansen Marg **Tel** *011 2371 8833*   **Map** *2 D5*

This dining room tucked away in the corner of the famous art gallery is discreet and homely. They offer a simple main course fare of *shammi* kebabs, vegetarian *pulao* and *aloo paranthas* with refreshing *chai* and snacks. Artists and lawyers (owing to the nearby courts) throng this quiet place every afternoon. Closed on Sundays.

NEW DELHI Have More

11-12 Pandara Road Market **Tel** *011 2338 7070*   **Map** *5 B3*

Located at a popular multi-cuisine restaurant complex, the restaurant has an array of popular Indian/Punjabi dishes on offer. Butter chicken, the staple favourite of most lovers of Indian food, is a speciality here. Other dishes recommended are *rogan josh*, *mutton do piaza* and *dal makhani*. This quiet complex comes alive in the evenings.

NEW DELHI The Big Chill

68 A, Khan Market **Tel** *011 41757588*   **Map** *5 B3*

This popular place has walls decorated with famous movie posters. The winners from their menu are the prawn and courgette (zucchini) salad, minestrone soup, the chicken in spicy *piri piri* sauce and the crisp pizzas. Stay away from the bakes and risottos. Their squidgy cake, banoffee pie and frozen yoghurts are much sought-after desserts.

NEW DELHI DV8

13 Regal Building, Connaught Place **Tel** *011 5150 0694*   **Map** *1 C5*

A lively bar-cum-restaurant that serves Indian, Oriental and European cuisine, with the best steaks in town for their price. Try Steak Diana or Steak Café de Paire. The Chinese dishes are best avoided although the pastas are well-made. The DJ spins good music, mostly rock and hip-hop. Live bands often play gigs at this venue.

NEW DELHI Gaylords

16-B Regal Building, Connaught Place **Tel** *011 2336 0717*   **Map** *1 C5*

Built in 1956, this used to be a sought-after place by artists and intellectuals alike. Try their coffee and snacks, while the kababs and grilled fillet o' fish are also recommended. The other European dishes can be avoided. Their vegetarian food is better than their non-vegetarian fare. Ideal for a secluded tête-à-tête rather than a hearty meal.

NEW DELHI Kwality

67 Regal Building, Connaught Place **Tel** *011 2374 2310*   **Map** *1 C5*

Delhi's first ice-cream parlor that later converted into a popular restaurant. The *chhola bhaturas* (spicy chickpeas eaten with deep fried fluffy bread) remains eternally popular among other Punjabi dishes served. Also worth trying are the kababs, especially the mutton *gilafi*. Leave some space to sample the wide range of Kwality ice-creams.

NEW DELHI Dhaba

The Claridges, 12 Aurangzeb Road **Tel** *011 2301 0211*   **Map** *5 A3*

Dhaba recreates the ambience of numerous little eateries lining North India's highways that serve authentic Punjabi cuisine. Hop onto their truck-seat and splurge on *balti* meat and tandoori prawns, amongst other fresh, spicy food that will tantalize your taste buds. Experience an Indian eating experience in all its charming rustic forms.

NEW DELHI Aqua

The Park, 15 Parliament Street **Tel** *011 23743000*   **Map** *1 C5*

A cool poolside lounge with tent-like alcoves perfect for a private evening. Aqua sees the city's who's who more often than anywhere else. Mediterranean and barbeque cuisine is served here. Grilled mushroom with basil and the falafel platter are mouthwatering. Their desserts are also scrumptious.

NEW DELHI Baluchi

Grand Intercontinental, Barakhamba Road **Tel** *011 2341 1001*   **Map** *2 D5*

Serving North-Western Frontier cuisine, Baluchi serve amazing tandoori dishes. *Jhinga masaledar* (skewered prawns in a secret-recipe marinade) and *murgh makhani tikka* (chicken marinated in a special butter-based sauce and grilled to perfection) are highly recommended. Their buffet is also worth trying.

Key to Symbols *see back cover flap*

NEW DELHI Daniell's Tavern

The Imperial, Janpath **Tel** *011 2334 1234*

Map 1 C5

Relive the days of the Raj through the eyes of William Daniell, a keen traveller and painter who captured the Colonial architecture of India on canvas . An elegant restaurant although the cuisine is not as impressive as the decor. Their *gosht shorba*, Hyderabadi *dum-pukht biryani* and *raan-e-dam* are all worth trying.

NEW DELHI House of Ming

Hotel Taj Mahal, 1 Mansingh Road **Tel** *011 2302 6162*

Map 5 B3

Arguably the premier Chinese restaurant in Delhi, this is spicy Schezuan and Cantonese at its best. The shark-fin soup and crispy thousand corner king prawns, Chef Wang's signature dish, are not to be missed. Also try the crispy fried spinach, among other vegetarian delicacies. For dessert, try their fried ice-cream.

NEW DELHI Kandahar

The Oberoi, Dr. Zakir Hussain Marg **Tel** *011 2436 3030*

Map 5 B3

Kandahar offers Indian and North-Western Frontier cuisine and much more. You can choose from their famous *galouti* kababs to the succulent tandoori *raan*. Try their *dal kandahar* for a rich home-cooked taste. The evenings in this popular restaurant are livened up by live *ghazal* performances.

NEW DELHI Lodi, The Garden Restaurant

Lodi Garden, Opposite Mausam Bhavan, Lodi Road **Tel** *011 2465 5054*

Map 5 A5

Under sprawling trees and pretty lanterns, this garden restaurant promises a fine dining experience. Start with *salata dijaj* or lamb Moroccan, braised meat in an exotic sauce, their chef's speciality. For vegetarians, the platter of garden vegetables is a good choice. Some of the world's finest wines are on their list.

NEW DELHI The Spice Route

The Imperial, Janpath **Tel** *011 2334 1234*

Map 1 C5

The historical route brought the spices of Southeast Asian countries to Europe. This restaurant presents them in the countries' exotic meals. The interiors reflect the journey and art and culture that flourished along this famous trail. The Sri Lankan *marris* curry and *phad phak ruam mitr* are recommended.

NEW DELHI Threesixty°

The Oberoi, Dr. Zakir Hussain Marg **Tel** *011 2436 3030*

Map 6 D4

Recently opened multi-cuisine restaurant that has become very popular. Their Japanese fare is highly recommended. Pizza lovers go in for chorizo and jalapeño pizza, baked in a wood-fired oven. Their excellent buffets offer a wide range of options. Top up with a glass of wine chosen from an extensive list.

NIZAMUDDIN Karim's

168/2 Jha House, Hazrat Nizamuddin West **Tel** *011 2435 0018*

Map 6 D5

Karim's is the hallmark of Delhi's authentic Mughlai cuisine, with recipes passed on from royal chefs to their heirs. The restaurant chain has retained its unforgettable taste. From *nihari* (popular meal made of marrow) to *barra* kabab and amazing *phirni* (creamy rice pudding), their diners are in for a treat.

OLD DELHI Karim's

16, Jama Masjid **Tel** *011 2326 9880*

Map 2 E2

Hailed throughout the country for serving the best Mughal cuisine, this was the first Karim's restaurant. It is located near the beautiful Jama Masjid, India's largest mosque. A non-vegetarian's culinary paradise, their Jehangiri chicken, *mutton burra* and tandoori *raan* are eternally famous and sought-after. Try their *phirni* for dessert.

OLD DELHI Chor Bizarre

Hotel Broadway, 4/15 Asaf Ali Road **Tel** *011 2327 3821*

Map 2 E3

Best known for its Kashmiri cuisine, Chor Bizarre is based on the concept of a thieves' market. Within their colourful walls, try the *yakhni* or *gushtaba*, pounded meat balls cooked in yoghurt, while the *thali*, offering an assortment of various dishes, should not be missed. Vegetarians must try the Kashmiri *dum aloo*.

FURTHER AFIELD (SOUTH) Sagar

18 Defence Colony Market **Tel** *011 2433 3110*

There's hardly a day when there isn't a queue outside this amazing South Indian restaurant. Every minute's waiting is worth it though. Try their long and crispy dome-shaped *dosas* with piping hot *sambhar* or the ever-popular South Indian *thali* as a main course, the *sooji halwa* for dessert and filter coffee to wash it down.

FURTHER AFIELD (SOUTH) Swagath

14 Defence Colony Market **Tel** *011 2433 0930*

Swagath is a good multi-cuisine restaurant that serves everything from Chettinad dishes to spicy Indian and Indianized Chinese cuisine. The "top of the list" dishes include Chettinad chicken, butter chicken, grilled prawns and garlic butter crabs. Hearty proportions and affordable prices make it a popular family restaurant.

FURTHER AFIELD (SOUTH) Aangan

Hyatt Regency Hotel, Bhikaji Cama Place **Tel** *011 2679 1234*

Earlier known as Delhi ka Aangan, the present restaurant has much more to offer on their menu. From their traditional "Delhi" cuisine, try the *raan-e-aangan* or the tandoori fish (including prawn and pomfret). Their *thali* presents a good assortment of popular Indian dishes.

FURTHER AFIELD (SOUTH) Diva

M-8 Greater Kailash II, M-Block Market **Tel** *011 2921 5673*

Opened by the restaurateur duo Gita and Ritu, this inviting place offers creative Italian dishes. Go for the antipasti platter for starters and *gamberoni de chardonnay* (prawns grilled with wine) and pizza alla Diva as a main course. It has a list of over 450 wines to choose from.

FURTHER AFIELD (SOUTH) Flavors

52-C Flyover Complex, Next to Moolchand Flyover, Defence Colony **Tel** *011 2464 5644*

Tarsillo Nataloni is the affable chef-owner at this Italian restaurant. The pizzas as well as the spicy pepperoni chorizo pasta and the sole mio are recommended. For vegetarians, the spinach and ricotta cheese ravioli is a must. For dessert, the mango cheesecake and crème brûlée are recommended.

FURTHER AFIELD (SOUTH) The Great Kebab Factory

Hotel Radisson, National Highway No. 8, Mahipalpur **Tel** *011 2677 9191*

A speciality restaurant serving scrumptious kebabs among other things. Eat a hearty meal with their "eat as much as you can" offer. The kebab platters are very popular. The *galouti* kebabs and *gosht babri seekh* for non-vegetarians and *malai* broccoli and *pudina paneer tikka* are highly recommended for vegetarians.

FURTHER AFIELD (SOUTH) It's Greek To Me

B-6/4 Commercial Complex, Safdarjang Enclave **Tel** *011 4101 2240*

The first restaurant in the city to serve Greek cuisine, it has vibrant interiors with decor that is truly Mediterranean. The lamb *moussaka*, chicken *vasilikos* and *souvlakis* are the menu toppers. The restaurant also provides a plate that you can break at the end of your meal, in true Greek style.

FURTHER AFIELD (SOUTH) Nanking

Opposite Delhi Public School, Vasant Kunj **Tel** *011 2613 8936*

The food at this Chinese speciality restaurant is quite simply stunning. Rated as one of the city's best, it offers fabulous duck along with crab and other seafood are served within its spacious interiors by friendly and helpful staff. They are also popular for their special dim sum lunches (veg/non-veg) which offers an extensive array of delicacies.

FURTHER AFIELD (SOUTH) Park Baluchi

Inside Deer Park, Hauz Khas **Tel** *011 2696 9829*

Strategically located amidst the lush greenery of the Deer Park and next to the exclusive boutique haven, Hauz Khas Village. Serving fine North-Western Frontier cuisine, Park Baluchi is a famous stopover for meat-lovers. The *murgh potli* and the *haryali choosa* are unique chicken dishes that taste great. The vegetarian fare, however, is avoidable.

FURTHER AFIELD (SOUTH) Seventy Seven

The Manor, Friends Colony West **Tel** *011 2692 5151*

The menu at Seventy Seven lashes together traditional Indian cuisine with contemporary Mediterranean and Norwegian fare. Enjoy the sprawling garden view, sip minestrone soup, follow it up by ravioli stuffed with spinach and mushrooms, and finally, splurge on Belgian waffle, their daily special dessert.

FURTHER AFIELD (SOUTH) Kylin

24 Basant Lok, Vasant Vihar **Tel** *011 4166 9799*

Kylin offers exotic cuisine from the Far East. Try the *gado-gado* peanut salad, Vietnamese prawn balls or *sui mai* dim sum followed by their special chilli squid and the *kai sen udon* (stir-fried noodles in oyster sauce). The cocktails are refreshing. Delhi fairly splits at the seams with Oriental restaurants but Kylin is a cut above the rest.

FURTHER AFIELD (SOUTH) La Piazza

Hyatt Regency, Bhikaji Cama Place **Tel** *011 2679 1234*

An extensive wine list, exquisite cuisine prepared by their Italian chef and the ambience of candlelit tables and woody interiors make La Piazza the most attractive Italian restaurant in town. The Antonio Gavi wine, the Pizza La Piazza, and grilled salmon are winners on the menu. Special fixed-price brunches every Sunday.

FURTHER AFIELD (SOUTH) TK's

Hyatt Regency, Bhikaji Cama Place **Tel** *011 2679 1234*

TK's is one of the city's most famous Japanese (teppanyaki) restaurants serving some of the best sushi in town. Try the Mongolian barbeque lunch along with some amazing sashimi especially imported from Japan. Their special interactive menu lets you not only decide what to eat but also lend a hand in cooking it.

FURTHER AFIELD (WEST) Sagar Ratna

The Ashok hotel, 50-B Chanakyapuri **Tel** *011 2687 8885*

Their name is synonymous with perhaps the best South Indian food served in the city. The deluxe *thali* is a popular choice, as it is an economical, hearty meal. The onion *rava masala dosa* and *idli* are highly recommended. The rates, however, are high compared to their Defence Colony counterpart.

FURTHER AFIELD (WEST) Basil and Thyme

Santusthi Shopping Complex, New Wellington Camp **Tel** *011 2467 4933*

A small eating joint with a peaceful ambience, the perfect place to relax after a hectic shopping spree at the popular Santusthi complex. Basil and Thyme serves Italian and other European cuisine. The chicken liver paté, quiche Lorraine and pasta bolognaise are the must-try list toppers.

Key to Price Guide *see p256* **Key to Symbols** *see back cover flap*

FURTHER AFIELD (WEST) China Town

The Ashok Hotel, 50-B Chanakyapuri **Tel** *011 2611 0101*

Although the ambience is a far cry from the quintessential Chinatowns of major cities worldwide, numerous exquisite dishes await vegetarians and non-vegetarians alike. Their native Chinese chef makes some delicious starters and main course dishes such as crispy spinach and the golden fried jumbo prawns.

FURTHER AFIELD (WEST) Bukhara

ITC Maurya Sheraton Hotel and Towers, Diplomatic Enclave **Tel** *011 2611 2233*

Once featured on the cover of *Time* magazine, Bukhara has had among its patrons, numerous international politicos. Famous for its appetising kebabs and mouthwatering *tikkas*, these dishes are served within lovely stone walls, crossed by dark wooden beams. Try the *Sikandari raan* or the *murgh malai* kebabs.

FURTHER AFIELD (WEST) Dum Pukht

ITC Maurya Sheraton Hotel and Towers, Diplomatic Enclave **Tel** *011 2611 2233*

Serving the best Awadhi and Hyderabadi cuisine in the city, this critically acclaimed restaurant has an excellent menu. Try the *kakori* kebabs and the grilled king prawns. Their famous *dum-pukht* or *kachchi gosht ki biryani* is highly recommended. Excellent food and a majestic ambience make for an unforgettable experience.

FURTHER AFIELD (WEST) Kumgang

The Ashok hotel, 50-B Chanakyapuri **Tel** *011 2611 0101*

A Korean speciality restaurant, Kumgang has ingredients flown in directly from Korea. Their Korean chef prepares the choicest delicacies. *Dubu kimchi*, a special Korean salad, *naengmyeon*, a popular noodle-soup, and *kimchi jeongal*, a special stew, are recommended among their other popular dishes.

FURTHER AFIELD (WEST) Orient Express

Taj Palace Hotel, 2 Sardar Patel Marg **Tel** *011 2611 0202*

The famous Orient Express train that passed through major European cities has inspired this restaurant's name and decor. Speciality European cuisine such as rack of lamb and tender steak along with gorgeous chocolate desserts are served. The five-course, fixed price menu is also a good option.

FURTHER AFIELD (WEST) Tea House of the August Moon

Taj Palace Hotel, 2 Sardar Patel Marg **Tel** *011 2611 0202*

Named after the famous movie starring Marlon Brando, this restaurant is surprisingly authentic. Their Chinese chef makes the best Peking duck in town, apart from perfectly cooked seafood dishes that go best with steamed *hofan* noodles. Inspired by traditional Chinese teahouses, it has lovely artwork on the walls.

NORTH OF DELHI

HARIDWAR Ahaar

Upper Road, Haridwar, **Tel** *No telephone.*

Although not as famous as Chotiwala in Rishikesh, Ahaar is nonetheless still a favourite joint among tourists for a quick snack. Serving a combination of Punjabi, Continental and Chinese dishes, the restaurant, however, is most popular for *mattar paneer* and butter *naan* followed by a tall glass of frothy sweet or salty *lassi*.

HARIDWAR Bestee

Shiv Murti Chowk, Jassa Ram Road **Tel** *01334 227 210*

Bestee is tucked away near Hotel Panama on Shiv Murti Marg. The restaurant offers some good South Indian and Continental food at very affordable rates. Go for a vegetarian club sandwich with a chocolate milkshake or simply enjoy the butter *masala dosa* followed by a tall glass of fresh mango shake.

HARIDWAR Chinkara Hills

Haridwar-Rishikesh Road, Raiwala **Tel** *0135 2484361*

This halt offers quick snacks to tourists en route to Haridwar. They offer standard Indian, Chinese and Continental fare. The attraction, however, is the promise of non-vegetarian food and liquor, both banned in Haridwar, but freely available here. The favourite combination seems to be beer and a plate of fried chicken.

HARIDWAR Mid-Way Resort

Near Raiwala Railway Bridge, Rishikesh-Haridwar Road **Tel** *0135 248 4208*

Essentially a tourist stop along the stretch between Rishikesh and Haridwar which is good for a quick refreshing drink and hot snack. The food is of a reasonable standard, nothing fancy or exotic, but the prices are relatively cheap and the service quick and efficient.

HARIDWAR Shivalik

Station Road **Tel** *No telephone.*

Specializes in Gujarati food from West India, which is primarily vegetarian and uses a large amount of millet, yoghurt, buttermilk and sesame seed in the preparation of their dishes. This restaurant also offers the other usual fare of Indian and Continental as well as the ubiquitous "Chinese" dishes.

RISHIKESH Chotiwala

Swargashram **Tel** *0135 243 0070*

A tour of the holy city of Rishikesh is incomplete without a meal at this 40-year-old restaurant. Their vegetarian menu offers a variety of Indian dishes but the favourite is their famous special *thali* and South Indian *bhojanam* followed by delicious, creamy *rasmalai* (dumplings soaked in sweet, thickened milk).

RISHIKESH Danapaani

Hotel Baseraa, Ghat Road **Tel** *0135 243 0720*

Located in the heart of the local market near the colourful Triveni Ghat, this restaurant serves excellent food, clean and freshly prepared. Definitely a good place to soak in the lively local atmosphere while enjoying a plate of piping hot food and a refreshing non-alcoholic drink.

RISHIKESH German Bakery

Lakshman Jhula **Tel** *0135 244 2089*

This airy restaurant is situated on the first floor of a building that offers a lovely view of the Ganges and the surrounding hills. The service is friendly and the food great. Most of the non-vegetarian dishes are good, while vegetarians should try the aubergine lasagne. The yak cheese sandwiches and fruit pancake are also recommended.

RISHIKESH Rangoli

16 Veerabhadra Road **Tel** *0135 243 1658*

Housed in Hotel Ganga Kinare (*see p.239*), and considered to be one of the top end hotels in Rishikesh, Rangoli offers lovely river views. This warm, friendly coffee shop serves fresh, light meals that are purely vegetarian as well as a variety of hot and cold refreshments.

RISHIKESH Kautilya Restaurant

Dehradun Road **Tel** *0135 243 1099*

Open from noon to 3pm and then for dinner from 7 to 11pm, Kautilya restaurant serves reasonably good North Indian, Chinese and Continental dishes. They have a separate smoking and non-smoking area. A good ambience makes this a place worth visiting for a meal.

ROORKEE Cheetal Grand

Delhi-Mussorie Road, Khatauli **Tel** *01396 272 468*

This pleasantly landscaped restaurant-cum-hotel has a lovely lawn and pretty flower beds amongst which you can enjoy a meal. Midway between Meerut and Roorkee, they serve quick, hot multi-cuisine dishes coupled with polite and friendly service. A special favourite is the fluffy cheese omelette and stuffed *paranthas*.

AGRA AND AROUND

AGRA Only Restaurant

45 Taj Road **Tel** *0562 222 6834*

This traditional restaurant is ideal for families with kids as they have a park outside with a playground. The reliable, if mundane, Indian, Continental and Chinese food served here is accompanied by live Indian and Rajasthani music as well as puppet shows in the evenings. The favourites are *kadhai* chicken and *kadhai* paneer.

AGRA Capri

Hari Parvat **Tel** *0562 252 2171*

This popular restaurant is located right at the entrance to Agra. It serves North Indian and Mughlai food and is famous for its butter chicken and *malai kofta* (vegetarian substitute for meat balls in a thick, rich curry). Ideal for a relaxed evening out.

AGRA Dasaprakash

Meher Theatre Complex, Balu Ganj, Gwalior Road **Tel** *0562 236 3535*

This restaurant, run by a reputed chain, specialises in well cooked and reasonably priced meals. From their vegetarian South Indian food menu, any one of the eight types of *dosas* and the special *thali* is recommended. They also provide kids with various activities and offer takeaway services.

AGRA Pizza Hut

8 Handicrafts Nagar, Fatehbad Road **Tel** *0562 233 3051*

All those who have a craving for American fast food would find this familiar and popular restaurant a comforting sight. They offer interesting Indian-style pizzas with tandoori chicken or *paneer tikka* toppings. However, it is best to avoid the rather unimaginative salad bar.

AGRA Bagh-E-Bahar

Welcomgroup Mughal Sheraton, Taj Ganj **Tel** *0562 233 1701*

An attractive speciality restaurant, set in the architecturally splendid Mughal Sheraton hotel. It offers magnificent views of the sparkling pool and green landscaped gardens. Delectable multi-cuisine fare is served to the lively strains of Western music in the evenings.

Key to Price Guide *see p256* **Key to Symbols** *see back cover flap*

AGRA Olive Garden

Holiday Inn, M G Road, San Jay Place **Tel** *0562 252 3460*

This multi-cuisine restaurant offers an interesting blend of various international cuisines. Its speciality is the buffet served for breakfast, lunch and dinner, although it does have an à la carte option as well. It offers a wonderful view of the lovely front lawns of the hotel.

AGRA Taj Bano

Welcomgroup Mughal Sheraton, Taj Ganj **Tel** *0562 233 1701*

Be prepared to eat lip-smacking food at this Indian, Chinese and Continental speciality restaurant. Although there are no snacks served, complete meals from a wide choice of cuisines are on offer. Also available is a gourmet buffet at which there is an interactive counter .

BHARATPUR Hotel Pelican

Near Keoladeo National Park Entrance **Tel** *05644 224 221*

Located in the hotel that is situated on the fringes of the famous bird sanctuary, this restaurant is an obvious favourite with bird-watchers. However, the food served here, a mix of Indian and Western, is also good.
The North Indian and Israeli dishes especially are must-try items.

BHARATPUR Spoonbill

Behind RTDC, Hotel Saras **Tel** *05644 223 571*

Located a stone's throw away from Keoladeo National Park, the in-house restaurant of this hotel is a popular eatery, serving reasonably good Indian and Chinese food. There are folk dance performances around a campfire in the evenings, perfect to unwind after a long day of sightseeing.

BHARATPUR Bharatpur Forest Lodge

Inside Keoladeo National Park **Tel** *05644 222 722*

Attached to the pleasant ivy-covered bungalow inside the park, this small state-run restaurant has scrumptious Indian and Continental buffets laid out for hungry bird-watchers. Although the place could do with some refurbishment, there is a handy in-house bar serving a wide array of beverages and snacks.

BRINDAVAN ISKCON Bhojanalaya

Bhakti Vedanta Swami Marg, Raman Reti **Tel** *0565 254 0021*

A part of the clean and hygienic ISKCON guesthouse, wholesome vegetarian food at good prices is served here.
An à la carte menu is available for breakfast while *thalis* are offered for lunch and dinner. They also have a selection of delicious sweets and confectionery items.

FATEHPUR SIKRI Gulistan Tourist Complex

Fatehpur Sikri Complex **Tel** *05613 282 490*

The cheery and peaceful environs of this garden restaurant does not quite enhance the appeal of its rather mundane menu. The food is standard and run-of-the-mill, although it is popular with tourists looking for a suitable, pleasant stopover point.

GWALIOR Volga

Jayendraganj, Lakshar **Tel** *0751 232 1092*

This old Gwalior restaurant is, in fact, the very first to open in the area in 1961. Although there is nothing Russian about it, it lives up to its reputation as one of the best Indian food places in the city. It is also popular because of its economical prices.

GWALIOR Kwality

M L B Road, Deen Dayal Market **Tel** *0751 242 3243*

One of Gwalior's most popular restaurants, Kwality specializes in Indian cuisine and their *kakori* chicken is a particular favourite. Their special chicken *malmal* is also worth trying. The food is fresh, the service is good and friendly and the prices are fairly reasonable.

MEERUT Alfa

Bombay Bazaar, Meerut Cant **Tel** *0121 266 0532*

A centrally air conditioned, multi-cuisine restaurant located in the heart of Meerut. The Indian tandoori food at Alfa is delicious and the long list of must-try dishes includes the *paneer butter masala* and butter chicken.
The garlic and mustard flavoured *tikkas* are also highly recommended.

ORCHHA Sheesh Mahal

Orchha, Dist Tikamgarh **Tel** *07680 252 624*

Considered one of the best eating places in Orchha, the Sheesh Mahal restaurant is located within the Jahangiri Mahal. The fortifying breakfasts and buffet dinners here are served on the terrace, the latter being perfect for a romantic evening. The accompanying folk music and singing also add extra charm.

ORCHHA Kaleva

The Orchha Resort, Kanchana Ghat, Tikamgarh **Tel** *07680 252 222*

Imaginatively designed and conveniently located, this restaurant offers a choice of both vegetarian buffet and à la carte meals. Cuisines include Indian, Chinese and Continental for snacks and main meals. The evenings are enlivened by regional folk dances.

JAIPUR AND ENVIRONS

AJMER Bhola Hotel

Agra Gate, Subzi Mandi **Tel** *0145 243 2844*

The restaurant section of a hotel, this is a good family place for vegetarian food, especially the *thali* which constitutes a complete and hearty meal. Their speciality, *gatta* fry (deep-fried gram flour fritters mixed with spices) and *dal* fry are popular favourites. They also provide a separate dining hall for chauffeurs.

AJMER Honey Dew

Near KEM resthouse, Station Road **Tel** *0145 262 2498*

Established in 1962, this popular tourist joint now focuses mainly on regular Indian, Chinese, and Continental meals rather than fast-food. However, they still serve pizzas and Indian-style burgers. Their deliciously cooling banana *lassi* remains a popular favourite.

ALWAR Prem Bhojanalaya

Near old bus stand **Tel** *0144 270 0544*

An unpretentious vegetarian eatery with reasonably priced snacks. The speciality here is their inexpensive *thali* meal. The popular items are the fresh, spicy *dahi vada* (doughnut shaped snack made out of lentils in yoghurt, garnished with mint, masala and tamarind sauce) and the sweet, creamy *kheer* (Indian rice pudding).

ALWAR Hotel Aravali

Near Railway Station **Tel** *0144 233 2883*

This restaurant and bar in this hotel serves standard Indian and Indian-style Chinese dishes. The outdoor tables near the poolside are a perfect place to dine under the stars, especially if accompanied by a glass of one of their Indian or imported wines. Live entertainment takes place on Saturdays only.

JAIPUR Indian Coffee House

MI Road **Tel** *0141 236 2024*

The aroma of freshly ground coffee will lead you straight here for the best-brewed cup in town. A well-known chain run by the Indian government, the coffee house has an old-world charm about it and offers a modest range of snacks. Decent breakfast options are also available although there are no full meals served.

JAIPUR Lassiwala

Opp Niros, MI Road **Tel** *No telephone.*

You would definitely need to queue up for Lassiwalla's irresistible North Indian *lassi*, a thick, creamy sweet or salty drink made with curd. The *lassi* is variously flavoured, freshly whipped up in front of you and served in terracotta tumblers. This popular place, which has been around for over 50 years, is a must-stop for tourists.

JAIPUR Bake Hut

Arvind Marg, MI Road **Tel** *0141 236 2811*

The name says it all – guests will find oven-fresh, take-away breads, croissants, pastries, doughnuts and other such treats here. Also available is a wide range of cakes in various flavours. Do try their shakes and ice-creams. It remains a popular joint with youngsters, locals and tourists alike.

JAIPUR Copper Chimney

Maya Mansion, Opp GPO, MI Road **Tel** *0141 237 2275*

High standards of hygiene and service distinguish this Kwality chain restaurant, which has a good selection of traditional and local dishes, such as the spicy *lal maas*, a Rajasthani mutton dish. Also popular for its sizzlers and Continental dishes. Beer and Indian wines are served here.

JAIPUR Midway Motel Behror (RTDC)

Jaipur Highway No. 8, Behror **Tel** *01494 220 049*

This cafeteria is run by the state's tourism department. It serves Indian, South Indian and Rajasthani food. Its speciality is the Rajasthani *thali*. There is also a buffet and snacks are served 24 hours. The attached bar offers tandoori snacks, vegetarian as well as non-vegetarian, and a range of beverages.

JAIPUR Bhuwaneshwari

Bissau Palace, outside Chandpol **Tel** *0141 230 4371*

Located in a grand palace heritage hotel, with elegant and traditional decor, this restaurant offers authentic local Rajasthani delicacies served with style. Their menu also includes an exciting array of Continental and Asian cuisine. Service is friendly and efficient. Poolside seating is offered during fine weather.

JAIPUR Laxmi Mishtan Bhandar
Johari Bazaar **Tel** *0141 256 5844*

This is Jaipur's oldest and most famous vegetarian restaurant serving vegetarian *thalis*. It also offers an à la carte menu and boasts of the largest selection of Indian sweets and savouries made by its traditional *halwais*. It is famous for its *chaat* (a mixture of fritters, chickpeas, potatoes, yoghurt and spicy sauces).

Key to Price Guide *see p256* **Key to Symbols** *see back cover flap*

JAIPUR Nahargarh Fort Resturant

Nahargarh Fort **Tel** *0141 514 8044*

A brilliant place to enjoy a stunning view of Jaipur city over a steaming cup of coffee or a cool sundowner. This little restaurant is located inside the magnificent Nahargarh Fort. The restaurant is run by the state's tourism department and offers typical North Indian fare.

JAIPUR Hightz

Hotel Mansingh Tower, Sansar Chandra Road **Tel** *0141 511 8771*

A wonderful view of the city is available from this rooftop restaurant of the centrally located Mansingh Hotel. There is an excellent range of *thali* meals along with traditional Rajasthani dishes. A bar serving multi-cuisine snacks has also been recently added.

JAIPUR Niros

MI Road **Tel** *0141 237 4493*

This popular eating place offers Indian, Continental and Chinese food. Try the refreshing American ice-cream soda. A restobar serves beer and wine. Also try the Rajasthani specialities, *lal maas* (spicy mutton curry), *sula* meat and the divine *kulfi falooda* (cardamom flavoured ice-cream, vermicelli and sweet syrup).

JAIPUR Rajasthan Hotel

Jaipur Highway No. 8, Dughera, Behror **Tel** *01494 220 087*

A highly recommended midway stop for the hungry bus or car traveller on the Jaipur-Agra highway. Delicious buffets as well as hearty *thalis* are served here. Both the bar and restaurant are air conditioned. Cold and hot beverages are available through the day.

JAIPUR The Marble Arch

Jacob Road, Civil Lines **Tel** *0141 222 3636*

Within elegant surroundings and boasting warm, efficient service, this restaurant is reputed for its Rajasthani *thali* and juicy, garlic flavoured chicken *tikkas*. The menu offers a wide range of Thai, Continental, Chinese, Indian and Italian food. Recent refurbishment has made its decor more Westernized.

NAWALGARH Apani Dhani

Jhunjhunu Road **Tel** *01594 222 239*

In this exceptionally well designed eco-farm guests will be served wholesome vegetarian food made from garden-fresh vegetables organically grown on the premises, to be eaten in traditional Indian style. The food is also cooked with bio-gas or solar heaters keeping in mind their eco-friendly principles.

NAWALGARH Roop Niwas Palace

Hotel Roop Niwas Palace **Tel** *01594 222 008*

Excellent vegetarian, non-vegetarian and special Rajasthani meals from a fixed menu are served here along with good buffets. This is a good place to refresh yourself after an expedition to the Nawalgarh Fort. Their bar is well-stocked with a wide collection of wines and other beverages.

NEEMRANA Amaltasse

Neemrana Fort, Neemrana **Tel** *01494 246 007*

In the enchanting environs of the magnificent Neemrana Heritage Hotel, this unusual French restaurant offers a gourmet four-course, candle-lit dinner that is worth the drive from Delhi. There are also live music performances. Advanced booking is a definite must.

PUSHKAR Om Shiva

Chhoti Basti **Tel** *0145 277 2647*

One of the few places in Pushkar that offers an excellent breakfast, complete with cereal, fruit, wholemeal bread and a choice of peanut butter, cheese or jam to go with it. They also do good buffet meals; the one at lunchtime is recommended for its soups, fresh vegetables and crispy falafels. It also provides a great view of the temple town.

PUSHKAR Sun-n-Moon

Near Bramha Temple **Tel** *0145 277 2883*

This mellow open-air restaurant caters to the foreign traveller offering a selected menu of dishes ranging from curry to mashed potatoes and Italian to Israeli. Try the delicious apple pie. It lies in the vicinity of the Brahma Temple and has tables placed around a *bodi* tree making it a peaceful, pleasant place to eat.

PUSHKAR Sunset Café

Hotel Sunset **Tel** *0145 277 2725*

Although the Indian and Continental food here is nothing special, its scenic position near the lake and lovely garden makes it a good place to enjoy a light snack, especially at sunset, when the crowds gather. Try the wide selection of pancakes on offer. There is usually dancing in the evening.

PUSHKAR Pushkar Palace

Pushkar Palace **Tel** *0145 277 3001*

Prices here are relatively high for Pushkar, but the ambience, the buffet and the meals offered justify the rates. The vegetarian multi-cuisine dishes include Indian, Continental and Chinese and can be served either indoors or out on the lawns overlooking the lake. Rajasthani dance and folk music performances also enliven the evening.

SHOPS AND MARKETS

The colourful markets of the region carry a vast and exciting range of handicrafts. The government-run state emporia are well stocked with merchandise at fixed and reasonable rates. Shopping arcades of larger hotels cater to travellers who are hard-pressed for time, though their more sophisticated boutiques are usually pricier. For the more adventurous, there are the street

Puppet

stalls and bazaars that offer glimpses of local colour, and where bargaining is a way of life. Delhi has some of the region's most elegant shops *(see pp118–19)*, but the charming bazaars of Jaipur and Agra offer visitors a chance to actually observe skilful craftsmen at work. In the smaller towns beyond the main cities, local crafts are often sold in quaint village stores or on the roadside.

Pavement hawkers in Jaipur

OPENING HOURS

Most shops usually open at 10am and shut down by 7:30pm, though the smaller markets keep longer hours. The government-run emporia close an hour earlier. Markets for fresh produce open at dawn and stay open until late evening, while the temporary bazaars that spring up at different localities on festivals or particular week days gather the crowds until late at night. In Jaipur and Agra, the closing day is Sunday, but in

Delhi, each locality has its own weekly holiday. Shopping centres in the New Delhi area are closed on Sundays, but in South Delhi and Karol Bagh, the closing days are Monday or Tuesday. By law all shops are required to remain closed on the three main national holidays, that is, Republic Day (26 Jan), Independence Day (15 Aug) and Mahatma Gandhi's birthday (Martyr's Day, 2 Oct).

HOW TO PAY

The rupee is accepted everywhere. The bigger stores accept international credit cards such as VISA, MasterCard, American Express and Diners, and usually display signs prominently inside the shops. But they are still not very common in the smaller shops and towns, and it is always sensible to keep some cash handy when travelling. Traveller's cheques can be encashed at local branches of the State Bank of India *(see p288)*, but again, this facility may not be available in the smaller towns.

Bright glass and plastic bangles

BARGAINING

Bargaining is an essential part of the shopping experience in India, and at the smaller markets, prices are quoted with the expectation that customers will haggle. Some of the most familiar scenes at all bazaars are those of local shoppers indulging in long and often acrimonious discussions with shopkeepers about price and quality. Most shopkeepers are tourist savvy today and will usually quote a higher price to foreigners. The best way to check out prices is to browse through a fixed-price shop like a government emporium. This will also give you an idea of quality. However, the price you offer to pay should be realistic and not so low that you miss out on a good purchase altogether. If this price is still unacceptable to the shopkeeper, an old and usually very effective bargaining tactic is to walk away feigning indifference.

All the bigger and fancier shops and boutiques, retail outlets of manufacturers and the government emporia have fixed prices with no scope for bargaining. Increasingly, in fact, more shops are tagging their goods with labels that clearly indicate item prices.

Connaught Place shopping complex, Delhi

Paper kite stall in Jaipur

RIGHTS AND REFUNDS

By law all shops are obliged to give you a receipt or cash memo for all purchases. When buying insist on getting one to which sales tax, generally seven or ten per cent of the total cost, has been added. Often the shopkeeper will say that you can save on the tax if you do not take a receipt, but do insist on one nevertheless. Refunds or the exchange of damaged goods are impossible without one and it is absolutely essential for the more expensive purchases. Bigger shops can be fussy about taking back goods but you can talk to the manager if absolutely necessary.

Delicately inlaid marble

If the shop is going to ship your purchases, make sure that you know all the costs involved, including taxes. Also, insist that all the paperwork is done correctly and you have copies of it all. If you wish you can also ship the larger purchases yourself through the international courier services *(see p291)*.

ANTIQUES

Antiques and art objects that are more than 100 years old cannot be taken out of the country. If in doubt about your purchases, consult the office of the Archaeological Survey of India *(see p279)*. You should also get a certificate from the shop stating the age of the artifact.

TOUTS

In the larger markets that are frequented by tourists, persistent touts can be a problem. Ignore the offers of fantastic bargains because the prices you pay are often suspect. Also beware of polite young men inviting you home for a cup of tea because "home" will be a shop down the lane. Tourist buses will of course stop at their selected shops but you don't have to buy anything from them. Try to shop for expensive things at big shops with price tags on their goods and beware of of shops with "government-approved" boards as these are usually private enterprises.

BAZAARS

A visit to a traditional Indian bazaar is worth the experience rather than the actual shopping. These lively places offer fantastic bargains and a colourful atmosphere. Most bazaars are located in the heart of the old cities. where narrow lanes are lined with rows of shops selling a variety of merchandise from car spare-parts, machinery, cooking utensils and provisions to textiles and jewellery. Vegetables and other fresh produce are sold on the roadside. Most cities also have the weekly bazaars, and rural India has seasonal *haats* that travel from village to village for the local people to shop for everything from agricultural equipment to clothes to pots and pans. The bazaars in Agra and Jaipur were originally craft guilds and some still specialize in specific local crafts such as textiles, jewellery, marble inlay and leatherwork, where you can watch the craftsmen at work, admire their skills and buy directly from them.

A streetside stall where bargaining skills are essential

GOVERNMENT EMPORIA

The central government and the state governments all run shops selling handicrafts and handloom textiles that are special to their region or state. The prices are fixed and the products genuine. Rajasthali, the Rajasthan emporium, concentrates on handicrafts from Jaipur. While Delhi is a centre for emporia from all the states, neither Agra nor Jaipur offer the same range of regional products. October is a good time for bargains and discounts.

Roadsides flooded with colourful, seasonal fruit

Anokhi, Jaipur, combining traditional designs with modern-day use

SHOPPING IN AGRA

The exquisite *pietra dura* work on the Taj Mahal is still practised in Agra by descendants of craftsmen who worked on the historic monument. Replicas of the delicate semi-precious stone inlay designs are found on marble and alabaster boxes and bowls, tabletops, chess-boards and trays readily available in Agra's bazaars. Large wall panels and ornate sofa backs can be made to order and shipped directly abroad. Plain marble, red sandstone and soapstone items are also popular. Another beautiful craft is *zardozi* embroidery done on silk or velvet with gold and silver thread and sequins to create dress material, bags, jackets and shoes.

Agra is renowned for its shoe industry. The designs are somewhat basic, but the shoes are sturdy and certainly worth their price.

You can also shop for cotton *dhurries* woven in modern or traditional designs.

NORTH OF DELHI

Smaller towns near Delhi have their own craft specialities. There are several weaving centres producing pile carpets which are sent to Delhi and other cities to be sold. **Panipat** is famous for its attractive cotton floor coverings and woven home furnishings. In **Saharanpur**, you will find all kinds of woodcarved items in intricate designs and brass inlay work ranging from tables and screens to boxes and ashtrays.

SHOPPING IN JAIPUR

Jaipur is truly a shopper's paradise. The range of textiles and handicrafts available here includes an irresistible selection of fabrics (embroidered, block-printed, tie-and-dyed), as well as ready-made garments. Rolls of colourful quilts in light layered cotton, but surprisingly warm, are piled high on streetside shops, and government emporia and larger shops stock the beautiful Mughal designed woollen carpets that are made in Jaipur. The city is known for its jewellery which ranges from folk designs in silver to the elegant and more pricey gold jewellery in *meenakari* and *kundan* work *(see p187)*.

Jaipur blue pottery

There is also a wide variety of handmade leather goods from *jootis* and bags to saddles and wallets, while in furniture, there is a dazzling choice of carved and painted tables, chairs, screens, wall brackets, candle and lamp stands.

Jaipur was a centre of miniature painting, and artists now sell perfect reproductions at a fraction of the price of originals. Both the religious *pichhwai* and the narrative *phad* cloth paintings make wonderful wall hangings. Blue pottery is another of Jaipur's traditional crafts, using delicate Persian, Turkish and Indian designs on vases, door-knobs and tiles.

AROUND JAIPUR

Both Sanganer and Bagru *(see p204)* are famous for their blockprinted textiles dyed in vegetable colours. In Rajasthan every village has its own artisans. The cobblers produce brightly decorated sandals and bags, potters mould clay into delightful terracotta bowls and plates, and the wood-carver will have wide-eyed puppets hanging on the walls of his workshop. The village markets teem with brightly dressed men and women responding to the cajoling and loud calls of hawkers. Among the traditional metal cooking pots and modern clothes made of synthetic fabric, there are toys and trinkets, lacquer bangles and silver jewellery.

Weaving a carpet on a traditional pit-loom

DIRECTORY

GOVERNMENT EMPORIA

Oswal Emporium
30 Munoro Rd, Sadar Bazaar, Agra.
Tel (0562) 222 5710.

Handloom House
MI Rd, Jaipur.
Tel (0141) 236 5331.

Khadi Ghar
MI Rd, Jaipur.
Tel (0141) 237 3745.

Rajasthali
MI Rd, opp Ajmeri Gate Jaipur.
Tel (0141) 237 2974.

Rajasthan State Handloom Dev. Corp. Ltd.
Chomu House, Jaipur.
Tel (0141) 237 1109.

JEWELLERY

Koh-i-Noor
41 MG Rd, Agra.
Tel (0562) 246 0855.

Munshi Ganeshi Lal & Son
9 MG Rd, Agra.
Tel (0562) 233 0168.

Amrapali
Tholia Building, MI Rd, Jaipur.
Tel (0141) 237 7940.

Bhuramal Rajmal Surana
Johari Bazaar, Jaipur.
Tel (0141) 257 0429.

Dwarka's
H 20 Bhagat Singh Marg, C Scheme, Jaipur.
Tel (0141) 236 0301.

Gem Palace
MI Rd, Jaipur.
Tel (0141) 237 4175.

Surana Jewellers
B 73, Surana Encl, Jaipur.
Tel (0141) 237 2544.

Silver Mountain
Chameli Mkt, Jaipur.
Tel (0141) 237 7399.

TEXTILES

Anokhi
2 Tilak Marg, Jaipur.
Tel (0141) 222 9247.

Naika
Tholia Building, MI Rd, Jaipur.
Tel (0141) 236 2664.

Rashid
Shri Govind Dev Colony, Tal Katora Rd, Jaipur.
Tel (0141) 231 3237.

Ratan Textiles
Papriwal Cottage Ajmer Rd, Jaipur.
Tel (0141) 222 2526

Shilpi Handicrafts
Near Siliberi, Sanganer.
Tel (0141) 273 1106.

Soma Shop
5 Jacob Rd, Civil Lines, Jaipur.
Tel (0141) 222 2778.

EMBROIDERED TEXTILES

Indian Crafts Gallery
Fatehabad Rd, Agra.
Tel (0562) 223 0336.

Thar Inc.
65, Mathur Vaishya Nagar, Tonk Rd, Jaipur.
Tel (0141) 272 1913.

CARPETS AND DHURRIES

Kanu Carpet Factory
18/160/1-A, Purani Mandi Taj Ganj, Agra.
Tel (0562) 233 0167.

Ambika Exports
Moti Doongri Rd, Jaipur.
Tel (0141) 260 7665.

Ankur Exports
2 Udhistar Marg, Jaipur.
Tel (0141) 222 8668.

Jaipur Carpets
G 250 Mansarovar Industrial Area.
Tel (0141) 239 8948.

PAINTINGS AND OBJETS D'ART

Shree Ganpati Arts
S-17 Golimar Garden, Amer Rd, Jaipur.
Tel (0141) 267 2212.

Saurashtra Oriental Arts
Opp Ayurveda College, Inside Zoravar Singh Gate Amer Road,

Juneja Art Gallery
Lakshmi Complex, MI Rd, Jaipur.
Tel (0141) 236 7448.

Ved Pal Sharma Banno
Chanakya Marg, Subhas Chowk, Jaipur.
Tel (0141) 260 3450.

BLUE POTTERY

Kripal Singh Shekhawat
B 18a Siva Marg, Bani Park, Jaipur.
Tel (0141) 220 1127 (by prior appointment).

HANDMADE PAPER

Salim's Paper
Gramodyog Rd, Sanganer.
Tel (0141) 273 0076.

BOOKS, TEA AND SPICES

Saroj Handicrafts and Arts
A-2 Tilak Marg, C-Scheme, Nandanam Apts, Jaipur.
Tel (0141) 511 0927.

Maharaja Exports
Fatehabad Rd, Agra.
Tel (0562) 400 5622.

Golden Tips Tea Co
Grah Sangrah Dept Store, Khasa Kothi Circle, Jaipur..
Tel (0141) 220 0271.

Books Corner
MI Road, Jaipur.
Tel (0141) 236 6323.

The Book Shop
Rambagh Palace, Bhawani Singh Rd, Jaipur.
Tel (0141) 238 5030.

SHOES

Yogi Shoes & Leather Crafts
Fatehabad Rd, Agra.
Tel (0562) 233 0029.

Bharat Boot House
Johari Bazaar, Jaipur.
Tel (0141) 256 4914.

Mojari
Bhawani Villa, Gulab Path, Chomu House, Jaipur.
Tel (0141) 237 7037.

MARBLE INLAY

Ganesi Lal International
Clarks Shiraz, Agra.
Tel (0562) 222 6126.

Akbar International
289, Fatehabad Rd, Agra.
Tel (0562) 233 0076.

UP Handicrafts Complex
Fatehabad Road, Agra.
Tel (0562) 233 1666.

BAZAARS

Agra
Johari Bazaar
Cotton dhurries.
Kinari Bazaar
Jewellery and zari work.
Taj Ganj
Marble inlay.

Jaipur
Johari Bazaar, Gopalji ka Rasta, Haldiyon ka Rasta
Jewellery and tie-and-dye textiles.
Khajanewalon ka Rasta
Marble carving.
Kishanpol Bazaar
Tie-and-dye textiles.
Maniharon ka Rasta
Lac bangles.
Nehru Bazaar
Embroidered jootis.
Ramganj Bazaar
Shoes.

What to Buy

The bazaars, markets and boutiques of Delhi, Agra and Jaipur showcase the wide range of the region's arts and crafts. In many places there is the joy of watching artisans at work and buying directly from them. The quality can vary, but the range is unbelievable, from exotic, aromatic spices, to ceramics and handicrafts, carpets, textiles and jewellery. There are also elegant contemporary interpretations of traditional design.

A bronze monkey

Jewelled and enamelled armband

Jewellery
Antique and jewellery shops stock exquisite pieces of gem-encrusted kundan *and enamelled* meenakari *jewellery. Also available are the silver ornaments worn by local men and women.*

Silver anklets, bracelet and armband

Hand-crafted cutlery

A pencil holder

Metal
Bronze and brass objects of everyday use, such as pots, lamps or boxes, are widely available along with an exciting range of artifacts in silver and other metals created by contemporary designers.

A goblet in mixed metal

Brass pots (lotas)

Silver fan (pankha)

Pottery
Abundant earthenware vessels and toys made by local potters can be seen stacked along the roadside. Commonly found are a sophisticated range of patterned tableware from Khurja, and Jaipur's famous blue pottery.

Door-knobs

Terracotta votive figure

Jaipur blue pottery jar with lid

A folk animal in terracotta

Tiles with floral motifs

Textiles

Blockprints and silk and cotton woven textiles in a dazzling choice of colours and designs can be bought as yardage or ready-made garments, scarves and saris. Floor coverings are either the thick pile carpets or the colourful cotton dhurries used in Indian homes.

Pile carpet with floral design

Window blinds

Scarves by Abraham & Thakore

Light-weight cotton quilts

Herbal Products

Traditional natural remedies have been re-invented to suit the contemporary need for eco-friendly cosmetics, soothing oils and lotions, tea and joss sticks (incense).

Joss sticks (agarbatti)

Traditional perfumes (attar)

Ayurvedic cosmetics

Soap

Herbal tea

Natural Rosewater

Handicrafts

Materials such as handmade paper, leather, stone and wood are used to make decorative and functional objects such as shoes, plates, boxes and puppets.

Handmade paper box

Embroidered slippers

ENTERTAINMENT

Except for Delhi, which offers a wide range of cultural entertainment round the year *(see pp120-21)*, options in most other cities are often restricted to the cultural fare offered by the hotels. Although both Agra and Jaipur have a strong tradition of folk and classical performing arts, these can only be seen during the peak season. One reason for this is that most Indians prefer to spend their evenings or holidays with the family. As outings invariably include children, the cinema is a favourite, while religious festivals, which offer free entertainment, are also popular. However, dining out is a rising fad among the urban elite.

Folk entertainer

INFORMATION SOURCES

Your travel agent is the best source of information on what is happening, where and when. Otherwise, calendars of cultural events are available from the tourist offices and also at hotels. Local newspapers also list daily events and advertise major cultural festivals, such as the Taj Mahotsav *(see p40)*. Small tourist oriented local publications, such as *Jaipur Vision*, available at book shops and hotel receptions, also carry listings of cinemas, restaurants and bars, swimming pools and shops.

BOOKING TICKETS

All the larger hotels in the region have regular evening performances of classical music and dance in their main restaurants. The dinner cover charge usually includes the performance. But if a show at a theatre or hall is announced, the tickets are available at the venue and your hotel or travel agent will be able to book them for you.

CLASSICAL MUSIC AND DANCE

Kathak and Hindustani music *(see p28)* flourished in this region, patronized first by the Mughal, and later by the regional courts. In an attempt to revive these traditional art forms, classical dance and music festivals are now held regularly in the cities during the peak tourist season sponsored by various cultural organizations. Among auditoria, the **Sur Sadan** in Agra, and in Jaipur, **Ravindra Manch** and **Panghat** are the most popular venues, while on special occasions, well-known dancers also perform before the main deity of the Govind Dev Temple in Jaipur. In Mathura and Brindavan the religious festivals of Holi and Janmashtami also attract classical dancers and singers.

A Rajasthani folk dancer

The devotional Sufi qawwali, originally based on the classical *raga* idiom *(see p28)*, is now a popular concert form. However, the best places to hear authentic qawwalis are at the Sufi shrines at Ajmer and Fatehpur Sikri where they are a daily ritual, while during the Urs festivities, special all-night soirées are held.

FOLK THEATRE, MUSIC AND DANCE

Few areas in this region can match the colour and vibrancy of Rajasthan's indigenous folk forms. Sadly, folk theatre and itinerant storytellers like the *phad* bards are fast losing their audiences and can often only be seen in smaller places. Yet, since Jaipur is the capital of the state, some of the best bards and dancers come here to perform at urban centres such as the **Jawahar Kala Kendra**. The *ghumar* dance, performed by women during religious festivals and

The *bhopa* musicians performing round a campfire

weddings, and the *kalbelia* or snake dance of a nomadic tribe can be seen at hotel shows. Folk singers, such as the *bhopas*, the Manganiyars or Langas, come regularly to the Pushkar Fair and smaller towns, attracting people with their rich and expressive repertoire of folk ballads.

During the Janmashtami festival (Aug–Sep) the Raslila, an enactment of the story of Lord Krishna, is held in the Brajbhumi area of Brindavan and Mathura *(see p162)*. Local Ramlilas *(see p37)*, are staged all over North India during Dussehra (Oct–Nov). These folk productions, often loud and melodramatic, have a unique vivacity and charm.

PUPPET SHOWS

Puppetry is a strong folk tradition practised by the Bhatt pastoral community in Rajasthan. String puppets, called *kathputlis,* play out heroic stories of popular folk and legendary characters. The romance of Dhola and Maru, royal lovers who were separated only a few weeks after they were betrothed but finally united, is one of the most popular puppet shows. The riveting performances of these travelling puppeteers is seen at every fair and festival.

CINEMAS

Cinema is still the country's most popular form of entertainment, and even the smallest town has a theatre screening the latest Hindi blockbuster. Jaipur's cinema halls are famous, and the **Raj Mandir**, actually a theatre hall with a flamboyantly kitschy interior, even screens World Cup cricket matches! Indian films are a fantastic mix of action and romance, song and dance, shot in fabulous sets and locales. The films range from the crass to the brilliant.

Dubbing in Hindi of Western mega-hits is the new rage, with films like *Star Wars* and *The World is Not Enough* taking the lead. Though art films have won many international awards, and directors such as Satyajit Ray are considered among the world's best, their films are rarely shown commercially. Nevertheless, a visit to the local cinema will give you an insight into the Indian people's most frequented form of popular entertainment.

Crowds jostling for tickets to a Hollywood mega-hit dubbed in Hindi

NIGHTLIFE AND BARS

Except for the five-star hotels, options for nightlife in Agra and Jaipur are limited. The luxury hotels all have their own bars where there is a good choice of both local and foreign liquors and the atmosphere is pleasant. A few other places in both the cities are licensed to have bars. The choice of spirits is limited but the atmosphere is lively.

DIRECTORY

PERFORMING ART CENTRES

Sur Sadan
Mahatma Gandhi Rd, Agra.
Tel (0562) 281 1009.

Birla Auditorium
Statue Circle, Jaipur.
Tel (0141) 238 5224.

Jawahar Kala Kendra
Jawaharlal Nehru Marg, Jaipur.
Tel (0141) 270 5879.

Panghat
Rambagh Palace, Bhawani Singh Rd, Jaipur.
Tel (0141) 221 1919.

Ram Niwas Bagh
Behind Central Museum, Jaipur.
Tel (0141) 256 5244.

Ravindra Manch
JN Marg, Jaipur.
Tel (0141) 261 9061.

Welcomgroup Rajputana Palace Sheraton
Palace Rd, Jaipur.
Tel (0141) 510 0100.

CINEMAS

Anjana
MG Rd, Agra.
Tel (0562) 285 0371.

Sanjay Talkies
Sanjay Place, Agra.
Tel (0562) 215 0384.

Shree
MG Road, Agra.
Tel (0562) 285 3737.

Ankur
Jaipur.
Tel (0141) 260 0531.

Laxmi Mandir
Jaipur.
Tel (0141) 274 1504.

Entertainment Paradise
Jawahar Circle, Jaipur.
Tel (0141) 512 7777.

Moti Mahal
Jaipur.
Tel (0141) 220 1723.

Space 1-2-3
City Plaza, Bani Park, Jaipur.
Tel (0141) 220 8444.

Raj Mandir
Jaipur.
Tel (0141) 237 9372.

BARS

Cheeta
Hotel Jaipur Ashok, Jaipur.
Tel (0141) 220 4491.

Polo Bar
Rambagh Palace, Bhawani Singh Rd, Jaipur.
Tel (0141) 221 1919.

Rajwada Library Bar
Rajvilas, Jaipur.
Tel (0141) 268 0101.

Rana Sanga Roof Top Bar
Mansingh Palace, Jaipur.
Tel (0141) 237 8771.

SPORTS AND OUTDOOR ACTIVITIES

Previously, only the traditional sports such as cricket and polo provided visitors with opportunities for participating in outdoor activities. But today, the tourism industry offers a vast diversity of choices for specialist holidays. For sports lovers, the main cities, especially Delhi and Jaipur, offer clubs and grounds for golf, tennis, swimming and riding. Those in search of adventure can explore the foothills of the Himalayas and

After a polo match

the Aravallis by trekking or rock climbing, while the tumultous mountain streams above Rishikesh are ideal for white-water rafting and kayaking.

A camel or horse safari is a good way to experience the haunting beauty of the Rajasthan desert, and wildlife enthusiasts can visit the national parks for tiger-spotting and birdwatching. For those wishing to delve deeper into the mystique of the region, there are centres for yoga and meditation, naturopathy and spiritual studies.

SPECTATOR SPORTS

Cricket has emerged as the main national sport and, no matter where you travel you will see men and boys batting, bowling and fielding. India hosted the 1996 World Cup, an event that further fuelled the passion for the game and its players, who enjoy a celebrity status equal to film stars. Each year, especially in winter, several international cricket teams come to India, and test matches are played at various cities. The scenic Feroze Shah Kotla ground in Delhi is a major venue. All-night matches are played at the Jawaharlal Nehru Stadium, lit up especially for the occasion. In Jaipur, the Mansingh Stadium is the main cricket playing ground.

Advertisements for national and international matches appear well in advance in all the newspapers, and tickets (usually on sale ten days earlier), are in great demand

even though the more important matches are broadcast on the national network and sports channels.

Indian football is yet to reach international standards, and world-class matches are rarely held in the country. However, passions run high at the Ambedkar Stadium in Delhi where national tournaments are held, and a view from the stands can be a very enjoyable experience on a sunny winter afternoon.

TENNIS AND SWIMMING

In Delhi, the Lawn Tennis Association maintains some excellent tennis courts. So do some of the city's clubs and sports complexes. In Jaipur, the main tennis courts are at the **Jai Club**, just off Mirza Ismail (MI) Road. Both these cities are venues for the Davis Cup matches, and with India winning the 1999 Wimbledon doubles championship, there is a rapidly growing interest in this international sport.

A tennis match

However, because of the scarcity of public tennis courts they are often booked in advance and the best option for a quick game is at your own hotel's tennis court.

Come summer and all clubs, sports centres and five-star hotels in the region open their swimming pools. The most easily accessible to visitors are in the five-star hotels, usually with attached saunas and fitness centres. Non-residents can take temporary membership or pay a fee to use hotel pools.

GOLF

All major cities have well-maintained golf courses. In Delhi, the oldest and most prestigious course is at the **Delhi Golf Club**, located next to The Oberoi Hotel. This 27-hole course, creatively developed around a cluster of beautiful medieval pavilions, hosts many international

The Jawaharlal Nehru open air Stadium in New Delhi

tournaments in the winter season. Military cantonments, both here and at Agra, have their own golf courses. Just outside Delhi, the **Classic Golf Resort** is publicized as a weekend getaway, but is open to golfers through the week. In Jaipur, the Rambagh Palace Hotel has its own golf course and offers golf sets on hire for residents to play on the premises. Most golf clubs offer temporary membership to visitors for a fee.

RIDING

Both Delhi and the Jaipur area have excellent riding clubs which non-members may use for a nominal fee. The **Delhi Riding Club** has a stable full of well-groomed horses for hire. In Shekhawati, the heritage Dunlod Fort *(see p243)* has a polo ground, organizes horse safaris and teaches equestrian skills.

Visitors on a horse safari in Rajasthan

POLO

Polo was once the preserve of royalty and the army, and the Jaipur maharajas used to personally lead their teams to tournaments abroad. Corporate sponsorship has now revived interest in the game, and a major attraction is the gaiety, pomp and glamour attached to it. Winter is the main polo season in Delhi and Jaipur. Most tournaments in Delhi are played at the polo grounds adjacent to the Race Course on Kamal Ataturk Road, and in Jaipur, matches are played at the **Rajasthan Polo Club** near the Rambagh Palace Hotel.

A golfer teeing off beneath the ramparts of Jaipur's Moti Doongri Fort

Ramgarh and Dundlod are major polo centres, where the game is also taught. In March, visitors may see some traditional elephant polo at Jaipur's Chaugan Stadium.

HELI-TOURISM

Helicopter package trips are a new departure for the tourism industry in India. Apart from the transport by helicopter, they include lodging, meals and sightseeing. Heli-getaways in the region, organized by **Deccan Aviation** for those who can afford it and are strapped for time, so far include Agra, Jaipur-Sariska, and Jaipur-Ranthambhore. From Delhi, **World Expeditions India** organizes heli-skiing in winter, and also cycling tours.

JEEP AND DESERT SAFARI

An adventurous way to see the countryside is by safari. For wildlife sanctuaries, jeep safaris are common with camping along the way. Camel safaris, organized by travel agents from Jaipur, and by

most heritage hotels especially in Kishangarh *(see p215)*, Mandawa and Nawalgarh *(see p246)*, promise unexpected glimpses of desert life and a first-hand acquaintance with the ship of the desert. Prices vary, depending on the duration of the safari. Camping out in the desert is a romantic experience, especially at night around a campfire with your camel driver relating thrilling stories of desert lovers and villains. Elephant and horse safaris can also be organized for groups through private travel agents.

CHILDREN'S ACTIVITIES

Delhi offers much to amuse children, beginning with a sprawling Zoo. The Appu Ghar Amusement Park has several roller coasters, water rides and other thrilling games. The **National Science Centre** and the **Nehru Planetarium** organize special shows for children on certain events, such as eclipses. The Rail Museum is also a great hit with children, and offers rides on a special toy train.

Experiencing desert life on a camel safari in Rajasthan

Rock climbing

CAMPING, TREKKING AND ROCK CLIMBING

The Himalayan foothills above Rishikesh have ideal locations for camping, trekking and rock climbing. As most of Rajasthan's forts nestle in the craggy slopes of hillsides, they also offer excellent opportunities for rock climbing and exploring the neighbouring countryside. Just beyond South Delhi, near Sohna in Gurgaon, there are many attractive hiking trails. The best source of information on these activities is the **Indian Mountaineering Federation**, and private operators, such as Milestones and Outdoor Adventures *(see p231),* who specialize in organizing treks. Most organizers can provide reliable guides, as well as campsite equipment such as tents and sleeping bags, though you may feel more comfortable carrying your own things. The best time for this activity is in the summer months from April to June, and after the monsoon from October to early December, before the weather gets too cold.

ECOTOURISM

This relatively new concept in tourism, which combines various aspects of nature study along with participation in conservation activities, is steadily gaining ground in India. There are three main national parks in Rajasthan. Ranthambhore *(see pp224–5)* and Sariska *(see pp210–11)* are known for their tiger populations, while bird-watchers will find many exotic inhabitants at Bharatpur's Keoladeo Ghana *(see pp168–9).* Tours can be arranged through Rajasthan Tourism. Near Delhi are smaller sanctuaries such as the Sultanpur Sanctuary *(see p116).* The **World Wide Fund for Nature, India (WWF),** with its headquarters in Delhi, has an active programme of activities, such as camps, film shows and seminars.

CULTURAL STUDIES

Yoga and meditation are taught at ashrams found in most cities. In Delhi, at the **Shivanand Yoga Vedanta Nataraja Centre** there is a good programme all year round. The best centres are, however, found in Rishikesh, where some of the best gurus conduct courses of yoga and Hindu philosophy all year round, and an International Yoga Festival is held here every year *(see p41).* Naturopathy and ayurveda, two Indian systems that rely on the healing powers of

Logo of a yoga centre in Rishikesh

natural foods and herbs, are also practised and taught at many centres, such as the **Ayurveda Kendra Clinic.** In Delhi, the **Kairali Health Resort** specializes in ayurvedic oil massages. Pranic healing, a method that channels positive forces through the *chakras* or energy centres in the body, is taught at the **Aurobindo Centre.** Those who are interested in Buddhist philosophy will find information on this area of study in Tibet House and at the **Toshita Mahayana Meditation Centre.** The **Sadhan Sansthan** can provide details of courses in *vipassana,* an old and efficacious form of meditation, while astrology and palmistry are taught at the Bharatiya Vidya Bhavan. Triveni Kala Sangam *(see p76)* holds short courses in classical singing, dance and in painting. Crafts skills can be studied at the Crafts Museum. Some travel agencies have devised special interest tours on subjects such as architecture, traditional crafts and spiritualism, and can draw up itineraries and organize tours to suit individual choices. These agencies have government recognition and are members of international organizations. A "Gourmet Journey through India" is one such tour on the agenda of **Indo Asia Tours** who engage specialists as their consultants.

A yoga asana

Trekking in the Himalayan foothills

River rafters relaxing on the banks of the Ganges

KAYAKING AND RIVER RAFTING

Just north of Rishikesh, a series of rapids on the Ganges as it rushes down the mountains make for excellent kayaking and river rafting *(see p145)* opportunities. A normal trip stretches over three days as participants are carefully introduced to the intensity of the rapids. The best time for rafting and kayaking is from September to April, when campsites are set up along the pristine beaches along the river both by the Uttar Pradesh State Government *(see p279)*, and professionally trained private groups, such as Outdoor Adventures *(see p231)* and **Himalayan River Runners**. All the required equipment – tents, rafts, life-saving jackets and helmets – is supplied, as well as meals.

FISHING

Fishing is permitted in many of the region's rivers and lakes. But you must obtain a licence to do so from the designated local authority on site. In Delhi, the Okhla Barrage, as well as the nearby Suraj-kund and Badkhal lakes are popular with amateur anglers. Further north, where hill streams join the Chandrabhaga and the Ganges, particularly above Haridwar and Rishikesh, the rivers yield a good catch of the local variety of carp and other fish, though rarely trout.

WATER SPORTS

Ramgarh lake *(see p197)* near Jaipur, where some events of the 1984 Asian Games were held, is being developed by Rajasthan Tourism as a venue for water sports with facilities for parasailing, water-skiing and wind surfing. Currently, you can hire rowing, pedal and motor boats for a ride on the lake. Also, in and around Delhi a number of man-made lakes have facilities for boating and water sports.

White-water rafting on the River Ganges

DIRECTORY

SPORTS

Classic Golf Resort
NH8 (to Gurgaon),
Distt Gurgaon.
Tel (0124) 2378841/42.

Delhi Golf Club
Zakir Hussain Marg,
Delhi. **Map** 5 C4.
Tel (011) 2436 2768.

Delhi Riding Club
Safdarjung Rd,
Delhi. **Map** 4 F5.
Tel (011) 2301 1891.

Jai Club
Mahaveer Marg,
C Scheme, Jaipur.
Tel (0141) 237 2321.

Rajasthan Polo Club
Ambedkar Circle, Near
Rambagh Palace, Jaipur.
Tel (0141) 238 3580.

HELI-TOURISM

Deccan Aviation
G-11 Haus Khas Market,
Delhi.
Tel (011) 3295 9042.

CHILDREN'S ACTIVITIES

National Science Centre
Bhairon Marg, Delhi.
Map 6 D1.
Tel (011) 2337 1893.

Nehru Planetarium
Teen Murti House, Delhi.
Map 4 E3.
Tel (011) 2301 4504.

CAMPING AND TREKKING

Indian Mountaineering Federation
Benito Juarez Road, Delhi.
Tel (011) 2467 1211.
www.indmount.com

ECOTOURISM

WWF India
Max Mueller Marg,
Delhi. **Map** 5 A4.
Tel (011) 4150 4184.

CULTURAL STUDIES

Aurobindo Centre
Off Aurobindo Marg,
Delhi.
Tel (011) 2651 2491.

Ayurveda Kendra Clinic
Rishikesh.
Tel (0135) 243 0626.

Indo Asia Tours
C–28 Housing Society,
South Extn I, Delhi.
Tel (011) 2469 1733.

Kairali Health Resort
120 Andheria More,
Mehrauli, Delhi.
Tel (011) 2680 2106.
www.kairali.com

Sadhan Sansthan
16 Hemkund Towers,
Nehru Place, Delhi.
Tel (011) 2645 2772.

Shivanand Yoga Vedanta Nataraja Centre
52 Community Centre,
East of Kailash, Delhi.
Tel (011) 2924 0869.

Toshita Mahayana Meditation Centre
9 Padmini Enclave, Delhi.
Tel (011) 2651 3400.

RIVER RAFTING

Himalayan River Runners
N-8 Green Park Main,
Delhi. *Tel (011) 2696 6981.*
www.hrrindia.com

World Expeditions India
G-1 MG Bhavan,
Madangir, Delhi.
Tel (011) 2905 3358.

SURVIVAL GUIDE

PRACTICAL INFORMATION 278–291

TRAVEL INFORMATION 292–301

PRACTICAL INFORMATION

The country's most popular travel circuit, the three cities of Delhi, Agra and Jaipur, receives the majority of the 2.5 million tourists who visit India annually. Because of this, the range of transport, accommodation and information offered here is among the best in India. The more remote areas are still not equipped to cater to the international traveller who may seek better banking facilities or prefer to pay by credit card. The government-run Department of Tourism (DOT) has

Logo of the Department of Tourism

a centrally located office in Delhi and many overseas branches. You can also get the latest and most relevant information at the local state tourist departments of Delhi, Rajasthan and Uttar Pradesh. There are innumerable travel agencies, but it is wise to approach a reputable one when booking accommodation, travel tickets and sightseeing tours. It is also wise to plan and book ahead if you wish to make a visit in the winter months, since this is the peak tourist season.

WHEN TO GO

The finest weather for travelling in North India is from October to March. This season also coincides with an abundance of festivals and cultural events, especially from October to December *(see pp40–41)*. Though it can get quite cold at night in winter (Dec–Jan), the days are crisp and sunny, and the brief spring of February and March is beautiful, with the flowers in full bloom. Try to avoid the summer (Apr–Jun), and rainy season (Jul–Sep) if possible. Summer in North India is unbearably hot, dry and dusty, compounded by power cuts, and during the monsoon, the humidity accentuates the heat, making travelling very uncomfortable. Climate and rainfall charts can be found on pages 38–41.

Brightly coloured blossoms adorning a Delhi roundabout

WHAT TO TAKE

The clothes you need will depend on the time of year that you visit. At the height of the winter you will need warm clothes – a jacket or a thick pullover, socks and warm trousers, especially during the early mornings and nights, although the days can be much warmer. For autumn and spring, pack light woollens and clothes in natural fibres that are easy to wash. In summer only loose cotton clothes are comfortable. Indian-made ready-to-wear cotton shirts and women's outfits are available everywhere. Choose easy-to-remove footwear as you will have to take off your shoes in places of worship. A first-aid kit is a must *(see p286)*. An umbrella or light raincoat is a good idea, and a powerful torch could be packed for unexpected power cuts.

ADVANCE BOOKING

Since all three cities are both tourist and commercial centres, it is advisable to have confirmed advance bookings for your accommodation and travel, especially during the peak tourist season. Airline tickets are easier to obtain at short notice, but as you can get confirmed train bookings at least two months in advance, it is wise to book ahead for train travel. Hotels and travel agents also book coach tours within Delhi, as well as to Agra and Jaipur as they are within a comfortable distance of each other.

VISAS AND PASSPORTS

Everyone needs a visa to enter India. There are three types of visa for tourists, available from Indian Consular Offices around the

Visitors in local attire enjoying a rural festival

◁ **The annual Pushkar camel fair, a riot of colour**

world: the 15-day single/double entry visa, the 90-day, or the longer multiple entry visa for six months.

Getting a visa extension beyond 15 days is a complicated procedure. First, you must collect an extension form from the **Ministry of Home Affairs** office, then ill and submit it to the **Foreigners' Regional Registration Office (FRRO)**, who will stamp it. Finally, you must go back to the Ministry of Home Affairs for the actual visa extension.

There are certain places in India that are "Restricted Areas" and for which special permits are required. These include Sikkim, all the Northeastern states, Andaman and Nicobar Islands and Lakshwadweep.

EMBASSIES AND CONSULATES

Most countries have diplomatic missions in Delhi, but no representation in the other two cities. Consular officials can re-issue passports and help in case of theft, imprisonment, hospitalization or other emergencies. Some embassies have been shortlisted on page 281.

CUSTOMS INFORMATION

When entering India, visitors are allowed the usual duty-free 950 ml of alcohol and 200 cigarettes along with one laptop computer. In case the value of an item exceeds the duty free allowance, duty shall be calculated on the excess of the amount. Regarding currency, if you are carrying more than $10,000 in cash or traveller's cheques, you are expected to fill in the Currency Declaration Form at the airport, to be attested by a customs official.

Antiques over a hundred years old cannot be taken out of the country. Neither can wildlife products, such as animal pelts, shahtoosh shawls or ivory. Consult the **Archaeological Survey of**

Tourist bargaining with a vendor

India (ASI), or the **Ministry of Environment & Forests** for more details of these rules.

The trafficking of narcotics and psychotropic substances is a serious offence, punishable by imprisonment.

IMMUNIZATION

There are no official immunization requirements unless you travel from designated countries in Africa, South America and Papua New Guinea, in which case you will need a valid vaccination certificate for yellow fever. Vaccination against tetanus, typhoid and hepatitis A and B is a good idea. You can also start a course of anti-malarial tablets before you arrive in India, after consulting a reliable physician about the course.

INSURANCE AND DRIVING LICENCE

Before arriving in India do take out an insurance policy for medical emergencies and theft. In fact, if you are planning to take part in any adventure activities or sports, medical insurance is a necessity. To drive in India an International Driving Licence is required, which you should get before leaving for India. **The Automobile Association of Upper India (AAUI)** (see p299) can help with a temporary driving licence, but you will have to take a driving test for one.

Visa stamp

DIRECTORY

TOURIST OFFICES

Government of India Tourist Offices
88 Janpath, Delhi. **Map** I C5.
Tel (011) 2332 0008.
191, The Mall, Agra.
Tel (0562) 222 6378.
State Hotel, Khasa Kothi, Jaipur.
Tel (0141) 237 2200.
www.tourismindia.com

Delhi Tourism
N-36, Middle Circle, Connaught Place, Delhi. **Map** I C5.
Tel (011) 2331 5322.
www.delhitourism.nic.in

Rajasthan Tourism
Bikaner House, Shahjahan Rd, Delhi. **Map** 5 B2.
Tel (011) 2338 9525.
TRC Govt Hostel, MI Road, Jaipur.
Tel (0141) 511 0598.
www.rajasthan-tourism.com

Uttar Pradesh Tourism
Chandralok Building, 36 Janpath, Delhi. **Map** I C5.
Tel (011) 2371 1296.
64 Taj Rd, Agra.
Tel (0562) 222 6431.
www.up-tourism.com

USEFUL ADDRESSES

Archaeological Survey of India
Janpath, Delhi. **Map** 5 A2.
Tel (011) 2301 5273.

Foreigners' Regional Registration Offices
8, East Block, RK Puram Sector I, Delhi.
Tel (011) 2671 1443.
16 Idgah Colony, Agra.
Tel (0562) 221 7629.
Police Headquarters, Behind Hawa Mahal, Jaipur.
Tel (0141) 261 8508.

Ministry of Environment & Forests
Bikaner House, Delhi. **Map** 5 B2.
Tel (011) 2436 1147 / 2436 1669.

Ministry of Home Affairs
Lok Nayak Bhavan, Khan Market, Delhi. **Map** 5 B3.
Tel (011) 2469 3334.

TOURIST INFORMATION

The Department of Tourism offices have information on travel throughout India, and its tourism counter in the arrival hall of Delhi's international airport also provides essential information. However, the state tourism departments *(see p279)* will provide more reliable and detailed advice on the three cities. The staff are helpful, with plenty of practical information on sightseeing, travel and accommodation. Tourist brochures and maps are usually distributed free of charge.

Tourist brochures

ADMISSION CHARGES

Most museums, historical monuments and wildlife parks charge an entry fee. This is often a modest amount, though admission to World Heritage Sites costs more. There are often additional fees for cameras and video cameras. Most places of worship do not have any admission fee, but often have a donation box.

HOLIDAYS AND OPENING HOURS

All banks and government offices remain closed on the three national holidays of Republic Day (26 Jan), Indep-

endence Day (15 Aug) and Martyr's Day (2 Oct) *(see p39)*, when markets too are closed. Each year a new holiday list is issued by the Indian government, which includes all major religious festivals whose dates change according to the lunar calendar. Certain religious holidays are termed "restricted", so while the office may be open, the required official may be on leave. Monuments and museums normally open from 10am to 6pm, and generally close on Mondays and on government holidays. Shop timings are usually from 10am to 7:30pm. In Delhi, the markets are shut on different days of the week, but in Agra and Jaipur, they are closed on Sundays. Government offices work from Monday to Friday from 9:30am to 6pm, with a half hour lunch break. Senior officials often work overtime.

GUIDES

All tourist offices, travel agents and hotels can arrange a certified expert for you at fixed hourly rates. At popular sights amateur guides swarm around tourists hoping to be hired. You should ignore them and look instead for English-speaking guides wearing a metal badge that certifies government tourist department approval.

BACKPACKERS

For students and young travellers, each of the three cities has branches of the **Youth Hostels Association of India (YHAI)**. In Delhi, check with the **Vishwa Yuvak Kendra**. There is also a comfortable **YMCA** in Delhi. If you plan to travel by bus and train, you should bring a sturdy backpack that can take rough handling. The safest way to carry money is in a pouch fixed to your belt.

FACILITIES FOR THE DISABLED

Facilities for the disabled are still not well developed in public buildings and places of interest, as ramps or rails are seldom provided. However, airports and all main railway stations do have wheelchairs, ramps and escalators, and porters to carry your luggage. Pavements are difficult to negotiate in a wheelchair as they are often bumpy. Few hotels are equipped for the needs of the disabled traveller. The staff, however, are always helpful.

TRAVELLING WITH CHILDREN

Child-minding services for tourists are rare, but Indians love children so they can accompany parents to most places. However, they must be protected against the fierce sun, and drink only mineral water. Most well-known restaurants have food that children may safely eat.

PLACES OF WORSHIP

The three cities have a number of temples, *gurudwaras*, churches, mosques and, in Delhi, a synagogue, holding regular services. Since many are also places of historical or archaeological interest, they are open to foreign tourists. However, certain rules of etiquette *(see pp282–3)* must be observed. Most of these places are open till late in the night, but it is safer, and preferable, to visit them during the day.

Visitors enjoying a camel ride at the Pushkar fair

INDIAN STANDARD TIME AND CALENDAR

In spite of its size, India has only one standard time. India is 5.5 hours ahead of Greenwich Mean Time (GMT), 4.5 hours behind Australian Eastern Standard Time, and 10.5 hours ahead of US Eastern Standard Time.

For all official work, the Western Gregorian calendar is used in India. This avoids the confusion of traditional calendars, which vary between religions and regions. For example, at the Millennium, the official Indian calendar (Saka era) had reached only 1922, whereas the old Hindu calendar, which follows the Samvat era, reads as 2057.

MEASUREMENTS AND CONVERSION CHART

The metric system is most commonly used all over the country.

Imperial to Metric
1 inch = 2.5 centimetres
1 foot = 30 centimetres
1 mile = 1.6 kilometres
1 ounce = 28 grams
1 pound = 454 grams
1 pint = 0.6 litres
1 gallon = 4.5 litres

Metric to Imperial
1 centimetre = 0.4 inches
1 metre = 3 feet 3 inches
1 kilometre = 0.6 miles
1 gram = 0.04 ounces
1 kilogram = 2.2 pounds
1 litre = 1.8 pints

Little photo shops in a tourist area, offering quick photo services

LANGUAGE

There are many regional languages spoken in India, and in the northern region, both Hindi and English are used as official languages. In the cities, some English is spoken by a wide range of people, especially by those who deal with tourists – taxi drivers, guides – and in hotels, shops and offices. However, it is useful to know a few basic phrases in Hindustani, the colloquial language of the region *(see p320)*. Road signs and numbers are both in English and Hindi.

A range of plugs

ELECTRICITY

The electrical current is 220-240 volts, 50 Hz. Supply is erratic in summer when power cuts can last for hours, but more reliable in winter. Triple round-pin sockets are the norm, but adaptors for other varieties are available at large markets, as are transformers, needed for some appliances. Do bring along a power surge cable to protect your laptop computer againt voltage fluctuations.

PHOTOGRAPHY

Colour camera film, easily available at most photo shops, is best bought at large shops. Such shops also have excellent developing and printing facilities and offer quick services. It is courteous to ask permission before photographing people or places of worship. Photographing security sensitive areas is strictly prohibited. Notice boards indicate where photography is not allowed.

Etiquette

Friendly and easy-going by nature, Indians consider hospitality intrinsic to their culture and religion. Guests are treated with immense courtesy, and people on the street will go out of their way to help you. If you have any doubts on issues regarding fares, rates or directions, it is better to be patient but firm, rather than arguing or becoming aggressive. As there are diverse religions, castes and social hierarchies in the region, it is safest to address everyone with respect without making allusions to their religious, ethnic or regional group. Public demonstrations of love, such as kissing, are frowned upon. Customs and rules of etiquette still follow traditional Indian norms, except in very Westernized sections of urban society.

Devotees with heads covered in a place of worship

GREETING PEOPLE

The most common form of Indian greeting is the *namaskar or namaste* (pronounced "namastey") when meeting or parting. The palms are pressed together, raised towards the face, and the head is bent slightly forward. Greetings and gestures may vary with religion or regional group. Muslims raise their right hand towards the forehead with the words *adaab* or *salaam aleikum*.

In North India, *"ji"* usually follows the name as a term of respect. On the first meeting, however, it is best to address someone formally with a Mr or Mrs or even Madam before their name. The use of first names is a sign of familiarity. However, the Western handshake is also commonly used, though Indian women still prefer to greet visitors with a *namaskar*.

Namaskar, the traditional greeting

In many traditional families, it is a polite gesture to touch the feet of elders when greeting them. As a rule, elders are never addressed by their first names. However, a courteous greeting in any form will be acknowledged. Personal questions about subjects which a foreigner may find intrusive, such as one's salary or relationship with one's mother-in-law, are not really considered offensive in Indian society. Seldom seen as an intrusion, they reflect a friendly interest in a new acquaintance.

BODY LANGUAGE

Indians tend to shake their heads a lot while talking, and it can be very confusing because sometimes what seems to be a negative shake is actually a sign of agreement. Indians also tend to talk loudly and gesticulate with their hands, giving the impression of being very agitated when they are actually having a perfectly normal conversation.

The head is considered to be the spiritual centre, and an elder will touch the head of a younger person in blessing. The feet are considered the lowliest part of the body, and shoes are treated as unclean. In many traditional Indian homes, you may have to slip them off at the door or before you enter the kitchen. At gatherings where the seating is on the floor, try to sit with your feet crossed or tucked away and not stretched out before you. When food is offered to you, it should be accepted with the right hand.

PLACES OF WORSHIP

Every major religion of the world is practised in India. The etiquette differs in the places of worship of each religion, but everywhere a simple decorum is expected. If in doubt about what you should do, it is best to observe those around you. Do not disturb people at their prayers by taking photographs or talking loudly. In any case, you should ask permission to take photographs. Clothes should be clean and unrevealing, and the head covered. Women should wear dresses that cover the upper arms and are

A devotee bathing a linga in milk in a Shiva temple

at least mid-calf length, and men should avoid shorts. At most places of worship, shoes are taken off at the door, and you should sit with your feet turned away from the image or the central holy book.

In Hindu temples, it is permissible to offer flowers and incense for worship. Apart from the central deity, the temples often have subsidiary shrines in other parts of the temple precincts. Do not sit or lean against them. Even those in ruins are considered holy. Some Hindu temples do not welcome non-Hindus, but this is rarely the case. However, if stopped at the door, please do not take offence. In mosques and in *gurudwaras*, the head should be covered with a scarf or large handkerchief when you enter, but not with a hat. You should avoid entering a mosque during prayers, and men should stay away from the women's enclosure.

SUITABLE DRESS

The Indian style of clothing is relatively modest and covers the body well. In small towns, women still prefer the traditional sari or the *salwar-kameez* and seldom wear Western outfits, though very small girls can be seen in skirts or dresses. Delhi has a more cosmopolitan attitude, and in the trendier parts of the city, jeans, short skirts and shorts are common. However, Indian men tend to stare a lot at women, so be prepared for this, whatever you wear. Agra

and Jaipur are much more conservative cities where short skirts and shorts might well attract unwanted attention.

Do dress a little formally when visiting Indian homes, as Indians like to dress up for occasions. In fact, owning a couple of Indian outfits makes great sense. Ready-made clothes for both men and women are available in most markets at reasonable rates, and are easy and comfortable to wear.

BARGAINING

Bargaining is a part of life in India, but do not get aggressive about it. Firmly state what you would like to pay and walk away if the shopkeeper does not agree. Larger shops usually have fixed price tags and do not readily discount.

EATING INDIAN STYLE

Most Indian meals are eaten with the fingers to tear the chapati or bread, and to scoop up rice and curry. At best, a spoon may be given to you. It is considered impolite to use your left hand. Most restaurants provide finger bowls at the end of the meal.

TIPPING

There are no fixed norms for tipping, or *baksheesh,* as it is called. Most restaurants add a service charge to the bill; a ten per cent tip over that is quite adequate. In smaller eateries, the waiter would be happy with less. Hotel staff, porters and most taxi drivers expect to be tipped. So do hairdressers. A small tip given to the person who minds your shoes outside a place of worship will be happily accepted.

The traditional Indian **thali** meal, eaten with the right hand, seated on the floor

Shoes left at the entrance to a religious place

Traditional village women in *ghunghat*, veiling their faces

SMOKING AND ALCOHOL

Though cigarette kiosks abound, and pavement sellers even sell one cigarette at a time, in Delhi smoking is officially banned in public places like airports, railway stations and offices (though in practice the ban is often ignored). Only certain restaurants are licensed to serve alcohol, and you are not allowed to drink in parks, buses or trains. Drinking near a place of worship can lead to arrest. It is also considered very offensive.

BEGGARS

Travellers can find beggars difficult to handle as they target foreigners and can be extremely persistent. Tourists who give money to one soon find themselves surrounded by a raucous throng demanding *baksheesh*. Be careful of being pickpocketed in the confusion. Beggars are found in the largest numbers around places of worship as people always give them alms or even food there. But it is best not to encourage them and to walk on till they leave you alone. If necessary, complain to a nearby policeman.

If you do want to help monetarily, your hotel may have a donation box and the staff will be able to suggest a few charitable institutions.

Personal Security and Health

Police officer's badge

The three cities of Delhi, Agra and Jaipur are well equipped with an efficient police force and a number of good hospitals. As long as you take a few simple precautions, there is little need to worry. For instance, do not get too friendly with strangers, protect your valuables and do stay and eat only in places that look clean. If you face a difficult situation, take the help of a policeman or file a report at the closest police station.

Policemen in uniform

IN AN EMERGENCY

The national emergency number for police is 100, the fire brigade is 101, and for an ambulance it is 102. Your embassy can also advise you in an emergency. If in need of immediate medical attention, your hotel's doctor-on-call can refer you to a private clinic. Otherwise, all public and most privately owned hospitals and clinics run a 24-hour service for casualty and emergency cases.

GENERAL PRECAUTIONS

Travelling in the region is relatively safe for tourists. Since Delhi, Agra and Jaipur are major tourist centres, there are bound to be touts, beggars and pickpockets who target the tourist. Take simple safety measures, such as wearing a money belt under your shirt in which to keep important documents, such as your passport. Protect your camera and avoid wearing jewellery or carrying large amounts of cash in crowded areas. You can leave your valuables in the hotel safe but insist on a receipt. While shopping, make sure that the shopkeepers make out a bill and process your credit card in front of you. It is also advisable to use a padlock, available at railway stations, during train journeys.

Some shopkeepers lead tourists into believing that goods bought in India can be sold back home at great profit. Unless you can judge a product's authenticity, it is best not to invest your money on such dubious purchases.

A word of caution about dealing with the police. If you find yourself in any trouble, for instance, if you have lost your passport or valuables, you must inform the nearest police station and file an FIR (first information report), but it is also advisable to contact your embassy for advice about the correct procedure.

NARCOTICS

The image of India as a country that is tolerant of drug use is not true. Possession of all drugs, from hashish to heroin, is banned by law, and penalties for possession, use and trafficking in illegal drugs are strictly enforced. Drug convictions lead to a minimum sentence of ten years without parole or remission. As a precaution, do not leave your luggage unattended or unlocked at public places, and by no means carry anything for strangers or check in their luggage at airports.

WOMEN TRAVELLERS

Women, both Indian and foreign, face a certain amount of unwanted attention from men in North India, even though "eve-teasing" is a punishable offence. When travelling alone, women can face problems – from being stared at, to more active harassment such as suggestive comments and unwanted body contact on buses and in other crowded places.

Take your cue from Indian women who continue with their independent lifestyles despite such hazards. Avoid wearing clothes that can be thought of as provocative, such as shorts, skimpy dresses and mini skirts at public places, though they can be safely worn inside the hotel. Ignore men lounging at street corners, and if their attention gets offensive, walk towards a policeman. Beware of men who try to draw you into a conversation, and threaten to call the police if they continue to do so.

Avoid moving about alone in quiet places and in the rougher parts of the city. When hiring a car or a taxi, get the hotel to make the booking for you. Hitchhiking is not advisable under any circumstances. A confident attitude, common sense and wariness can help women travellers tackle problems that arise from travelling alone.

A Delhi police jeep

A hospital ambulance

LEGAL ASSISTANCE

Legal problems are very rare for travellers, but if you do find yourself in a legal tangle, immediately contact your embassy *(see p281)*. Always carry your passport and keep a photocopy handy. Do not hand your travel papers over to anyone until your embassy has been informed. Some insurance policies also cover legal costs for certain emergencies such as accidents.

PUBLIC TOILETS

Wayside public toilets have poor hygiene. However, though still few in number, those public toilets, known as Sulabh Shauchalayas, located on main city roads are a great civic invention. Attractively designed, they are easy to spot, extremely clean, and charge a very nominal amount for use. They are, however, of the Asian-squat kind and can be difficult to handle. Some restaurants and hotels allow you to use their toilets, but it is best to carry some spare toilet paper as not all public toilets are equipped with it.

Sign identifying a toilet

HOSPITALS AND MEDICAL FACILITIES

Do take comprehensive medical insurance before arriving in India. **MASTA** (Medical Advisory Service for Travellers Abroad) in the UK can give a health update for travellers to India.

In Delhi, there are excellent private hospitals and medical specialists, and though it is crowded like other government hospitals, the renowned **All India Institute of Medical Sciences (AIIMS)**, is a highly advanced hospital and centre of research. Most of the embassies have a list of approved hospitals and clinics as well as the names of the best medical specialists and dental practititioners in town. The local **Indian Red Cross Society** is the safest option for blood transfusions.

A pharmacy situated in a local market

PHARMACIES

Most big markets in the three cities have well-stocked pharmacies (or chemist shops, as they are known in India). The pharmacists are often able to advise you on simple remedies. They also stock toiletries, sanitary napkins and tampons, cosmetics, infant food and disposable diapers. If you are taking any special medication, it is advisable to carry the prescriptions, or show the packaging with the generic name if the brand is unfamiliar to the pharmacist. Most pharmacies are open between 9am and 7:30pm. Public hospitals such as AIIMS usually have round-the-clock pharmacies which are also open to non-patients.

Pavement quacks peddling concoctions of a dubious nature

HEAT AND SMOG

Summer in north India is dry and very hot, and the monsoon months that follow are oppressively humid. It takes time to get acclimatized to this weather, so take things at a relaxed pace in the first few days. The best way to beat the heat is to drink lots of fluids at regular intervals, and add a little salt to your food to prevent dehydration. Bathe often and avoid going out in the hottest part of the day, between noon and four o'clock. While walking, try to rest in the shade at regular intervals, for continuous exposure to high temperature can cause heat stroke.

It is advisable to wear light shoes and loose-fitting cottons that cover your arms and legs, as exposed skin can get badly sunburnt. Polyester clothing and covered shoes and socks trap perspiration and can lead to annoying prickly heat and fungal infections. Prickly heat powder is available at most pharmacies. Wear a wide-brimmed hat and sunglasses and use sun-screen to protect your skin.

In the winter, the city air can get quite smoggy. Asthmatic travellers should carry their medication at all times.

Sugarcane and other juices sold on the street, tempting but best avoided

FIRST-AID KIT

Most first-aid items are readily available at the pharmacies in the cities, and while going on excursions or day-long trips, it is advisable to carry a basic first-aid kit. This should include any personal medication, aspirin or painkillers for fevers and minor aches and pains, and antiseptic and calamine lotion for cuts and bites, an anti-fungal ointment, plaster and crêpe bandages, scissors, insect repellent and tweezers; antihistamines for allergies, anti-diarrhoea tablets and, water purification tablets; lip

balm, a couple of disposable syringes and a thermometer.

There are some effective herbal remedies, but you should buy only brands recommended by a reliable practitioner or pharmacist.

MINOR STOMACH UPSETS

Diarrhoea is a common stomach disorder among travellers, usually caused by a change of diet, water and climate. Since Indian food is mostly hot and spicy, it can lead to digestive disorders. In such cases, it is best to eat plain boiled food without spices until the attack subsides. Most import-antly, make sure you drink plenty of liquids to replace your body fluids. Avoid tap water and opt for sealed bottles of mineral water, such as Evian or Bisleri, if available. Most known international brands of carbonated drinks are widely available, and are clean and safe, as is fresh coconut water. No matter how tempting the food looks, it is advisable not to eat from streetside food carts. If you do want to eat in a *dhaba*, it is best to go to one that seems popular with the local people. The food there is more likely to be fresh and

A hand fan

of a reliable quality. However, it is best to avoid raw salads, cut fruit, cold cuts and fresh juices at wayside eateries.

A good pharmacist will suggest standard diarrhoea medication. In the case of a severe attack, with nausea, cramps and exhaustion, it is best to consult a doctor. You must immediately take oral rehydrating salts (ORS), which are commercially available under the popular Indian brand names of Electral or Electrobion. An effective homemade remedy of half a teaspoon of salt and three teaspoons of sugar mixed in boiled water which has been cooled also helps to keep the body fluids in balance.

INSECT-BORNE DISEASES

The summer and monsoon months are the seasons for malaria, though it can occur at any time of the year. Its symptoms include violent shivering followed by high fever and sweating. Caused by a parasite carried in the saliva of the female *Anopheles* mosquito, the incubation period can vary from a few days to several weeks. Another serious mosquito-borne disease is dengue fever, carried by the *Aëdes egypti* mosquito. The symptoms are similar to malaria and include severe pain in the joints and muscles, and often, rashes. The dengue

Vicks Vaporub, a decongestant

LEGAL ASSISTANCE

Legal problems are very rare for travellers, but if you do find yourself in a legal tangle, immediately contact your embassy *(see p281)*. Always carry your passport and keep a photocopy handy. Do not hand your travel papers over to anyone until your embassy has been informed. Some insurance policies also cover legal costs for certain emergencies such as accidents.

PUBLIC TOILETS

Wayside public toilets have poor hygiene. However, though still few in number, those public toilets, known as Sulabh Shauchalayas, located on main city roads are a great civic invention. Attractively designed, they are easy to spot, extremely clean, and charge a very nominal amount for use. They are, however, of the Asian-squat kind and can be difficult to handle. Some restaurants and hotels allow you to use their toilets, but it is best to carry some spare toilet paper as not all public toilets are equipped with it.

Sign identifying a toilet

HOSPITALS AND MEDICAL FACILITIES

Do take comprehensive medical insurance before arriving in India. **MASTA** (Medical Advisory Service for Travellers Abroad) in the UK can give a health update for travellers to India.

In Delhi, there are excellent private hospitals and medical specialists, and though it is crowded like other government hospitals, the renowned **All India Institute of Medical Sciences (AIIMS)**, is a highly advanced hospital and centre of research. Most of the embassies have a list of approved hospitals and clinics as well as the names of the best medical specialists and dental practititioners in town. The local **Indian Red Cross Society** is the safest option for blood transfusions.

A pharmacy situated in a local market

PHARMACIES

Most big markets in the three cities have well-stocked pharmacies (or chemist shops, as they are known in India). The pharmacists are often able to advise you on simple remedies. They also stock toiletries, sanitary napkins and tampons, cosmetics, infant food and disposable diapers. If you are taking any special medication, it is advisable to carry the prescriptions, or show the packaging with the generic name if the brand is unfamiliar to the pharmacist. Most pharmacies are open between 9am and 7:30pm. Public hospitals such as AIIMS usually have round-the-clock pharmacies which are also open to non-patients.

Pavement quacks peddling concoctions of a dubious nature

HEAT AND SMOG

Summer in north India is dry and very hot, and the monsoon months that follow are oppressively humid. It takes time to get acclimatized to this weather, so take things at a relaxed pace in the first few days. The best way to beat the heat is to drink lots of fluids at regular intervals, and add a little salt to your food to prevent dehydration. Bathe often and avoid going out in the hottest part of the day, between noon and four o'clock. While walking, try to rest in the shade at regular intervals, for continuous exposure to high temperature can cause heat stroke.

It is advisable to wear light shoes and loose-fitting cottons that cover your arms and legs, as exposed skin can get badly sunburnt. Polyester clothing and covered shoes and socks trap perspiration and can lead to annoying prickly heat and fungal infections. Prickly heat powder is available at most pharmacies. Wear a wide-brimmed hat and sunglasses and use sunscreen to protect your skin.

In the winter, the city air can get quite smoggy. Asthmatic travellers should carry their medication at all times.

FIRST-AID KIT

Most first-aid items are readily available at the pharmacies in the cities, and while going on excursions or day-long trips, it is advisable to carry a basic first-aid kit. This should include any personal medication, aspirin or painkillers for fevers and minor aches and pains, and antiseptic and calamine lotion for cuts and bites, an anti-fungal ointment, plaster and crêpe bandages, scissors, insect repellent and tweezers; antihistamines for allergies, anti-diarrhoea tablets and, water purification tablets; lip

Sugarcane and other juices sold on the street, tempting but best avoided

balm, a couple of disposable syringes and a thermometer.

There are some effective herbal remedies, but you should buy only brands recommended by a reliable practitioner or pharmacist.

MINOR STOMACH UPSETS

Diarrhoea is a common stomach disorder among travellers, usually caused by a change of diet, water and climate. Since Indian food is mostly hot and spicy, it can lead to digestive disorders. In such cases, it is best to eat plain boiled food without spices until the attack subsides. Most importantly, make sure you drink plenty of liquids to replace your body fluids. Avoid tap water and opt for sealed bottles of mineral water, such as Evian or Bisleri, if available. Most known international brands of carbonated drinks are widely available, and are clean and safe, as is fresh coconut water. No matter how tempting the food looks, it is advisable not to eat from streetside food carts. If you do want to eat in a *dhaba*, it is best to go to one that seems popular with the local people. The food there is more likely to be fresh and

A hand fan

of a reliable quality. However, it is best to avoid raw salads, cut fruit, cold cuts and fresh juices at wayside eateries.

A good pharmacist will suggest standard diarrhoea medication. In the case of a severe attack, with nausea, cramps and exhaustion, it is best to consult a doctor. You must immediately take oral rehydrating salts (ORS), which are commercially available under the popular Indian brand names of Electral or Electrobion. An effective homemade remedy of half a teaspoon of salt and three teaspoons of sugar mixed in boiled water which has been cooled also helps to keep the body fluids in balance.

INSECT-BORNE DISEASES

The summer and monsoon months are the seasons for malaria, though it can occur at any time of the year. Its symptoms include violent shivering followed by high fever and sweating. Caused by a parasite carried in the saliva of the female *Anopheles* mosquito, the incubation period can vary from a few days to several weeks. Another serious mosquito-borne disease is dengue fever, carried by the *Aëdes egypti* mosquito. The symptoms are similar to malaria and include severe pain in the joints and muscles, and often, rashes. The dengue

Vicks Vaporub, a decongestant

mosquito is more active at daytime, unlike others that are active in the dark, between sunset and dawn.

If you are sleeping in a room without air-conditioning, keep the screened windows closed at all times. You can also ask the hotel for a mosquito repellent gadget, as well as a net over your bed. Avoid wearing dark clothing and strong perfumes as these attract mosquitoes. If going outdoors in the evenings, you should wear shoes and clothes that completely cover your arms and legs, and rub mosquito repellent cream on any part of the skin that is exposed.

Mosquito repellent coil and cream

If you do experience symptoms of malaria, it is best to seek medical help immediately. You must take courses of preventive anti-malarial drugs before, during and after your trip. For the latest information on malaria medication, call a travel clinic or MASTA (see p285) who post details free of charge.

CUTS AND BITES

Insect bites are a common problem in the rainy season. Many monuments have huge beehives, so you should carry a good antiseptic ointment and antihistamine that would help in case of wasp and bee stings. Snake bites are rare, but if bitten, tie on a tight crêpe bandage, keep the limb immobile and seek immediate medical help. Clean all cuts with an antiseptic solution and cover with sticky plaster or a light bandage.

FOOD- AND WATER-BORNE DISEASES

Travellers must guard against two types of severe intestinal infection, known as dysentery. The first, bacillary

dysentery, is accompanied by severe stomach pains, vomiting and fever, but rarely lasts longer than a week. Amoebic dysentery has similar symptoms but takes longer to manifest itself. If not treated with a course of prescription drugs, this can later become a recurring, chronic ailment. The same is true of Giardiasis, a type of chronic diarrhoea, caused by contaminated water.

Some forms of hepatitis, a serious liver ailment, such as Hepatitis A and B, can be prevented with a vaccine. Its symptoms include extreme fatigue, body aches, fever, severe chills and jaundice. The only treatment is plenty of boiled water, rest and a strictly controlled diet.

If you are visiting a site ravaged by floods you must get yourself vaccinated early enough against cholera, a serious disease that can be fatal unless the patient is rushed to hospital for re-hydration and medication.

Typhoid, which has a vaccine, is another gastro-intestinal disease transmitted through contaminated water or food. Early symptoms may seem like flu, but develop into high fever, leading to acute dehydration and weight loss. A doctor should be immediately consulted for the right antibiotics.

Since they are the most common ailments faced by travellers to India, certain common-sense precautions, such as eating only at clean places and drinking mineral water, are the best prevention against gastric infections.

Bottled mineral water

PEOPLE- AND ANIMAL-BORNE DISEASES

Awareness of sexually transmitted diseases such as HIV, which causes Acquired Immune Deficiency Syndrome

(AIDS), is still low, and screening at blood banks unreliable. In case blood transfusion is required, do contact the **Indian Red Cross Society** (see p285).

Meningitis, a severe inflammation of the membranes surrounding the spinal cord and brain, is accompanied by high fever and occasional seizures. Penicillin drugs are effective in combating it, but patients must be rushed to a hospital straight away.

To avoid getting rabies if you are bitten by an animal, clean the wound immediately with an antiseptic solution and seek medical help at once, for treatment involves a course of injections. There is also a vaccination against rabies. Vaccination against tetanus is also essential while travelling. This potentially fatal infection is transmitted through open wounds, and its symptoms include lock-jaw, stiff muscles and fatal convulsions. You should clean the wound and go to a good doctor without delay.

Tuberculosis, commonly transmitted through coughing and close household contact with an infected person, is not a great risk for travellers.

Before an inoculation, buy your own disposable syringe, or insist that a new syringe and needle is unwrapped in front of you. Avoid shaves at dubious barber shops, and insist on a new razor blade. Any procedure using needles, such as tattooing and ear-piercing, is best avoided.

Delicious streetside food, often difficult to stomach

Banking and Local Currency

Logo of the State Bank of India

The three cities provide accessible banking facilities and also money exchange services, with English speaking staff at all the counters. Delhi has a good selection of international banks with a range of services. Exchange facilities are available at major banks and hotels, travel agencies, the international airport, and registered money changers. Unauthorized dealers and touts might offer enticing rates, but they are illegal operators. Some shops will also give better value for money against purchases in major foreign currencies. Traveller's cheques are the safest way to carry money, but always keep some small change and notes for telephones, transport, tips and purchases.

BANKS AND BANKING HOURS

There are many banks with branches across the country offering services, including international money transfers. Most national banks, such as the **State Bank of India**, have their head offices and several branches in Delhi, as well as in the other cities. The State Bank's counter at the international airport, Central Bank of India at the **Ashok Hotel** *(see p231)* and select branches of **Standard Chartered** in Delhi offer 24-hour banking services. The Ashok also offers 24-hour money exchange facilities. Foreign banks have offices in Delhi, though not always in the other two cities. Indian banks with branches abroad and foreign banks with branches in India can also wire money by telex from their various offices.

Banking hours are between 9:30/10am–2pm (Mon–Fri), and 9:30/10am–12 noon (Sat). Banks can be closed on regional and national holidays *(see p39)*, and occasionally they shut down without any notice at all in response to public protests or strikes.

American Express, offering money changing and banking facilities

CHANGING MONEY

Most hotels change money for resident guests, but banks offer the best rates. Visitors staying at government hotels require a receipt to show that they have changed their money in a bank. The State Bank of India, in Agra the **Allahabad Bank**, and the **Rajasthan Bank** in Jaipur are the best places in the region. Agents such as **Thomas Cook** *(see p297)* and **LKP Forex Ltd** also change money at the official rates, but with higher service charges. Newspapers publish exchange rates for major international currencies. The "black market" in India offers better rates than the official ones, but it is safer to go to authorized dealers.

CREDIT CARDS

International credit cards such as VISA, MasterCard, Amex and Diners Club are accepted in the larger shops, hotels and restaurants. Look out for the credit card sticker on shop windows. Cards can also be used to book rail and air tickets. American Express in Delhi gives traveller's cheques in US dollars or pounds sterling. Against some cards you can get a cash advance in rupees at many international banks. But credit card related fraud is on the increase, so keep your cards safely, and insist that receipt vouchers at shops are made out in front of you.

DIRECTORY

INTERNATIONAL BANKS

American Express Bank
Hamilton House,
Connaught Place,
Delhi. **Map** 1 C4.
Tel (011) 2332 7602.

Standard Chartered
Narian Manzil,
Barakhamba Road,
Connaught Place, Delhi.
Map 2 D5.
Tel (011) 4152 4403.

Citibank
Jeevan Bharti, Connaught
Place, Delhi. **Map** 1 C5.
Tel (011) 2371 4211.

Hongkong and Shanghai Bank
Birla Towers, Barakhamba
Road, Delhi. **Map** 2 D5.
Tel (011) 2371 6000.

INDIAN BANKS

State Bank of India
Sansad Marg, Delhi.
Map 1 B5.
Tel (011) 2336 2635.

MG Rd, Agra.
Tel (0562) 225 2076.
Tilak Marg, Jaipur.
Tel (0141) 510 1547.

MONEY CHANGERS

American Express
Connaught Place,
Delhi. **Map** 1 C4.
Tel (011) 2332 7602.

LKP Forex Ltd
M-56 Connaught Place,
Delhi.
Map 1 C4.
Tel (011) 4151 8000 .

Allahabad Bank
Hotel Clarks Shiraz,
54 Taj Rd, Agra Cant.
Tel (0562) 222 6531.

Thomas Cook
Jaipur Towers, MI Rd,
Jaipur.
Tel (0141) 236 0940.

Only Delhi offers 24-hour foreign exchange services at these counters: State Bank at the airport, Central Bank at Ashok Hotel and Thomas Cook at New Delhi Railway Station.

CURRENCY

The unit of currency is the rupee (Rs), divided into 100 paisas. Among the coins the most commonly used are the 50 paisa and the one, two and five rupee ones. Currency notes range from Rs10 to the newly minted Rs1,000.

Be careful with the 100 and the 500 rupee notes which are quite similar in colour. Also, be wary of accepting torn or taped notes, as banks and shops are very often reluctant to accept or even change them for you.

TRAVELLER'S CHEQUES

The well-known names in traveller's cheques in US dollars or pounds sterling are easy to cash, and can be

The ATM at Citibank, Connaught Place, New Delhi

exchanged at all banks and exchange counters. Banks have the lowest surcharge so they give the best value. They always charge a small fee per cheque, so using large de-nomination cheques at a time is much more economical. Traveller's cheques give better exchange rates than cash.

ATM SERVICES

All the foreign and some Indian banks have ATM (automatic teller machine) counters accepting VISA, Master Card, Amex or Diners Club cards. Instructions are displayed in English, and the cash dispensed is in rupees.

Bank Notes
All currency is minted by the Reserve Bank of India. The notes have either Mahatma Gandhi or the Ashoka lions on one side.

10-rupee note

20-rupee note

50-rupee note

100-rupee note

500-rupee note

Coins
The following silver coins are in circulation, with variations of the Rs1 coin. All bear the national insignia.

50 paisa   **1 rupee**   **Rs 2**   **Rs 5**

Communications

Telephone booth sign

The post and telecommunications systems in India are now fairly sophisticated. In addition to the government network, several reputable international courier agencies have offices here. All the main hotels have business centres, and most markets have shops from which international calls can be made, e-mail and faxes sent and the Internet accessed. A wide range of newspapers and magazines is sold in the three cities and, particularly in Delhi, most international newspapers and magazines are available in bookshops.

Stamps in five-rupee denomination

POSTAL SERVICES

The Indian postal service is efficient and reliable. It offers general or registered mail, parcel, *poste restante,* speed post and courier services. Most post offices are open from Monday to Friday between 10am and 5pm, and on Saturdays, only until 12 noon. The closing time for certain services, such as registered mailing, is usually earlier.

Letters sent *poste restante* are held at the post office for up to a month. In Delhi, the **Foreign Post Office**, and in Agra and Jaipur, the **General Post Office (GPO)** will hold your letters for you, but accessing them may take some time. Letters should be addressed with the surname underlined and in capital letters c/o Poste Restante, followed by the name and place of the post office. American Express also provides this service to its clients, and so does the India Tourist Office at Janpath in Delhi *(see p279).* The procedure for sending parcels is not very simple, so check the details before trying to do so on your own.

In some places your hotel sells stamps and may offer to post letters and smaller parcels for you. Indian letter boxes are colour coded: local letters, green; metropolitan and other cities, red; Quick Mail Service (QMS), yellow.

A regular post box

FAX AND TELEGRAPH SERVICES

Fax services are available at main post offices and also at market ISD/STD booths which, though often easier to access, charge more. The business centres of all large hotels have centralized telecommunication services, but these are open for use only to those who are staying there.

INTERNET AND E-MAIL

The internet is widely used in Indian cities and most larger hotels offer net access to guests. Privately operated cyber cafés with the latest facilities are more common in Delhi than in the other two cities. Libraries, such as the British Council and United States Information Centre in Delhi, have Internet facilities which can be used for a small payment to browse the web and to use for e-mailing.

COURIER SERVICES

While it is better to ship larger items such as furniture by regular land, sea or air cargo, letters, documents or smaller parcels are better sent through a courier agency, even though it may be more expensive. **United Parcel Service (UPS)**, an international courier agency, has a widespread network of branches all over the world. Many shops offer to send purchases by courier, but except for the government emporia and well-known shops, you will be doing so at your own risk. If necessary, send the parcel yourself, even though it may be bothersome.

TELEVISION AND RADIO

The state-run Doordarshan television network has programmes in English and the major regional languages. With the arrival of satellite TV, the choice has become much wider. Cable TV is available almost everywhere, including most hotel rooms. Through it you can watch international channels, such as the BBC World Service, CNN, Discovery, National Geographic and the Hong

General Post Office or Gole Dak Khana, New Delhi

Further Reading

Architecture

Delhi and its Neighbourhood Sharma, Y.D., Archaeological Survey of India, Delhi 1982.

Delhi, the City of Monuments Dube, D.N. and Ramanathan, J., Timeless Books, New Delhi 1997.

Fatehpur Sikri Brand, M. and Lowry, G.D. (eds.), Marg Publications, Mumbai 1987.

Indian Architecture Brown, P., (2 vols), D.B. Taraporevala Sons & Co. Pvt. Ltd., Bombay 1964.

Mughal Architecture Koch, E., PRESTEL-Verlag, Munich 1991.

Mughal India Tillotson, G.H.R., Penguin, London 1991.

Sacred Architecture Pereira, J., Islamic Books & Books, New Delhi 1994.

Stones of Empire Morris, J., Oxford University Press, Oxford 1983.

Taj Mahal: The Illumined Tomb Begley, W.E., Aga Khan Program for Islamic Architecture, Massachussetts 1989.

The Architecture of India Grover, S., (2 vols), Vikas Publishing House Pvt. Ltd., New Delhi 1981.

The Forts of India Fass, V., Collins, London 1986.

The History of Architecture in India Tadgell, C., Phaidon, London 1990.

The Palaces of India Fass, V. and Maharaja of Baroda, Collins, London 1980.

The Penguin Guide to the Monuments of India (Vol 2) Davies, P., Viking, London 1989.

Culture and Crafts

A Second Paradise Patnaik, N., Sidgwick and Jackson Ltd., London, 1985.

Catalogue of the Crafts Museum New Delhi 1982.

Curry and Bugles Brennan, J., Penguin, London 1992.

Dance of the Peacock Bala Krishnan, U. and Kumar, M.S., India Book House, Mumbai 1999.

The Essence of Indian Art Goswamy, B. N., Mapin International, San Francisco 1986.

Hanklyn-Janklin Hankin, N., Banyan Books, Delhi 1992.

Indian Art Dehejia, V., Phaidon, London 1997.

Indian Painting Randhawa, M.S. and Galbraith, J.K., Vakils, Feffer & Simon Limited, Bombay 1982.

Masterpieces from the National Museum Collection Gupta, S.P., National Museum, New Delhi 1985.

Paradise as a Garden Moynihan, E.B., George Braziller Inc., New York 1979.

The Arts of India Birdwood, G.C.M., Nanda Book Service, Delhi 1997.

The Golden Calm Kaye, M.M. (ed.), Webb & Bower, Exeter 1980.

The Painted Walls of Shekhawati Nath, A. and Wacziarg F., Croom & Helm, London 1982.

The Splendour of Mathura Art and Museum Sharma, R.C., DK Printworld (P) Ltd., New Delhi 1994.

Fiction

A Passage to India Forster, E. M., Penguin, London 1924.

A Suitable Boy Seth, V., Viking, New Delhi 1993.

City of Djinns Dalrymple, W., Flamingo, London 1994.

The Raj Quartet Scott, P., Heinemann, London 1976.

Train to Pakistan Singh, K., Ravi Dayal Publisher, Delhi 1988.

History

A History of India (Vol 2), Spear, P., Penguin, London 1956.

A Princess Remembers Gayatri Devi, Rupa and Co., New Delhi 1995.

Annals and Antiquities of Rajasthan Tod, J., Oxford University Press, Oxford 1920.

Delhi Between Two Empires Gupta, N., Oxford University Press, Delhi 1981.

Delhi and its Monuments Spear, P., Gupta N. and Sykes, L., Oxford University Press, New Delhi 1994.

Freedom at Midnight Lapierre, D. and Collins, L., Vikas Publishing House Pvt. Ltd., Delhi 1976.

India Britannica Moorhouse, G., Paladin Books, London 1984.

Indian Mythology Ions, V., Paul Hamlyn, London 1967.

Jaipur Nath, A., India Book House, Mumbai 1993.

Lives of the Indian Princes Allen, C. and Dwivedi, S. London 1985.

Myths and Symbols in Indian Art and Civilization Zimmer, H., Harper and Brothers, New York 1962.

Symbols in Art and Religion Werner, K. (ed.), Motilal Banarsidass Publishers Pvt. Ltd., Delhi 1991.

The History of India Dodwell, H. H. (ed.), 6 vols, Cambridge University Press, Cambridge 1934.

The Great Moghuls Gascoigne, B., Dorset Press, London 1971.

The Wonder that was India Basham, A.L., Rupa and Co., New Delhi 1966.

Nature and Wildlife

Bharatpur: Bird Paradise Ewans, M., Lustre Press, New Delhi 1992.

Book of Indian Animals Prater, W., Bombay Natural History Society, Bombay 1948.

Book of Indian Birds Ali, S., Bombay Natural History Society, Bombay 1941.

The Garden of Life Patnaik, N., Doubleday, New York 1993.

In Danger Manfredi, P., Ranthambhore Foundation, New Delhi 1997.

Indian Wildlife Israel S. and Sinclair T. (eds.), APA Publications, Singapore 1989.

Nature Watch Singh, K. and Basu, S., Lustre Press, New Delhi 1990.

Birds of India Grewal, B., Local Colour, Hong Kong 2000.

Tigers: The Secret Life Thapar, V., Elm Tree Books, London 1989.

Photography Permissions

Dorling Kindersley would like to thank the following for their kind permission to photograph their products: Preeti Paul.
The publishers would also like to thank the following for permission to photograph at their establishments: Biotique, New Delhi; City Palace Museum, Jaipur; Crafts Museum, New Delhi; Gem Palace, Jaipur; Mathura Museum, Mathura; Maulana Abul Kalam Azad Arabic & Persian Research Institute, Tonk; The Next Shop, New Delhi; Ogaan, New Delhi.

Picture Credits

t = top; tl = top left; tlc = top left centre; tc = top centre; tr = top right; cla = centre left above; ca = centre above; cra = centre right above; cl = centre left; c = centre; cr = centre right; clb = centre left below; cb = centre below; crb = centre right below; bl = bottom left; b = bottom; bc = bottom centre; bcl = bottom centre left; br = bottom right; d = detail.

The publishers are grateful to the following individuals, picture libraries and companies, for permission to reproduce their photographs:

Avinash Pasricha: 28cla/clb, 28 & 29c, 29bl, 120b, 292c, 293t; Bobby Kohli: 54 & 55c, 55b, 56 & 57c, 57tr; B. R. Chopra Films: 209b; British Library, London: 43b; Crafts Museum, New Delhi, Pankaj Shah: 86tr/ca/cb, 87tl/tc/cb; Dean K Brown: 78t; DK Classic Asian Cook Book: 254tc/crb; DK Picture Library: Rowan Greenwood Collection 11br; DN Dube: 52bl/b, 53cr, 75bc, 170tr, 171t, 172tr/c.

Fotomedia Picture Library: 9 (inset), 29tr, 52tc, 54clb, 55tr, 56cb, 105b, 120c (4 pics), 133 (inset), 295bl; Aditya Arya: 295br; Akhil Bakshi: 21t, 22bcr, 28br/b, 29b, 32clb, 195b, 272t, 289t, 294t/b/bl; Amar Talwar: 60cl, 172b, 251clb, 269b, 296t; Amita Prashar Gupta: 266b; Ashim Ghosh: 21bl, 22bcl, 50b, 58cb, 173b, 271t, 278b, 280b, 281b, 283t, 301t; Ashish Chandola: 168b; Ashish Khokar: 283c, 297t; Ashok Dilwali: 150b, 170tl, 172tl; Ashok Kaul: 61tl, 215b; Bimla Verma: 20tl, 22t, 23cr, 49bl, 93b, 141bl, 163b, 268br/bcr; BN Khazanchi: 36c, 37br, 272c; BPS Walia: 143br, 270c; Christine Pemberton: 15c, 40cl; Deepak Budhraja: 40b; Dharmendar Kanwar: 266t; E Hanumantha Rao: 18tl/clb/bc, 211trc, 225cb/b; François Gautier: 21b; J Saha: 20b; Jatinder Singh: 20tr; Jitendra Singh: 22bc; Joanna van Gruisen: 18cra/b/bl,19cra/bl, 48cb, 61ca, 210b, 224cl; M Balan: 33bcl, 169b; Manu Bahuguna: 39b, 71b, 91b, 232b/bl, 273t; Marie D' Souza: 33cr, 60t, 180t, 269br; Mathew Titus: 23br; Mohit Satyanand: 274b; MS Oberoi: 22br, 254t; Nagaraja: 211t; Neeraj Mishra: 18cla; Nihal Mathur: 224tr; NP Singh: 32b, 184bl; NPS Jhalla: 268bc; NS Chawla: 27c; Pallava Bagla: 18tr, 19tl/tr/tc/trc, 38t, 210tl; Pankaj Sekhsaria: 169trc; Pradeep Das Gupta: 255tc; Pradeep Mandhani: 40cl, 61t, 272b; Prakash Israni: 17tl, 22cl, 37b, 163tlc, 173bl, 274t; Prem Kapoor: 37c, 38b, 46t, 60b, 60 & 61c, 61br; Raj Salhotra: 32cla; Ravi Kaimal: 17c; RK Wadhwa: 23cra; RS Chundawat: 18crb, 116b, 210tr, 211b; S Nayak: 168c; S Venugopal: 141c; Sanjay Saxena: 32cl, 145c, 185b; Sanjeev Saith: 16b,137b, 275t/b; Sanjiv Misra: 41t; Shalini Saran: 20c, 28tr, 30cl, 32 & 33c, 37t, 38c, 46br, 49tl, 50 & 51c, 52br, 53br,

54br, 57tl, 63 (inset), 73t/b, 88, 107b, 114t, 147b, 150tr, 152tl, 153b, 173tl, 174b, 216tl, 249b; SK Panda: 19cla; Subhash Bhargava: 17b, 23ca, 36t/b, 39c/bl, 50cb, 54cla, 58t, 144b, 164t/cl/b, 165ca/b, 184t, 192c/bl, 200b, 225t, 228c, 254c, 268cr, 273c/b, 274tr; Sudhir Kasliwal: 48c, 187t/b/bl/cl, 195t, 268tr/trc, 276 & 277; Tarun Chopra: 49br; Thakur Dalip Singh: 33bc; Toby Sinclair: 18br, 19crb/clb, 33bl, 122, 210cb, 224tl/c/b, 225ca, 270b; TS Satyan: 19br, 76c, 141t, 197b, 228t, 252b (2pics), 255b; V Muthuraman: 226 & 227, 251cb.

Frazer & Haws, New Delhi: 118c; Fredrik & Laurence Arvidsson: 2 & 3, 14, 66, 89t, 98, 132 & 133, 136, 146, 178, 179b; Ganesh Saili: 101b; Henry Wilson: 212t, 231t, 232c; Idris Ahmed: 10tr, 169crb, 264bl; ITC Hotel Ltd. Welcomgroup: 121t, 228b, 248b, 249c; Kamal Sahai: 45tr/cla, 47tl; Lonely Planet Images: Andrew Bain 10br, Patrick Horton 118bl; National Museum, New Delhi: 44t/cl/bl, 45b, 46c, 46cb, 46 & 47c, 47b, 50t, 51t/bl, 53tr, 72tl/tr/ca/cl/bl/br, 141br, 167b; JC Arora: 43t, 54bl, 55bl, 64b, 74tl/tr, 75t; RC Dutta Gupta: 29t, 44cla/clb/br, 44 & 45c, 45tlc/cl/cr, 46b, 47tr/cl, 48t/b, 52t, 54t, 74b, 75c/br; Neemrana Palace Hotels: 48ca, 49tr, 230b, 233c, 249t; The Oberoi Group of Hotels: 229b, 230t; Otto Pfister: 168t/bl, 169t/c, 211c, 270t; P ROY 187cr/cb.

Press Information Bureau: 58 & 59 c, 59cr; Rajnish Kashyap: 11tl; Satish Sharma: 22 & 23c, 23tl/tc/b, 34bl, 35tl; Syndications Today: 61cb; Teen Murti Memorial Library: 56bl/br, 57b, 58ca, 59tc/bl/br, 60cb; Textile Art Society: Benoy K Behl 33tc; Theatre and Television Associates: Gopi Gajwani 29br; Tulsi: Hemant Mehta 269tl; Courtesy of the Board of Trustees of the V & A Museum: 52cl/ca/cb.

Works of art have been reproduced with the permission of the following copyright holders: © National Gallery of Modern Art, New Delhi: 30 & 31 (all pictures except 30cl).

Special Assistance in Photography

Ajai Shankar, Director-General, Archaeological Survey of India, New Delhi; Aman Nath; Anjali Sen, Director, National Gallery of Modern Art, New Delhi; Aruna Dhir, The Oberoi Hotel, New Delhi; Dr Daljeet Kaur, National Museum, New Delhi; JC Grover, National Museum, New Delhi; Jyotindra Jain, Crafts Museum, New Delhi; OP Jain, Sanskriti Museum; Dr RD Chowdhouri, Director-General, National Museum, New Delhi.

Front endpaper: All special photography except Shalini Saran: tr.

JACKET
Front - DK Picture Library: Aditya Patankar bc, cb; Getty Images: Suzanne & Nick Geary main image; National Museum, New Delhi: J.C. Arora cbl. Back - DK Picture Library: Aditya Patankar t, b. Spine - Getty Images: Suzanne & Nick Geary.

Every effort has been made to trace the copyright holders, and we apologize for any unintentional omissions. We would be pleased to insert the appropriate acknowledgments in all subsequent editions of this publication.

Acknowledgments

Dorling Kindersley would like to thank the following people whose contributions and assistance have made the preparation of this book possible.

Contributors

Anuradha Chaturvedi is a consultant on architectural conservation with the Indian National Trust for Art and Cultural Heritage (INTACH).

Dharmendar Kanwar is a well-known travel writer based in Jaipur. She has published several books on the architecture and culture of the region.

Partho Datta teaches Indian history at a college in Delhi University. He is interested in modern urban studies on which he has written several papers.

Premola Ghose is a gifted writer and illustrator of children's books. She is the Programme Officer at the India International Centre, New Delhi.

Ranjana Sengupta is a journalist and author of books on Ajanta and contemporary Indian society. She is currently writing a book on Delhi after 1947.

Subhadra Sengupta is a freelance journalist based in Delhi who writes on travel and tourism for several Indian newspapers and magazines.

Consultants

Ajai Shankar is a senior civil servant with the Government of India and is the Director-General of the Archaeological Survey of India (ASI).

Aman Nath has written extensively on the crafts and architecture of Rajasthan. He is involved in the restoration of heritage properties in this region.

Daljeet Kaur is the curator of the Indian miniature paintings section in the National Museum, New Delhi and has written several books and articles on this subject.

Ebba Koch has travelled extensively in the sub-continent and is an internationally acknowledged expert on the art and architecture of the Indo-Islamic and Mughal periods.

Giles Tillotson is Senior Lecturer in South Asian Art at SOAS (University of London), and the author of books on architecture in India during the Mughal, Rajput and British periods.

Jyotindra Jain is the founder-director of the Crafts Museum, New Delhi, and has authored several books on Indian crafts.

Kishore Singh is one of India's leading travel writers and is with the *Business Standard* in Delhi. He has written several books on Rajasthan.

Kumkum Roy is an Associate Professor of Ancient History at the Jawaharlal Nehru University, New Delhi. She writes for several prestigious academic journals.

Martand Singh is one of the country's best-known experts on textiles. He is based in Delhi and is a founding member of the Indian National Trust for Art and Cultural Heritage (INTACH).

Narayani Gupta is a Professor of Modern Indian History at Jamia Millia Islamia in New Delhi. Her book on the history of Delhi is widely regarded as an authoritative text.

RV Smith is a journalist who writes on the history and legends of Delhi. His column, "Quaint Corner", has been a regular feature in *The Statesman* for over 25 years.

Satish Grover heads the Department of Architecture at the School of Planning and Architecture, Delhi. He has written three seminal books on the history of Indian architecture.

Sunil Kumar is an Associate Professor in Medieval Indian History at Delhi University. He has a special interest in the Sultanate period and is currently writing a book on the subject.

Vijayan Kannampilly is a journalist and painter based in Delhi and has a special interest in Indian design and contemporary art.

Editorial and Design
Publisher Douglas Amrine
Editorial Director Vivien Crump
Art Director Gillian Allan
Senior Managing Editor Louise Bostock Lang
Production Marie Ingledew

Map Coordinator
David Pugh.

Design and Editorial Assistance
Ipshita Barua, Nandini Mehta, Kiran Mohan, Vandana Mohindra, Kate Molan, Janice Erica Pariat, Priyanka Thakur, Tara Sharma, Sadie Smith.

Cartography Assistance
Kishorchand Naorem, Shivanand.

Proof Reader
Abha Kapoor.

Fact Checking
Ranee Sahney

Indexer
Bibhu Mohapatra.

Additional Contributors
Anirudh Goswami, Rani Kalra, Ira Pande, Ranee Sahaney.

Additional Illustrations
Aniket Vardhan, Arun P, Mugdha Sethi.

Additional Photography
Anal Shah, Anand Naorem, Benu Joshi, Ipshita Barua, Mugdha Sethi, Rajnish Kashyap.

DTP Designers
Jessica Subramanian, Shailesh Sharma.

Special Assistance
Dorling Kindersley would like to thank all the regional and local tourist offices in Delhi, Agra and Jaipur for their valuable help. Particular thanks also to: Ajai Shankar, ASI, New Delhi; Dr Daljeet, National Museum, New Delhi; Malaynil Singh, TCI; Delhi School of Planning and Architecture; Siraj Qureshi and RVI Singh in Agra

Tripolia Bazaar 184, **186**
Tripolia Gate 186
Trivandrum (Thiruvananthapuram) 292
Triveni Ghat 144
Triveni Kala Sangam 76, 120, 121, 274
Tropic of Capricorn 36
Tuberculosis 287
Tudors of England 52
Tughlaq architecture 115
Tughlaqabad Fort **107**, 114
Tughlaq dynasty 50, 137
Tughra 218
Tulsi 118, 119
Turkish Sultana's House 170, 172
Turkman Gate 89, **96**
Typhoid 287

U

Udaipur 196, 197, 295
Ugrasen's Baoli **76**
Ujjain 144, 192
United Parcel Service (UPS) 290
  UPS courier service
  Agra 291
  Delhi 291
  Jaipur 291
United Kingdom (UK) 229, 281, 291
US Eastern Standard Time 281
USA 291
  embassy 281
United States Information Centre (Delhi) 290
University of Roorkee 143
Unnatansha Yantra 192
UP Handicrafts Complex (Agra) 267
Upanishads 22, 45, 137
Urs
  Ajmer 37, 40, 218, 220–21
  Nizamuddin 38, 82
Useful dialling codes and numbers 291

V

Vadehra Art Gallery (Delhi) 121
Vajpayee, AB 61
Valley of Monkeys 196
Vana Vihar Ram Sagar Wildlife Reserve 167

Varanasi 44, 45, 73, 190, 192
Varsha 37
Vasant 36
Vasant Panchami 36, 41
Vasantasena 47
Ved Pal Sharma Banno (Jaipur) 267
Ved Vyas 141
Vedas 22, 137
Vegetarian food 249, 250, 254
Veroneo, Geronimo 153
Viceroys of India 56
  house of, 64, 67, 70
Victoria 56
Vidyadhar ka Bagh 196
Vijay Chowk 68, 69, **70**
Vijay Mandal 114
Vijay Mandir Palace **207**
Vijay Sagar Lake 207
Vijaya Dashami 37, 40
Vinay Singh 208
Vindhya mountains 224
Vintage Car Rally (Delhi) 41
Viratnagar 209
Visas and Passports **278**
Vishnu 24, 25, 112, 176, 196, 203, 218
Vishram Ghat 161
Vishwa Yuvak Kendra (Delhi) 280, 281

W

Wajid Ali Shah 55
War Graves Cemetery 104
Water sports 275
Welcomgroup Maurya Sheraton, Delhi 231
Welcomgroup Rajputana Palace Sheraton (Jaipur) 271
WelcomHeritage (Delhi) 229, 231
Western Court 78
Wetlands 21
What to buy **268–9**
  Handicrafts 269
  Herbal products 269
  Jewellery 268
What to eat **250–53**
What to take 278
When to go 278
Where to eat **248–63**

Where to stay **228–47**
White ibis 168
White-throated Kingfisher 169
Lord Willingdon 103
Lady Willingdon 79
Captain Willoughby 101
Wimbledon championship 272
Wine and drinks 249
Women travellers 284
Woodpeckers 211
World Bank 61
World Book Fair 85
World Cup 272
World Expeditions India (Delhi) 275
World Heritage Sites 147
World Trade Centre 85
World War I 68, 71, 78
World War II 58, 104
World Wide Fund for Nature (WWF) 214, 274, 275

Y

Yagna Stambha 199
Yamuna, River 20, 21, 64, 84, 95, 107, 147, 148, 149, 150, 158, 161, 162
Yashoda 162
Yellow Boys 101
Yoga asana 74, 274
Yogi Shoes & Leather Crafts (Agra) 267
Youth Hostel International 230
Youth Hostels Association of India (YHAI) 280, 281
YMCA 230, 280, 281
YWCA 40
Yudhishthira 209

Z

Zabita Khan's Mosque 143
Zafar Mahal 110
Zakir Hussain 31
Zakir Hussain College 96
Zardozi 266
Zinat Mahal 96
Zinat-ul-Masjid **97**
Zinat-un-Nisa Begum 97

Kong-based Star TV network. Star Sports and ESPN are exclusive sports channels whereas Channel V and MTV are the music channels.

India also has a wide radio network, with programmes in English and local languages. It is still the best form of information, especially in the rural areas. FM channels are now available in many cities. You should check the daily papers for interesting television and radio programmes.

Some of the major English-language newspapers

NEWSPAPERS AND MAGAZINES

India has a wide variety of national English language newspapers. Leading papers like *The Times of India* and *The Hindustan Times* make for lively reading with fierce debates, cartoons and good sports coverage. Weekly magazines, such as *India Today* and *Outlook,* provide excellent coverage of local and international news. Readily available monthly magazines, such as *Delhi Diary* and *First City* list restaurants, films, exhibitions and other events in Delhi. Agra and Jaipur also have local newspapers in English and Hindi which give details of current cultural programmes.

INTERNATIONAL AND LOCAL CALLS

All major hotels offer international subscriber dialling (ISD) services. You can also book a trunk call from a private telephone. Most markets also have ISD/STD (subscriber trunk dialling) booths from which local and international calls can be made at cheaper rates than the hotels. Look for the yellow ISD/STD sign above the shop. To make an international call you will need to dial: the international access code, followed by the country code, the area code and the local number. Domestic long-distance calls are made on the STD lines, and the service covers a large part of the country, including villages. STD rates depend on the distance and time of the call. These calls are cheapest between 11pm and 6am Indian time. Local calls can also be made from public STD telephone booths. The latter take new one rupee coins, renewable for every additional three minutes.

Easy-to-operate public telephone

DIRECTORY

Foreign Post Office
Kotla Marg, Near ITO, Delhi.
Map 2 F4.
Tel (011) 2323 1281.

General Post Office
Ashok Rd, Delhi. **Map** 4F1.
Tel (011) 2336 4111.
The Mall, Agra.
Tel (0562) 236 2867.
Mirza Ismail Rd, Jaipur.
Tel (0141) 236 8740.

UPS Courier Service
Tel (011) 2638 9323. Delhi.
Tel (0141) 511 3800. Jaipur.

ADDRESSES

The older sections of Indian cities are often a maze of lanes and alleyways. Some road signs can be confusing and hard to decipher, and sometimes there may not even be a road sign. If you are lost, a passerby will always help, but the best bet is to get directions from a taxi or auto-rickshaw driver. The newer residential localities are divided into blocks, and the block number usually appears with the house number. So B4/88 Safdarjung Enclave would be: house number 88 in the B4 block of Safdarjung Enclave colony.

Various services, advertised through large signboards

USEFUL DIALLING CODES AND NUMBERS

- To make an inter-city call, dial the STD code of that city and the local number. For Delhi, dial 011; Agra, dial 0562; and for Jaipur, dial 0141.
- To make an international call (ISD), dial 00, the country code, area code and the local number.
- Country codes are: UK 44; France 33; USA & Canada 1; Australia 61; Ireland 353; New Zealand 64; South Africa 27; Japan 81.
- Dial 180 to book a Trunk call in the country, and 186 for international calls.
- For directory assistance dial 197 in Delhi, Agra and Jaipur.
- For the morning alarm, dial 116 in Delhi, Jaipur and Agra.

TRAVEL INFORMATION

Most international visitors to India arrive by air, and though road and ferry links are used between India and her neighbours, such as Pakistan, Bangladesh and Sri Lanka, this method of travel can be a complicated one. Travelling within the country, and especially between the three cities of the Golden Triangle is possible by air, train and road. Whatever your mode of transport, you should be prepared for delays and unexpected detours that

The Maharaja, mascot of Air India

may test your patience. The distance between the three cities is less than 250 km (155 miles) and only takes a few hours by road or rail. The state-run Indian Airlines has the widest network of air routes. Private airlines like Sahara and Jet Airways also cover many cities in this region. Indian Railways is one of the world's largest networks, and travelling first class is a good way to see the country. The long-distance luxury coach is another easy option.

![Aeroplanes lined up on the international airport tarmac]

Aeroplanes lined up on the international airport tarmac

ARRIVING BY AIR

All the major international airlines land in India, normally as stopovers on air routes between East and West. The international airports are at Delhi, Bombay (Mumbai), Calcutta (Kolkota), Madras (Chennai), Trivandrum (Thiruvananthapuram) and Goa, from where connecting domestic flights cover the rest of India. A direct flight from London to Delhi takes approximately nine hours. From Delhi there are several connecting flights onwards to Agra and Jaipur.

AIR FARES

Air fares can vary according to the airline and the season. Before buying your ticket, do find out from a few travel agents about special offers or discounted fares. Cheaper fares are offered during the off-peak season, but usually stipulate the route and duration of the journey.

CUSTOMS

The green channel is for those who do not have dutiable goods as listed in the Immigration Certificate. The Red Channel is for passengers with goods that attract customs duty, including money in excess of US$2,500.

INTERNATIONAL AND DOMESTIC AIRPORTS

The main airport in Delhi is called Indira Gandhi (IG) International Airport. It has two terminals: Terminal I for domestic flights, and Terminal II for those coming from abroad. The latter has more facilities, with 24-hour currency exchange counters, left luggage services and an air-conditioned visitors' lounge. Travel agencies located in the arrivals area can help you organize your tour itinerary and onward bookings, while

Licence plate of a taxi

the hotel counters, also located here, can arrange accommodation in a reliable hotel. Terminal I (domestic) is at Palam, 7 km (4 miles) from Terminal II. If transferring to a domestic flight from an international one (or vice versa), do allow enough time to get between the two terminals (approximately 15 minutes driving time). Airport coaches run hourly between the two during peak hours when most international flights arrive, and offer free transfers.

GETTING TO AND FROM THE AIRPORT

The domestic terminal is 12 km (7 miles), and the international terminal, 19 km (12 miles) southwest of the city centre (Connaught Place). Coaches run regularly between these destinations free of charge. You can also book a pre-paid taxi from a counter outside the arrivals area. The rates of these are fixed – about Rs 750 from Terminal II and Rs 500 from Terminal I to the city centre. If you are booking your accommodation in advance, do check if your hotel is offering a free pick-up service. The trip from the airports to the city centre can take up to 50 minutes, but if your flight arrives or departs in the early hours of the day, it should certainly take less.

Passengers in the airport lounge

TRAVEL PACKAGES

Indian (Airlines) offers two travel packages if paid in US dollars. The "Discover India Fare" for 15 or 21 days is about $700–900, and allows unlimited travel with certain route restrictions. "India Wonder Fare" for about $300 is for seven days of travel in one region. It does not include the Andaman Islands.

DOMESTIC FLIGHTS

While Indian Airlines offers the largest choice of routes and the most frequent services, the two major private-run airlines, Jet Airways and Sahara Airlines, also connect a wide network of cities. Delhi is connected to all Indian airports, while Agra and Jaipur, an hour's flight from Delhi, offer fewer connections. While all domestic airlines have their own booking offices, tickets can also be booked through travel agents *(see p297)*.

Air tickets

CHECK-IN

International flights usually ask you to check-in three hours ahead of the flight departure time. For most domestic flights, it is normally one hour, except when security checks are more stringent, for places such as Kashmir. There is a restriction on the amount of baggage you can carry with you. Most airlines allow 20 kg per person in the hold and one item of hand baggage, though some international airlines allow two full suitcases plus one item of hand baggage. Excess baggage charges can be high.

TAX CLEARANCE CERTIFICATE

If you stay in India for more than 120 days from the date of issue of the visa, you need a tax clearance certificate to leave the country. You should apply for the certificate to the **Income Tax Department** Foreign Section. This is to prove that you have financed your trip with your own foreign exchange and not by working in India. Do keep all documents about travel finance in case they are needed later.

DEPARTURE TAX

When leaving India, you have to pay a Foreign Travel Tax of Rs 500, unless already included with your ticket. But if travelling to Pakistan, Nepal, Sri Lanka, Bhutan, Burma (Myanmar), the Maldives or Afghanistan, only Rs 150 has to be paid.

DIRECTORY

INCOME TAX DEPARTMENT (ITO)

IP Marg, Delhi. **Map** 2 F5.
Tel (011) 2337 9161.

AIRPORT ENQUIRIES PRE-RECORDED

Indian Airlines (IA)
Tel 140 General.
Tel 142 Arrival.
Tel 143 Departure.

Air India
Tel 144 Arrival.
Tel 145 Departure.

AIRLINES OFFICES

Air France
Tel (011) 2346 6262.

Air India
Tel (011) 2373 1225.

British Airways
Tel (95124) .

Indian
Delhi.
Tel (011) 2331 0517, C Place.
Tel (011) 2462 0566, Safdarjung.
Agra
Tel (0562) 222 6821.
Jaipur
Tel (0141) 274 3500.

Japan Airlines
Tel (011) 2332 7108.

Jet Airways
Delhi.
Tel (011) 3984 1111, 2334 7729.
Jaipur.
Tel (0141) 511 2222.

KLM/North West Airline
Tel (011) 2335 7747.

Qantas
Tel (011) 2332 1344.

AIRPORT	INFORMATION	DISTANCE TO CITY CENTRE	AVERAGE JOURNEY TIME
Delhi (IG Domestic) Terminal I	(011) 2567 5121/26	12 km (7 miles)	Road: 30 minutes
Delhi (IG International) Terminal II	(011) 2565 2021	19 km (12 miles)	Road: 50 minutes
Agra (only charters)	(0562) 222 6821	16 km (10 miles)	Road: 45 minutes
Jaipur (Sanganer)	(0141) 272 3655	13 km (7 miles)	Road: 30 minutes

Travelling by Train

Indian Railways logo

Travelling through India by train is a truly unforgettable experience. It can be extremely relaxing or uncomfortable, a lot of fun, or frustrating. But if you can spare the time, it is the best way of getting to know the Indian people and seeing the countryside. India has a well organized railway network but it is also extremely busy, so plan your train journey carefully and do book your tickets well in advance. There are computerized ticket counters at railway stations, and most travel agents can buy tickets for you. The journey between Agra, Delhi and Jaipur takes only a few hours.

A modern diesel engine train

THE RAILWAY NETWORK

The Indian railway network is divided by region and the three cities of Agra, Delhi and Jaipur are served by Northern Railways. Delhi has three major railway stations: Delhi Main, New Delhi and Nizamuddin, so check from which station your train will be leaving. Most fast trains for Agra, such as the Shatabdi Express, (New Delhi) and the Taj Express (Nizamuddin) take less than three hours. This makes a day trip to Agra possible. Another Shatabdi Express runs between Delhi and Jaipur and takes about five hours after an early start from New Delhi. The Gangaur Express runs between Agra and Jaipur.

TRAINS AND TIMETABLES

There are three kinds of trains: passenger, express and mail. It is best to take the express trains as they have

Train timetable

fewer stops and offer better facilities and services. Avoid passenger trains as they stop at all the small stations, sometimes for long periods, and are always very crowded. The major cities are connected by air-conditioned super-fast trains, such as the Rajdhani and Shatabdi Express, which make minimal stops. Their fares include meals, and the Rajdhani also provides its overnight passengers with bedding. Trains have a first and second class, chair-cars, and two- and three-tiered sleeper coaches. Where these are air-conditioned, the fares will increase. Sleeper coaches are a comfortable option on longer journeys, and save useful daytime hours. Train timings are subject to change; these are listed in the updated railway timetable, *Trains at a Glance,* a handy 100-page guide is available at all major railway stations, and even at some bookshops.

TRAIN TICKETS AND FARES

Be sure to buy your tickets in advance with reserved seat numbers noted on them. Your hotel travel counter or your agent can arrange this for you. Avoid buying tickets from touts, as this is both illegal and unreliable. Reservation fees are nominal and tickets can be booked six months in advance. An **International Tourist Bureau**, on the first floor of New Delhi Railway Station, meant only for foreigners, is open Mon–Sat, from 7:30am to 5pm. The tickets, payable in US dollars or pounds sterling, get priority reservation and are exempted from reservation fees. Though refundable, the tickets are still subject to any cancellation charges. Other railway booking centres are located at **Nizamuddin** and **Sarojini Nagar**.

INDRAIL PASS

If you are planning to travel extensively around India, the Indrail Pass is a convenient option, saving on hours of queueing time and also on reservation charges. It offers unlimited travel across the country, either first or second class, from 7 to 90 days. It can be bought in India or abroad, but must be paid for in foreign currency. The pass, however, may work out more expensive than buying tickets for individual trips. Ensure that you have a confirmed seat number for each journey.

A crowded railway platform

Railway ticket booking centre at New Delhi Railway Station

SERVICES

At the station look for the licensed porters or *coolies* who wear a red shirt and an armband with a metal tag bearing a licence number on it. Note the porter's number because you could lose sight of him in the chaos. The tariff varies according to weight, although Rs10–20 per item is an acceptable rate. You would be wise to settle on a fee at the time of hiring your porter.

Railway waiting rooms are the best place to spend the night if you are unable to go elsewhere. Go to the Upper Class Waiting Rooms. The Rail Yatri Niwas, at New Delhi station, offers very basic facilities, but is a convenient and safe night halt. Left luggage facilities, called cloakrooms, are offered at most stations. On a day trip to a city, you can leave heavy bags here for a small charge. Avoid stalls with uncovered food and use the station canteens that are reasonably clean and provide reliable mineral water and hygenically-packed meals.

Porters in red, easy to recognize

ON BOARD

Indians travel with a lot of luggage and like making friends on a train, so unless you bury yourself in a book, be prepared to spend time talking about yourself! Try to get a window seat or the uppermost sleeper. Toilets are of the Indian and Western kind. Carry your own toilet paper, soap and towel.

THE ROYAL TRAINS

Travel like the maharajas in the most luxurious trains in India – the **Palace on Wheels** and the **Heritage on Wheels**. From September to April, the Palace on Wheels operates week-long tours through the finest sights of Rajasthan, covering Jaipur, Udaipur, Jaisalmer, Jodhpur, Bharatpur and Agra. The Heritage on Wheels goes through the relatively unexplored regions of Bikaner and Shekhawati. In opulent coaches, re-created to look like the saloons of erstwhile royalty, you will be impeccably served and royally pampered.

Insignia of the Jaipur State Railway

Royal service in the Palace on Wheels

Travelling Around by Coach

All the major Indian cities are well connected by a network of roads, and the highways linking Delhi, Agra and Jaipur are among the busiest in North India. The advantage of travelling by long-distance coaches over trains is that you have a wider choice of timings and stops. Deluxe coaches

Logo of the India Tourism Development Corporation (ITDC)

run by the state tourist departments are comfortable and run on time. The Transport Ministry-owned buses running throughout the day from city bus depots, though cheaper, can be crowded. Travel agencies and private tour operators have a wide choice of itineraries between the three cities and their surrounding areas.

Boarding a luxury coach

Buses for various destinations at the ISBT, Delhi

DEPARTMENT OF TOURISM-RUN BUSES

Guided tours around the three cities are organized by the state tourism departments as well as the Indian government's **Ashok Tours & Travels**. Addresses of state tourism offices are given on page 279. The Government of India Tourist Office in each

Delhi Tourism organizes a variety of innovative package tours

city offers the latest information on timings and pick-up points. Buses run by the tourism department are by far the best option; they are clean, uncrowded and comfortable, and make less frequent midway stops than ordinary buses which may be much cheaper. Delivery and pick-up points are usually in the city centres.

The Uttar Pradesh Tourism Department (UPTDC) buses also pick up tourists coming from Delhi to Agra by the Taj Express at the railway station. After the day's city tour, the passengers are dropped back at the station in time to catch the evening train to Delhi.

The best option to go to Jaipur from Delhi is by the Rajasthan Tourism Pink Line which leaves at 1:30pm from Bikaner House (see p279). It is a good idea to buy tickets

in advance though they can also be bought on the spot for all buses. The five-hour journey breaks midway for refreshments. From Jaipur, state tourism buses leave from a stand outside Hotel Sheetal.

STATE GOVERNMENT-RUN COACHES

The transport department of the three states also run buses to these three and other cities of India. The main bus station in Delhi is the **Inter-State Bus Terminus (ISBT)** at Kashmiri Gate. It is a chaotic place, so do arrive early to book your ticket. Then check at the enquiry counter to find the stand where your bus will arrive. Finally, be prepared for a lot of jostling as the passengers push to get to the best seats. Rajasthan state buses leave from Bikaner House. Buses for Agra leave from another bus station at **Sarai Kale Khan (SKK)**, a comparatively less crowded bus stop near Nizamuddin railway station. The trip takes about four hours to Agra and almost five to Jaipur. From Agra and Jaipur, buses leave hourly for the other two cities, at Agra from the **Idgah** bus stand, and at Jaipur, from **Sindhi Camp**.

RTDC coach ticket

PRIVATE TOUR OPERATORS

Tour buses run by private operators and travel agencies leave regularly from Delhi for places in the region during the tourist season. To Agra it is a day's trip, unless

An overcrowded bus – a common sight

you take in Fatehpur Sikri and all the Agra sites and also want to shop, in which case it involves at least a night's stopover, as it does for Jaipur. Most hotels and travel agents also organize the night's accommodation at a reasonable place. If you are on a travel agent's tour bus, then a guided tour is usually part of the package and the fare includes a guide as well as the overnight stay at a hotel. Most travel agents have a tie-up with luxury buses that pick up tourists from designated hotels. You can make reservations through your hotel's reception desk or through any of the travel agencies who operate in the region.

Logo of the Rajasthan Transport Corporation

COACH TICKETS AND FARES

Bus or coach fares are much less than train fares and depend on the kind of transport you are taking. There is a good choice – from ordinary to deluxe and deluxe air-conditioned coaches. Ordinary buses are slow,

uncomfortable and usually very crowded. A deluxe bus is good for a trip in winter, but in the hot weather, air-conditioning is the only way to survive long-distance travel. If opting for a deluxe bus, you can book your ticket in advance and can also reserve your seat.

PACKAGE TOURS

There are places in and around the three cities within easy travelling distance that should be seen. These include religious sites, places of historical interest and wildlife sanctuaries. State tourism departments have a wide range of itineraries and package tours. These are also offered by private tour operators and agencies who can arrange tours to suit your individual interests. Tourism offices and travel agents who specialize in adventure tours (see p275) offer excursion packages that include transport, guides and a few days' stay in these places.

(see p275)

DIRECTORY

STATE BUS STATIONS

Delhi
Tel ISBT (011) 2386 0290.
Tel SKK (011) 2435 8343.

Agra, Idgah
Tel (0562) 236 4557.

Jaipur, Sindhi Camp
Tel (0141) 511 6031.

TRAVEL AGENTS

American Express Travel Related Services
Enkay Cen, A1 & A2 Udyog Vihar, Gurgaon.
Tel (95124) 239 8555.

Ashok Tours & Travel
L1 Connaught Circus, Delhi.
Map 1 C4.
Tel (011) 2341 5331.

Cox & Kings
H Block, Connaught Place, Delhi. **Map** 1 C4.
Tel (011) 2373 8811.

Mercury Travels
Jeevan Tara Building, Sansad Marg, Delhi.
Map 1 B5.
Tel (011) 2336 2008.
Hotel Clarks Shiraj, 54 Taj Rd, Agra.
Tel (0562) 222 6531.
www.mercury-india.com

Sita World Travel
F 12, Connaught Place, Delhi. **Map** 1 C5.
Tel (011) 2331 1122.
www.sitaindia.com

Travel Corporation (India) Ltd
35 C Block, Connaught Place, Delhi. **Map** 1 C4.
Tel (011) 2341 5636.
Hotel Clarks Shiraz, 54 Taj Rd, Agra.
Tel (0562) 222 6521.
19–C, Gopal Bari, Jaipur.
Tel (0141) 236 2075.

Thomas Cook
85-A, Rishyamook, Panchkuian Rd, Delhi. **Map** 1 B4.
Tel (011) 2334 2171.
www.thomascook.com

A clean and comfortable luxury bus run by Rajasthan Tourism

Travel by Road

Milestone with distances in kilometres

Driving is a comfortable and leisurely way to travel between the three cities. It gives you the opportunity to do the trip at your own pace and visit places along the way. Hiring a chauffeur-driven car makes sightseeing or shopping within the cities much easier as one is relieved of the stress of negotiating traffic and locating destinations. Cars can be hired from car rental companies, hotel and other taxistands.

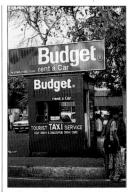

An international company offering car rental services in India

RENTING A CAR

If you plan to bring your own vehicle into India, it will have to be done under a carnet. This means you take it out after your visit or else must pay exorbitant taxes. Alternatively, there is a good choice of international and local car rental companies in Delhi. Among them, **Hertz, International Travel House** and **Budget** offer both self-driven and chauffeur-driven cars which can be hired through travel counters at larger hotels or from tourist offices. Rates are fixed on a daily rental and minimum mileage basis, with each extra mile carrying an extra cost. Fuel and other running costs are extra and a security deposit is taken in advance to be refunded only if there is no damage to the car when you return it. If you plan to drive yourself, make sure you are carrying your international driving licence. If you fail to do so, you might be able to get a temporary one from the

Logo of the Automobile Association

Automobile Association of Upper India (AAUI), Delhi, provided you have a passport or a valid driving licence from your own country. You may also be required to take a driving test, though this may not always be the case.

A wiser and more common option is to hire a chauffeur-driven car. It is usually cheaper than hiring a self-drive car and fairly hassle-free. If lucky, you may find a driver who could double up as a guide and an interpreter.

HIRING A CHAUFFEUR-DRIVEN CAR

Unless you are mentally geared to cope with the not-so-well-maintained Indian roads and driving conditions, you should rent a chauffeur-driven car. The drivers are familiar with Indian traffic rules and you won't have to worry about parking either. Taxis with DLY or DLZ number plates can be hired through travel agents, hotels and some taxistands. They have permits to travel beyond

city limits, and you can insist on getting a driver who is familiar with the city you plan to visit. Certain companies require foreign nationals to pay rentals in foreign currency. But some are willing to accept payment in rupees after negotiating a per kilometre rate payable in cash. Car companies in these cities normally charge a fixed rate for

Logo of a car rental company

a minimum of four hours or 40 km (25 miles), or up to 80 km (50 miles) for eight hours. Rates differ according to the type of car and from where you rent it.

FUEL AND FUEL STATIONS

Highways and main roads have petrol (gasoline) pumps at regular intervals, usually closer to a town. Most fuel stations now carry unleaded petrol. All three cities have some fuel stations that are open 24 hours; some on the highways are also open round-the-clock. Most cars run on petrol, though some newer ones are being made with diesel engines. Taxis usually run on diesel, which is about half the price of petrol. It is a good idea to use the fuel station's toilet facilities before the next leg of the journey. City stations often have a telephone booth, but only for local calls.

Fuel stations, found at regular intervals along the highways

ROAD SIGNS AND ROAD MAPS

Good maps are available for the three major cities as well as some of the smaller ones. The placement of road signs is erratic and at times these are not in English. Road names have also changed, particularly in Delhi, from the old English names, to names of well-known Indian or international figures. For Delhi there is the excellent *Eicher City Map*. Agra and Jaipur also have fairly clear state tourism city maps which display the major roads and sights. All are in English.

If you are travelling by road between the three cities, you should acquire a road map of North India from the **AAUI (Automobile Association of Upper India)**. The government **Survey of India** also has a good collection of detailed maps available at their office. Maps also indicate lesser known places and road categories. Road signs will also inform you of approaching motels and eateries on the highway.

DLY and DLZ taxis which travel beyond the city limits

Licence plates with bold and clear lettering

RULES OF THE ROAD

Though there are established traffic rules, such as lane driving and the discreet use of high-beam lights, traffic can be chaotic on Indian roads. All too frequently, traffic lights do not function, and though major crossings have policemen to guide you, this is more often

the exception than the rule. Bear in mind that there are numerous types of road users, from pedestrians to cyclists, bullock carts and containers. On the highways, be wary of trucks which muscle in whenever possible. There are also some unwritten rules which should be kept in mind. Few adhere to lane driving, and overtaking, meant to be from the right, is often from the opposite side, with no warning. Crossing red lights is one of the biggest hazards, the cause of most accidents, and horns are used even in "No Horn" areas.

PARKING

Parking can be a serious problem in busy shopping centres and in the commercial complexes of the three cities. With the boom in car production in recent years, parking lots are unable to cope with the number of cars driving in. Private parties are contracted by the state to ensure car safety and facilitate parking for a fee ranging from Rs 5 to Rs 10. You should keep your key but will have to leave your car in neutral gear so that it can be moved back and forth. Make sure the attendant gives you a receipt and check that you pay no more than the amount that is written on it. In New Delhi, Connaught Place is one of the few places which has a tiered and neatly planned and protected car parking lot.

Hand-cart prohibited

Bullock-cart prohibited

No horn please

Bicycle crossing

DIRECTORY

24-HOUR CAR RENTALS

Budget Rent-a-Car
104, FF Ansal Bhawan, Kasturba Gandhi Marg, Delhi. **Map** 1 C5.
Tel (011) 2331 8600.

Avis Oberoi Hotel
Zakir Hussain Marg, Delhi.
Tel (0562) 233 1771.

International Travel House
14 A&B, Basant Lok, Vasant Vihar, Delhi. *Tel (011) 2619 1348.*
Mughal Sheraton, Agra.
Tel (0562) 233 0350.
Shri Gopal Tower, Krishna Marg, C–Scheme, Jaipur.
Tel (0141) 236 1268.
www.travelhouseindia.com

Hertz
434 Westend Green Farm House Road, Mahipalpur, Delhi.
Tel (011) 4166 7232.

AAUI
C-8 Qutub Institutional Centre, Delhi.
Tel (011) 2685 2052.
www.aaui.org

ROAD MAPS

Survey of India
24 Janpath Barracks, Delhi.
Tel (011) 2332 2288.

24-HOUR PETROL STATIONS

Queens Rd Service Stn
Vasant Vihar, Delhi.
Tel (011) 2614 7843.

Inter Club
L1/15 Haus Khas, New Delhi.
Tel (011) 2651 2605.

Local Transport in the Cities

Logo of the Delhi Transport Corporation

The choice of local transport in the three cities is immensely varied. It ranges from buses and taxis to horse-drawn *tongas* and sputtering auto-rickshaws. All three cities are notorious for their traffic jams, and the narrow lanes of the older sections are best negotiated by the smallest vehicle possible. Here, a cycle-rickshaw is often the smartest option. Parking is a real problem, and in some of the extremely crowded areas, there are stringent car parking rules. Though there is a wide choice of local transport, a taxi or hired car is usually the most comfortable and stress-free way to travel. The drivers often speak some English.

Taxistands, found in all areas

GETTING AROUND

Delhi, Agra and Jaipur are all old cities with historic areas that can be congested. The roads carry vehicles that range from ambling bullock carts to expensive Mercedes Benzes. In between there are others such as bicycles, rickety cycle-rickshaws, horse carriages, three-wheelers, taxis, tempos, buses, trucks and, in Jaipur, carts pulled by benign but doleful looking camels.

Perhaps the best way to move around in these three cities is to hire an auto-rickshaw (also known as scooters or autos), or a taxi. In the crowded older city areas, a cycle-rickshaw is the best option. Almost all deluxe hotels have a travel desk to help you with car or taxi hire. It is advisable to avoid public buses which, though cheap, are crowded, especially during peak traffic hours.

TAXIS

The black-and-yellow taxis in Delhi move within the city limits. Unlike in other cities, they do cruise the streets, though it is safer to hire one from a taxistand. Large hotels have taxis on their premises, and these are always well-maintained with the meters in good working order. There is usually more than one stand in a locality, and taxis can be summoned by telephone provided you have the name and number of the stand. Another type of taxi, which is licensed to run inter-state, is usually white in colour and has a DLY or DLZ on its numberplate. These can be hired through car rental companies, travel agencies and a few taxistands.

In Agra and Jaipur, the only option is the tourist taxi

Taxi meter

which does not run by the meter, but charges according to distance or by the day, or a pre-fixed rate. Your hotel or travel agent will tell you what the latest rules are for hiring these taxis. Many drivers have a tie-up with certain shops which give them a commission on sales, so you must be firm about where you want to go.

AUTO-RICKSHAWS

You can't miss them on the roads. The three-wheeled, black-and-yellow or green-and-yellow auto-rickshaws zigzag through the traffic like buzzing bees. They offer a noisy, bumpy ride but are still a better option than buses and cheaper than taxis. In Delhi, they can carry up to three passengers, but in smaller towns, where they look a little different, they are often jammed with people and baggage. Auto-rickshaws are useful for travelling short distances or through crowded localities.

Auto-rickshaw, a cheaper travelling option

FARES AND METERS

All auto-rickshaws and taxis in Delhi have meters, but this is not so in Agra and Jaipur where fares should be negotiated in advance. You should insist on paying by the meter in Delhi. Starting at Rs 13 for taxis and Rs 8 for auto-rickshaws, the meters register a fare increase proportionate to the number of kilometres travelled. As rates keep changing according to the

Different modes of transport jostling in the streets of Jaipur

Cycle-rickshaws, convenient for covering short distances in inner city areas

increase in fuel prices and meters are not always simultaneously calibrated, the drivers of taxis and auto-rickshaws always carry an updated fare chart to enable you to calculate the exact amount from the meter reading. Both day and night fares are given separately on either side of the fare chart. Be sure to check the correct column before you pay. Night fares, from 10pm to 6am, are up to 20 per cent extra.You also have to pay an extra charge for luggage.

At railway stations and the airport, you should look for the pre-paid taxi and auto-rickshaw booths where you will be asked to pay a fixed amount in advance according to the distance you travel. You will be given a receipt, to be handed over to the driver at the end of the journey. Also, do carry smaller notes and small change, as very often, the drivers do not have the correct amount to return. It is not necessary in India to tip the drivers, but if you do, they will gladly accept it.

RICKSHAWS, TONGAS AND TEMPOS

The cycle-rickshaw is the most common mode of transport in the small towns and congested older sections of Indian cities. A convenient means of covering short distances, these are most commonly seen in the walled city of Old Delhi. In Agra and Jaipur, these are the most popular means of local transport. Always fix the fare beforehand. In small towns, the creaky horse-drawn carriages called *tongas* and *ikkas* offer a leisurely ride. Tempos are wagons with the rear half fitted with seats. They are not very comfortable, and start a trip only when all seats are occupied.

BUSES

The bus service in most Indian cities is never adequate for the large numbers who can only afford this means of travel, and so buses are always crowded. You buy the bus ticket from a conductor once you have boarded the bus. However, if a bus is full, it will not stop, and bus stops are usually seen full of waiting commuters. Delhi's bus drivers are notorious for their reckless driving. Even the so-called luxury buses drive at great speed. Avoid the experience even though it is the cheapest way to travel.

DELHI METRO RAILWAY

Delhi has a ring railway, encircling a core area and facilitating connections between some of the outer localities to the city centre. The recently launched Metro Rail is now operational between Shahdra and Rithala, with 18 stations en route. Safe and efficient services run from 6 am to 10 pm. It has been planned with underground and overhead railway lines, well integrated with other modes of transport and availability of parking areas.

Auto-rickshaws like this, called Vikram, which ply in smaller cities to the north of Delhi

The "new look" Maruti Omni which is quickly replacing the old Ambassador taxis in Delhi

General Index

Page numbers in **bold** type refers to main entries

A

Aapki Pasand 119
Aath ("eight") Havelis 213
Abbottabad (Pakistan) 104
Abdar Khana 172
Abdur Rahim Khan-i-Khanan 105
Abhimanyu 209
Abraham & Thakore (Delhi) 119
Abu'l Fazl 191, 206
Accommodation *see* Hotels
Achariyon ki Haveli 196
Acquired Immune Deficiency
    Syndrome (AIDS) 287
Act of 1858 56
Adhai Din ka Jhonpra **218**
Adham Khan 82, 85
    Adham Khan's tomb 111, **113**
Adi Granth 21
Adilabad 114, 115
Admission charges 280
Advance booking 278
Aëdes egypti (mosquito) 286
Afghan cuisine 248
Afghanistan 18, 47, 293
Afsarwala Tomb 83
Afzal Khan 158
Agra 11, **150–61**
    hotels 239–40
    map 151
    restaurants 260–2
    shopping 266
Agra and around **146–77**
    exploring Agra and around 148–9
    hotels 239–42
    restaurants 260–61
Agra Club 153
Agra Fort 11, 24, 147, **150**, 166
Ahmad Shah Abdali 140
Air travel **292–3**
    air fares 292
    airport enquiries 293
    departure tax 293
    international and domestic
        airports 292
    travel packages 293
Airlines offices 293
    Air France 293
    Air India 293
    British Airways 293
    Indian 293
    Japan Airlines 293
    Jet Airways 293
    KLM/North West Airline 293
    Qantas 293
Ajabgarh 209
Ajitgarh 103
Ajmer 134, **218–19**, 221, 270

Ajmer (cont.)
    hotels 243
    map 219
    restaurants 262
Ajmeri Gate **96**
Akbar II 113
Akbar, Mughal emperor 52, 111, 150,
    152, 160, 170, 191, 202, 223
Akbar's Mosque 221
Akbari Mosque 203
Alai Darwaza 26, 51, 112
Alamgiri Koran Sharif 222
Alauddin Khilji's tomb 112
Albert, Prince of Wales 194
Alexander, the Great 45, 161
All India Institute of Medical Sciences
    (Delhi) 285
Allahabad 144
Allahabad Bank (Agra) 288
Alliance Française (Delhi) 120
Alwar 134, 181, **206–7**, 208, 210
    hotels 243
    map 207
    restaurants 262
Amanat Khan 157
Amar Singh Gate 150
Amaravati (Andhra Pradesh) 74
Ambala 101, 138
Ambedkar Stadium (Delhi) 272
Amber 200–203
    history 179, 180, 181,182,183, 209
    fort 11, **200–202**
    township **203**
Ambika Exports (Jaipur) 267
Ambikeshwar Mahadev Temple 203
American Express Bank
    (Delhi) 288, 290
American Express Travel Related
    Services (Delhi) 297
Amir Khan 222
Amir Khusrau 51, 81, 82
Amoebic dysentery 287
Amrapali (Jaipur) 267
Amritsar 58
Anaji 219
Anangpal 117
Anangpur Dam 117
Anasagar Lake 218, **219**
Ancient empires **46–7**
Ancient Monuments Preservation
    Act 1904 57
Andaman and Nicobar Islands 58,
    279, 293
Anglo-Afghan War II 57
Anglo-Afghan War III 71
Anglo-Arabic School 96
Anglo-Indian community 21
Anguri Bagh 150
Anhilwad 49
Anjana (Agra) 271

Ankh Michauli 171
Ankur Exports (Jaipur) 267
Ankur (Jaipur) 271
Annakut 37
Annual Camel Fair *see* Pushkar
Anokhi 79, 118, 267
Anoop Talao 170, 172
Anopheles (mosquito) 286
Antarctica 60
Antiques 265, 279
Apartheid 59
Appu Ghar 85, 273
Arab ki Sarai 83
Arab traders 20
Aram Bagh
    Agra 158
    Jaipur 202
Aram Mandir 199
Aravallis 17, 20, 104, 134, 179, 180,
    208, 224, 272, 274
Arayish 198
Archaeological Survey of India 105,
    203, 218, 265, **279**
Architecture **24–6**
    colonial features 27
    early Indian architecture 26
    fort architecture 28
    glossary of 29
    history of 26
    palace architecture 28
Arjuna 141, 209
Art Heritage (Delhi) 121
Aryabhatta 47
Aryan settlements 17
Aryans 43, 44
Asiatic Society of Bengal 55
Ashley, Edwina (Mountbatten) 103
Ashok Tours & Travel
    (Delhi) 296, 297
Ashoka tree *(Saraca indica)* 21
Ashoka, Mauryan emperor 46, 208
    Ashokan edict 46
    Ashokan pillars 97, 103
Asian Games Village Complex 108
Atamsukh 190
Atgah Khan's tomb 82
Athpula 79
ATM services 289
Attar 91
Aurangabad 190
Aurangzeb, Mughal emperor 53, 73,
    94, 97, 150, 182, 183, 206, 222
Aurobindo Centre (Delhi) 274, **275**
Australia 281, 291
Australian Eastern Standard
    Time 281
Automobile Association of Upper
    India (AAUI) 279, 298, **299**
Ayurveda Kendra Clinic
    (Rishikesh) 274, **275**

B

Baba Kharak Singh Marg 77
Babur Nama 32, 74, 206
Babur, Mughal emperor 52, 84, 140,
 143, 158, 167, 214
Bacillary dysentery 287
Backpackers **280**
Badal Mahal 182
Badi Chaupar 11, 186
 Street-by-Street **184–5**
Badi Ganeshji Temple 216
Badkhal Lake 275
Badshahi Darwaza 173
Baghera 218
Bagichi Masjid 110
Bagru 180, **204**, 205, 266
Bahadur Shah Zafar 94, 96, 97,
 110, 113
Baha'i House of Worship (Delhi)
 115, 281
Baha'i sect 115
Bahlol Lodi's tomb 79, 108
Bahri & Sons (Delhi) 79
Bairat **208**
Baisakhi 36, 38
Baker, Herbert 27, 68, 70
Baker's Oven 27
Bala Qila **206**, 208
Balban 50
Balban's tomb 111
Balloon Mela (Delhi) 40
Bandipol 210
Bandung Conference 60
Banganga, River 197, 209
Bangladesh 292
Bani Thani 215
Banke Bihari Temple 163
Banking and local currency 288
 banks and banking hours 288
 changing money 288
 credit cards 288
 international banks 288
Banyan tree *(Ficus bengalensis)* 224
Bara Darwaza 84
Bara Gumbad 79
Bara Hindu Rao 103
Baradari 202
Baramasa 33, 191
Bari **167**
Bars 121, 271
Barsana **162**
Basilica 142
Bath 76
Bayabani, Hazrat Shah Turkman 96
Bazaars 265, **267**
Beating Retreat 41, 70
Beauty parlours 228
Beetli Hill 218
Begg, John **104**

Beggars 283
Begum Bagh 92
Begum Samroo 55, 137, 142
Begum Skinner 140
Begumpuri 96
Begumpuri Mosque **109**
Bengal 48, 54, 162, 202
 Bengal famine (1770) 54
 Bengal partition 57
 Bengal renaissance 31
Ber (Zizyphus mauritiana) 212
Besant, Annie 58
Betwa, River 135, 176
Beyond Delhi **132–225**
 Agra and around 146–177
 beyond Delhi at a glance 134–5
 Jaipur and environs 178–225
 North of Delhi 136–145
Bhagavad Gita 47, 137, 141
Bhai Duj 37
Bhajans 30
Bhakti Movement 18
Bhangarh **209**
Bhansali tribe 86
Bharany's (Delhi) 118
Bharat Boot House (Jaipur) 267
Bharata Natyam 120
Bharatiya Janata Party 61
Bharatiya Vidya Bhavan 274
Bharatpur 147, **166**, 168, 179, 295
Bharatpur Fort 54
Bharatpur kings 163, 164
Bharmal ki Chhatri 203
Bhartiya Haveli 29
Bhatt (pastoral community) 271
Bhim ki Doongri 209
Bhopa musicians 270
Bhopal 149
Bhuramal Rajmal Surana (Jaipur) 267
Bhutan 293
Bihar 48, 87
Bijak ki Pahadi 208
Bijasan Mata (Durga) 223
Bijay Mandal 109
Bikaner House 279, 296
Bir Singh Deo 174, 176
Birbal ka Chatta 140
Birbal's House 172
Bird Hospital 92
Birla Auditorium (Jaipur) 271
Birla, GD 77
Birla Mandir **77**
Birla Planetarium 195
Birlas 78, 194, 212
Bismillah Khan 31
Biyani Haveli (Sikar) 212, 213
Black-necked stork 168
Blockprinted textiles 205, 266
Blue pottery 204, 266, 267
Body language 282

Bodyline 117
Boileau, JT 153
Bombay (Mumbai) 23, 55, 212, 292
Book Shop (Jaipur) 267
Books Corner (Jaipur) 267
Bose, Subhash Chandra 59
Bougainvillea 104
Bourbon family 153
Bradman, Donald 61
Brahma 25, 216
Brahma Temple 216
Brahmapuri 145
Brahmpuri 198
Brahmasar 140
Brahmi inscriptions 103
Brahmi script 97
Brajbhumi **162**
Brendish & Pilkington 101
Brindavan 18, 38, 39, 147, **162–3**,
 182, 270, 271
BBC World Service 290
British Council (Delhi) 120, 121,
 290
British Crown 18, 56
British East India Company 18, 23 43,
 54, 55, 56, 113, 166
Buddha, Gautam 23, 45 47, 74, 104
Buddha Jayanti 37, 38, 104
Buddha Jayanti Park
 (Delhi) 38, **104**
Buddhism 22, 23, 43, 46, 47, 74, 161
Buddhist Art, Gandhara (Pakistan)
 47, 161
Buddhist kingdom 17, 148
Buddhist philosophy 274
Budget hotels and tourist
 lodges 229
Budget Rent-a-Car (Delhi) **299**
Bugatti cars 207
Buland Darwaza
 Dargah Sharif (Ajmer) 221
 Fatehpur Sikri 52, 173
Bulbulekhan area **96**
Bundela kings 135, 175, 176
Bundelkhand 175
Burma (Myanmar) 293
Bustan-e-Sadi 74
Buxar Battle 54
By bus 301
 state bus stations 297
By bus (cont.)
 state government-run coaches 296
By coach **296–7**
 coach, tickets and fares 297
 package tours 297

C

Calcutta (Kolkata) 57, 59, 103, 160,
 212, 292
Calligraphy 50, 73, **157**

Calligrapht (cont.)
  calligraphic panels 155
Camping, trekking and
  rock climbing **274**
Canada 291
Lord Canning 56
Carnatic music 120
Car rental 298, 299
  hiring a chauffeur-driven car **298**
Carpet Cellar, The 118, 119
Castle Mandawa **232**
Cellular Jail (Andaman Islands) 58
Central Asian antiquities 75
Central Cottage Industries (Delhi) 118
Central Post Office (Agra) 153
Ceramic tiles 50
Chahamanas 49
Chaitanya Mahaprabhu 162
Chaitya hall 208
Chakra Yantra **192**
Chakravarty, Vidyadhar 183, 186
Chaksu 36, 181, **222**
Chalukyas 49
Chambal ravines 16
Chambal, River 20, 21
Champaran Satyagraha 58
Chandellas 49
Chand, Nihal 191, 215
Chand Pol 203
Chandigarh 138
Chandni Chowk 89, **92**, 93, 118, 119,
  Street-by-Street **90–91**
Chandragupta 45
Chandragupta I 47
Chandragupta II 47
Chandra Kumari Ranawatji 195
Chandra Mahal 182, 188, 189,
  198, 212
Chandrabhaga, River 144
Changing money 288
Channel V 291
Char Chowk Haveli 213
Char Dham pilgrim route 144
Char Qutbs 140
Charbagh 105, 155, 160, 165, **167**,
  182, 196
Chatar ki Burj 183
Chatta Chowk 94
Chaturbhuj Temple 176
Chaugan 183
Chaugan Stadium 38, **183**, 273
Chauhan, Prithviraj **48**, 50, 107, 219
Chauhans 179
Chaunsath Khamba 82
Chaurasi Kos ki Yatra 162
Chausa Battle 52
Chawri Bazaar 93
Check-in 293
Cheeta (Jaipur) 271
Cheetal (Indian spotted deer) 20
Cheltenham 76

Chhipa Mohalla 205
Children's activities **273**, 275
Children's Day 40
China 47, 75, 248
Chini ka Rauza **158**
Chini ki Burj 183
Chiragh Delhi **108**
  Raushan Chiragh-i-Dehlvi 108
Chishti, Khwaja Moinuddin 37, 40,
  134, 218, 220
Chishti, Salim 170
Chishti sect 82, 140
Chittorgarh 203
Chittor 221
Chola dynasty 74
Cholera 287
Chomu **212**
Chor Minar 106
Chhoti Chaupar 184
Chowsingha 211
Christian Armenian community 23
Christianity **23**
Christmas 37, 41
Chrysanthemum Show (Delhi) 40
Churches
  Cathedral Church of the
    Redemption (Delhi) **71**, 281
  Cathedral of the Immaculate
    Conception (Agra) 281
  Church of North India (Delhi) 102
  Roman Catholic Church of the
    Sacred Heart (Mathura) 161
  Sacred Heart Cathedral (Delhi) 281
  St George's Church (Agra)153
  St James's Church (Delhi) 102
  St John the Baptist Church
    (Roorkee) 143
  St John's Church (Meerut) 142
  St Martin's Church (Delhi) 104
Church Missionary Society 152, 160
Churiwali Gali 93
Cinema *see* Entertainment
Citibank (Delhi) 288
City Palace
  Alwar **206**
  Jaipur 11, 183, 186, 199
City Palace Museum (Jaipur) **188–191**
  Arms Gallery 191
  Art Gallery 190
  Textiles and Costumes Gallery 190
City Palace Museum (cont.)
  Transport Gallery 191
  Plan 189
Civil Disobedience Movement 59
Civil Lines 99, 100, **102**
Classic Golf Resort 273, 275
Classical music and dance **270**
CNN 290
Lord Clive 54
Coffee shops **249**

Colonial architecture **27**, 142
Communications **290–91**
Company Bagh
  Alwar **207**
  Saharanpur 143
Company School of Painting 33
Conference centres 228
Congress Party 58, 60, 69
Duke of Connaught 76
Connaught Place 64, **76**, 78, 118,
  292, 299
Constitution of India 22, 70
Consulate General of Malta 76
Contemporary Indian art 33
Contemporary theatre 31
Cooch Behar 194
Cooke & Kelvey (Delhi) 118
Coolies (licensed porters) 295
Coronation Durbar 57
Coronation Memorial **103**
Coronation Park 71
Correa, Charles 85, 195
Courier services **290**
Cox & Kings (Delhi) 297
Crafts Museum 11, **86–7**
  Crafts Museum shop 87, 118, 119
  Floor Plan 86–7
  Gallery Guide 87
Credit Cards **288**
Crested serpent eagle 20, 211
Cricket 61, 272
Cunningham 218
Currency **289**
Lord Curzon 57, 111, 170, 218
Customs **292**
Customs information **279**
Cuts and bites **287**

D

Da Milano 118, 119
Dabra 175
Dacca *see* Dhaka
Dalai Lama 23, 104
Lord Dalhousie 56
Dalmias 212
Damoh 167
Dandi Salt March 59
Daniells 71
Dara Shikoh 83
Dargah Bazaar 221
Dargah Qutb Sahib 110, **113**
Dargah Sharif 218, **220–21**
Dariba Kalan 91, 93, 118, 119
Darlington 105
Darter cormorants 168
Darter or snake bird 21
Daryaganj 119
Datia 147, **174**, 175
Datia Palace 174
Daulat Bagh 219

Davis Cup 272
Deccan Aviation (Delhi) 273, 275
Deeg **163**
Deeg Water Palace **164–5**
Degs 221
Delhi airport 114
Delhi cantonment **104**
Delhi College 96
Delhi Diary 120, 291
Delhi Gate 150, 152
Delhi Gliding Club 105
Delhi Golf Club 272, 275
Delhi Metro Railway 77, **301**
Delhi Riding Club 273, 275
Delhi Sultanate **50–51**, 112,
Delhi Tourism 40, 279
Delhi University 99, **103**
Delhi **62–131**
    day trips 116–17
    Delhi at a glance 64–5
    entertainment 120–21
    further afield 98–117
    hotels 234–6
    New Delhi 66–79
    Nizamuddin to Purana
    Qila 80–87
    Old Delhi 88–97
    restaurants 256–7
    shopping 118–19
    Street Finder 122–131
Demetrius 46
Demoiselle cranes 116
Dengue fever 286
Department of Tourism 278
Department of Tourism-run
    buses **296**
Departure tax 293
Devanagari 97
Dhak (Butea monosperma) 20, 211
Dhaka (Bangladesh) 58, 190
Dhar 49
Dhamma 46, 103
Dhanna Bhagat Temple 216
Dharamshalas and ashrams 229, 231
Dharma 141
Dhola and Maru 271
Dholpur **166**, 167
Dhrupad 163
Dhrupad Festival (Delhi) 41
Dhurries 266
Digamber Jain Mandir 92
Dilaram Bagh 202
Dilkusha Kothi 142
Dilli Haat 118, 119
Diners Club 288
Dinpanah 84
Directorate of Film Festivals 120
Disabled travellers **231**
Discover India Fare 293
Discovery channel 290

Diwali 37, 40, 197, 199
Diwan-i-Aam
    Amber 201, 202
    City Palace (Jaipur) 189, 190
    Fatehpur Sikri 170
    Red Fort 95
Diwan-i-Khas
    Amber 201, 202
    City Palace (Jaipur) 189, 190
    Fatehpur Sikri 170
    Red Fort 94
Diva Burj 199
Doctrine of Lapse 56
Domestic flights **293**
Doordarshan 290
Draupadi 141, 209
Drinks 251, 255
    Evian or Bisleri 286
Driving 298
Dry days 249
Dry deciduous forests 20
Duleh Rai 197
Dundlod Fort 213, 273
Dun-huang (China) 75
Durbar of 1903 57
Durga 25, 36, 77, 223
Durga Puja 37
Dussehra 30, 37, 40
Dutch East India Company 153
Dwarka's (Jaipur) 267

E

Early civilizations **44–5**
Early Indian architecture **26**
Eastern Court 78
Eating Indian-style 283
Ecotourism 274
Edward VII of England 157
Egrets 116, 168
Egyptian artifacts 74
Eicher City Map 299
Electricity 281
Elephant Festival (Jaipur) 38
Elizabeth I 152
Embassies and consulates 279
Embassies in Delhi 281
Embroidered textiles 267
Emergency numbers 284, 285
England *see* UK
Entertainment 120, **270–71**
    booking tickets 270
    cinemas 271
    performing art centres 271
Escorts Heart Institute 285
ESPN 291
Etiquette **282–3**
European mercenaries 54
European traders and colonizers **54**
Everest, Mount 60
Eve-teasing 284

Exchange Stores (Delhi) 102
Expo Plus (Jaipur) 267

F

Fabindia (Delhi) 118, 119
Facilities for children **231**
Facilities for the disabled 231, **280**
Fa Hsien 47
Fakr-ul-Masjid 100
Falaknuma 85
Faqir Chand's (Delhi) 79
Fariburz Sahba 115
Fateh Burj 166
Fateh Jang's Tomb **207**
Fatehpur 54, 213
Fatehpuri Begum 92
Fatehpuri Masjid 92
Fatehpur Sikri 147, **170–73**
    Plan 171
Father Santos 153
Fax and telegraph services 290
Ferghana 167
Ferozabad 97, 107
Feroze Shah Kotla **97**, 272
Feroze Shah Tughlaq 51, 103, 104,
    107, 109, 112, 140, 167
Festivals in India **36–7**
Firoz Khan Khwajasara's tomb **153**
First City 120, 291
First-aid kit 286
Fishing 275
Fitness centres 228
Five-star luxury hotels 228
Flame of the forest (*Butea
    monosperma*) 34, 104
Food
    Flavours of Delhi, Agra and Jaipur,
    The 250-51
    Flavours of the Tandoor, The
    252-53
Food and water-borne diseases 287
Foreign Post Office (Delhi) 290, 291
Foreign travel tax 293
Foreigner's Regional Registration
    Offices
    in Agra 279
    in Delhi 279
    in Jaipur 279
Forest Essentials 119
Fraser, William 101
Freedom Movement **58–9**, 78
French Cultural Centre 120
Fuel and fuel stations 298
Full Circle 79, 119
Further Afield (Delhi) **98–117**
    Area map 99
    Street-by-Street 100–101

G

Gaitor **198**, 203
Sage Galav 196

Galis and *katras* 89
Galta 181, **196**
Gandhak ki Baoli **111**
Gandhara sculpture 47
Gandhi, Indira 60, 61
Gandhi, Kasturba 78
Gandhi, MK 58, **59**, 68
  birthday 40, 97
  writings 78
Gandhi, Rajiv 60, 61, 78
Gandhi Samadhi 59
Gandhi Smriti **78**
Gandhi, Sonia 60
Ganeriwala family 213
Ganesh Pol 201, 202
Ganesh Temple 223
Ganesha 24, 25
Ganga Canal Irrigation Project 143
Ganga Canal Workshop 143
Ganga Devi 87
Gangaur festival (Jaipur) 38, 213
Ganges, River 25, 43, 144, 230, 275
Ganges Valley 44, 45, 46
Ganjifa 141
Garden tomb 29
Garganery teal 168
Garuda 25, 218
Gauri 38
Gauri Shankar Mandir 92
Gayatri 216
Gayatri Devi 194, 195
Gayatri Temple 216
Gem Palace (Jaipur) 267
General elections 60, 61
General Post Office (GPO)
  in Agra 290, 291
  in Jaipur 290, 291
  Old Delhi **101**
George V of England 71, 76, 103
George Walter 103
Getting around in the
  cities **300–301**
  general precautions while
  travelling 284
Ghalib Academy 82
Gharial (Gavialis gangeticus) 21
Ghata ("cloud") Mosque 97
Ghat ke Balaji **196**
Ghat ki Guni **196**
Ghazi-ud-Din 96
Ghazi-ud-Din's grave 96
Ghazi-ud-Din's madrasa 96
Ghiyasuddin's tomb 115
Ghumar dance 270
Giardiasis 287
Gita Jayanti 140
Gita Research Centre 140
Glasgow 105
Goa 152, 292
Godse, Nathuram 78

Goenkas 212, 213
Gokul 162
Golden Temple (Amritsar) 23
Golden Triangle 10, 228, 292
Gole Market 76
Golkara 105
Gondophernes 46
Good Earth (Delhi) 119
Gopal Bhavan 164
Gopal Sagar 164
Gopalji ka Rasta (Jaipur) 185,
  187, 267
Gopinath Temple 163
Gourmet restaurants 228
Govardhan **162**
Govardhan, Mount 37
Govardhan Puja **37**
Government Central Museum
  (Albert Hall) **194**
Government emporia **265**, 267
Government Museum
  (Mathura) 161
Government of India Tourist
  Offices 279
Govind Dev Temple **182**, 199, 270
Govindeoji Temple
  (Brindavan) 162
Grand Trunk road 138, 140,
  150, **160**
Great Indian horned owl 211
Green channel 292
Greenwich Mean Time (GMT) 281
Greeting people 282
Gregorian calendar 281
Grey herons 168
Grey partridge 211
Grishma 37
Grover, Satish 85
Guesthouses **229**
Guides **280**
Gujarat 52, 75, 86, 172
Gujari Mahal 174
Gujjar tribe 114
Gulistan 206
Gupta empire 43, 46, 47, 74, 161
Gurjara-Pratiharas 48
Guru-ka-Tal 160
Gurukul Kangri University 144
Guru Purab 37
Gwalior 147, 153, **174**, 175
Gwalior Fort 174
Gwalior Gharana (Music) **174**

H

Hailey Road 76
Haji Begum 83
Haldiyon ka Rasta (Jaipur) 187, 267
Hall of Nations and Industries 85
Hamams 94
Hammonds (London) 195

Hamsadhwani Auditorium 85
Handicrafts *see* What to Buy
Handloom House (Jaipur) 267
Hansi 101, 137, **140**
Hanuman 24, 25, 37, 48, 196, **197**
Haram Sara 172
Harappan Culture 17, **44–5**, 74, 75
Hardayal Library 92
Hardinge, Lord 103, 152
Haridwar 135, 137, **144**, 229, 275
Har-ki-Pauri 144
Harsha Vardhana 47
Haryana Tourism 117
Hastinapur 141
Hathi Pol 172
Hauz Khas **106**
Hauz Khas Village 118, 248
Hauz Suiwalan 96
Hauz-i-Shamsi 110
Havelis **29**, 212
Havelock Memorial Church 153
Hawa Mahal
  Fatehpur Sikri 172
  Jaipur 11, **186**
Hazarilal 96
Heat and smog 286
Heli-tourism 273, 275
Hemant 37
Henry IV of France 153
Hepatitis A 287
Hepatitis B 287
Herat 190
Herbal Products *see* What to Buy
Heritage hotels **232–3**
Heritage Hotels Assocation of India
  229, 231
Herons 116
Hertz car rentals 298, 299
Hessing, John 153
Hill Fort (Kesroli) **233**
Hillary, E 60
Himachal Pradesh 76
Himalayan River Runners (Delhi) 275
Himalayas 20, 134, 138, 144, 272, 274
Hindola Gate 174
Hindu astrology 144
Hindu festivals 36
Hindu gods and goddesses **24–5**
Hindu Shahis 49
Hinduism **22**, 115
Hindustan Times 291
Hindustani classical music **30**, 270
Hiran Minar 172
Hissar 140
History, Delhi, Agra and Jaipur **42–61**
  Ancient Empires 46–7
  Colonial Period 54–5
  Delhi Sultanate 50–51
  Early Civilization 44–5
  Freedom Movement 58–9

History, Delhi, Agra and Jaipur (cont.)
India Today 60–61
Mughal Dynasties 52–3
Pax Britannica 56–7
Rajput Dynasties 48–9
Timeline 44–61
Lieutenant Hodson 97
Holi 36, **38**, 163
Holidays and opening hours **280**
Banks 288
Holika 36
Hollywood 271
Holy Trinity 25
Home Rule League 58
Hongkong & Shanghai Bank (Delhi) 288
Hospitals and medical facilities **285**
Hotels
Ashok Group 228, 229, 231
Ashok Hotel 288
booking, checking in and out 230
budget hotels and tourist lodges 229
facilities for children 231
hidden extras 230
hotel chains 231
hotel grading and facilities 228
how to pay 264
Hiuen Tsang 47
Hujra 173
Humayun, Mughal emperor 52, 65, 83, 84, 107, 220
Humayun's Gate 84
Humayun's library 84
Humayun's Tomb 10, 29, 52, 65, 81, **83**
Huns 43
Husain, MF 71
Hyderabad 75, 96
Hyderabad House 71
Hyenas 211

I

Ibn Batuta 109
Ibrahim Kothi 117
Ibrahim Lodi 52, 106, 140
Ibrahim Shah Sur 140
Id-ul-Fitr **37**
Illbert Bill 57
Iltutmish 50, 51, 110, 112, 114, 220
Iltutmish's tomb **113**
Immigration certificate 292
Immunization **279**
Indika 45
Income Tax Department (Foreign Section) 293
Independence day 39, 179, 280
Indergarh **223**
India Gate 10, 57, 67, 68, **71**, 103
India Habitate Centre 120, 121

India International Centre 120, 121
India International Travel and Tourism Show 85
India Today 291
India Tourism Development Corporation (ITDC) 229
India Tourist Office (Delhi) 279, 290
India Trade Promotion Organization 85
India Wonder Fare 293
Indian Board for Wildlife 223
Indian consular offices 278
Indian Council Act (ASI) 1861 56
Indian Council for Cultural Relations (ICCR) 120
Indian Crafts Gallery (Agra) 267
Indian design **34–5**
Indian elephants 20
Indian Express building 97
Indian flag 60
Indian food
glossary of **254–5**
Indian Made Foreign Liquor 249
Indian Mountaineering Foundation (Delhi) 274, 275
Indian Mutiny or Great Revolt of 1857 54, 55, 65, 89, 142, 147, 153, 175
Indian National Airport 105
INA Market **105**
Indian National Congress *see* Congress Party
Indian pine *(chir)* 20
Indian Red Cross Society **285**, 287
Indian roller bird 225
Indian Standard Time and calendar 281
Indian trees **20**
Indira Chowk 76
Indira Gandhi (IG) International Airport 292
Indira Gandhi National Centre for the Arts 71, 121
Indo Asia Tours (Delhi) 274, 275
Indo-Islamic architecture 111, 112, 172
Indo-Pakistan War 60, 71
Indo-Saracenic architecture 27, 194, 219
Indra 37
Indraprastha 84
Indrail pass 294
Indus (Sindhu), River 43, 44
Indus Valley 43, 44, 45, 72, 74, 137
Information sources **270**
Insect-borne diseases **286**
Insurance and driving licence **279**
Inter State Bus Terminus 102
Inter State Bus Terminus (ISBT), Kashmiri Gate 296
International and local calls 291

International Film Festival 120
International Tourist Bureau 295
International Trade Fair (Delhi) 40
International Travel House
Agra 299
Delhi 299
Jaipur 299
International Triennale Exhibition 76
International Yoga Festival (Rishikesh) **41**, 274
Internet and e-mail **290**
Ireland 281, 291
Iris 156
Iron pillar **112**
Isfahani, Abdullah 191
Ishwar Lat 184
ISKCON Temple 163
Islam *see* Muslims
Islamic architecture 26, 111, 112
Islamic art 222
Italy 248
ITC Sangeet Sammelan (Delhi) 38
Itimad-ud-Daulah's Tomb 11, 53, **158**

J

Jackal 211
Jacob, Sir Samuel Swinton 194, 197
Jagat Shiromani Temple 203
Jahanara Begum 81, 82, 90, 150, 151
Jahan e Khusrau (Delhi) **38**
Jahangir, Mughal emperor 52, 150, 156, 158, 173, 176, 191, 206, 209, 218, 221
Jahangiri Mahal 150, **176**
Jahangiri Mahal's museum 176
Jahanpanah 99, 107, **109**
Jahaz Mahal 40, 110
Jai Mandir 200, 202
Jai Niwas Bagh **182**
Jai Prakash Yantra 77, 193
Jai Singh, Alwar 207
Jai Singh I 191, 200,
Jai Singh II 182, 184, 188
Jai Van 199
Jai Vilas Palace 174
Jaigarh 198, 199
Jaigarh Fort 200, 203
Jain, OP 114
Jain votive plaque (Mathura) 74
Jainism 23, 204
Digambaras 23
Svetambaras 23
Tirthankaras 204, 219
Jaipur **182–199**
hotels 243–5
restaurants 262–3
Jaipur and environs **178–225**
exploring Jaipur and environs 180–181
hotels 243–7
restaurants 261–3
Street-by-Street (Jaipur) 184–5

Jaipur and Environs (cont.)
  Street-by-Street (Pushkar) 216–7
Jaipur House 71
Jaipur Vision 270
Jaisalmer 295
Jal Mahal 140, **199**
Jalan havelis 213
Jaleb Chowk 202
Jalianwala Bagh 58
Jamali-Kamali Mosque and
  Tomb **111**
Jama't Khana Mosque 82
Jamawar shawl 75, 118
Jami Masjid
  Agra 150, **151**, 152
  Fatehpur Sikri **173**
  Jaipur 185
  Mathura 161
  Meerut 142
  Old Delhi 89, 91, **92**
Jamvai Mata 197
Janata Party 60
Janmashtami 37, 39, 163, 182
Janpath 67, 71, 77, 78, 118
Jantar Mantar
  Delhi **77**
  Jaipur 11, 184, **192–3**
Japan 248, 291
Japan Airlines 293
Jas Mandir 200, 202
Jawahar Burj 166
Jawahar Kala Kendra **195**, 271
Jawahar Mela 164
Jawaharlal Nehru Stadium
  (Delhi) 272
Jeep and desert safari 273
Jewellery **187**
Jews 23
Jhansi 148, 149, **175**
Jhor 167
Jinnah, MA 59
Jodha Bai's Palace 172
Jodhpur 295
Jogi Mahal 224
Jogmaya Temple 40, 113
Johari Bazaar
  Agra 151
  Jaipur 185
Johari Mal, Gulab Singh 119
John Brothers (Delhi) 118
Jones, William 55
Jorawar Singh Gate 199
Judah Hyam Synagogue
  (Delhi) 281
Jugal Kishore Temple 163
Juneja Art Gallery (Jaipur) 267

K

Kabul 49, 158, 160
Kachhawahas 179, 190, 197, 198, 200,
  202, 204, 206

Kachi-ki-Sarai 160
Kadamba *(Anthocephatus cadamba)*
  21
Kagazi Mohalla 205
Kair (Capparis decidua) 211
Kairali Health Resort (Delhi) 274, 275
Kala Hanumanji 199
Kala Pani 58
Kalan Masjid 96
Kalbelia 271
Kali **25**, 115
Kalidasa 46
Kalighati 210
Kalinga War 46
Kaliya 74
Kaliyamardan (Chola Bronze) 74
Kalkaji Temple **115**
Kamagata Maru 58
Kamani Auditorium 76, 120
Kamaraj, Nadar 69
Kamasutra 47
Kamsa 161, 162
Kanak Vrindavan Temple 199
Kanch Mahal 160
Kanchana Ghat 176
Kandy (Sri Lanka) 153
Kanishka 46, 47, 161
Kannauj 48
Kans Qila 161
Kantha embroidery (Bengal) 75
Kanu Carpet Factory (Agra) 267
Kanvinde, Achyut 85
Karbala 36
Kargil 61
Karim's 90
Karnal 96, 103
Karnataka 87
Karol Bagh 264
Kartik 217
Kartik Purnima 179
Kaserat Bazaar 151
Kashmir 46, 61, 100, 190, 293
Kashmiri Bazaar 151
Kashmiri Gate
  Street-by-Street **100–101**
Kasumbhil 106
Katcheri (court) Bagh 166
Kathak 31, 120, 270
Kathak Bindadin Mahotsav (Delhi) 41
Kathak Kendra 41
Kathak Utsav (Delhi) 40
Kathakali 120
Katra Neel 93
Katras 93
Kauravas 140, 141, 209
Kayaking and river rafting 275
Kennedy, Jacqueline 195
Keoladeo Ghana National
  Park **168–9**
Kerala 87
Kesar Kyari Bagh 202

Keshav Bhavan 164
Keshi Ghat 163
Ketu 140
Khadi 78
Khadi Ghar (Jaipur) 267
Khair-ul-Manazil 81, **85**
Khajanewalon ka Rasta
  (Jaipur) 267
Khajuraho temples 49
Khalsa 23, 38
Khan Abdul Ghaffar Khan 79
Khan, Amjad Ali 30
Khan, Chenghiz 50
Khan, Nawab Faiz Ali 186
Dr Khan Sahib 79
Khan, Ghazi-ud-Din 96
Khan, Iqbal 106
Khan, Isa 83
Khan Market 11, **79**, 118, 119
Khan-i-Jahan Junan Shah 96, 109
Khari Baoli 92, 93
Khas Mahal 95, 150
Khazana 119
Kheri Gate 203
Khilji, Alauddin 51, 106, 107, 108,
  112, 223
Khilji period 106
Khirkee 96, **109**
Khoja Mortenepus 152
Khuni Darwaza 97
Khwabgah
  Red Fort 95
  Fatehpur Sikri 170, 172
Kikar 104
Kimkhabs 190
Kinari Bazaar 90, 93, 151
  Agra 267
King Cobra 21
King Lear 31
King Virat 209
Kingfishers 116, 211
Kingsway 67
Kishangarh 180, **215**
Kishangarh's School of
  Painting **215**
Kishanpol Bazaar (Jaipur) 267
Kaudiyala 145
Koh-i-Noor (Agra) 267
Koran 22, 37, 82, 112, 206, 222
  illuminated Koran 73
  illustrated Koran 50
Koran-e-Kamal 222
Kos minar 138, 140, 148
Kosi 162
Kotwali 92
Krishna **25**, 36, 37, 74, 141, 161,
  162, 163
Krishna Cult 18, 140, 162, 163,
Krishna Katha 39
Krishna Museum (Kurukshetra) 140

Kuanwalji (Lord Shiva) 223
Kubera 72
Kufic script 73, 218
Kumbh Mela 135, **144**
Kundankari 75, 187
Kuru tribe 140
Kurukshetra 138, **140**, 141, 209
Kushak Mahal 78
Kushak-i-Shikar 103
Kushanas 17, 46, 72, 161
Kusum Sarovar 162
Kutch 86

L

Laburnum 104
Lachhmangarh 213
Ladliji Temple 162
Laghu Samrat Yantra 192
Lahore 187, 190
Lahore Gate 28, 91, 94
Lake Palace (Udaipur) 199
Lakshman 37
Lakshman Jhula 145
Lakshmi 24
Lakshmi Narayan Mandir
    (Delhi) **77**
Lakshmi Narayan Temple
    (Jaipur) 194
Lakshwadeep 279
Lal Darwaza 84
Lal Kot 99, 110
Lal Kuan Bazaar 96
Lalit Kala Akademi 76
Landscape and Wildlife **20–21**
Langas 271
Language, official 281
Lanka 37
Laxmi Bai 147, 175
Laxmi Mandir (Jaipur) 271
Laxmi Niwas 199
Laxmi Vilas Palace (Bharatpur) **233**
Left Book Club 78
Legal assistance 285
Legislative Assembly 102
Lehenga 30
Lentils 252, 254
Linga 92
LKP Forex Ltd 288
Local transport in the cities **300–301**
    rickshaws, tongas and tempos 301
Lodi dynasties 79
Lodi Estate 79
Lodi Gardens 11, **79**
Lodis 51, 110
Lohagarh Fort 166
Lohri 36, 41
Lok Sabha 70
London 72, 189, 292
Lord Lake 166
Lotus 35

Lotus Garden 167
Lotus Pool 155
Lotus quoins 165
Lotus Temple 115
Ludo 172
Lunar calendar 36
Lutyens, Edwin Landseer 27, **68**, 70,
    78, 104, 167
Luxury hotels **228**

M

Machchhi Bhavan 150
Machkund 167
Madan Mohan Temple 163
Madhavendra Bhavan 198
Madhi Masjid 110
Madho Singh I 184, 199, 222
Madho Singh II 188, 189, 193, 195,
    198
Madhubani painting 87
Madras (Chennai) 292
Maffi, Bernardino 153
Mahabharata 47, 77, 84, 137, 140,
    141, 191, 209, 222
Mahal Khas 166
Maham Anga 85
Maharaja Exports (Agra) 267
Maharaja of Gwalior 233
Maharaja of Jaipur 233
Maharaja of Kishangarh 232
Maharaja Sawai Man Singh II
    Museum *see* City Palace Museum
Maharana Pratap 102
Maharana Sangram Singh 75
Maharani ki Chhatri 199
Mahavira 23, 204
Mahesh Yogi 144
Mahishasura 25, 223
Mahmud of Ghazni 50
Makar Sankranti 36, 41
Makhdum Shah Wilayat 142
Makrana **214**
Malachite 156
Malaria **286**
Maldives 293
Malik Talao 224
Man Mandir 174
Man Prakash (Jaipur) 271
Man Sagar 199
Man Singh I **49**, 162, 187, 191, 199,
    200, 202, 203, 204
Man Singh II 194, 195, 199
Manchester 105
Mandalas 162
Mandawa 213
Mandi House Complex **76**
Mangala Devi Temple 209
Manganiyars 271
Mango Festival (Delhi) 39
Maniharon ka Rasta (Jaipur) 267

Mansa Devi Temple 144
Mansabdar 53
Mansingh Stadium (Jaipur) 272
Mansur 32
Mant, Charles 219
Maota Lake 200, 202
Marathas 54, 140, 150
Marble inlay *see* Pietra Dura
Marco Polo 51
Mariam Zamani's Tomb 160
MASTA (Medical Advisory Service for
    Travellers Abroad, UK) 285, 287
Master Card 288, 289
Mathura 17, 18, 44, 47, 147, 148, 149,
    161, 192, 270, 271
Mathura School of Art **47**, 161
    The Drunken Courtesan 47
Matka Pir 81, **85**
Maulana Abul Kalam Azad Arabic
    and Persian Research Institute 222
Max Mueller Bhavan 120, 121
Max Medcentre 285
Lord Mayo 219
Mayo College **219**
Mazar Sharif 220
McDonalds 248
Measurements and conversion
    chart 281
Mecca 82, 218
Medd, Henry Alexander 71
Medical facilities 285
Meena Bazaar 150
Meena tribe 197, 198
Meenakari 75, 187, 266
Meerut 103, **142**
Megasthenes 45
Mehfil Khana 220
Mehmankhana (Lodi Gardens) 79
Mehrauli 110, 113, 118
Mehrauli Archaeological
    Park **110–11**
Menander 46
Mercury Travels
    Agra 297
    Delhi 297
    Jaipur 297
Mesopotamia 44, 74
Metcalfe, Sir Thomas 102
Metcalfe House 102
Metric system 281
Mexico 248
Middle Eastern cuisine 248
Middle-range hotels **229**
Milad-ul-Nabi 36
Mildenhall, John 152
Milestones 230, 231, 274
Military Works Department 104
Mina Masjid (Agra Fort) 150
Miniature painting 266
Ministry of Civil Aviation 105

Ministry of Defence 102
Ministry of Environment &
   Forests 279
Ministry of External Affairs 70
Ministry of Home Affairs 279
Minor stomach upsets **286**
Mir Qamar-ud-Din 96
Mira Bai 203
Mirak Mirza Ghiyas 83
Miran Sayyid Hussain 218
Mirza Ghalib 81, 82
Mirza Ulugh Beg 192
Misra Yantra 77
Missionaries of Charity 102
Mithi (sweet) Id 37
Miyan Bhuwa 106
Modems 228
Prophet Mohammad 22
Mohenjodaro 74
Monkeys
   langur 20, 210
   rhesus 20
Monsoon architecture **165**
Montagu-Chelmsford
   Reforms (1919) 70
Moosi Maharani ki Chhatri **206**
Moth ki Masjid **106**
Mother Teresa 102
Moti Burj 183
Moti Doongri, Jaipur **194**
Moti Doongri Palace, Alwar 207
Moti Mahal (Jaipur) 271
Moti Masjid 94, 113, 150
   Agra Fort 150
   Red Fort (Delhi) 94
Motilal Banarsidas 119
Mountbatten, Lord Louis 59, 103
Mrignayani 174
MTV Asia 291
Mubarak Mahal 188, 190, 191
Mughal architecture **27**, 159, 188
Mughal art **52**, 75
Mughal Gardens 41, 70
Mughal Marble Swing 164
Mughal miniature paintings 32, 72,
   190, 194
Muhammad Ghaus's tomb 174
Muhammed Ghori 50, 206
Muhammad Shah 77, 102, 105
   tomb of 79
Muhammad Shah Rangila 81
Muhammad-bin-Tughlaq 107, 108,
   109, 115, 143
Muharram 36
Multan 114, 158
Mumbai see Bombay
Mumtaz Mahal 135, 150, 154
Muni-ki-Reti 144
Munjeeta Travel 229, 231
Munshi Ganeshi Lal & Son (Agra) 267

Musamman Burj 150
Museums
   Archaeological Museum (Gwalior)
      174
   City Palace Museum (Alwar) 206
   City Palace Museum (Jaipur)
      188–91
   Crafts Museum (Delhi) 11, **86–7**
   Government Museum (Ajmer) **218**
   Government Museum (Mathura)
      161
   Government Central Museum
      (Jaipur) 194
   Jawahar Kala Kendra (Jaipur) **95**
   Kitchen Museum 70
   Krishna Museum and Gita Research
      Centre (Kurukshetra) 140
   Museum of Indology
      (Jaipur) **194**
   Maulana Abul Kalam Azad Arabic
      and Persian Research Institute
      (Tonk) 222
   National Gallery of Modern Art
      (Delhi) **71**
   National Museum (Delhi) 10,
      72–5
   National Rail Museum
      (Delhi) 10, **104**
   Nehru Memorial Museum and
      Library (Delhi) **78**
   Purana Quila Museum 84
   Sanskriti (Delhi) **114**
   Scindia Museum (Gwalior) 174
Music, Dance and Theatre **30–31**
Muslims
   Shias 22
   Sunnis 22
Muslim League 58, 59
Mutiny Memorial 103

N

Nadir Shah 54, 89, 90, 92
Nag kings 175
Nagina Masjid
   Agra Fort 150
   Fatehpur Sikri 172
Nagphas 206
Nahar Singh 198
Nahargarh **198**
Nai ki Mandi (Agra) 267
Nai Sarak 93
Naidu, Sarojini 58
Naika (Jaipur) 267
Najaf Khan 142
Nakul 209
Namazgah (Fatehpur Sikri) 173
Nand 162
Nand Bhavan 164
Nandgaon 162
Nandi 25

Guru Nanak 23, 37
Naqqar Khana 94
Narada 24
Narasing Dev 203
Narain Niwas Palace
   (Jaipur) 232
Narcotics 284
Narivalaya Yantra 192
Narmada Bachao activists 61
Narmada Dam 61
Narnaul **140**
Narsimha Temple 203
Nasik 144
Nasiruddin Mahmud 108
Nasiruddin 82
Nasiyan Temple 219
National Archives 71
National Film Festival (Delhi) 39
National Gallery of Modern
   Art **71**, 121
National Geographic 290
National Museum (Delhi) 10, **72–5**
   Ancient and Medieval Sculpture
      Gallery 74
   Bronze Gallery 74
   Central Asian Antiquities
      Gallery 75
   Coins and Scripts Gallery 72
   Dara Shikoh's Marriage
      Procession 72
   Decorative Arts Gallery 75
   Floor Plan 72–73
   Gallery Guide 73
   Indus Valley Gallery 74
   Key to floorplan 73
   Manuscripts and Wall Paintings
      Gallery 74
   Indian Miniatures Gallery 75
   Textiles, Arms, Armour and
      Musical Instruments Gallery 75
National Parks
   Keoladeo Ghana National
      Park **168–9**
   Sariska National Park **210–11**
   Ranthambhore National
      Park **224–5**
National Parks and Camping
   Sites 230, 231
National Rail Museum 10, **104**
National School of Drama
   (Delhi) 39, 76, 120
National Science Centre
   (Delhi) 85, 273, 275
National Stadium 68
National Theatre Festival 120
Naturopathy 274
Natya Shastra 31
Naubat Khana 172
Nauchandi Mela 38
Navaratna 75

Navaratri 36, 37, 251
Nawab Saheb ki Haveli 186
Nawabganj 143
Nawalgarh 213
Neem *(Azadirachta indica)* 21
Neemrana Fort Palace 233
Neemrana Shop 119
Nehru Bazaar (Jaipur) 267
Nehru family 60
Nehru, Jawaharlal 22, 59, 60, 61, 78, 113
  private collection 78
Nehru Memorial Museum
  and Library 10, **78**
Nehru Planetarium 10, 78, 273, 275
Nepal 74, 293
New Delhi **66–79**
  map 67
  Street-by-Street 68–9
New Delhi Railway
  Station 294, 295
New year's eve 37, 41
Newspapers and magazines **291**
Nicholson Cemetery **102**
Nicholson, John 102
Nidhivana 163
Nightlife and bars 271
Nikumbh Mahal 206
Nikumbh Rajputs 206
Nilgai (Blue Bull) 169
Nili Masjid 106
Nizam Gate 221
Nizam of Hyderabad 220
Nizamuddin Auliya 22, 38, 51, 81, 82, 108
Nizamuddin Auliya's
  Dargah 82, 114
Nizamuddin Complex 81, **82**,
  map 81
Nizamuddin to Purana Qila **80–87**
  Area map 81
Nizamuddin Railway Station 294, 295, 296
Non-cooperation Movement 58
Norgay, Tenzing 60
North of Delhi **136–45**
  Exploring North of Delhi 138–9
  hotels 234–6
  restaurants 256–67
Northern Railways Office 101
Northern Ridge 103
North-West Frontier Province
  (Pakistan) 71, 79
Nur Jahan 53, 150, 158

O

Oberoi Group **121**, 231, 272
Oberoi Maidens Hotel **102**
Odissi 120
Odyssey 141

Okhla Barrage 275
Old Central Jail 142
Old Delhi **88–97**
  area map 89
  bazaars **93**
  Street-by-Street 90–1
Old Rohilla Fort 143
Old Secretariat 102
Open-bill stork 168
Orchha 135, 147 175, **176**
  Plan 177
Oswal Emporium (Agra) 267
Ottomans of Turkey 52
Oudh 55
Outdoor activities **272–5**

P

Pachikari 156
Pachisi Court 171, 172
Package tours **297**
Padam Talao 224
Painted floral patterns 159
Painted havelis of Shekhawati 212
Painted stork 21, 116, 169
Paintings and objets d'art 267
Painting **32–33**
  Company School of Painting 33
  Contemporary Indian art 33
  Mughal paintings 32, 75
  Pahari paintings 33, 75
  Rajput paintings 32, 33, 75
Pakistan 17, 19, 22, 59, 74, 292, 293
Palace on Wheels 181, 295
Palladio's Church of II Redentore 71
Panch Mahal 171
Pandavas 84, 140, 141, 209
Pandupol 210, 211
Pandupol Temple 210
Panghat (Jaipur) 270, 271
Panipat 54, 103, 137, **140**, 266
Panna Mian ka Kund 203
Panni Gali 151
Paradise Garden **167**
Paramars 49
Parampara Festival 40
Parking 299
Parliament House 59, 68, 70
Parshuram Temple 216
Parsis 23
Parthians 43
Partition of India 19, 59
Parvati 25, 38, 39
Pashmina (shawl) 118
Patachitra 141
Pataudi 116, **117**
Patna 44
Paying guests **229**
  paying guest accommodation 231
Peacock Throne 95, 150

Pelicans 116
People and Culture, India 19
People- and animal-borne diseases
  287
Peregrine falcon 168
Performing art centres 271
Performing arts 30
General Perron 153
Persia 23, 150
Persian wheel 50
Personal computers 228
Personal security and health **284**
Phad 49
Pharmacies 285
Phool Mahal 215
Phoolwalon ki Sair (Delhi) 40, 113
Photography 281
Pichhwai 266
Pietra dura 35, 155, 156, 159, 205, 266
Pipal tree *(Ficus religiosa)* **21**, 104
Pir Ghaib 103
Pishtaq 155
Pizza Hut 248
Places of worship 280, 281
Plassey Battle 54
PM Allah Buksh & Sons (Jaipur) 267
Poddar 213
Polo **195**, 273
Polo Bar (Jaipur) 271
Poppy 156
Postal services 290
Pragati Maidan 40, 81, **85**, 120
Pratap Singh 206, 208
Prices and discounts 230
Prices and tipping 249
Prime Minister's Office 68
Prince Philip 195
Prince Salim 221
Prinsep, James 97
Pritam Chowk 188
Private Spier 104
Private tour operators 296
Project Tiger 210, 223, 224
Prophet Mohammad 22
Protestant missionaries 23
Public toilets 285
Pundarik ki Haveli **198**
Pundarik, Pandit Ratnakar 198
Puppet shows 271
Purana Qila 81, **84**, 85, 107
  Purana Quila Museum 84
Purjan Vihar 207
Purnanand Ashram 144
Pushkar **216–17**, 273, 278
  Street-by-Street 216–17
Pushkar Fair 37, 40, 180, **217**, 218, 271
Pushkar Lake 216

Q

Qila-I-Kuhna Mosque 84
Qalandar Shah 140
Qawwalis 30, 220, 270
Qila Rai Pithora 99, 107, 110
Qudsia Begum 102
Qudsia Gardens **102**
Queen Mary's Library 153
Quit India Movement 59
Qutb Festival (Delhi) 40
Qutb Minar 99, 109, 110, 111, **112**
Qutb Minar complex 50, 51,
    112–13, 218
Qutb Sahib 110
    dargah of **113**
Qutbuddin Aibak 48, 50, 51, 107, 110,
    112, 218
Qutbuddin Bakhtiyar Kaki 40, 113
Quwwat-ul-Islam Mosque 50,
    112, 218

R

Rabab 30
Rabies 287
Rabindra Bhavan 76
Radha 77, 162, 163, 203, 215
Radha Raman Temple 163
Radhakund 163
Radisson Hotel 228, 231
Raga 51, 75
Raga Todi 31
Ragamala 31, 32, 75, 191
Rahu 140
Rai Pithora 48
Rai Praveen Mahal 176
Rail Yatri Niwas 295
Railway booking centres
    in Delhi 295
Railway enquiries 295
Railway services 295
Rainfall chart 40
Raisina Hill 61, 64, 68, 70
Raj Mahal 176
Raj Mahal Palace **195**
Raj Mandir (Jaipur) 271
Raj Rewal 85
Raja Indrasal 223
Raja Kedarnath 115
Raja ki Mandi 152
Raja Ravi Varma 71
Raja Sansar Chand 33
Raja Sawant Singh 215
Raja Suraj Mal 163, 164, 166
Raja Ugrasen 76
Rajamal ka Talab 183
Rajasthali (Rajasthan Emporium) 265,
    Jaipur 267
Rajasthan Bank (Jaipur) 288
Rajasthan Polo Club 273, 275
Rajasthan state buses 296

Rajasthan State Handloom
    Dev. Corp. Ltd. (Jaipur) 267
Rajasthan Tourism 181, 275, 279
    Delhi 279
    Jaipur 279
Rajbagh 224
Rajbagh Talao 224
Rajendra Pol 188
Rajgarh **208**
Rajgarh Palace 174
Rajghat **97**
Rajiv Chowk 76
Rajiv Gandhi Foundation 38
Rajon ki Bain 111
Rajpath 10, 41, 61, 67, 70, **71**
Rajput art 49
Rajput Bundela architecture 176
Rajput Bundela kings 148
Rajput dynasties **48–9**
Rajput miniature paintings 32, 33, 194
    Krshna revealing his Divinity as
    Vishnu to his parents 33
Rajputana Museum 218
Rajputana 206
Rajwada Library Bar (Jaipur) **271**
Rajya Sabha 70
Raksha Bandhan 39
Ram Niwas Bagh (Jaipur) 271
Ram Niwas Gardens 194
Ram Raja 176
Ram Singh II 186, 191, 194, 195, 199
Ram Yantra 77, 192
Rama 25, 37, 40, 197
Ramadan or Ramzan 37
Ramakrishna Mission (Delhi) 229, 231
Ramayana 37, 40, 47, 77, 191,
    197, 222
Rambagh **158**
Rambagh Palace **195**
Rambagh Palace Hotel (Jaipur)
    11, 248, 273
Ramganj Bazaar (Jaipur) 267
Ramgarh **197**
Ramgarh Lake 275
Ramlila 30, 37
Ramnavami 36
Rana Sanga Roof Top Bar
    (Jaipur) 271
Randiyon ka Mahal 209
Rang Mahal 95
Rangaji Temple 217
Ranthambhore Fort 223, 224
Ranthambhore National Park 222,
    223, **224–5**, 233
Rao, Narasimha 61
Rao Shekha 213
Rashid (Jaipur) 267
Rashivalaya Yantra 193
Rashtrapati Bhavan 64, 67, 68, **70**,
    72, 78

Raslila 30
Rathors 179, 198, 215
Ravana 37, 40, 197
Ravi Shankar 30
Ravindra Manch (Jaipur) 270, 271
Ravissant 118, 119
Ray, Satyajit 271
Razia, Sultana
    grave of 96
Razmnama 191
Red channel 292
Red Fort (Delhi) 39, 65, 89, 90, 92,
    94–5, 280
    Plan 95
Reinhardt, Walter 142, 152
Religions **22–3**
    gods and goddesses **24–5**
    religious symbols 24
Remembrance Day 104
Republic Day Parade 41, 61, 67, **71**,
    264, 280
Restaurants
    coffee shops 249
    prices and tipping 249
    South Indian eateries 249
    speciality restaurants 248
Restricted areas in India 279
Rickshaws, tongas and tempos 301
Rights and refunds 265
Rig Veda 44, 45
Rishabhdeva 219
Rishikesh 137, **144**, 145, 230, 274,
    275
River rafting 275
River rafting campsite 230
River tour along the Ganges **145**
Riverine areas **21**
Road signs and road maps 299
    rules of the road 299
Roadside and market food stalls 249
Roe, Sir Thomas 218
Rolls Royce cars 166
Roman Catholic Cemetery (Agra) **152**
Roopangarh Fort **215**
Roorkee 135, 139, **143**
Roshanara 150
Round Table Conference 58
Royal Academy's Burlington
    House 72
Royal Trains
    Palace on Wheels 295
    Heritage on Wheels 295
RTDC (Jaipur) 231
RTDC Tourist Village (Pushkar) 231
Rudraman 46
Russell, Robert Tor 76, 78

S

Sa'adi 206
Sabha Niwas 190

Sadhana Sansthan (Delhi) 274
Safdarjung
  aerodrome 105
  tomb of 99, **105**
Sagar 203
Sahara Airlines 292
Saharanpur **143**, 266
Sahdev 140, 209
Sahitya Akademi 76
Sal tree (Shorea robusta) 20
Salar Masa-ud Ghazi's maqbara 142
Salim Mahal 206
Salim's Paper (Sanganer) 267
Samarkand 192
Sambar 20
Sambhar Salt Lake **214**
Samode **212**
Samode Bagh 212, 230
Samode Palace 28, **232**
Samrat Yantra 77, 193
Samvat 281
Sanganer 180, 181, 190, 196, **204**, 266
Sanganeri motifs 205
Sangeet Natak Akademi 76
Sanghi Jutharam Temple 203
Sanghiji Temple 204
Sangin Burj 172
Sanjay Talkies (Agra) 271
Sanjhi craft 163
Sannahit Sarovar 140
Sansad Bhavan 68, 70
Sanskriti (Museum) **114**
Sarai Kale Khan 296
Saraswati 24
Sardhana 137, 139, **142**
Sariska 209, 274
  flora 211
Sariska National Park 134, 180, 206,
  208, **210–11**
Sariska Palace 210
Saroj Handicrafts and Arts
  (Jaipur) 267
Sarojini Nagar 118
  Railway booking centre 294
Sarus crane 116, 168
Sas-Bahu ka Mandir 174
Sati Burj 161
Sati pillars 176
Sati sites 48
Satpula 109
Sattais Katcheri 202
Savitri Temple 216
Savitri 216
Sawai Jai Singh Benevolent Trust 195
Sawai Jai Singh II (Jaipur) 77, 134,
  161, 182, 183, 191, 192, 194, 195,
  196, 198, 199
Sawai Madhopur **222**
Sawai Madhopur Lodge 231, **233**
Sawai Pratap Singh 186

Sayyids 50, 51, 69, 79
Scindias 147, 152, 174
Scindia Museum 174
Scott, Alfred 102
Scott, Ida 102
Scythians 43
Sen, Amartya 61
Serindian collection 72
Shah Jahan Mughal Emperor 53, 89,
  92, 94, 107, 135, 150, 151, 153, 154,
  158, 190, 191, 207, 219, 220, 222
Shah Jahan's court **53**
Shahjahanabad 53, 89, 92, 96, 107
Shahjahani Masjid 220
Shah Nazar Khan 152
Shah of Persia 191
Shah Pir's Maqbara 142
Shah Quli Khan 140
Shahi chirag 151
Shahji Temple 163
Shahpur Jat 108
Shahtoosh shawls 279
Shakti 48
Shakuntalam Theatre 85
Shankaracharya 48
Shankarlal Sangeet Sammelan
  (Delhi) 38
Shanti Kunj Ashram 144
Sharad 37
Sharan Rani 75
Sheesh Gumbad 79
Sheesh Mahal
  Agra 150
  Alwar 206
  Amber 200, 202
  Rajgarh 208
  Samode 212, 232
Sheikh Hasan Tahir 109
Shekhawat, Kripal Singh 267
Shekhawati frescoes 212
Shekhawati 29, 179, 180, **213**, 273
Sher Mandal 84
Sher Shah Gate (Lal Darwaza) 84
Sher Shah Sur 84, 97, 107, 140, 160
Sher Shah's mosque 84
Shergarh Fort 167
Shergarh 84, 107
Shergill, Amrita 71
Shesh Nag 24
Shiha-bu'd-Din Ahmed Khan 85
Shila Devi Temple 201, 202
Shila Devi 200, 201
Shilpi Handicrafts (Sanganer) 267
Shishir 36
Shitala Ashtami 36
Shitala Devi 36
Shitla Mata 222
Shiva Temple
  Keoladeo Park 168
  Moti Doongri (Jaipur) 194

Shiva 25, 36, 38, 72, 86
Shivalik Hills 137
Shivanand Yoga Vedanta Nataraja
  Centre 274
Shivpuri 145
Shivaratri 36, 41
Shoosmith, Arthur Gordon 104
Shopping arcades 228
Shopping around Jaipur 266
Shopping in North of Delhi 266
Shops and markets **264–7**
  around Agra 266
  around Jaipur 266
  bargaining 264, 283
  carpets and dhurries 267
  Delhi 118–9
  North of Delhi 266
Shree (Agra) 271
Shree Ganpati Arts (Jaipur) 267
Shri Aurobindo Ashram,
  (Delhi) 229, 231
Shri Ganesha, Ranthambhore 223
Shriram Bharatiya Kala Kendra 40
Shyam ki Burj 183
Shyam Ahuja 118, 267
Siberia 168
Siddharth Carpet Mfg Co. (Jaipur) 267
Sikandar Lodi 106, 109, 160
  tomb of 79
Sikandra 27, **160**
Sikar 213
Sikhism **23**
Sikhs 37
Sikkim 279
Siliserh **208**
Siliserh Lake 208
Silk Route (Chinese Turkistan) 47,
  72, 75
Silver Mountain (Jaipur) 267
Simla 207
Sindhi Camp 296
Singh, Gobind 23, 38
Singh, Ishwari 184
Singh, Jagat 199
Singh, Kishan 215
Singh, Maharaja Bakhtawar 206
Singh Manmohan 61
Singh Pol 164
Singh, VP 61
Singhania 213
Sireh Deori Bazaar 186
Siri Fort 51, 99, 106, 107, **108**
Siri Fort Auditorium 38, 39, 108, 120
Sisganj Gurudwara 90, 92
Sisodia Rani ka Bagh **196**
Sita World Travel
  Delhi 297
Sita 37, 197
Sind 47
Sivanand 144

Skinner, James 101, 137, 140
Skinner's Horse 101, 140
Slave dynasty 50
Slopka 211
Sloth bear 225
Smoking and alcohol 283
Snacks 254
Snake bird 168
Solani, River 143
Soma Shop (Jaipur) 267
Someshwar Temple 209
Sonagiri 175
South Africa 59
     Embassy 281
Spear, Percival 103
Spectator sports 272
Spinal Injuries Centre 114
Sports and outdoor activities 272–5
Sri Krishna Janmabhoomi
     Temple 161
Sri Lanka 292, 293
Sri Ram Centre 76, 120
Sri Ranganathji 162
St John's College **152**
St Stephen's College 103
St Thomas 23, 46
St Thomas's Church 143
Standard Chartered Bank (Delhi) 288
Star TV network 291
Star Wars 271
State Bank of India
     Agra 288
     Delhi 264, 288
     Jaipur 288
State tourism departments 279, 280
Statue Circle **195**
Stein, Joseph Allen 85
Stein, Sir Aurel 72, 75
     Stein's Serindian collection **72**
Steppe eagle 168
Storks 168
Stylized floral motif 156
Subhat Niwas 199
Subramanyam, KG 71
Subz Burj 81
Sufi 22, 51
Sufi dargah 140
Sufi qawwali 270
Sugar & Spice (Delhi) 79
Suitable dress **283**
Sukh Niwas 201, 202
Sukhi Baoli 111
Sulabh shauchalayas
     (public toilets) 285
Sultan Ghari **114**
Sultan Mahal 212
Sultanate architecture **26**
Sultanpur (bird) Sanctuary **116**, 274
Summer Theatre Festival (Delhi) 39
Sundar Horticulture Nursery 81

Sundar Nagar Market 81, 118
Sunehra Makan 172
Sunehri Bagh 69
Sunehri Kothi 222
Sunehri Masjid 90, 92
Sungas 46
     panel 64
Sunshine chart 39
Sur dynasty 137
Sur Sadan (Agra) 270, 271
Suraj Bhavan 165
Suraj Mahal 182
Suraj Pol 202, 203
Surajkund 41, **117**
Surajkund crafts mela **117**
Surajpal 117
Surat 190
Survey of India 299
Surya Temple 196
Svarna Nagari Hall 219
Swami Haridas 163
Swami Shraddhanand's statue 92
Swimming pool 228

T
Tabla 31
Tadolini of Rome 142
Tagore, Rabindranath 33, 58
Tagores 71
Taj Group 231
Taj Mahal 11, 29, 53, 83, 135, 147,
     153, **154–7**, 214, 266
Taj Mahotsav (Agra) 41, 270
Taklamakan Desert 72
Talab Shahi 167
Taliqi Darwaza 84
Talkatora (Jaipur) 182, **183**
Talkatora Stadium (Delhi) 39
Talvriksha 210
Tandoori food 252–3
Tansen Festival 40
Tansen 163, 170, 174
Tara 74
Taragarh Fort **218**
Taragram 175
Tasbih Khana 95
Tax clearance certificate 293
Taxes 230
Taxila (Pakistan) 17
Taxis 300
Teej (Jaipur) 39
Teen Murti 59, 78
Guru Tegh Bahadur 90
Telegraph Memorial 101
Television and radio 290
Teli ka Mandir 26, 174
Temperature chart 41
Tendulkar, Sachin 61
Tennis and swimming 228, **272**
Tetanus 287

Thailand 248
Thana 55
Thar Desert 20, 134, 179
Thar Inc. (Jaipur) 267
The Bookworm (Delhi) 119
The Far Pavilions 212
The Statesman 41
Thomas Cook 288, 297
Thomson Civil Engineering
     College 143
Thomas, George 140, 142
Three- and four-star hotels 228, 229
Tibet House 119, 274
Tibetan Buddhists 23
Tibetan food 248
Tibetan market 77
Tibetan thangkas 74
Tie-and-dye *(bandhini)* 190, 266
Tiger 20, 210, 223, 225
Tikamgarh 176
Tilak, BG 58
Timeless Book Gallery 119
Timur the Lame 51, 97
Tipping 231, 283
Toilets 285
Tomar Dynasty 117
Tonk 180, **222**
Toshita Mahayana Meditation Centre
     (Delhi) 274, 275
Tourist information 280
Tourist lodges 229
Tourist park 102
Tours
     Driving tour, Brajbhumi **162–3**
     Driving tour, Bundelkhand **175**
     Driving tour, Shekhawati **213**
     River tour along the Ganges **145**
Touts 231, 265
Traditional houses **27**
Travel agents **297**
     Ashok Tours and Travels 296
     Sita World Travel 297
Travel by road 298
Travel Corporation of India (TCI)
     in Agra 297
     in Delhi 297
     in Jaipur 297
Travel information **292–301**
Travel packages 293
Traveller's cheques 289
Travelling by train **294–5**
     Indrail pass 294
     enquiries 295
     on board 295
     royal trains 295
     services 295
     tickets and fares 294
     trains and timetables 294
Travelling with children 280
Trekking and camping 275

Glossary

ARCHITECTURE

ashram: hermitage

bagh: garden

bangaldar: curved roof derived from Bengali hut *(see p26)*

baradari: pavilion with 12 pillars *(see p196)*

basti: settlement *(see p81)*

charbagh: quadripartite garden *(see p27)*

dharamshala: charitable rest house for pilgrims

ghar: house, crypt *(see p114)*

gali: lane

jaali: carved lattice work on stone screens *(see p25)*

katra: side lane *(see p89)*

khirkee: window

kotla: a citadel or fortified area within a city

kund: pool, tank *(see p117)*

mahal: palace

mardana: men's quarters in a palace

maqbara: burial-palace, mausoleum, sepulchre *(see p142)*

masjid: mosque

mehmankhana: guesthouse

minar: freestanding tower

minaret: tower in mosque for calling the faithful to prayer

pol: gate *(see p183)*

toshakhana: state treasury *(see p190)*

zenana: women's quarters in a palace

CRAFT AND CULTURE

bandhini: tie-and-dye *(see p86)*

dholak: drum *(see p97)*

Dhrupad: style of North Indian classical music *(see p28)*

ganjifa: set of playing cards *(see p141)*

gharana: school of classical music or dance *(see p28)*

ikat: tie-and-dye yarn woven in a pattern

katha: epic tale *(see p29)*

matka: earthenware pot

mela: fair, fête

patachitra: painted scroll with mythological tales *(see p141)*

phad: painted cloth scroll from Rajasthan *(see p194)*

pichhwai: cloth painting depicting Krishna lore

raga: melodic structure with a fixed sequence of musical notes *(see p28)*

rasa: mood; essence *(see p29)*

shahtoosh: a fine shawl, now banned, that can pass through a ring. It is woven from the down of the endangered chiru antelope.

tala: rhythmic cycle of varying beats *(see p28)*

thal-posh: dish cover *(see p190)*

DRESS

burqa: concealing cloak worn by Muslim women

chador: ceremonial pall of cloth or flowers placed over a Muslim tomb *(see p82)*

dhoti: unstitched garment of Hindu men which covers the lower half of the body

gota: gold or silver frill

jootis: slippers *(see p186)*

khadi: hand-woven, hand-spun cloth popularized by Gandhi *(see pp58–59)*

lehenga: flounced skirt *(see p93)*

mukut: crown *(see p186)*

zari: gold thread

RELIGION

aarti: ritual of Hindu worship

ahimsa: non-violence

amrit: sacred nectar of the gods *(see p23)*

Balaji: one of Hanuman's many names in North India *(see p197)*

bhajan: devotional song *(see p28)*

Chishtiyas: followers of the 12th century Sufi saint, Moinuddin Chishti *(see p82)*

dharma: duty, calling *(see p141)*

kalasha: urn *(see p115)*

lila: divine sport *(see p163)*

linga: phallic emblem of Lord Shiva *(see p86)*

madrasa: Islamic theological college

Mahabharata: famous Hindu epic *(see p141)*

namaaz: ritual prayers of Muslims

pir: Muslim saint *(see p82)*

puja: ritual prayer *(see pp22)*

Ramayana: epic on the legend of Lord Rama

samadhi: memorial platform over site of cremation *(see p97)*

sati: practice of self-immolation by a widow on her husband's funeral pyre

Shaivite: followers of Shiva

tirthankara: Jain prophet

Upanishads: philosophical texts regarded as sacred scripture, dating to the later Vedic age *(see p20)*

Vaishnavite: followers of Vishnu

Vedas: texts codifying Aryan beliefs and principles, these were orally transmitted until transcribed into Sanskrit as the *Rig Veda*, *Sama Veda*, *Yajur Veda* and *Atharva Veda* *(see p20)*

yagna: vedic rite

MISCELLANEOUS

badal: cloud *(see p182)*

bahi khatha: cloth bound account book *(see p186)*

charpoy: string cot

chowkidar: watchman

Doctrine of Lapse: this gave the British the right to take direct control of princely states that did not have an undisputed heir *(see p56)*

haat: open-air market

ikka: pony trap *(see p191)*

jheel: shallow lake

katar: two-sided blade

loo: hot westerly wind that blows over North India from April to June

machan: look-out post

mohur: Mughal gold coin

nawab: a Muslim prince

pachisi: a ludo-like dice game *(see p171)*

Raj: the period of British rule in India *(see pp56–57)*

Satyagraha: a form of moral protest started by Gandhi *(see pp58–59)*

thakur: Hindu chieftain

Phrase Book

Hindi is the national language of India and even though it is not the mother tongue of a major proportion of the population, it is spoken widely in this region. All nouns are either masculine or feminine and the adjective agrees with the noun. Most masculine nouns end with –aa (as in rather), most feminine nouns end with –i (as in thin), while all plural nouns end in –e (as in hen). Verb endings also differ if it is a man or woman speaking. In the present tense, a man ends his verbs with –a, a woman ends hers with –i.

In an Emergency

Help!	Bachao
Stop!	Roko
Call a doctor!	Doctor ko bulao
Where is the nearest telephone?	Yahan phone kahan hai?

Communication Essentials

Yes	Haan
No	Na/ naheen
Thank you	Dhanyavad/Shukria
Please	Kripaya/Meharbani se
Excuse me/sorry	Kshama karen/Maaf karen
Hello/goodbye	Namaste
Halt	Rook jao
Let's go	Chalo
Straight ahead	Seedha
Big/Small	Bara/Chhota
This/That	Yeh/Voh
Near/Far	Paas/Door
Way	Raasta
Road	Sarak
Yesterday	Beeta hua kal
Today	Aaj
Tomorrow	Aane wala kal
Here	Yahaan
There	Wahaan
What?	Kya?
Where?	Kahaan?
When?	Kab?
Why?	Kyon?
How?	Kaise?
Up	Upar
Down	Neeche
More	Aur zyada
A little	Thora
Before	Pehle
Opposite/facing	Saamne
Very	Bahut
Less	Kam
Louder/harder	Zor se
Softly/gently	Dheere se
Go	Jao
Come	Aao

Useful Phrases

How are you?	Aap kaise hain?
What is your name?	Aapka naam kya hai?
My name is ...	Mera naam ... hai.
Do you speak English?	Angrezi ati hai?
I understand	Samajh gaya/gayi
I don't understand	Nahin samjha/samjhi
What is the time?	Kya baja hai?
Where is ...?	...Kahaan hai?
What is this?	Yeh kya hai?
Hurry up	Jaldi karo
How far is ...?	... Kitni door hai?
I don't know	Pata nahin
All right	Achha/Theek hai
Now/instantly	Abhi/Isi waqt
Well done!	Shabash!
See you	Phir milenge
Go away!	Hat jao/Hato
I don't want it	Mujhe nahin chahiye
Not now	Abhi Nahin

Useful Words

Which	Kaun Sa
Who	Kaun
Hot	Garam
Cold	Thanda
Good	Achha

Bad	Kharaab
Enough	Bus/Kafi hai
Open	Khula
Closed	Bund
Left	Baayan
Right	Daayan
Straight on	Seedha
Near	Paas/Nazdeek
Quickly	Jaldi
Late	Der se
Later	Baad mein
Entrance	Pravesh
Exit	Nikas
Behind	Peechhe
Full	Bhara
Empty	Khali
Toilet	Shauchaalaya
Free/no charge	Nih shulka, muft
Direction	Disha
Book	Kitab
Magazine	Patrika
Newspaper	Akhbaar

Shopping

How much does this cost?	Iska kya daam hai?
I would like…	Mujhe ... chahiye.
Do you have…?	Kya aap ke paas ... hai?
I am just looking	Abhi dekh rahen hain
Does it come in other colours?	Yeh dooserey rangon main bhi aata hai kya?
This one	Yeh wala
That one	Voh wala
Black	Kaala
Blue	Neela
White	Safed
Red	Lal
Yellow	Peela
Green	Hara
Brown	Bhura
Cheap	Sasta
Expensive	Mehanga
Tailor	Darzi

Bargaining

How much is this?	Yeh kitne ka hai?
How much will you take?	Kya loge?
That's a little expensive	Yeh to mehanga hai
Could you lower the price a bit?	Daam thoda kam kariye
How about XX rupees?	XX rupeye lainge?
I'll settle for XX rupees.	XX rupeye mein dena hai to dijiye

Staying in a Hotel

Do you have any vacant rooms?	Aapke hotel mein khali kamre hain kya?
What is the charge per night?	Ek raat ka kiraya kya hai?
Can I see the room first?	Kya mein pehle kamra dekh sakta hoon?
Key	Chaabhi
Soap	Sabun
Towel	Tauliya
Hot/cold water	Garam/thanda pani

Eating Out

Breakfast	Nashta
Food	Khaana

Water	Pani
Ice	Baraf
Tea	Chai
Coffee	Kaufi
Sugar	Cheeni
Salt	Namak
Milk	Doodh
Yoghurt	Dahi
Egg	Anda
Fruit	Phal
Vegetable	Sabzi
Rice	Chaawal
Pulse (lentil, split pea etc)	Dal
Fixed priced menu	Ek daam menu
Is it spicy?	Mirch-masala tez hai kya?
Not too spicy, ok?	Mirch-masala kam, theek hai?
Knife	Chhuri
Fork	Kanta
Spoon	Chammach
Finish	Khatam

Numbers

1	Ek
2	Do
3	Teen
4	Char
5	Panch
6	Chhe
7	Saat
8	Aath
9	Nau
10	Dus
11	Gyarah
12	Barah
13	Terah
14	Chaudah
15	Pundrah
16	Solah
17	Satrah
18	Atharah
19	Unnees
20	Bees
30	Tees
40	Chalees
50	Pachaas
60	Saath
70	Sattar
80	Assi
90	Nabbe
100	Sau
1,000	Hazar
100,000	Lakh
10,000,000	Karod (crore)

Time

One minute	Ek minit
One hour	Ek ghanta
Half an hour	Aadha ghanta
Quarter hour	Pauna ghanta
Half past one	Derh
Half past two	Dhai
A day	Ek din
A week	Ek haftah
Monday	Somwar
Tuesday	Mangalwar
Wednesday	Budhwar
Thursday	Veerwar
Friday	Shukrawar
Saturday	Shaniwar
Sunday	Raviwar
Morning	Subah
Afternoon	Dopahar
Evening	Shaam
Night	Raat

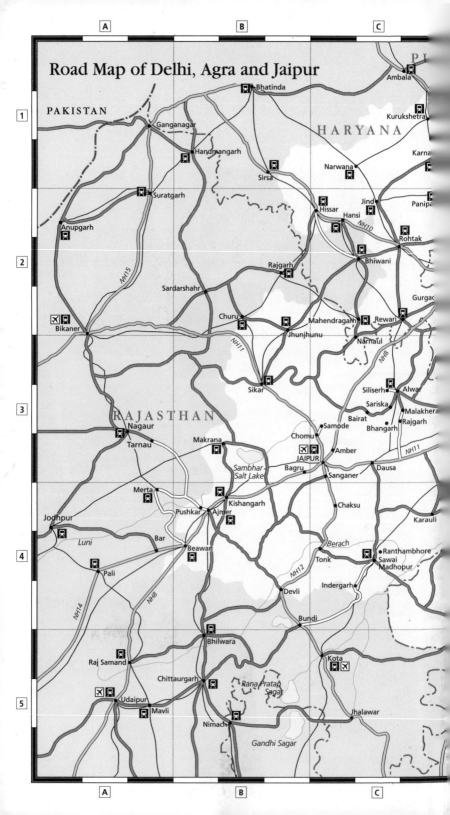

Road Map of Delhi, Agra and Jaipur